Writing Children's Books

FOR

DUMMIES®

2ND EDITION

by Lisa Rojany Buccieri and
Peter Economy

WILEY

John Wiley & Sons, Inc.

Writing Children's Books For Dummies®, 2nd Edition

Published by
John Wiley & Sons, Inc.
111 River St.
Hoboken, NJ 07030-5774
www.wiley.com

WILEY

About the Authors

Lisa Rojany Buccieri has written over 100 children's books, including several award-winning and bestselling titles. She is also a publishing executive and editor with over 20 years of professional experience in the industry and is the lead writer for *Writing Children's Books for Dummies*. Her latest Young Adult (YA) title, *Surviving the Angel of Death: The True Story of a Mengele Twin in Auschwitz,* with Eva Kor, got a stellar review by Archbishop Desmond Tutu.

As well as spearheading four publishing startups, Lisa has simultaneously run her own successful business, Editorial Services of L.A. She is also publisher and editor in chief for www.nyjournalofbooks.com, a well-respected, online-only book review site. She has been editorial/publishing director for Golden Books, Price Stern Sloan/Penguin Group USA, Intervisual Books, Gateway Learning Corp. (Hooked on Phonics), and other established publishing houses. Lisa loves working with fiction and general nonfiction writers for all ages, helping them make their work the best it can be. She lives with her family in Los Angeles. Lisa can be contacted at www.EditorialServicesofLA.com or EditorialServicesofLA@gmail.com.

Peter Economy is a bestselling author, ghostwriter, and publishing consultant with more than 60 books to his credit. Peter is coauthor of *Writing Fiction For Dummies; Managing For Dummies; Consulting For Dummies; Giving Back: Connecting You, Business, and Community; Creating an Orange Utopia; Enterprising Nonprofits: A Toolkit for Social Entrepreneurs;* and many more books. Peter is also associate editor of *Leader to Leader,* the award-winning journal of the Leader to Leader Institute. Check out Peter's Web site at www.petereconomy.com.

Dedication

To writers and illustrators everywhere, aspiring and published, who use their creativity, imagination, perseverance, and courage to create children's books that make a difference.

Authors' Acknowledgments

We would like to thank Tim Bowers, Michael Cart, Michael Green, Emma Walton Hamilton, Allison Higa, Randy Ingermanson, Maryglenn McCombs, Leslie McGuire, Erin Molta, Stephen Mooser, Glenn Murray, Don Panec, Susan Patron, Jennifer Christopher Randle, Susan Goldman Rubin, Barney Saltzberg, Rhonda Sturtz, Peggy Tierney, Doug Whiteman, and Debra Mostow Zakarin. Your words of wisdom and experience are deeply appreciated — and any errors are all our fault. We are also grateful to the authors, illustrators, and publishers who gave us permission to reprint book covers and interiors. Thanks as well to the folks at Wiley who cared enough to make this second, updated edition the best it could be: Tracy Boggier, Susan Hobbs, David Lutton, Jill Santopolo, and Jennifer Tebbe.

Lisa's additional thanks: Thanks to Peter Economy, my brother, my friend. To Ana Guadalupe Sierra de Gonzales: *Su amistad y cariño me enseñan muchissimo cada día.* Ted and Rhonda Sturtz: Any venture with you two is an adventure. To my closest girlfriends and sister for those soul-nourishing breaks in Malibu and the Strand. To Kristian, a better person I have never met. To my children, the lights of my life. And to Shane: *Enfin. Je t'ai attendu toute ma vie. Maintenant que tu es là, chaque moment est encore plus fort, plus enrichissant et magique. Aucun mot ne saurait exprimer à quel point je t'aime.*

Peter's additional thanks: A thousands thanks are not enough to acknowledge the debt of gratitude I owe my coauthor Lisa Rojany Buccieri for putting her heart and soul into this book — twice! You are a joy to work with — a real pro — and I am honored to be your writing partner and friend.

Publisher's Acknowledgments

We're proud of this book; please send us your comments at http://dummies.custhelp.com. For other comments, please contact our Customer Care Department within the U.S. at 877-762-2974, outside the U.S. at 317-572-3993, or fax 317-572-4002.

Some of the people who helped bring this book to market include the following:

Acquisitions, Editorial, and Vertical Websites

Project Editor: Jennifer Tebbe

   (Previous Edition: Tere Stouffer)

Acquisitions Editor: Tracy Boggier

Copy Editor: Susan Hobbs

   (Previous Edition: Corbin Collins)

Assistant Editor: David Lutton

Editorial Program Coordinator: Joe Niesen

Technical Editor: Jill Santopolo

Editorial Manager: Christine Meloy Beck

Editorial Assistant: Rachelle S. Amick, Alexa Koschier

Cover Photo: © Images.com / Alamy

Cartoons: Rich Tennant (www.the5th wave.com)

Composition Services

Project Coordinator: Sheree Montgomery

Layout and Graphics: Carrie A. Cesavice, Jennifer Creasey, Joyce Haughey

Proofreader: Debbye Butler

Indexer: Potomac Indexing, LLC

Publishing and Editorial for Consumer Dummies

   Kathleen Nebenhaus, Vice President and Executive Publisher

   David Palmer, Associate Publisher

   Kristin Ferguson-Wagstaffe, Product Development Director

Publishing for Technology Dummies

   Andy Cummings, Vice President and Publisher

Composition Services

   Debbie Stailey, Director of Composition Services

Contents at a Glance

Table of Contents

Introduction

· ·

*I*f you've gone through the trouble and expense of buying this book, we're going to take a wild guess: You dream of writing your own children's book and getting it published. Your desire may come from a deep-seated yearning to communicate with young people or to share experiences with them. Or it may stem from an interest in a subject you think children may also delight in. Regardless of where your desire comes from, we want to help you turn that passion into a well-written, saleable manuscript. Our goals in writing this book are to help you understand the children's book writing process and give you the tools you need to turn your children's book dream into reality. Many people think writing a children's book is child's play. Actually, it's not. It takes a lot of hard work.

We've seen plenty of people just like you attempt to tackle the process of writing a children's book. Some haven't the slightest idea where to start. Others have a good idea where to start, but don't know what to do with their manuscript after they've written it. Still others have published a children's book or two, but would like to try writing a new type of children's book. Good news: We understand the process and what it takes to move through it with as little stress as possible. In the pages that follow, we provide you with the very best advice our many years of experience have to offer.

About This Book

There's a lot more to writing a children's book and getting it published than simply knocking out a manuscript and mailing it to a publisher. If you're serious about getting your book published, then you need to understand the entire process of how a children's book comes into existence and how to deal with the different challenges that present themselves along the way. Where do you start? How do you get your manuscript in front of an editor? Should you consider self-publishing? How can you use social media to promote your book? This book answers these questions, and hundreds more like them, in an easy-to-use reference you can take with you anywhere. Also, throughout the book we sprinkle a generous helping of insightful, candid interviews with publishing pros who answer common questions with incredible candor and honesty — and often a great sense of humor.

Conventions Used in This Book

We use the following conventions throughout the text to make everything consistent and easy-to-understand:

- ✔ All Web addresses appear in `monofont`.
- ✔ New terms appear in *italics* and are closely followed by an easy-to-understand definition.
- ✔ **Bold** text indicates keywords in bulleted lists or highlights the action parts of numbered steps.

What You're Not to Read

Sidebars are the shaded boxes that appear here and there throughout the book. They contain fun facts, interesting asides, and interviews with industry experts. Of course, we hope you read each and every one, but if you're just not interested or don't have the time, don't worry about them.

Foolish Assumptions

We wrote this book with some thoughts about you in mind. Here's what we assume about you, our reader:

- ✔ You've long fantasized about writing your own children's book and getting it published.
- ✔ You may have already written a children's story but aren't sure how to prepare it for submission. You may have already had a children's book published, but would like to experiment writing a different type of children's story. Or you may even be an experienced children's book author who is looking for new perspectives on the industry.
- ✔ You're looking for a comprehensive guide that demystifies children's book writing by focusing on the information that's most worth knowing.
- ✔ You want to improve your writing skills and hone your craft.
- ✔ You're willing to take the time to become knowledgeable about the conventions in the children's book world to separate yourself from the wannabes.
- ✔ You're interested in exploring different publishing options, including self-publishing and e-books.

✔ You want to know how to promote and market your book to improve sales.

✔ You want to know what you need to do to find an agent or publisher.

How This Book Is Organized

This book is divided into six parts. The following sections explain what you'll find in each one.

Part 1: The ABCs of Writing for Children

In this part, we introduce you to the world of children's books and take an in-depth look at the many different formats of children's books, as well as who actually buys children's books and why.

Part 11: Immersing Yourself in the Writing Process

Above all, writing a children's book involves *writing*. In this part, we help you get a jump on the writing process, looking at how to set up your workspace, develop great story ideas, and build on your great idea with research.

Part 111: Creating a Spellbinding Story

A spellbinding story has a plot that makes sense (and doesn't leave out details that make the story believable), characters you care about and root for, dialogue that sounds real, and a setting that transports you to a different world. This part helps you create all of that and more, whether you're writing a picture book, a leveled reader, a young adult (YA) novel, or a work of nonfiction.

Part 1V: Making Your Story Sparkle

In this part, we show you how to rewrite and edit your manuscript yourself and where to get outside help. We also look into formatting your manuscript for submission and illustrating your manuscript. Finally, we give you some information about where to find other writers and great teachers.

Part V: Getting Published and Promoting Your Book

After you've written your book, it's time to sell it. In this part, we consider the pros and cons of working with literary agents versus approaching publishers directly yourself. We provide detailed information on book deals and contracts and give you some quick tips on dealing with copyright law. We also take a close look at self-publishing and give you the information you'll need to become your own publisher quickly and easily.

Additionally, we consider how you can promote and publicize your book, explaining how to use social media to get the word out about your book to as large an audience as possible.

Part VI: The Part of Tens

This part includes quick resources that provide information in an easy-to-digest fashion. We explore some classic children's book storylines and consider some of the most prestigious children's book recognitions and awards.

Icons Used in This Book

To make this book easier to read and simpler to use, we include some icons in the margins so you can easily find and fathom key ideas and information.

This icon highlights important information to store in your brain for quick recall at a later time.

These tidbits provide expert advice to help you save time, money, or frustration in the book-writing process.

Avoid mistakes by following the sage words of advice appearing alongside this icon.

Where to Go from Here

The great thing about this book is that *you* decide where to start and what to read. It's a reference you can jump into and out of at will. Just head to the table of contents or the index to find the information you want.

Part I

The ABCs of Writing for Children

The 5th Wave · By Rich Tennant

"To get a feel for middle-grade books, I've focused my reading on books reflecting a common idea: that they end in fewer than 200 pages."

In this part . . .

The universe of children's books can be a bewildering and foreign place for the aspiring author. The diversity of products — and customers — is unequaled in any other corner of publishing, which is why in this part we provide you with a broad overview of the world of children's books.

After covering the basics, we take a detailed look at all the different formats of children's books, from board books to chapter books to young adult novels (and much more). We also explore different genres of children's books — including fantasy, horror, biography, and historical fiction — and then delve deeply into the children's book market so you can find out about the institutions and people (aside from the children themselves) who make up the market's key players.

Chapter 1

Exploring the Basics of Writing Children's Books

In This Chapter

▶ Defining the children's book world

▶ Diving into the writing process

▶ Creating a powerful story for children and polishing until it shines

▶ Publishing your book and spreading the word

For many, dreams of writing or illustrating a children's book remain just that — dreams — because they soon find out that writing a really good children's book is *hard*. Not only that, but actually getting a children's book published is even harder. If you don't know the conventions and styles, if you don't speak the lingo, if you don't have someone to advocate for your work, or if you or your manuscript don't come across as professional, you'll be hard pressed to get your manuscript read and considered, much less published.

Consider this chapter your sneak peek into the world of children's publishing. We fill you in on the basics of children's book formats, creating a productive writing zone, employing key storytelling techniques, revising your manuscript, and getting your story into the hands of publishers who sell to the exact children's audience you're targeting.

 Every bestselling children's book author started with a story idea — just like yours. Also, many of today's most successful writers were rejected time after time until they finally found someone who liked what he or she read or saw and decided to take a chance. Follow your dreams. Feed your passion. Never give up. The day your children's book is published, we'll be cheering for you.

Knowing Your Format and Audience

Before you do anything else, figure out what kind of children's book you're writing (or want to write). Manuscripts are published in several tried-and-true formats, with new ones developed every year. *Formats* involve the physical characteristics of a book: page count, *trim size* (width and height), whether it's color or black and white, has lots of pictures or lots of words, is hardcover or softcover, comes as an e-book or an app — or both. There are also lots of genres your book may (or may not) fall into. So figuring out your format and genre will help you determine exactly how to write and present your book. Chapter 2 has lots of examples of published books that do a great job in each format.

You also need to ask yourself: Who is my audience? Believe it or not, *children* isn't the correct answer. Children of a particular age bracket, say *infant to age 2*, or *ages 3 to 8,* may come closer to defining the target age you're trying to reach, but are they really the ones who buy your book? Because books are ushered through the process by grown-ups — signed up by agents, acquired and edited by editors, categorized by publishers, pushed by sales reps, shelved and sold by booksellers, and most often purchased by parents and other adults — your audience is more complicated than you may think. In Chapter 3, we tell you all about the different people you need to impress before you get your book in the hands of children.

Getting into a Good Writing Zone

If you thought you could just grab a pen and paper and jump right in to writing, you're right! But you may also want to consider what will happen when your life starts to intrude on your writing time. How do you work around the children needing to be fed and your desk being buried under mounds of bills and old homework? How do you figure out when it's best to write? In Chapter 4, we talk about the importance of making a writing schedule and sticking to it. We also emphasize finding a space of your own for writing and making that space conducive to productivity and creativity.

After you figure out how to get to work, you have to decide what you're going to write about. Coming up with an interesting idea for a story isn't necessarily as easy as you may think, which is why we provide lots of ways to boot up your idea factory in Chapter 5. We also have ways to get you unstuck if you find yourself with a mysterious case of writer's block.

As soon as you have your good idea, it's time to get out there and research to make sure the idea fits your target audience. We cover the hows and whys of researching your audience, of figuring out what children like and what is important in their lives, and then researching the topic itself in Chapter 6.

Transforming Yourself into a Storyteller

By making sure your fiction story features these key elements, you'll be one step closer to publishing success:

- ✔ **Memorable characters:** Whether it's a child who can fly, a really hungry wolf, a boy and a slave floating down the Mississippi River, or a smelly green ogre, characters are the heart and soul of children's books. So how can you create characters who jump off the page and into your readers' hearts? Chapter 7 reveals how to build and flesh out great characters and how to avoid stereotyping and other common pitfalls.

- ✔ **An engaging plot:** What exactly is a plot, and how does one figure out what constitutes a beginning, a middle, and an ending? That's the territory of Chapter 8, as are conflict, climax, and resolution.

- ✔ **Realistic dialogue:** Kids can tell when dialogue doesn't sound right. This is why Chapter 9 features tips and step-by-step advice for writing realistic, age-appropriate dialogue for each of your characters. We also look at ways to keep your characters sounding different from one another.

- ✔ **Interesting settings:** One way to engage young readers is to set your story in places that intrigue them. We give you some pointers on how to create interesting settings that ground your story in a particular context and draw in your reader in Chapter 10.

Of course, you also need to consider your author voice or *tone.* Do you want to sound playful by incorporating word play, rhyming, and rhythm (the music inherent in words well matched)? Or do you want to make youngsters giggle uncontrollably? We give you the tools you need to create your character's voice in Chapter 11. And if you're struggling with sticking to a consistent point of view, Chapter 11 can help you out there, too.

Interested in writing nonfiction? Then turn to Chapter 12. It's chock-full of good advice on jump-starting your nonfiction project by choosing a kid-friendly topic, organizing your ideas into a comprehensive outline or plan, and fleshing out your ideas with all the right research.

Polishing Your Gem and Getting It Ready to Send

After you've written your first (or tenth) draft, you may be ready for the revising or editing process. Revising and editing aren't just exercises to go through step by step; they are processes in which the writer gets to know his story inside and out. Characters are fleshed out, the story is honed and sharpened, the pacing is fine-tuned, and the writing is buffed and polished.

In Chapter 13, we guide you through the steps of revising and editing, addressing in detail how to fix everything from dialogue issues to awkward writing, advising when to adhere to the rules of grammar (and when it's okay not to), and giving you a few simple questions to ask yourself to make the process much smoother and less complicated.

In the process of rewriting and editing your story, you may find that you have some serious questions about your manuscript, such as "Is this really final, or does it need work?" or "Is this supporting character turning into more of a distraction than anything else?" Seek out feedback from others to help you find answers to any and all questions you may be asking. You can join (or start) a local writer's group, attend book conferences or writing workshops, or participate in writing message boards. For the full scoop on all things feedback-related, see Chapter 15.

In the publishing world, first impressions carry a lot of weight. Your thoroughly revised, well-written, and engaging manuscript may fail to wow editors if it looks unprofessional. Trust us: Proper formatting goes a long way toward making your submission look as professional and enticing as possible. (Flip to Chapter 13 for some formatting tips.)

And what about illustrations? Should you illustrate your book yourself, or should you partner with or hire an illustrator to create the pictures you envision to complement and enhance your manuscript? For writers wondering about whether art should be included with their manuscript, we give you the pros and cons of partnering with an illustrator. For those with artistic talent to pair with their writing skills, Chapter 14 also provides step-by-step examples of what illustrating a picture book really looks like.

Selling Your Story

After you have a well written, carefully edited, perfectly formatted manuscript in your hands, you're ready to launch it on its first (or 17th) journey out into the big, bad world of publishing. At this point in the process, you have a few different options:

- ✔ You can send your manuscript to an *agent,* a person who will best represent your interests and do all the photocopying, query-letter writing, submitting, tracking, and negotiating on your behalf. The good ones are well worth the 15 percent they typically charge to take your career from amateur to professional. Finding the right one, getting her attention, and then negotiating your contract is a process unto itself, which is why we tell you all about that in Chapter 16.

✔ You can submit your book to publishers on your own. Finding the right match and submitting to only the "right fit" publishing houses is an art form requiring in-depth research and quite a bit of sleuthing. Turn to Chapter 17 for advice on finding the publisher who's looking for stories just like yours, as well as how to get what you want in your contract.

✔ You can opt out of the submissions game altogether and choose to publish your book all by yourself. Chapter 18 introduces you to the world of self-publishing, offering you tips, options, and guidelines about how and where to start with print or digital versions of your book.

Promoting Your Book

After you have your finished book or its actual publication date, how can you be sure anyone else will ever see it or buy it? If you're working with a traditional publisher, that company likely has a marketing team dedicated to spreading the word about your book, but you know what? The efforts your publisher is planning on making on your behalf may not impress you, which means you need to do some marketing and publicizing of your own if you want your book sell over the long run. Don't worry, though. Publicity professionals let you in on their secrets in Chapter 19, and we give you lots of ideas of how to get your book noticed. Marketing, planning, and promotion take you from book signing to lecture — all starring you and your fabulous children's book.

Unless you've been living under a rock, you're probably aware that social media has become a powerful force in promoting everything from products and politics to — you guessed it — children's books. Chapter 20 explains how to use social media (including Facebook, Twitter, and blogs) to introduce your book to the world, alert potential buyers to its existence, and keep it in the public consciousness long after its release date.

Improving your chances of getting published

We've worked in the publishing industry for a long time, and we have a pretty good idea of what works and what doesn't. Here are some insider tips that can significantly improve your chances of getting published. Some of these tips involve very specific advice, such as getting feedback before submitting; others provide less concrete (but just as important) tips about the etiquette of following up with publishers and how to behave if rejected.

Act like a pro. If you act like you're an experienced and savvy children's book writer, people perceive you as being an experienced and savvy children's book writer — provided you've really done your research. And because

(continued)

(continued)

the children's book industry tends to be more accepting of those people who already "belong to the club" than of the newbies pounding on the door to be let in, you'll greatly improve your chances of getting published by behaving as if you already belong. Some examples of this include sending a one-page query letter that addresses all the salient points, how to submit your carefully and thoroughly edited manuscript, and formatting your manuscript properly (discussed in Chapters 13 and 16).

Create magic with words. Writing a fabulous children's book isn't easy. A children's book editor has a very finely tuned sense of what constitutes a well-written book and what will sell in the marketplace. If you want to get your book published, your writing must be top notch — second best isn't good enough. If you're still learning the craft of writing, by all means get some reliable and knowledgeable feedback. And you might even choose to engage the services of a professional children's book editor or book doctor to help fix up your manuscript before you submit it to a publisher for consideration. Whichever avenue(s) you choose, the goal is putting your best effort forward.

Research thoroughly. To get published, your book needs to be both believable and factually correct (especially if you're writing nonfiction). If you're sloppy with the facts, your editor won't waste much time with your manuscript before pitching it in the trash. (Chapter 6 keeps you up on the latest developments in the world of children and ways to research your topic.)

Follow up — without stalking. After you submit your manuscript or proposal, expect to follow up with the agent or editor to whom you submitted it. But keep in mind that agents and editors are very busy people, and they probably receive hundreds if not thousands of submissions every year. Be polite and persistent, but avoid stalking the agent or editor by constantly calling or e-mailing for status. Making a pest of yourself will buy you nothing except a one-way ticket out of the world of children's books. See Chapters 16 and 17 for more on when and how to follow up.

Accept rejection graciously. Every children's book author — even the most successful and famous — knows rejection and what it's like to wonder whether her book will ever get published. But every rejection provides you with important lessons to be applied to your next submission. Take these lessons to heart and move on to the next opportunity. Head to Chapter 17 for more on rejection.

Practice until you're perfect. There's no better way to succeed at writing than to write, and no better way to get better at submitting your manuscripts and proposals to agents or publishers than to keep trying. Don't let rejection get in the way of your progress; keep writing and keep submitting. The more you do, the better you'll get at it — *it* being everything you discover in Parts II and III. And remember: Hope means always having a manuscript being considered somewhere.

Promote like crazy. Publishers love authors with a selling platform — that is, people who have the ability to publicize and promote their books as widely as possible. By showing your prospective publishers that you have the ability to promote your books — in the media, through your networks of relationships, and more — you'll greatly increase your chances of being published. (For more on promotion, see Chapters 19 and 20.)

Give back to the writing community. Both beginners and pros give back to their profession, to their readers, and to their communities. They volunteer to participate in writing groups or conferences to help new or unpublished authors polish their work and get published; they do free readings in local schools and libraries; and they advocate for children in their communities. When you give back like a pro, you improve your standing in the children's book industry, increasing your chances of getting published. And besides all that, you establish some good karma — and that can't hurt.

Chapter 2

Delving into Children's Book Formats and Genres

In This Chapter

▶ Getting to know the many children's book categories and formats

▶ Acquainting yourself with the various genres

Children are as different as the many different books catering to their many different interests and desires. Because of this, children's books offer a wealth of diversity in formats, shapes, sizes, intended audiences, and genres. In this chapter, we explain the different formats and genres children's books fall into. We also show you lots of examples of book covers to give you a feel for successful and representative formats selling in various channels of the children's book market.

Understanding Children's Book Categories and Formats

Children's books can be grouped into two overarching *categories:* fiction and nonfiction. *Fiction* is made-up writing, and it's a big plate that other derivative (and delicious!) morsels may fall on. *Nonfiction* is writing based on real facts, people, places, or events — see Figure 2-1.

Within those categories, children's books are also divided into *formats,* which are based on the various ages the books serve, as well as the book's size, shape, and content. Some examples of formats include picture books, board books, chapter books, and young adult (YA) books, all of which we describe in this chapter.

Figure 2-1:
*Art Against
the Odds:
From Slave
Quilts to
Prison
Paintings.*

By Susan Goldman Rubin. Reprinted courtesy of the author.

Formats help publishers group their titles by age appropriateness (that is, where children are developmentally), or physical characteristics, or both, which, in turn, helps children's book readers know what type of books are suitable for particular age ranges, interests, or goals. These format separations and identifications follow each title from conception through in-house production in the publishing company, to the sales team, and to the bookseller, who often organizes the books by format right in the store. So even the customers find books presented to them in specific formats — and don't necessarily realize it.

Always refer to your work's title and the format *together* — in the same sentence — as in, "*Alphababies* is a board book using photographs of babies to teach the alphabet to toddlers." That way, the person reviewing your work can immediately identify the format into which your book falls.

Many writers can't figure out their format until they have their story down and are in the editing process — way down the road from this point. But others find it helpful to know the parameters of the various formats ahead of time to help them make decisions along the way about plot complexity, word count, vocabulary level, and other elements that go into defining a format. And knowing about formats doesn't mean you can't start writing without figuring out which format your book should be. Nor does it mean that you can squeeze any story into any format.

Note: Digital downloadable versions across most children's book formats are now often released simultaneously with the print versions.

Inside and out: The anatomy of a book

Before we go dropping lots of terminology on you, we want you to have descriptions of the most basic parts of a book at your fingertips. Being at least a little familiar with these terms will help you when you're communicating about your book to other publishing professionals.

- **Cover:** The *cover* of your book is the face your book presents to the world after it is published. It can be a *hardcover* book (also known as a *hardback*), meaning it has paper glued over hard cardboard on all three sides (front cover, back cover, and spine); or it can be a *softcover* book (also known as a *paperback*), meaning it has thicker bond cardstock paper for all three sides.

  - A hardcover book's cover is called a case and is often one solid color that is stamped on the front cover and spine with the name of the book and author. The jacket is a sheet of paper that wraps around this case.

  - A softcover book's front cover usually features the title, the author's name, the illustrator's name, and some graphic image. The back cover can have sell copy (words that describe what the book is about in brief and why it's so great), the publisher's name, copyright info, a barcode, a price, and other information that helps retailers categorize and sell it.

  - When a hardcover book cover doesn't have a jacket and looks more like a softcover book cover, it's called a paper-over-board book, because the paper is wrapped around the cardboard without a jacket covering it. (***Note:*** For many board books and novelty books, the text and images begin right away on the inside front cover.)

- **Spine:** The *spine* is the part of the book that usually hides the *binding,* which is where the pages are glued or sewn together. The spine is between both covers and usually carries, at minimum, the title, the author's and illustrator's last names, and the publisher's name or logo.

- **Jacket:** A *jacket* is a separate piece of heavier-stock removable paper that may be wrapped around the cover and tucked under the front and back covers of the book. The jacket often repeats all the information and images found on the front cover, but sometimes the book's actual covers may be blank (as is often the case in picture books and hardcover young adult novels), with the jacket providing all the images and publishing information, including the title, credits, sell copy, author and illustrator bios, and the dedication.

- **Pages:** *Pages* are the sheets of paper onto which your story is printed. Illustrations also appear on the pages. Most children's books are published in *signatures* (groups) of 8 pages each, because of how the pages are printed, folded, and then cut at the bindery, so that's why you may notice that most children's picture books and leveled readers have pages in denominations of 8: such as 24 or 32 pages, 48 or 64 pages. As we move up into books with chapters, the signatures are 16 pages long, which is why the book pages come in multiples of 16.

- **Trim (or trim size):** *Trim* is the size of the book. *Page trim* refers to the size of the book's interior pages. *Cover trim* refers to the size of the cover, which may be larger than or the same size as the page trim.

- **Endpapers:** Most of the time, *endpapers* are not part of the books as printed. They are the double leaves of paper added at the front and back of the book before it's bound.

(continued)

(continued)

The outer leaf of each page is pasted to the inner surface of the cover (this is known as the *paste-down*), the inner leaves (or free endpapers) forming the first and last pages of the book when bound. Endpapers are mostly of heavier stock paper than the rest of the text pages and are often decorated or filled with mini-illustrations.

✔ **Front matter:** *Front matter* refers to the material that comes before the text or story of a book, including title and copyright pages, a table of contents, an introduction,

a dedication, and acknowledgments. Sometimes this information is moved to the back of the book as a design decision.

✔ **Back matter:** *Back matter* is composed of various sections that come after the main text: acknowledgements, index, citations — mostly supporting material.

✔ **Spread:** The left page and the right page of an open book constitute a *spread*. For example, pages 4–5 in a picture book usually constitute spread 2.

Baby and Toddler Friendly: Books with Pictures

What we loosely refer to as "books with pictures" describes any of the formats focusing mainly on heavy illustration and few words. Books with pictures are therefore perfect for babies and growing toddlers. Usually, parents read these to their kids, rather than the kids reading the books themselves. We walk you through the various formats we consider to be books with pictures in the next sections.

Board books

Get yourself a chunky book with a heavy stock, rounded corners, and bright, eye-catching pictures, and you've got yourself a *board book* (see Figure 2-2). Perfect gifts for little ones, these books are for the youngest readers — so young, in fact, that they don't even read yet! *What's Wrong, Little Pookie?* by Sandra Boynton (Robin Corey Books) and indeed most of Boynton's books are published as board books. Fabulous picture books that are republished as board books include *Goodnight Moon* and *Runaway Bunny,* both by Margaret Wise Brown (HarperFestival), *Jamberry* by Bruce Degen (HarperFestival), and *Hug* by Jez Alborough (Candlewick Press). We fill you in on the basics of board books — and how to write a great one — in the following sections.

Figure 2-2:
*1, 2, 3 in the
Sea* (a) and
*1, 2 at the
Zoo* (b).

a

b

Beginning with the basics of board books

Board books get their name because they're made of *cardboard* or *chipboard,* which makes their pages stiffer and heavier than regular paper — and able to withstand use by small hands that don't have the fine motor development to turn regular paper pages without tearing them. Board books are perfect for kids ages 0 to 3 years old.

Most board books are 10 to 14 pages long, with very little text, if any. We're talking a few sentences at most, and sometimes only one word to a page. These books vary in size, from 2×3 inches to 14×16 inches.

Other variations of books for children of the same age range — newborn to age 3 — are made of different materials, such as cloth books (which may include zippers, buttons, laces, pockets, and other pleasing fabrics), vinyl bath books, and books die-cut into interesting shapes.

Writing great board books

Terrific topics for board books include early learning concepts, such as shapes and colors and daily experiences like mealtime and naptime. But you don't need a lot of words to get your concepts across. Board books are the perfect place to employ simple rhyming text and lots of bright, colorful, engaging pictures to attract baby's attention.

To write a good board book, you need to make sure your content is unique. The only way to ascertain that is to research what's out there and take a good look at the board books that continue to sell and sell and sell, such as the ones we mention in the earlier "Board books" section. The best board books have a few elements in common:

- ✔ They feature simple concepts or story lines appropriate for babies and toddlers.

- ✔ They have minimal text per page, often only a word or two.

- ✔ Their text is illustratable (meaning there are no overly complex concepts, such as gravity or black holes).

- ✔ Their illustrations are clear and evocative; if the words were to disappear, the illustrations could tell the story by themselves.

 Many board books today are written by their illustrators. This is because the text is usually so short, and the pictures do most of the storytelling. Sandra Boynton and Rosemary Wells are board book author/illustrators who are worthy of study; however, if you're determined to sell a board book based on text only, in a market totally inundated with concept books and simple stories about everyday experiences, the text must be very unique indeed. The only way for you to make sure yours stands out is to study what's already out there so you can create an original concept and story.

Picture books

Picture books, like the ones with wildly different illustrative styles shown in Figures 2-3 and 2-4, are most often hardcover, heavily illustrated storybooks that cover almost every topic under the sun. They can be fiction or nonfiction, told in poetry or prose, and aimed at the literary or the mass/commercial markets. Teachers and parents with children from preschool age through early elementary years use picture books to speak to children about everything and anything the children might be experiencing at the moment: holidays, new siblings, moods, a fascination with birds or princesses — you name it, picture books cover it.

Figure 2-3: (a) *Wild Colt,* (b) *The Kissing Hand,* and (c) *Chester the Brave.*

 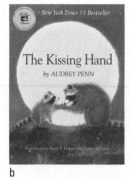 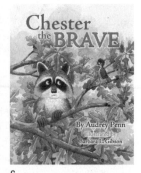

a   b   c

Figure 2-3a reprinted courtesy of Schiffer Publishing, Ltd. © 2012 Schiffer Publishing, Ltd.
Figures 2-3b and 2-3c reprinted courtesy of Tanglewood Books.

One of the most popular picture book series of all time is Ian Falconer's Olivia series (Atheneum/Anne Schwartz Books), a perfect example of picture book writing and illustrating in which the author/illustrator manages to create a fleshed-out character who looks, feels, and behaves just like the kid next door — even though she's a pig. The minimal text, limited color palette, and evocative yet restrained illustrations all work together in just the way they should in a picture book. Other bestsellers, all very different from one another include *Knuffle Bunny: A Cautionary Tale* by Mo Willems (Hyperion), Anna Dewdney's Llama Llama series (Viking Juvenile), *Seriously, Just Go to Sleep* by Adam Mansbach and illustrated by Ricardo Cortes (Akashic Books), and *Pete the Cat: Rocking in My School Shoes* by James Dean, illustrated by Eric Litwin (HarperCollins).

Figure 2-4:
(a) *Cindy Moo* and (b) *The Tiptoe Guide to Tracking Mermaids.*

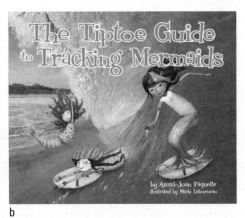

a   b

Figure 2-4a reprinted courtesy of HarperCollins Children's Books. Text © 2012 by Lori Mortensen. Illustrations © 2012 by Jeff Mack.
Figure 2-4b reprinted courtesy of Tanglewood Books. © 2012 by Ammi-Joan Paquette.

Pondering picture book basics

Picture books are perfect for readers 3 to 8 years old. Generally with 24, 32 — or less frequently, 40 — pages and anywhere from 100 to 1,500 words, these books can capture the vastly different interests and attention spans of kids in this age range. Picture books most often measure in at 8½ × 11 inches.

Following is a rundown of the not-so-standard picture book varieties:

✔ Softcover storybooks that are 8 inches × 8 inches are called *eight by eights* or *8x8s* in the industry. They're usually 8, 16, or 24 pages long, often star licensed characters, and come in pairs — if not series — of books. Sometimes these are also referred to as *picturebacks.* You can often find them in spinner racks at bookstores and markets.

Licensed characters are characters generally culled from popular television shows, toys, and movies. Some that have been around for a while and will probably stick around for a while more include Elmo, Barbie, and SpongeBob SquarePants.

✔ Board book adaptations of picture books are titles that have already had a successful run as a picture book and get a second life as a board book. In general, these *picture boards* are board books with the same text and illustrations as the original picture books (with sometimes an editorial nip and tuck here and there, but usually not enough to be noticeable to the casual reader).

✔ Softcover picture books (see Figure 2-5) come in many sizes and shapes besides the 8x8s shown here. It used to be that all picture books had a *first run* (the first printing of the book) as hardcovers. If the hardcover picture book was successful, then the publisher would follow up with the cheaper softcover. Nowadays picture book originals are often published directly into a softcover format, sometimes referred to as *picturebacks*.

Figure 2-5:
Countdown to Grandma's House and *Grandpa Lets Me Be Me.*

By Debra Mostow Zakarin. Reprinted courtesy of the author.

Becoming a picture book author

Although word count is a wild card, some picture books, such as Monique Felix's *Story of the Little Mouse Trapped in a Book* (Simon & Schuster Children's Publishing), have no words, and some are packed with words from the top of a page to the bottom, page after page. We're of the opinion that less is more. The best picture books are those whose spare, well-chosen text and well-structured stories complement the illustrations with zero fat (see Figure 2-6).

Figure 2-6:
(a) *My Dog, My Cat* and
(b) *Is a Worry Worrying You?*

a

b

Figure 2-6a reprinted courtesy of Tanglewood Books. © 2011 by Ashlee Fletcher.
Figure 2-6b reprinted courtesy of Tanglewood Books. © 2005 Ferida Wolff.

To break into the picture book market, you have to write a stellar story, which involves mastering the elements of writing we cover in Part III. When you're done with that, make sure your picture book does the following:

✔ Captures the essence of your story in no more than 750 to 1,000 words. (More than this and you risk losing the attention of the youngest of the picture book audience — and hence those who do the reading to them as well.)

✔ Makes every word work really hard, eliminating all descriptive baggage and every unnecessary word — especially those the illustrations will convey.

✔ Replaces ordinary words with richer, more evocative ones without getting wordy or too adult.

✔ Has a strong, multidimensional main character that a child can relate to.

✔ Takes your main character through a satisfying story arc including a beginning, a middle, and an end.

✔ Conveys concrete visual imagery (in action and dialogue throughout) that moves the plot ahead.

Other books with pictures

Although picture books and board books seem to dominate the field in illustrated books, that perception is not accurate. There are three other players in the category — coloring and activity books, novelty books, and graphic novels — one of which, coloring and activity, probably outdoes all the others combined in terms of units sold.

The potential problem with poetry

It is a well-accepted truism that most children's book editors feel pretty strongly about rhymed text. From those who despise it or merely tolerate it to those who adore it, editors are pretty picky about rhyme. Why? Because, authors often sacrifice the story for the sake of the rhyme — not to mention torturing the English language to create rhymes, with little attention paid to whether they make sense or not. Much more often than not, amateur writers of rhyme skimp on plot and character development, throwing in extra words just to make the rhyme work. The story and the language should come first; rhyme is secondary. A good rhyming story will always sell, but it has to be written as tightly as a story in prose.

If you are going to write poetry, take it from us: Dr. Seuss did a fabulous job with the particular rhyme schemes he used in his books, and he continues to sell tens of thousands of books a year despite not being among the living anymore. So if you want to rhyme, don't use Seussian meter; make up your own.

Coloring, activity, and how-to

With pictures to color and lots of activities, from mazes, dot-to-dots, and hidden pictures to word scrambles and crossword puzzles, coloring and activity books (or *C&A books*) offer kids fun — plain and simple. And some C&A books (like the ones in Figure 2-7) are educational.

Mad Libs (those great fill-in-the-word-blank games published by Price Stern Sloan) are fabulous for good, clean fun at sleepovers. Almost any arts and crafts book by Klutz (Klutz Press) keeps kids busy for hours. Dozens and dozens of choices are on the Klutz rack, including *Beaded Bands: Super Stylish Bracelets Made Simple, Paper Flying Dragons,* and *Coin Blasters: An Arcade Inside a Book.* (Consider getting one of these books for yourself on a road trip to drown out the cries of "Are we there yet?" and "He touched me!") Any activity you can think of that kids enjoy spending time doing or creating can be made into an activity or how-to book.

Although the sky is truly the limit when it comes to making a great coloring or activity book, we recommend you keep the following in mind:

- ✔ Have a well-known main character or set of characters hosting the book's content (this can be as simple as having a known or licensed character on the cover).

- ✔ Stick to one set of activities; for example, all games (word games, dot-to-dots, word searches, word scrambles, mazes, and the like), all coloring, or all preschool learning, but not a mishmash of everything.

- ✔ Do not try to be storybooks.

- ✔ Keep it simple and age-appropriate.

Figure 2-7:
*Cool Yule!
A Creative
and Crafty
Christmas!*
and
*Happening
Hanukkah:
Creative
Ways to
Celebrate.*

By Debra Mostow Zakarin. Reprinted courtesy of the author.

The cool thing about C&A books on the market today is that they often come with innumerable and novel extras such as punch-outs, stickers, crayons, paints, glow-in-the-dark markers — you name it. These extras actually cross-classify these C&A books as novelty books, which we talk about in the next section.

C&A book authors are often in-house editors at publishing houses or established writers with specific educational experience, firmly rooted in the publisher's stable of workhorse writers. Very rarely do new authors break into this format (though it's not unheard of if the concept is truly original). Another bummer: You won't always get to see your name on the front cover.

Novelty books

A *novelty book* is one that goes beyond just words and pictures on flat pages. It's often three-dimensional and always *interactive* (meaning the child must engage more than just his eyes in the experience). From pop-ups to pull-tabs, from juggling balls to paper dolls, innovative novelty books can really engage the imagination (see Figure 2-8 for an example.) When any type of children's book has something besides just flat paper and images in it, it moves into the novelty category.

Printing just words and illustrations on paper has become expensive — especially if the publisher prints only a few thousand to start. And novelty books always go beyond simply printed and bound paper. Once upon a time publishers could afford to print tens of thousands of copies of a novelty title right off the bat. But as the market became saturated (basically, lots of titles competing for reader attention along with the evolution of other — often more compelling to kids — storytelling media), it became unable to sustain all those titles and their brothers and sisters and cousins and knockoffs. So the publishers could no longer count on economies of scale to offset the extra costs of hand assembly or packaging or the items that came with the book. As such, there are very few players in the novelty book market today. What does that mean for you? Unless you are David A. Carter (a novelty book author who can write, illustrate, design, and paper engineer his own titles) or Robert Sabuda (another Renaissance publishing star of multiple talents in the novelty field), your chances of getting a novelty book to market are slim to none. Unless you self publish. (We fill you in on the world of self-publishing in Chapter 18.)

Graphic novels

Graphic novels (like the one in Figure 2-9) are books with lots of pictures *and* words aimed at older readers, namely middle-graders (ages 7 to 10), tweens (ages 9 to 12), young adult readers (12 and up), and even adults. Not surprisingly, every page of a graphic novel boasts graphics, which can come in the form of black-and-white illustrations, color illustrations, comics, or captured video/TV/movie photos. Most often, the illustrations look more comic-book-like than full-page picture book illustrations.

In most graphic novels, the text doesn't appear in freestanding blocks but rather in dialogue bubbles or with a line around it, like in comic books, near the relevant image. Graphic novels are often *digest sized* (5½ inches wide × 8½ inches high — about the size of a piece of paper folded in half) or slightly smaller at 6⅝ × 4⅞. Becoming a graphic novel writer generally requires the ability to illustrate in the style of graphic novels or comics. Another option is to pair up with someone who has that talent. (For information on illustrating your work, see Chapter 14.)

Figure 2-8:
*Hide and
Seek.*

Figure 2-9:
Jeremy Kreep: Fang Fairy.

Interview with Erin E. Molta, editor

Erin E. Molta is an editor who has worked across a broad spectrum of formats in children's publishing: from novelty books to licensed books to book clubs to young adult novels — even running her own editorial service. If novelty books are your passion, read on to discover what she looks for in novelty book submissions.

WCBFD: What formats, aimed at the youngest readers, sell the most year after year?

EEM: It's not so much the format but the author. Straight board books by Sandra Boynton sell continually, lift-the-flap board books by Karen Katz, as do classic board books reprinted from best-selling picture books, such as Eric Carle's *Papa, Please Get the Moon for Me* (Little Simon).

WCBFD: What are your favorite formats for the youngest readers to develop new writers into and why?

EEM: Again, the manuscript dictates a format, though we have certain formats that we consistently publish — mostly holiday or seasonal titles, like Sparkle N Twinkle or Sparkle N Shimmer series. They are holiday based and have glitter and/or sequins on each spread.

WCBFD: What formats for the youngest readers are you always looking for new ideas for?

(continued)

(continued)

EEM: The buzzwords these days are *new* and *innovative*. Everybody wants something different. So it can't just be a flap book, it must be a flap book with touch-and-feel or sound or pop-ups and foil, glitter, acetate — and it has to be able to be produced really inexpensively, too!

WCBFD: What are the most common pitfalls occurring to new writers who submit to you and in what formats do those pitfalls seem to occur most?

EEM: Everybody thinks they can write for children. It's easy, right? But most people are writing as an adult to a child rather than for — or with — a child. Kids want the text to be on their level. It doesn't mean it has to be childish — just child-appealing and childlike.

WCBFD: What grabs your attention the most?

EEM: New and innovative! The key to a successful format for the youngest reader is how it is integral to the text and art. If you have flaps in a book but there's no incentive to lift them and once you do, you don't care, then that is a bad use of the flap as a technique to further the story and enhance the reading experience. I'm looking for truly interactive books, where a child can spin a wheel to find an answer or press a button, or something pops up to stimulate understanding.

WCBFD: What do you look for in a submission that would make you immediately excited?

EEM: New and innovative! I'm looking for the perfect integration of an interactive element and lively text. Say you have animals and it's counting and the animals are night creatures — rather than on the farm (I'm sick of farm animal books). Or you're doing a book on colors, but it's in outer space. There are zillions of books about colors, shapes, counting, and opposites, but something out of the ordinary sparks my interest!

WCBFD: What would make you reject a submission almost immediately?

EEM: Tell me you read it to your students, grandkids, or even your very own children and they loved it. Of course they did! Would any kid say they didn't? Poor spelling doesn't help either, nor do farm animals.

WCBFD: How do new formats get developed? Do most of your ideas for new formats come from submissions, in-house, packagers, or combinations? Tell me how the process works for you.

EEM: We get ideas for new formats from brainstorming in-house or from packagers. I usually will come up with a format and see if I have a manuscript that fits *or* I get a manuscript and try and come up with a format that will make it stand out on the bookstore shelves! It's very much a collaborative process — taking a little bit of what's been done and tweaking it to make it new and innovative!

For younger readers, Dav Pilkey's *The Adventures of Super Diaper Baby: The First Graphic Novel* (Blue Sky Press/Scholastic, Inc.) is a stellar entry for middle-graders. For those in the middle, older middle-graders, Neil Gaiman's *Coraline* (HarperCollins) is a standout that was licensed into a movie of the same name. Comic books, anime, manga, graphic novels, and combinations thereof populate many shelves in the young adult section. (Interestingly, female teen readers are the most voracious in this category.)

Graphic novels today are very different from their comic book ancestors and are not simply just collections of comics or anthologies of comic book series from long ago. Graphic novels tell complex, sophisticated, and lengthy stories, and they often have more realistic subject matter than traditional comic books.

Working through Books with Lots of Words

In this section, we take a look at books that focus more on telling a story through words. This category includes early readers, first chapter books, middle-grade books, and YA books.

Early readers

Early readers (see Figures 2-10 and 2-11) are developed for children who are first learning their letters or perhaps even sounding out their first words. Experts in reading, teaching, learning, or curricula create particular programs around the theory of reading that the publisher has chosen to embrace, often a phonics-based or whole-language-based theory.

Figure 2-10:
(a) *Where Is My Frog?,*
(b) *Pat, Cat, and Rat,* and
(c) *Ants in Her Pants*

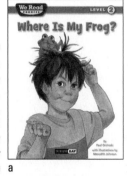

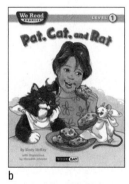

a   b   c

Figures 2-10a and 2-10b reprinted courtesy of Treasure Bay, Inc. Illustrations © 2010 by Meredith Johnson.
Figure 2-10c reprinted courtesy of Treasure Bay, Inc. Illustrations © 2010 by Jeffrey Ebbeler.

Developing an early reader program in a publishing house includes creating vocabulary lists and deciding on parameters for story development and illustration, page counts, and more — all designed to make the child's first reading experiences satisfying and logically progressive, and to encourage more reading.

Figure 2-11:
We Read
Phonics
series.

Surveying early reader basics and age levels

With anywhere from 10 pages to 64 pages, the amount of information and the word count in early reader books varies greatly, but one thing normally stays the same: the size. Most early reader books come sized at 6 inches × 9 inches. Early reader books (also known as *leveled readers*) are best for kids between the ages of 5 and 9, though they are divided into five levels, depending on the reading level of each child:

- ✔ **Level 1:** For readers who are just getting started, who know the alphabet, and are excited about reading their first books. Sometimes labeled for ages 3 to 6.

- ✔ **Level 2:** For readers who can recognize and sound out certain words but who may still need help with more complex words. Often labeled for ages 4 to 6.

- ✔ **Level 3:** For readers who are ready to tackle easy stories all by themselves. For kindergarten through third graders.

- ✔ **Level 4:** Many programs introduce chapter breaks here for children who are ready to jump into "bigger kid" books but are not yet ready for middle-grade topics or length. For second and third graders.

> ✔ **Level 5:** If the program goes this far, these books are actual chapter books with a few black-and-white illustrations scattered throughout. It's not unusual to find third and fourth graders still reading these.

Knowing how to write early readers

Turning word lists into fascinating stories is no easy task. Indeed, writing truly good early reader books requires a talent for minimalism, perfect word choice, a well-honed sense of whimsy and fun, and an understanding of how to keep plot, pacing, and character development on the move with the turn of each page. We go more into the latter elements of writing in Part III, but we maintain that to be able to write well in this format, you have to research the style, tone, and contents of each publisher's early reader series and then practice until you get better at it. As well, there are more often than not vocabulary lists to adhere to. Most publishers offer guidelines for submission into their programs that you can access on their Web sites.

Early readers can be fiction or nonfiction and cover topics that are often found in the curriculum taught in school for particular age ranges. As nationwide testing in reading comprehension and reading skills starting at the earliest grades becomes more prevalent, we expect even more curriculum-based reading programs to surface, supplementing what teachers are presenting in the classrooms.

First chapter books

A first chapter book is often a child's first real foray into reading books without full-color illustrations (see Figure 2-12). It can be a very exciting time in a child's life when they get to go the section in the bookstore or library that houses the big-girl and big-boy books. The subject matter is more mature, and the stories in first chapter books are more complex — as are the characters and their relationships with one another. Most, if they are illustrated at all, contain a few black-and-white images scattered randomly throughout. The plots are more complicated, and the pacing is maintained much more directly through story developments and conflict than through illustration or subtle suggestion. Some popular first chapter book series include the My Weird School and the My Weirder School series by Dan Gutman and Jim Paillot (HarperCollins) and Annie Barrows's and Sophie Blackall's Ivy & Bean series (Chronicle Books).

Focusing on the basics of first chapter books

As a child moves from Level 5 early readers to first chapter books, the books are longer, the illustrations switch from color to black and white, and the stories and vocabulary generally progress in complexity. These books are generally for kids in the 7 to 10 age range. With approximately 128 pages, first chapter books come in hardcover or softcover digest size, which is usually around 5½ × 8½ inches. They typically contain about eight or ten chapters of about eight to ten pages each.

Figure 2-12:
*Nancy
Clancy
Super Sleuth:
Book 1.*

*Nancy Clancy Super Sleuth, Book 1, reprinted
courtesy of HarperCollins Children's Books.
Text © 2012 by Jane O'Connor.
Illustrations © 2012 by Robin Preiss Glasser.*

Writing first chapter books

As with any other format, writing good first chapter books requires skill, and practice helps you develop that skill. First you must read, read, read examples of the format to get a feel for the ways in which the characters are developed, the story is created and fleshed out, vocabulary is used in both speech and narrative, the plot is kept progressing, and the pacing and interest are maintained at steady levels. You need to have an appreciation for children in the target age group of 7 to 10 years old (what they like, what they don't like, what they glom onto, and what they're likely to reject) — we reveal how to figure out some of that in Chapter 6.

Middle-grade books

Middle-grade fiction and nonfiction books are what many of us remember reading from our childhoods. These are the first books we read that were long and detailed and complex and dealt with subject matter that was much more intriguing (and potentially much more divisive) than most children's picture books. Some classic middle-grade books include *Stuart Little* and *Charlotte's Web,* both by E. B. White (both HarperTrophy), *The Secret Garden* by Frances Hodgson Burnett (HarperTrophy), and *The Phantom Tollbooth* by Norton Juster (Yearling).

Consider some of the issues covered in these classics: In *Charlotte's Web,* Wilbur, the main character, is a runt of a pig who is about to be killed before the farmer's daughter saves him; not lost or hidden or given away, but *killed!* This is big-kid stuff. Then think about the word play and complex relationships found in *The Phantom Tollbooth. The Secret Garden* delves into death and sickness (physical and emotional), not to mention social class discrepancies. Middle-grade books are often a child's first peek into the real world in which people die, are irredeemably bad, have to solve real problems, and even fail.

Getting down to the middle-grade basics

With an average page count that's anywhere from 96 to 156 pages, middle-grade books are written for 8 to 12 year olds and they normally come in the small 5½ × 8½ size. They can be hardcover or softcover. Many are developed into series, such as the *Series of Unfortunate Events* series by Lemony Snicket (HarperCollins), but just as many are *stand-alones* (meaning they stand alone and are never developed into series).

Gary Paulsen is a good example of the fluidity of age levels and labeling. While many bookstores categorize his fiction in the young adult section of the store, you are just as likely to find his books shelved with the middle-grade books. So which format are his books? Young adult novels or middle-grade fiction? The answer is up for grabs. The novels in Figure 2-13 are also good examples of middle-grade novels that skew toward the upper middle grades but might not appeal as much to young adults 14 and older.

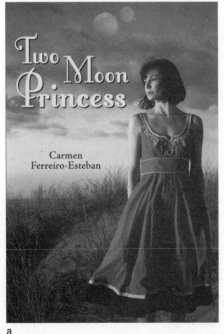
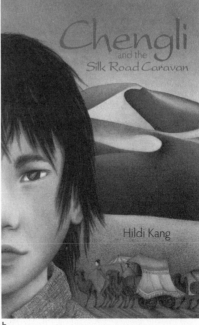

Figure 2-13: (a) *Two Moon Princess* and (b) *Chengli and the Silk Road Caravan.*

a
b

Figure 2-13a reprinted courtesy of Tanglewood Books. © 2007 by Carmen Ferreiro-Esteban, Cover illustration © 2007 by Sarah Brennan.
Figure 2-13b reprinted courtesy of Tanglewood Books. © 2012 by Hildi Kang.

Writing for the middle grades

When writing middle-grade books, you can't rely on lots of photographs or illustrations to help tell your story. The distinguishing factor that most children become aware of as they master this format is that these books have few or no interior illustrations. If illustrations are included at all, they're often limited to black-and-white sketches at chapter breaks.

Want to break into writing for this age group? What makes good middle-grade fiction good also makes YA novels good — and also makes grown-up books good:

- ✔ Strong, interesting, uniquely drawn characters who have a burning need or desire that drives them to action throughout the book
- ✔ Stories that grab you from the get-go and don't let you go until you've turned the last page
- ✔ Writing that uses language to paint pictures in the mind — writing with style (which we delve into in detail in Part III)
- ✔ A truly unique, standout voice
- ✔ Cliffhanger chapter endings
- ✔ A clear grasp of the audience and their concerns
- ✔ An ability to go back into space and time and put yourself into the shoes of a protagonist of that age without ever sounding like an adult or a younger child — a balancing act of the highest order

 You may start to notice that many of the skills required to break into children's book writing for any format or age group sound alike. And you would be right on target. As we discuss in Part III, the basic elements of good writing are the same for any format, for any age group, for any subject, and for fiction or nonfiction. Although the subject matter, topics, complexity, vocabulary, images, and other parts of the content and packaging change from format to format and age level to age level, the skills you need to develop are basically the same. Good writing is good writing. Period.

Young adult books

Young adult books are just what they sound like: books aimed at readers in their early to later teens (you can see examples in Figures 2-14 and 2-15). And although it used to be a common belief that young adults only read teen magazines and grown-up novels, bookstores are now creating separate sections devoted to material they believe addresses the issues, concerns, and interests of young adults.

It's not that there were never YA sections in bookstores and libraries. There were. But they were usually mixed right in with the board and picture books —

the "baby" books. Now these venues often physically separate out the books and the space to give teens their own hangouts.

Some classic YA titles include *Go Ask Alice* by the no-longer-anonymous Beatrice Sparks (Simon Pulse), *Catcher in the Rye* by J. D. Salinger (Little, Brown), Francesca Lia Block's *Weetzie Bat* books (HarperTrophy), *The Chocolate War* by Robert Cormier (Laurel Leaf), *Speak* by Laurie Halse Anderson (Penguin), *King of the Mild Frontier* by Chris Crutcher (Greenwillow), and *Forever* by Judy Blume (Atheneum).

Figure 2-14: (a) *Ashfall* and (b) *Ashen Winter.*

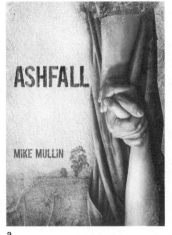 

a   b

Figure 2-14a reprinted courtesy of Tanglewood Books. © 2011 by Mike Mullin.
Figure 2-14b reprinted courtesy of Tanglewood Books. © 2012 by Mike Mullin.

Figure 2-15: *Mystery at Black-beard's Cove.*

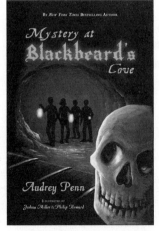

Reprinted courtesy of Tanglewood Books.
© 2004 by Audrey Penn.

Diving into YA basics

Young adult books fall into two main age groups: YA appropriate for children ages 12 and up, and YA for children 14 and up. While each YA novel differs from the next, we can attribute the split in age ranges *most of the time* to five issues: sexual intercourse, foul language, drug use, extreme physical violence, and graphic abuse. Those YA novels that overtly and unashamedly deal with these topics are usually saved for the older kids.

Does that mean that you will find an official section or publisher designation separating these two YA age ranges? Nope. And this is why movies are labeled G, PG, PG-13, and R. And why parental guidance and the child's individual maturity level need to be taken into account. Do we think there *should* be age labels on YA books? Certainly not; the First Amendment is sacrosanct, labels too infantilizing, and if a child decides she is going to read or do something no matter what the consequences, there is truly little an adult can do to prevent it.

Regardless of the specific age target (if there is one), YA novels are for those 12- to 18-year-olds who want to read novels about issues they face every day — or ones they merely wish they did.

With anywhere from 128 to 300+ printed pages, these books come in sizes ranging from 4¼ × 6¾ (also known as mass market or rack-sized books — you know, the fat paperback size that used to be sold only at supermarket and drug store checkout lines) or 6¼ × 9¼ tall (about the same size as standard grown-up hardcovers).

Young adult books are often cross-shelved with grown-ups' books, and sometimes the only distinction between the two is that the protagonists of YA novels are usually teenagers. The issues confronted in YA novels often center on coming-of-age issues of socially, economically, spiritually, emotionally, or politically marginalized kids (gay teenagers, straight teens in gay-parent families, cross-gendered teenagers, pregnant teens considering their options, teens experimenting with drugs and not completely messing up their lives or dying because of it, teens falling in love with older adults and acting on it, and the like). Other YA books focus on kids who seem to live perfect lives until you look under the surface, at orphans, or other teens in complex situations — and *complex* does not mean always weighty or incendiary because sometimes just being a teen at an exclusive prep school can present abnormally difficult situations, especially if it turns out your peers are all the walking undead.

In YA novels, the protagonists don't always win at the end. If they are human, they are buried in drama and trauma. If they are not human, their issues often parallel those of human teenagers: trying to fit in; making a difference; finding love; scouting out acceptance; breaking out of their parentally imposed limitations; seeking independence; proving their worth; conquering physical, emotional, and spiritual demons; and so on. With few exceptions today, the protagonists of YA novels have lost their innocence (different from losing their virginity), but that does not mean they've lost hope or strength or their ability to imagine a better life, a better self, and a better world.

Some YA books are considered *crossovers,* meaning they can serve as both a young adult book and a contemporary adult book. An example of a crossover title is Markus Zusak's *The Book Thief* (Knopf), which, though primarily designated a young adult novel (and made into a movie for kids), is also found in the adult section with his other books.

Writing YA books

Young adult books are filled mostly with words and rarely have any illustrations. So if you're hankering to break into the young adult field, you have to be ready to write well for 200 pages or more. Again, the criteria are similar to those required for writing good middle-grade fare, repeated here from the previous section with some real differences noted:

- ✔ Strong, interesting, uniquely drawn characters who have a problem — only they might not try very hard to solve it; in fact, they might wallow in it for awhile

- ✔ Storytelling that absolutely sparkles and makes all those apps on the young adult's smartphone or tablet nonexistent

- ✔ Writing that uses language to paint pictures in the mind and writing with style and voice (which we delve into in detail in Part III)

- ✔ A unique voice that stands out — some might argue this is the most important element of good YA fiction

- ✔ A clear grasp of the audience and their concerns (teenagers are serious about their lives and problems and issues, and people who write for them have to treat the subject matter seriously)

- ✔ An ability to go back into space and time and put yourself into the shoes of a protagonist of that age without ever sounding like an adult or a child — the balancing act of the highest order still holds here, perhaps even more than with middle-grade fiction

- ✔ An understanding of contemporary issues and culture and its effect on teens (this does *not* mean we're recommending you use slang or wear pants with the waist hanging down to your knees for you to be able to nail a character, but you should be at least a little bit hip to what it's like to be a teen today)

Dr. Donald Freeman, an aspiring YA writer, actually took our advice and sat down to read a dozen successful YA novels; he came up with the following list of similarities in most of them. (Granted, not every single one of these applies to any single YA book, but it's surely a good list of attributes to aspire to in your writing.)

✔ Word counts generally fall between 50,000 and 70,000 words.

✔ The main protagonist is in every scene, with limited point of view (see Chapter 11), whether the story is told in the first or third person.

✔ The main protagonist is already between 10 and 16 years of age at the beginning of the story; anything occurring before is revealed in flash-back or dialogue.

✔ The story begins at a moment of crisis.

✔ The protagonist's repeated efforts to rectify matters tend to backfire but can also lead to unexpected benefits (new friendships, improved self-awareness, and so on).

✔ The hero or heroine finds him- or herself in contention with an initially intimidating and harsh-seeming older adult, yet their relationship ends up being positive and rewarding.

✔ The parent figures are either ineffectual and in need of help themselves or else they're entirely out of the picture.

✔ Success ultimately crowns the protagonist's often bumbling and mis-guided efforts as helped along by others such as buddies or the adult (non-parent) figure.

✔ Overt sex is usually avoided.

✔ The protagonist is bright and energetic, but is initially hampered by lack of sophistication.

✔ Belonging (literal or figurative) and the quest to attain belonging are all-important and often define the theme.

✔ Both adults and peers experience a mixture of charm and alienation over the protagonist's "differentness," and it is his or her main develop-mental task to become socially effective without sacrifice of essential individuality.

Exploring the Genres

Genres are the general nature of major children's book categories. They're like big buckets into which a bunch of books written with certain similar conventions are thrown. For example, mystery fiction is a genre, as is action/adventure.

Conventions of a genre are customs or rules widely accepted because they've been in use that way for a long time. Basically, conventions are expectations a reader has for a genre because that's what he's used to reading; for example, it's a widely accepted convention that a book that falls into the mystery genre will have a problem that has to be solved, and a solution that isn't readily apparent, requiring discovery by the protagonist. Sometimes you want to stick to those conventions, and sometimes you want to veer away from them to make your story more interesting. Either way, it helps to know what genres are out there.

In the following sections, we explore the various genres in which children's books can be found. If a distinctive style, form, or content composes the very nature of certain genres, we talk about those, too. We also dip into the series pool, where single characters can take off into multi-book adventures.

If you aren't writing plays, poetry, or nonfiction, chances are you're writing fiction.

Science fiction

Writers of *science fiction* can manipulate settings to fit narratives or make up out-of-this-world settings altogether. Sci-fi writers rely on the utter *suspension of disbelief,* which is a fancy way of saying that you have to believe what you read no matter how implausible it may seem. If the writer of science fiction does his job, he sets up the story and characters in such a way that he seems to be describing something that can occur in the not-so-distant future because it's based on things that already exist today. Science fiction takes existing scientific principles and theories and uses them in the plot. It's meant to be understood literally, not metaphorically, and its characters ought to be believable even if the setting isn't.

Subgenres of sci-fi include apocalypse, space travel, utopia/dystopia, and messianic works. One of Peter's favorite books when he was in first grade (although it's hard to find today) was Louis Slobodkin's *The Space Ship Under the Apple Tree* (MacMillan). Current popular sci-fi titles include the YA books *Divergent* by Veronica Roth (Katherine Tegen), *Onyx* by Jennifer Armentrout (Entangled Teen), Pittacus Lore's *The Rise of Nine* (Harper Collins), the Maze Runner series by James Dashner (Delacorte), and the Uglies series by Scott Westerfeld (Simon Pulse).

Science fiction is usually targeted to older children, so the formats that work best for it include graphic novels, middle-grade, and young adult books.

Fantasy

Fantasy, like that in Figure 2-16, relies on the notion that real people in real settings can encounter magical things and can often perform magic. In other words, some people have special powers, whereas others don't. Fantasy can also involve mythical creatures such as fairies and unicorns, as well as talking animals that may or may not interact with humans. Subgenres of fantasy include urban fantasy, paranormal romance, fairy tale retellings, magical realism, high fantasy, and sword-and-sorcery tales.

Fantasy is appropriate for children of all ages from, say, three years of age and up, so the formats that work best for it include picture books, graphic novels, early readers, first chapter books, middle-grade, and young adult books.

Great examples of classic contemporary children's fantasy include Roald Dahl's *Charlie and the Chocolate Factory* and *Matilda* (Viking Books), J.K. Rowling's Harry Potter series (Arthur A. Levine Books), and Jenny Nimmo's The Children of the Red King series with titles such as *Midnight for Charlie Bone* (Orchard). For young adults, Stephenie Meyer's Twilight series (Little Brown Books for Young Readers) and Suzanne Collins's The Hunger Games series (Scholastic Press) have taken the reading world by storm.

Related to fantasy is the rich array of fairy tales, fables, folktales, myths, and legends. What they all have in common is that they come from old traditions of storytelling that can be traced to particular countries of origin. A few of the originating sources that are mined again and again include the Brothers Grimm, Charles Perrault, Hans Christian Andersen, Aesop, Russian folk tales, and Greek mythology. In fact, nearly every culture has a storytelling tradition that can be researched for material. Every year these stories inspire writers to write *retellings* and *adaptations,* stories that add to or change the source material in some unique way. *Ella Enchanted* by Gail Carson Levine (HarperTeen), *Beastly* by Alex Flinn (HarperTeen), and *Bound* are excellent examples of retellings.

Fantasy and science fiction can also be combined. This approach is especially popular for middle-grade and young adult readers. One example would be Philip Pullman's His Dark Materials series (Laurel Leaf). It has technological aspects to the plot as well as fantasy-type characters.

Figure 2-16: Blackbeard series.

Reprinted courtesy of Tanglewood Books.

Horror and ghost stories

Horror stories and *ghost stories* are the creepy, goose bump-inducing stories that make you leave the flashlight on under your sheets — even when you're done reading. Good ghost stories always suck you in because they're grounded in reality. After you really fall for the characters and the setting (as if the story were about the family next door), the plot springs something otherworldly on you. Neil Gaiman *The Graveyard Book* (HarperCollins), with illustrations by Dave McKean, is an example of good writing in the genre.

To break into writing horror, you need to demonstrate an appreciation for otherworldly content and hold-your-breath pacing — and you need to stick to formats for middle-graders and older.

Action/adventure

Often targeted to boys with very stylized, masculine covers, *action/adventure* focuses on young boys and girls who combat nature, industry, bad adults, and other evils. You usually find action/adventure stories in early readers, middle-grade books, young adult books, and graphic novels.

The best action/adventure stories are characterized by engaging, well-thought-out plots and a main character who's smart, self-reliant, and cunning. They have true a true danger element and often take place in territory unfamiliar to the reader. Gary Paulsen is a master of the genre and books of his, such as *Hatchet* (Atheneum) and *The River* (Delacorte), are great examples, as is Mike Mullins's *Ashfall* (Tanglewood Books).

Subgenres of action/adventure include thrillers and espionage (usually involving a spy who must protect her imperiled country, school, or family against an enemy), mysteries, crime-solving stories, and detective novels.

True stories

Who needs to make up a story when there are so many true stories out there simply waiting to be conjured into a children's book? One real-life subject that all children seem to gravitate toward is true stories about animals. One successful example is *Owen & Mzee: The Story of a Remarkable Friendship* by Isabella Hatkoff and Craig Hatkoff (Scholastic Press) about a baby hippo and a 130-year-old giant tortoise who adopt each other after a tragedy leaves the baby hippo orphaned.

Narrow down animals to dogs and cats and other domesticated beasts (who have a lot in common with children, after all) and you have another potentially winning formula. A moving example is *Marshall the Miracle Dog* written by Cynthia Willenbrock and illustrated by Lauren Hambaugh (see Figure 2-17) about a horribly mistreated and disfigured dog who, against the odds, finds a "forever home."

Many new writers swear they have an incredible tale, stranger than fiction and 12 times more lovely. Great! Go ahead and write it. Just beware that all the rules of writing good children's books apply to real stories just as much as they do to fictional ones.

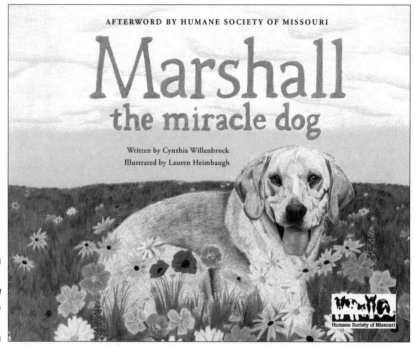

Figure 2-17:
Marshall the Miracle Dog.

Reprinted courtesy of Cynthia Willenbrock and The Marshall Movement © 2012 The Marshall Movement
www.marshallthemiracledog.com.

Historical fiction

Who needs to look further than one's own history to find exciting stories of heroes and heroines from all over the globe? Based on real events or on real people in history, *historical fiction* offers the best of both worlds if written well: exciting stories and stealthy learning. It works well with picture books, chapter books, middle-grade, and YA.

My America (Scholastic) is a successful middle-grade series in this category; see also Kathryn Paterson's *Bread and Roses, Too* (Clarion Books) and *Lyddie* (Puffin Books). In YA, there has been an explosion of writing in this genre, including *A Great And Terrible Beauty* (Ember) and *The Diviners* (Little, Brown), both by Libba Gray; *Revolution* by Jennifer Donnelly (Ember); and *The Luxe* by Anna Godbersen (HarperCollins). These books do well because they are well written and because teachers, parents, and children support the subject matter they cover.

To write good historical fiction it's important to keep in mind that the time and place provide the setting for the story, but the plot and characters are still the most important elements. Don't let the setting or time period take center stage. And remember that the characters live in this time, so they wouldn't remark upon how different it is from our time period, or even notice what we'd consider strange or different.

Biography

Biographies like that shown in Figure 2-18 are told in the third person and involve a lot of research. Biographies of historical, cultural, and scientific figures past and present can be very literary, whereas biographies of current hipsters and celebrities (both movie/TV stars and sports heroes) tend to read like *Teen People* magazine — and both have their readership. Biographies are generally written as picture books, middle-grade books, and YA.

Popular literary picture book biographies include Mordecai Gerstein's *The Man Who Walked Between the Towers* (Roaring Brook), *Snowflake Bentley* by Jacqueline Briggs Martin (Houghton Mifflin), and Kristin Armstrong's *Lance Armstrong: The Race of His Life* (Grosset & Dunlap).

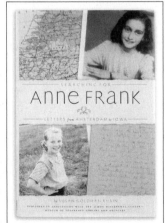

Figure 2-18: *Searching for Anne Frank: Letters from Amsterdam to Iowa.*

By Susan Goldman Rubin. Reprinted courtesy of the author.

The best biographies always reveal the most about the central figure's character and include enough details and tidbits about the character's personal life to make the reader feel as if he is getting a realistic and comprehensive look at another person's life.

Learning/educational

The most skilled writers disguise learning in the most elegant manner so that the reader doesn't even know she's learning. As a genre, you mostly find *learning/educational* in board books, picture books, early readers, coloring and activity books, and middle-grade nonfiction.

Workbooks, subject-based readers, leveled readers, and supplementary school materials fill up stacks and stacks of shelves in most chain bookstores, so if you have an educational or teaching background, you can likely find work writing for children. *Historical-figure biographies, activity,* and *how-to* all fall into this genre. Issue-based books on puberty, sex, divorce, race, adoption, understanding gays/lesbians, and all the hot-button issues of the day for children and teens generally are included as well, though a lot of fiction also covers these topics.

American Girl Publications has a few great entries in this category, such as *The Care & Keeping of You: The Body Book for Girls* by Valorie Lee Schaefer and *Help! The Absolutely Indispensable Guide to Life for Girls* by Nancy Holyoke (both Pleasant Company Publications). Or try *From Boys to Men: All About Adolescence and You* by Michael Gurian and Brian Floca (Price Stern Sloan).

David Macaulay's *The New Way Things Work* (Houghton Mifflin) is a bestselling example of a children's learning/educational book that's so well-written adults were grabbing it out of their children's hands and hiding in the other room to read it in peace.

A newer category in leveled reading developed by Treasure Bay for the educational market, but available to the mass market, is called the We Both Read series. In these books (see Figure 2-19), one page is written in more elevated language for the parent to read aloud and the opposite page is written in appropriate leveled language for the child to read. With titles in both fiction and nonfiction, these books are wonderful tools encouraging both learning to read and parent-child interaction. We think the series provides a pretty remarkable way for parents and kids to bond over reading and books.

Reprinted courtesy of Treasure Bay, Inc.

Figure 2-19:
We Both
Read series.

Religion and diversity

Religion as a genre includes stories related to the Bible, biblical characters, Christianity, Judaism, Islam, Kwanzaa, and any other religious affiliation and its attendant holidays, characters, or tenets. This genre permeates nearly every format of books — from board books to Bible story compilations for the middle grades. Diversity and multiculturalism are also big themes in school curricula, so titles focusing on these issues are often excerpted in textbooks — an added source of revenue for authors.

Books such as Maria Shriver's *What's Heaven?* (Golden Books Adult Publishing), Bryn Barnard's *The Genius of Islam* (see Figure 2-20), and *The Sandwich Swap* by Queen Rania of Jordan Al Abdullah and Kelly DiPucchio, and illustrated by Tricia Tusa (Hyperion Books for Children) fall into this genre.

Gender-oriented series books

Gender-oriented series books are series designed to appeal specifically to either boys or girls, but not both. From board books to picture books, licensed titles to novelty books, many are developed to cater to gender-specific themes or characters. And although many books up to and through middle-grade series (like *Mean Ghouls: A Rotten Apple Book* by Stacia Deutsch [Scholastic]; shown in Figure 2-21) are found in this genre, as we approach the YA audience, gender specificity tends to fall away.

The Baby-Sitter's Club series by Ann M. Martin (Scholastic) was probably one of the most famous series of girl-oriented titles after the Nancy Drew series (Grosset & Dunlap) and The Little House on the Prairie books (HarperCollins). Since that time, dozens and dozens of other series have sprouted up, focusing on what's still considered traditional "girly" fare, such as pets, ponies, fairies, and the like — even a more contemporary revamping of the Baby-Sitters Club seeking to capture some of the avid book reading (and collecting!) middle-grade audience.

Figure 2-20:
The Genius of Islam.

Reprinted courtesy of Knopf Books for Young Readers. © 2011 Bryn Barnard.

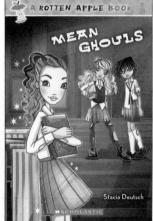

Figure 2-21:
Mean Ghouls: A Rotten Apple Book.

Reprinted courtesy of Stacia Deutsch.
© 2012 Stacia Deutsch.

Successful entries with lots of girl appeal include the Dear Dumb Diary series by Jim Benton (Scholastic) as well as his Franny K. Stein, Mad Scientist (Simon & Schuster Books for Young Readers) and his It's Happy Bunny series (Scholastic Paperbacks), as well as the Ivy & Bean series by Annie Barrows and Sophie Blackall (Chronicle Books).

Some stellar offerings in the nonfiction category specifically and unabashedly targeting girls include nearly every title produced in the American Girl series (Pleasant Company Publications), which also includes historical fiction series with multicultural girl protagonists across the ages. A classic to check out for girls is Louisa May Alcott's *Little Women* (Signet Classics).

For boys, the series list is also enormous. The Diary of a Wimpy Kid series by Jeff Kinney (Amulet Books), the Big Nate series by Lincoln Peirce [sic] (HarperCollins), and the Zack Files series by Dan Greenburg and Jack E. Davis (Grosset & Dunlap) are just a few.

Interestingly enough, Dav Pilkey's incredibly successful Captain Underpants graphic novel series was originally aimed at young middle-grade boys, but girls totally got into them, too, clamoring for the next title (which always seemed too long in coming) and welcoming the series offshoot *The Adventures of Super Diaper Baby* (both Blue Sky Press/Scholastic). Other crossovers for both genders (what we would simply refer to as skilled, hilariously funny writing), include the My Weird School series by Dan Gutman (HarperCollins) and The Spiderwick Chronicles series by Tony DiTerlizzi and Holly Black (Simon & Schuster Books for Young Readers).

Licensed character series books and books into brands

Licensed character series start out life basically in one of two ways: as characters in books (see Figure 2-22) or as characters in products, TV, apps, or other media. When they become popular, they're *licensed* (loaned out for a price) into other media and products.

When a licensed character or series of characters becomes so popular and gets licensed into so many product categories (bedding, stationery, toys, and so on), then it becomes a *brand.* That's just a fancy way of calling a licensed character a product instead of just the star of a book or TV series. If your children's book character ever gets developed into a plain old series of more books, you should consider yourself fortunate. If your children's book character becomes licensed out to, say, a TV series on Nickelodeon or an animated or live-action movie, consider yourself incredibly fortunate. And if your children's book character becomes a brand, well then you'll just be sitting on a fortune.

Publishers are almost always the people who assign TV and movie-based books to writers, so chances are unless you're the best friend of one of the stars, tied to the original movie or TV show, or already in the publisher's stable of frequently assigned adaptation writers, you won't be writing a movie or TV tie-in anytime soon.

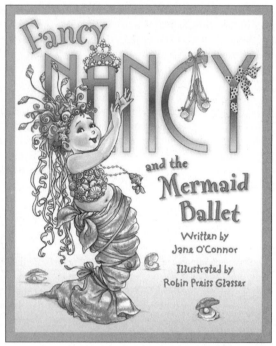

Figure 2-22:
Fancy Nancy and the Mermaid Ballet.

Fancy Nancy and the Mermaid Ballet. Reprinted courtesy of HarperCollins Children's Books. Text © 2012 by Jane O'Connor. Illustrations © 2012 by Robin Preiss Glasser.

Interview with Doug Whiteman, former president of Penguin Books for Young Readers

If you want to know what it takes to stand out, listen to Doug Whiteman, former president of Penguin Books for Young Readers. Having been in the publishing business for over two decades, Doug started out as a book sales rep and worked his way to the top. He's a publishing exec who still loves reading as much as he did when he first came to the company so many years ago.

WCBFD: Since we're talking about genres and series for children in this chapter, can you tell us how important you think it is that a writer understands the conventions of a children's book genre and sticks to what the readers expect?

DW: That's a really good question because we have different filters we're selling to, each of which has its own expectations. Our accounts and their buyers certainly expect things to fit into traditional molds, as do many parents, and many times I've seen books stopped cold if they couldn't be easily classified in a traditional way. Having said that, kids themselves are looking for the truly unique and original. So the best answer to your question is: Understand the conventions and know we will have to package and position your book in a relatively traditional way in order to get past the filters, but give us some sneaky originality inside the covers to captivate the kids.

WCBFD: As one of the largest publishing companies, with lots of divisions all publishing different kinds of books, what kinds of books are always hot?

DW: It seems to me that we're becoming increasingly cyclical, so there's very little that's *always* hot. Picture books, for example, seem to go into downturns every ten years or so. Series books are less cyclical than they used to be. And nothing is more cyclical than licensed publishing, which goes up and down like a roller coaster every few years. Probably the steadiest category is fantasy; everyone likes to think that *Harry Potter* "made" fantasy into a bestselling genre, but the truth is that people like Philip Pullman and Brian Jacques were selling huge numbers long before J.K. Rowling came along.

WCBFD: What kinds of books are most always *not* hot?

DW: Picture books with long texts, expensive books based on holidays that can't command high price points (like Halloween), and books that have depressing endings! I can't think of a genre, though, that's never hot.

WCBFD: What turns a one-off children's book title into a contender for a series?

DW: A wonderful character (or characters). People can enjoy a great book that doesn't have an impactful, memorable character, but a great character can supersede an otherwise mediocre book, leaving your readers clamoring for more.

WCBFD: If you could project into the next decade, what genre of books could you see being most successful?

DW: I see people increasingly looking for true "escapist" fiction, so I'm putting my money on fantasy, futuristic books, and books that have a lot of humor.

WCBFD: Any advice for new writers?

DW: Just what I've said already: Do your homework, and *listen!*

Chapter 3

Understanding the Children's Book Market

*Y*ou may think a children's book writer would be writing solely for children; however, the children's book universe is populated by all sorts of grown-ups who essentially serve as gatekeepers, judging your book at each stage of the publishing process and determining whether your book passes muster and is allowed to proceed on to the next step.

The chain of book business professionals whom you have to impress before even one child sees your book looks more or less like this:

Publisher/Acquisitions Editor or Agent → Marketing Pros and Sales Reps → Chain or big box store book buyer, Reviewer, or Critic → Bookseller → Librarian or Teacher → Parent → Child

Of the many grown-ups who stand between you and your audience (children), agents and acquisitions editors or publishers are the first ones you must impress. An agent serves as the eyes and ears for the publishers and acquisitions editors — and all three are looking for the same qualities: a unique, well written, absolutely worth-the-effort, *gotcha!* manuscript. Next in line are the publisher's in-house marketing and sales reps who take their cues from the editorial team and build out plans from there. These folks are followed by book buyers, reviewers, and critics. Then the booksellers get their hardcopies to shelve after the books are published. Finally, parents, teachers, and librarians become the most powerful links in the chain. *All these adults make choices before children ever set eyes on a book.* So every child without pocket change or an allowance of their own is out of your reach if you can't get these adults on your side. How do you ingratiate yourself with them? By paying attention to the information we share in this chapter.

We start by exploring these gatekeepers. We also look at your target audience — children — and what they like, what they don't like, even how you can tap into an unusual trend and perhaps write a book that rocks the ages.

Interview with Peggy Tierney, small press publisher

Peggy Tierney owns a successful and award-winning small publishing house, Tanglewood Books, www.tanglewoodbooks.com. In her position as owner/publisher, Peggy acquires every title on her list. Here, we ask her how she goes about choosing books in the categories described in Chapter 2.

WCBFD: There are so many formats and age categories to choose manuscripts for. How do you choose which format to publish when?

PT: I am more likely to sign something in a category that isn't glutted at the moment. A few years ago, there were simply too many picture books being published, so it was incredibly difficult to get a new title on the shelves. Publishers slashed their picture book category. I think the YA market is overwhelmed right now — particularly in certain areas such as supernatural romances or dystopian novels. That doesn't mean that I won't publish a book in a crowded category, but the manuscript would have to be truly outstanding for me to consider it. From what I know, bigger publishers also adjust the number of books in each category in the same way. As far as formats, I always publish a book in hardcover to begin with, then follow it with a paperback edition a year or two later. Sometimes a book will work in one format but not another — I always want to give a book the best chance it can have.

WCBFD: Is it important for a query or cover letter to indicate the format or target audience of the manuscript? Why or why not?

PT: For me, it's essential that the writers tell me who their audience is. It's something writers should know before they pick up a pen (or sit down at a computer). It also tells me that they've done their homework and are treating their submission like the professional endeavor it is. The most common thing I see is a picture book manuscript that's too long and too advanced as far as language level.

WCBFD: Once you choose the format that is missing from your seasonal publishing lineup (for example, perhaps you need a board book, two picture books, one middle grade novel with series potential, and a YA for the spring), how do you find the manuscripts?

PT: So far, I haven't had to actively search for a particular format. It seems like I get a nice variety of submissions, so I can always find a promising manuscript or two from each category. I am still much slower to sign a new picture book, though I get more picture book submissions than anything else.

WCBFD: What attracts you to a book?

PT: Characters that seem real; a plot that hasn't been done; great writing, which means being skilled at "show don't tell"; good pacing; and subtle character development.

WCBFD: What repels you from a submitted manuscript?

PT: A writer who clearly has not done his or her homework, and by that, I mean going to libraries and bookstores, studying what is on the shelves, reading everything you can. It will not only make you sound smart and savvy to your publisher, it will keep you from writing stories that have already been done — and it will make you a better writer overall.

As far as the writing itself, a common mistake new authors make is to try to open the book with all the background and character development. You can't wait for 50 pages to start telling the story. Character development and background have to be artfully woven in while moving the plot forward. I use the word "artfully" intentionally; writing well is an art.

WCBFD: When you find a manuscript you like — or more than one — in a format you need, how do you choose from among all the ones you like?

PT: There are a couple of ways I decide. The first one is just taking stock of my passion for a title or lack thereof. If I love a book, I will push harder for it to be successful. And in this day and age, with so many children's books being published, a book has to be outstanding, not simply okay or even good enough. It needs to be a book that makes me want to hug it after I've read it. And something else I do is to send books out to kids. I have kids and teens who read for me, and they are all smart, avid readers who give me honest opinions. They know I want honesty, even if it means they say they don't like something. If a book fails the kid test, I don't publish it.

WCBFD: What if a manuscript you like does not exactly fit into the boxes supported by the industry? (Brian Selznick's *The Invention of Hugo Cabret* [Scholastic Press] is a good example of this — and it became a huge success, even engendering a movie.) What do you do?

PT: I hesitate. I like to do things that are different, but I know my limitations. There have been a few times when I've thought a manuscript was outstanding, but I didn't think I could do it justice, and I've referred the author to an agent or editor who might give it a better home.

WCBFD: What advice do you have from a publisher's/acquisitions editor's perspective for beginning writers just breaking into the business?

PT: They've taken a great step by reading this book! Read, read, read. Go talk to librarians and booksellers and find out what they love and why — then read it. Join SCWBI or find a really good critique group — a group that is not just there to encourage you but to give you constructive criticism. Take a writing class.

WCBFD: Any final words?

PT: I would say to never underestimate the importance of your query letter. The synopsis should be a wonder of conciseness while still capturing the essence of the book and creating interest. If a synopsis is long and rambling, I assume the book is going to be the same. The writing in general should sparkle every bit as much if not more than the manuscript; I will start reading the manuscript already convinced you are a good writer. Tell me who the book is written for and how it fits into that market, such as what book is this like but how is it different? Tell me your background. While I love to hear about a writer's passion, keep it professional and don't sound like a diva. Let me know how hard you will work to make your book a success. In other words, sell yourself to me — that helps me sell your book to others.

Getting Insight into Book Buyers

In a retail store, the *book buyers* are the people who sit down with the sales representatives from the publishing companies or distributors hired by the publishers to handle sales and decide which books they are going to take, for which stores, and in what quantities.

Large chains, such as Barnes & Noble (B&N), may employ an entire department of buyers who purchase, say, only fiction; others may purchase only children's books. Costco has one main book buyer and a team of junior buyers she supervises. At the other end of the spectrum, a buyer may own an independent bookstore with only one or two locations and thus may be responsible for choosing and stocking all titles in the store.

The requirements of each of these buyers may be quite different, and sales reps must adjust their selling approaches to the buyers' unique needs. For example, one buyer may be on the lookout for middle-grade fiction targeting reluctant boy readers; another book buyer may insist that every children's book have a great cover illustration and a unique hook.

A chain bookstore buyer may share some independent bookstore buyers' discerning tastes, but the chain bookstore buyer has also to consider specific sections within the overall children's book area that he has to fill, which size books will fit in those sections, which books may go well in the store's book displays, and how often a section will have to be replenished with new product to keep it from looking stale to frequent customers.

The good news is that your editor will likely be very well versed in how to make your book shine no matter what kind of store it's sold in — big or small, chain or independent. But if you have your own suggestions for getting your book to stand out from the pack, don't be shy. Let your editor know what you think.

The following sections offer some insight into what different selling venues have to offer and how they set up their product to entice their customers.

For chain and big-box bookstores

In chain bookstores such as Barnes & Noble, the children's section has a very distinct organization that is largely duplicated at every store. Most often, inside the children's book section you will find books separated by the categories we explore in Chapter 2.

Although many Barnes & Noble stores still have Young Adult (YA) sections within the physically separate children's book section, featuring mostly classic, evergreen, and award-winning YA titles, most have established a totally separate YA section *physically outside* the children's book area. This has been done because older teens do not want to be thought of as children, so titles and series addressing that target audience get their own special area.

What does this division mean for you? Specifically, as a new children's book writer, you must write your manuscript to fit one of those widely accepted and specific categories or boxes.

Chain store book buyers are often concerned with more than just what's inside the book. The physical size and appearance of the book take on great importance, too. But whether a buyer is purchasing books for all the B&Ns in the country, all the Costcos in the Southwest, or one store in Los Angeles, she's looking for the best in each format for each age group.

Buyers for big-box retailers that don't specialize in just books, such as Target, Toys R Us, or Wal-Mart, may also have additional parameters a book must meet. For example:

- ✔ Does the book fit in the *planogram* (an aisle-long rack with tiered, face-out shelves fitting specific size books)?
- ✔ Is the book special enough to promote on an *endcap* (the end of an aisle)? Is the publisher willing to share the cost for this highly visible position in the store?
- ✔ Does it target the store's primary audience that parents buy for?
- ✔ Is it priced right to survive up to a 50 percent markdown if the sell-through is poor?
- ✔ How will it compete against all the licensed books, which comprise a large portion of the books sold in some venues?

Find out as much as you can about the book business, because after you become a published writer, this business becomes your business, too! So get out to those bookstores, chains, and warehouses, and study their offerings.

For independent bookstores

The buyers for independent bookstores may have the time to look a little more carefully at each book up for consideration. They can also exercise greater freedom in taking a chance on unknown authors and their works.

Here's how one independent book buyer, Jennifer Christopher Randle, defines her job:

> A buyer's job is to identify books that add value to the store — economic value and literary value both. We need to understand what our customers want, understand where sales trends are leading, be aware of which

authors and illustrators are making an impact on the market, and be able to highlight the importance of different formats and genres of books for children. With all of that information, we then meet with publishers' sales representatives at conventions, conferences, and in-store meetings to determine which titles we will acquire.

When asked how she chooses which books to buy for a) infant to three, b) picture books, c) leveled readers, d) middle grade, and e) YA, here's what she had to say:

a) For the youngest, I tend to look for bright colors, familiar images, bouncy rhymes, and simple stories. At this age, the goal is to introduce a love of books to the child.

b) Picture books help foster a child's imagination and wonder, helping children understand there is a bigger world out there. I was always drawn to different types of illustrators from Mo Willems to Gennady Spirin. The most important thing to me is the story — if it's good, it will be read over and over, the pictures will be closely analyzed, and a child will try to squeeze everything they can out of it. If the story is not successful, then most times even the illustrations can't save it. And yet some of the most memorable picture books are told entirely through the illustrations, rewarding because without the leading hand of the author, great imagination is required.

c) Leveled readers are more commonly seen in the educational/library market. They are a great way for children to feel pride in mastering each level and help grow a child's confidence in reading and reading comprehension. This is an underserved market, and I think it is also the most challenging for authors based on the constrictions. You have to use limited language, it can't be too long, and you want to tie the illustrations to the words on the page.

d) Middle-grade fiction is, to me, the most exciting group of books. It is here that a reader has his first taste of genre fiction, which can grow to a lifelong passion. Give a child *The Hobbit,* and I can almost guarantee he will be reading George R. R. Martin in high school. I look for a wide assortment of titles crossing many different genres, because you never know which one will be the spark that ignites a child's interest. Whether funny, scary, historical, or adventure-driven, story is king. Middle-grade fiction has little to no illustration to support it. I always ask myself, "Can I see it?" If I can't picture my protagonist in the story he's starring in, then I would pass. I have a very active imagination, so if I can't picture your world, what chance does a ten-year-old child have?

e) YA is tricky because you have to define it. Is it dumbed down adult fiction? If it's good, should it be YA or "promoted" to general fiction? Usually, it boils down to how it's marketed. With YA, it is important to stay informed by reading reviews, watching award lists, and reading.

Story is key: You need to have complex characters with believable conflicts carrying real consequences. I think that's true of all fiction, really. The early teen years are when kids are pushing boundaries and testing limits. Reading can be an escape, a way of finding perspective, and a constant companion.

Interview with Jennifer Christopher Randle, book buyer for Daedalus Books & Music (independent)

WCBFD: How does your job as an independent bookstore buyer differ from that of a buyer for a chain such as B&N or a big-box retailer such as Costco?

JCR: For Daedalus, I purchased children's titles for one store. We were a remainder book store, so we had the luxury of being able to see past sales history of a title; however, we were also able to find overlooked titles that were great books but just didn't rise as high as some of the other titles. We also had a solid understanding of our customer base: a very literate, educated customer who was looking for a book to share their love of books with their children. All of these factors made it easy to meet with sales representatives at the store or at conventions like BEA (BookExpo America) or CIROBE (the Chicago International Remainder and Overstock Book Exposition). We would be able to quickly go through known titles and familiar authors and illustrators, and spend more time sifting for the forgotten gems.

As an independent bookstore, we were not tied to marketing contracts for book placement or told how to arrange displays according to a corporate office. We could also — much more than large chain stores — take chances on unknown titles. Everybody had a say in which titles were displayed, and we constantly educated one another.

WCBFD: How have bookstores and book buying at the independent level changed in the last few years?

JCR: Both have become more cautious and more volume driven. Buyers are not taking as many chances, focusing their buying power on tried and true books. There is closer scrutiny at the sales history of authors, genres, and publishers making for a tight market that pushes out a lot of participants. The independent bookstore is becoming an endangered species, and everyone is still nervous about the impact of e-books. A lot of it is economically driven, yet we need independent bookstores to provide both great books and great guidance. A customer is more likely to purchase a title if a bookseller can handsell it. That means having a wide selection and an educated staff. Readers like being around other readers, and independent bookstores provide a community lacking in other venues.

WCBFD: What advice would you offer beginning children's book writers?

JCR: Recognize that children are smart and able to pick up on dishonesty faster than most adults. If you write in a condescending way, children will pick up on that. Don't be afraid to be honest if you're writing on a difficult subject. This is how children are able to conquer their own fears, frustrations, and sorrows. People forget that childhood is a very difficult and challenging period when you are essentially powerless amid giants. Authors and illustrators help children understand their own feelings and thoughts, expand their world past their front door, and encourage them to be curious, creative kids.

Recognizing What Reviewers Offer

Reviewers and critics come in many forms and can seriously affect how a book is received in the publishing community. Before committing to buy copies for their stores and schools, booksellers and librarians regularly review such book trade publications as *The School Library Journal, Publishers Weekly, The Library Journal,* and others.

Online reviews such as New York Journal of Books also play a big role for book consumers, as do respected bloggers who focus on children's book reviews. The more respected a venue or blog, the more influence it has on buying choices.

Michael Cart is a book critic, editor, and lecturer who spends a lot of time reading and evaluating books for young adults for various publications and online venues. In his words:

> After 60 years of avid reading, I find the things I look for more than any others are originality and freshness. Give me a story I haven't read countless times before, and I'm a happy chappie! Also, because I think it's imperative that every kid be able to see his or her face reflected in the pages of a good book — especially if that kid has been marginalized for whatever reason (race, religion, place of national origin, sexual identity, and so on) — I look for books featuring characters who have been absent from traditional YA fiction. I also look for books that are creatively venturesome, playing with considerations of structure, voice, and narrative strategy. Some recent favorites include *The Children and the Wolves* by Adam Rapp (Candlewick Press) and *Dying to Know You* by Aidan Chambers (Amulet).
>
> As for nonfiction, I look for high-interest, non-curriculum-related topics that may be offbeat but that will capture the attention of teens with limited time for reading. To that same end, I look for books with strong narrative content and also for books that are eye-catching in terms of design and visual content.

Michael recommends *Master of Deceit* by Marc Aronson (Candlewick) and *Moonbird* by Phillip Hoose (Farrar Straus Giroux) as good examples of nonfiction to check out.

Discovering What Librarians Add to the Mix

Every book buyer looks at content to one extent or another, but public librarians and school librarians are among the most discerning when choosing books for their collections. The American Library Association (`www.ALA.org`) offers lots of reference tools on how to build a library collection, and annual ALA conferences help librarians stay current in a fast-changing field. Great library service to children and young adults assumes a close knowledge of the community and a carefully developed collection. We could attempt to explain generally how librarians make their selections, but we think you'll find more value in hearing from a distinguished former librarian.

In Susan Patron's former position as Juvenile Materials Collection Development Manager at the L.A. Public Library, she concentrated on providing books to serve a large and diverse community in the city of Los Angeles. Part of this task included consideration of a huge system of satellite library branches. Each branch serves its own community and has its own budget, so although she compiled a wide monthly selection of books of all types, not every branch would buy every title.

For example, if considering a new book on skateboarding, she would first examine her existing collection to see whether those holdings addressed the age and interest range of her target audience (meaning appropriate for readers ages 5 to 11, those most likely to want to read about skateboarding) or if she could use a new book not already in the collection. Does the book in hand add anything — better illustrations, for example, or useful safety information?

Other considerations for nonfiction:

- ✔ Well researched, not dated material
- ✔ Pictures appropriate for the audience
- ✔ Contents arranged logically
- ✔ Text readable and inviting
- ✔ Text and illustrations well matched
- ✔ No fictionalized dialogue
- ✔ Source material cited
- ✔ Table of contents and index
- ✔ Is the author passionate about the subject

Susan says that children want a lot of variety on the page. The text shouldn't be too dense, and illustrative material should be clearly marked and ample. All ages of readers enjoy seeing illustrations or photographs that amplify and augment the text. Additionally, trade nonfiction titles should strive for economy of words because most kids will invariably select a thin book over a thick one. An example she gives is *Balloons Over Broadway* by Melissa Sweet (Houghton Mifflin). This book won the American Library Association's Sibert Medal for the best informational book of the year in 2012; the list of Sibert winners and honor books is a useful one for writers of nonfiction: (`www.ala.org/alsc/awardsgrants/bookmedia/sibertmedal/`).

Susan emphasized that libraries seek to maintain a balanced collection, including books on controversial topics that present a variety of points of view. Writers should not avoid subjects for fear of offending some readers — as long as the information is not sensationalized and the sensibilities of the target audience are kept in mind. For example, Susan recommended the excellent sex education books by Robie H. Harris and Michael Emberley, including *It's So Amazing* and *It's Perfectly Normal,* as well as their many other titles for preschoolers to teens.

In terms of picture books, Susan said librarians and reviewers look for an original idea that has not been done before, or if it has, that this incarnation provides a new twist.

> A child protagonist has to solve the problem, not the adult or some magical creature, and the story should be told from a child's perspective. The pictures and words should work well together, and every page should offer enough interest, suspense, drama, or humor to keep the reader (or the person reading to the child) turning the pages. Linda Ashman's *How to Make a Night* (HarperCollins) infuses a well-worn subject, bedtime, with fresh originality and vitality and is entirely child-centered.

In terms of younger middle-grade fiction, kids are interested in subjects such as friendship, siblings, animals, fantasy worlds, and school. These themes are explored in chapter books over and over, and Susan finds that the most popular books work because they're written from the heart and have a unique voice. This audience loves humor and strong protagonists. Susan recommends as a page-turning example Helen Fox's *Eager* (Wendy Lamb Books) and its sequels about a robot who is almost human.

Susan says the library also purchases lots of board books for babies and toddlers, including ones with flaps and die-cuts. The best board books have very few words, and the text directly relates to the very young child's experience. To facilitate access, children's librarians actually place board books in baskets on the floor in the picture book area because they want the target audience (who may still be crawling) to be able to find them. An example of a book that perfectly addresses its audience's experience is *Where's Spot?* by Eric Hill (Penguin Books for Young Readers):

> It's the perfect two-year-old's book because over and over again the text repeats a favorite word of that age group: "NO!" It's funny, suspenseful, interactive, and reassuring because by the end we know that Spot's mom cares more about him than anything in the world. Sandra Boynton, Lucy Cousins, and Rosemary Wells also produce brilliant board books to engage babies and very young children.

Susan astonished us with the fact her library even purchases pop-up books, which we thought would be a no-no due to their fragility. (But as we figured, novelty books with pieces that can be separated from the book are not purchased.)

Even if a pop-up or novelty book is likely to be ephemeral in the collection, we will often buy it for display and story time. We want kids to see how fun and inventive and beautiful books can be. Well-done pop-up books, like those of David A. Carter and Robert Sabuda, are great for story time because they project to a group and can be seen at the back of the room. Plus, they are often packed with audience-pleasing surprises.

Libraries occasionally even buy coloring books and activity books, but very selectively. For example, Susan says that if they relate to topics or information kids are asking for with school assignments, the library will provide them as supplementary material.

Susan hopes new writers will enlist the help of their local children's librarians in becoming knowledgeable and informed about the current field of children's literature.

Public librarians can be a writer's best friend. We want books that engage and delight children, books that make them want to read for pleasure, and we love to help writers in their research — whether by tracing the source of a folktale, checking what's available on a given subject, providing tools such as recommended reading lists, or discussing what topics are of current interest to kids.

Interview with Susan Patron, librarian turned bestselling, award-winning author

In an interesting twist to our original 2005 interview, two years later librarian Susan Patron became a bestselling, award-winning author when her book, *The Higher Power of Lucky* (Simon & Schuster/Richard Jackson), won the coveted Newbery Award in 2007. We asked her a few questions about the experience:

WCBFD: What was the genesis of the idea that became your book, *The Higher Power of Lucky?*

SP: The setting came before the story itself: I'd fallen in love with the remote, harsh, seemingly barren environment of California's Eastern Sierra high deserts, where my husband and I often traveled on vacations. I wondered what it would be like to grow up in a tiny, impoverished community there.

WCBFD: How do you think your experience as a youth services librarian contributed to your writing sensibilities?

SP: I learned the power of story: Well-told/well-written ones can mesmerize a group of wriggly preschoolers, transform apathetic readers into enthusiastic ones, and bring tears to the eyes of a cynical 11-year-old. I discovered it's counterproductive to identify trends or write fiction that tries to correspond to what is currently popular — better to search instead for the story I was *compelled* to tell. I believe this is the way for a writer to find that elusive quality called "voice": Write the story that's banging its hand on the door to your heart.

(continued)

(continued)

WCBFD: How long did the process of writing and finally getting a publication date take? And how did you feel when you finally got to hold the first printed copy of the book?

SP: Since I was working full time, *The Higher Power of Lucky* took over 10 years — maybe more like 12 — with various drafts submitted over those years. I was fortunate to be working with the brilliant editor Richard Jackson, who was patient and wise and kept saying, "It's not quite ready yet." When it was finally published, I was already focused on *Lucky Breaks*, the second book in the trilogy.

WCBFD: How did you transition from your former job to a job that now entails sitting down every day and writing, writing, writing?

SP: When I still had a day job, I got used to spending weekends and vacations with the novel for that long incubation period. Fortunately, I'm married to the world's most supportive husband. He understands about allowing me solitude. So our routine, in which I sit at the keyboard and stare out the window for hours at a time, is well established. Since the act of writing makes me happy — when I'm not being driven crazy by it! — sitting down every day to write is a wonderful job. Holding a printed and bound copy of a novel I have written and published is a great joy.

WCBFD: We heard that there was some ridiculous brouhaha involving the book and attempts to ban it from libraries or bookstores. Can you tell us a little about it?

SP: On the first page a dog is bitten on its scrotum by a rattlesnake. On a private list-serv, some school librarians discussed being uncomfortable with the word *scrotum*, and the conversation was leaked, eventually leading to a page-one article in the *New York Times*. This set off a tremendous national dialogue about censorship. The book was strongly endorsed and supported by the American Library Association's Intellectual Freedom Committee, the Society of Children's Book Writers and Illustrators (SCBWI), The International Reading Association, the National Coalition Against Censorship, and by many individual authors and librarians. Parents may determine whether a particular book is appropriate for their children — but *only* for *their* children.

WCBFD: Do you have any sage advice to offer prospective writers of upper middle-grade or YA fiction?

SP: Write every day. Every. Single. Day. And if you haven't already done so, join SCBWI.

WCBFD: Is there anything our readers should keep an eye out for in terms of future books from you?

SP: A historical novel, *Dear America: Behind the Masks* (Scholastic) came out early in 2012. I'm now working on what might be called a domestic fantasy. Readers can check out my Web site, www.susanpatron.com, for any breaking news.

Taking a Look at Teachers

Teachers have various concerns and issues they want books in the classroom to address. Of course, for teachers of middle school and higher, a lot depends on the subject taught, but most teachers buy books across a wide range of subjects. For example, a preschool director will buy a lot of books dealing with the behaviors, experiences, and concerns of preschoolers. *Hands Are Not for Hitting* by Martine Agassi (Free Spirit Publishing), *The Way*

I Feel by Janan Cain (Parenting Press), and many of Jamie Lee Curtis's books are all good examples of preschooler-targeted titles.

We asked one of our favorite teachers, Jodi Feinstein, a mother of four young adults, what kinds of books she looks for as a kindergarten through sixth-grade teacher. She believes the age and reading level of the child determines her needs, along with whether she's choosing a book to get a child to read or to supplement the core curriculum. For those in primary grades — kindergarten through third grade — Jodi feels that it depends on the reading level of the students, whether she's looking for picture books to read to the class or providing the first chapter/picture books they will see.

> Pictures are essential, and they must be bright and eye-catching. Humor is an absolute must, because it draws in children, they love to laugh at others like them, and if the protagonist does obviously dumb or silly things, so much the better.

Jodi likes picture books that can lead to meaningful discussions in the classroom no matter the grade level. An added bonus is if the book may stimulate the children's analytical skills. She stays away from trendy, commercial, and licensed books.

For the middle primary years — grades four and five — she says,

> The pictures are not so essential anymore, but humor is still quite important. I tell parents with reluctant readers to let them read anything you can get them to read — even comic books — while constantly introducing other genres of books along the way. And books with main characters their age involved in interesting and exciting adventures that fourth through sixth graders can relate to are always appreciated — especially those with sequels that extend the story, thereby piquing the child's interest and keeping him reading. On the other hand, children of this age also like to read a lot of fantasy that is completely removed from real life, but just might have the *possibility* of being possible.

And we find that not much has changed for middle-school-aged readers:

> Kids this age are invariably caught up in a world in which they are the center of the universe. They think everything in their lives generally sucks and that their life is really hard, that nothing is fair. As such, they like to read about kids who have it worse. So books such as *It Happened to Nancy: By an Anonymous Teenager, A True Story from Her Diary* by Beatrice Sparks (Avon), *Go Ask Alice* also by Beatrice Sparks (Simon Pulse/Aladdin), and *A Child Called "It": One Child's Courage to Survive* by Dave Pelzer (HCI) are the kinds of stories they really get into: real-life, horrible things that happen to average boys or girls. I think these kinds of books actually make these readers feel better, feel they can overcome — even if just for a moment.

When the curriculum calls for supplemental reading, Jodi likes to tie in books with whatever her students are learning in history and with what's going on in the real world, not just their world. Other teachers might assign books by topic or issue to get the children discussing subjects of relevance both in school and out in the bigger world.

Teachers are always looking for books to supplement, enhance, and reinforce the curriculum. If you are a writer unsure of a topic, go ask a teacher what subjects she can always use more reference for. Whatever holes exist in the juvenile publishing spectrum, teachers (and librarians) are the ones most keenly aware of them.

Considering Parents' Perspectives

Parents of the very youngest readers (the ones who prefer to use their books as teething rings rather than reading them) buy books that have great art, are bright and eye-catching, and are made of tasty board material. So if you as a new writer aim to create a board book, make sure it focuses on a baby's experiences and has bright art.

It's not until your child starts really paying attention to the content of the books that you have to be very, very, very careful of which books you buy. Because if you buy a book that you will not enjoy reading 5,000 times in a row, you only have yourself to blame. So this is where great story and excellent art really come into play.

As your child grows, your taste in books may be less issue-oriented and more media-oriented, such that you find a lot of licensed books (based on popular television, film, cartoon, or toy characters) creeping into your collection. Or not. And issue-oriented books for older children are just as important as they were back when your child was teething. This is what parents look for most: books told from a child's perspective, starring unique child protagonists who can help their own children become better people, dealing with their issues in a positive and hopeful manner.

If you want to appeal to parents, get down and dirty — literally, get down in the sandbox and listen to what's really going on in children's minds and hearts. And then write from that perspective: what a child wants to hear, not what you as a parent feel he has to hear.

Thinking Like a Kid

Something happens to children when they grow up: They forget what it's like to have magic in their lives. They forget that an ant on the sidewalk can be a source of endless entertainment and speculation. They forget that the need to right injustices and make things fair is as necessary as breathing. They forget that most of the world is black and white, with unbreakable divisions between what's right and what's wrong, what's good and what's bad.

And most pivotally, adults forget that for children, the line between fantasy and reality is blurred. What may seem miraculous or outlandish to an adult is simply part of life to a child.

As a result of this amnesia, many new writers (and sorrowfully, quite a few published writers, although not the truly successful ones) write down to children. They write about what they think children should learn; they lecture, chide, preach, and tell stories instead of showing readers a special storybook world.

So how do you, as a new writer, write for children and not for your own peers? Keep reading. The next sections reveal a little about what children want and, of course, what they don't want.

Speaking to children on their level doesn't mean speaking down to them or using baby talk. It means getting into their heads and their lives and writing about what is relevant and of interest to them.

Going after what kids like — regardless of Mom and Dad

Sometimes writing about what children like may offend adults. Stephenie Meyer's Twilight series, because it has vampires, magic, May-December paranormal love, and other (what some consider to be) dystopian or inappropriate content in it, has been banned in many areas of the United States. Yet the books in the series have won multiple awards.

So you have a choice: You can play it safe with topics children love (and adults don't mind), or you can take a chance with topics children love (and adults definitely mind). Entirely up to you.

Here are some themes children respond to (usually at different ages), adults be darned:

- ✔ Little people can indeed triumph over grown-ups.

- ✔ Poopoo, peepee, tushies, passing gas, burping, underwear — all are hilarious.

- ✔ Turning things upside down is funny — as long as those things make sense in the first place right side up.

- ✔ Magic can occur as a logical reaction to an action.

- ✔ Regular children can go on implausible missions regardless of what the grown-ups say or do.

- ✔ Paranormal and dystopian realities work.

- ✔ Having dead or missing parents makes for better adventures.

- ✔ Taboo activities that older children might indulge in — cutting, drugs, sex (straight or gay is okay, but avoid graphic depictions), drinking, smoking, and so on — are appropriate subjects for upper-grade young adult books.

When writing for children, remember this: Their world is not constrained by the same limitations and consequences ours is. In general, unless they have been abused or suffered extreme peril, children have not yet learned to be cynical or hopeless. There is always a chance for everything to work out — and that chance is lurking just beyond the next page.

Knowing what kids don't like

We guarantee that kids do not and will not embrace the following:

- ✔ Books that preach, condescend, or lecture

- ✔ Books with no real story (nor a plot with beginning, middle, end)

- ✔ Picture books so packed with text you wonder what happened to the editor

- ✔ Nonfiction books so packed with text and so lacking in design and visuals you wonder what happened to the book designer

- ✔ Books whose main characters are boring, uninteresting, or adult

- ✔ Books with main characters who have a problem they don't actively solve, hence they don't change by the end of the book

- ✔ Books that tell instead of showing, using narrative as a soapbox and destroying any semblance of immediacy, making the story feel like old news from page one

Part II
Immersing Yourself in the Writing Process

The 5th Wave   By Rich Tennant

"And now, if you'll hand me my sippy cup, I can begin the first draft of my children's book."

In this part . . .

To write creatively and efficiently, set up your writing workspace to be free from pinging e-mails and texts, spilled juice, screaming children (and spouses or significant others), and all the other distractions of daily life. This part shows you how to make a room of your own, conducive to both creativity and productivity.

After you settle into your writing space, you can begin to work on ideas, big and small, and start researching both the children who will read your story and the subject matter of your story.

Chapter 4

Setting Up Your Workspace

In This Chapter

▶ Scheduling your writing time

▶ Finding your best place to write

▶ Ignoring outside distractions

Guess what? Before you can revel in all those copies flying off the book-store shelves and into online shopping carts — you have to write a book! For some fortunate writers, this is the easy part; for others, it's like waiting at the dentist's office for a root canal.

If you're a natural for the job — someone from whom the words spill out by the gallon — then you probably have little use for this chapter. But if you're wondering how to get started, you may need to gain some understanding of how best to prepare for writing up a storm, so that's exactly what we show you in this chapter.

Finding Time to Write

Effective writers know when they're most productive and create a writing schedule around those times — then they stick to it. In the following sections, we help you pinpoint when *you're* most productive. We also give you some pointers on creating a schedule that makes you want to write and evaluating how that schedule is working for you.

Figuring out when you're most productive

Are you a night owl? A morning person? Are you at your best after you've had a cup of coffee and a chance to read the morning paper or after you've run five miles? Is your house quiet for long periods of time, or is the atmosphere routinely punctuated with noise and distractions — kids running up and down the hallway or a construction project next door? The answers to these questions determine when you're most fertile and inventive as a writer.

Zero in on when you're most productive and then do the majority of your writing during that period of time. Every successful writer has a sweet spot: the time when he or she gets the most done. Check out these tips for finding yours:

✔ Try writing for an hour at different times of the day and night. When do you feel the most creative and prolific? Be sure to give every possible time a try before you settle into a routine.

✔ Shift your writing time around specific everyday events in your life: before or after breakfast, before or after you shower or exercise, before or after you watch TV. Play with your schedule and see what feels good.

✔ You can also accommodate your writing time and your job by taking a laptop, tablet, or pad of paper with you to work. Go in early, or get away to a park or café during lunch.

Not all writers function the same way. Some enforce strict writing schedules at the same time every day; others make sure to devote a certain amount of hours daily to their craft, sneaking them in whenever they can. And some writers vary the amount of time they spend writing. Whatever you choose, make sure it works best with when you're most productive writing-wise and with your *daily* schedule.

Writing once a week won't get you where you want to go; commit to at least every *other* day if every day is not a realistic option.

Sticking to a writing schedule

If you want to be a serious writer — and a successful children's book author — you can't leave your writing to chance. Include writing in your schedule and then do it! Unfortunately, in many ways this is the hard part. Why? Because it requires discipline and focus.

But here's why you need to do what you can to make a schedule work:

✔ By setting aside a specific time every day to write, you soon make writing a habit. As everyone knows, habits are hard to break (and when it comes to writing, that's a good thing).

✔ After you settle into a writing routine, you take a large amount of the stress of the writing process off your shoulders. And a relaxed writer is a more effective and prolific writer.

✔ When you set a regular time to write, you indicate to others (family, friends, and co-workers) that this time is for you and your writing — and not to bother knocking when your keyboard is a-rocking.

Calendars and planners are absolutely essential tools for keeping organized and on track during the course of the day. Lisa is assured she has no other obligations if she enters *writing time* into her smartphone's calendar. So buy a calendar or daily planner, or use your smartphone's or electronic tablet's built-in calendar — and use it regularly.

Evaluating whether you're a one-shot wonder or a committed writer

Think about how your writing feels after a few weeks of sticking to your trial schedule. Are you relaxed? Energized? Distracted? Creative? Asleep? Assess your temporary schedule to find a time that works best for you.

You may sincerely want to make writing a priority in your life, but when the time comes to write something always gets in the way — taking care of the kids, paying bills, or watching a favorite TV show. If this is the case, ask yourself whether writing a children's book is truly important to you. If the answer is yes, recommit to the process and prioritize it in your life. If the answer is no, then consider waiting a few weeks or months (or even years) before you again take up your children's book. Sometimes a break can give you a lot more energy for your project when you come back to it.

Then again, you may just have a temporary case of writer's block, when the words don't seem to flow no matter what you do with your schedule. We reveal how to deal with writer's block in Chapter 5.

Optimizing Your Writing Environment

Just as important as finding the right time to write is finding the right place to write. Even if you've zeroed in on the very best time of the day to avoid distractions and focus on wordsmithing, it will do you no good if your writing environment is, for one reason or another, unsuitable for the task at hand. The next sections present some ways to find your special place while making that place even more conducive to writing.

Locating your special writing spot

Every writer needs a place to write that's comfortable and cozy, stimulates creativity, and has the necessary writing tools. Have a look at some possible places to write:

- A dedicated office in your home

- Another room in your home, such as a den, dining room, or family room — we strongly advise against using your bedroom as your special writing place if you have someone else who routinely occupies it with you

- An inspiring outdoor space

- A local library

- A coffeehouse or café

- A bookstore with tables and chairs available for patron use

- A train station or bus station — you'd be surprised how many places offer free Wi-Fi

- A shopping mall or shopping center

The point is that anyplace can be your special place — you just have to keep looking until you find it. Instead of just settling at the first place you land, try a variety of different locations until you find the one that feels just right. You'll know it when, all of a sudden, everything clicks and the words flow like someone just turned on the tap.

Getting organized

Although different people have different preferences when it comes to the amount of organization they need in their lives, many people work better and more effectively when they're organized. Consider some tips for getting organized — sooner rather than later.

- **Clean up your desk.** The busier your life, the less time you have to clean up the old coffee cups, the wadded up pieces of paper, the reference books, and all the other things that naturally seem to make their home on your desk. As all this stuff piles up, however, it becomes harder for you to write, not only because you have less space in which to work but also because things start getting lost — never to be seen again.

- **Separate obligations.** If you use your writing desk to pay bills, run your philanthropic endeavors for the children's schools, or conduct your other home business, separate out those obligations from your writing ones. Get file holders that physically keep other tasks separated from your writing and that can be moved out of the way if they prove distracting.

- **Clean up your office.** Just as your desk will accumulate progressively deeper layers of stuff, everything from empty boxes and stacks of shoes to tossed waste paper that missed the basket and old candy bar wrappers will find their way into your office. The solution? Clean it up!

✔ **Revisit your office layout.** Consider where you have your desk, your chairs, your computer, your filing cabinet, and anything else, and make sure it's all in the best place to support your writing efforts.

✔ **Schedule regular organizing sessions.** Schedule a regular time to clean up — say every Saturday afternoon or on the first of the month.

✔ **Eliminate distracting clutter.** Consider replacing clutter with a few items that stoke your creativity. Lisa likes to be in an environment with little toys and other objects she finds ingenious or humorous, such as an iron fairy, a set of stone hands filled with tiny rocks, a clutched fist made of wax — all items that make her feel whimsical and lighthearted, the perfect mood pieces for her creative juices to flow in her hyper-organized space.

✔ **Get organized now.** This one speaks for itself. Don't just think about getting organized, *get organized.* Right now! The sooner you get it over with, the sooner you can start writing.

Preventing and dealing with interruptions

Your telephone or computer can be one great big distraction that can keep you from focusing on doing the writing that needs to be done. Ignoring a ringing phone or chiming text message or that inbox full of e-mails is almost impossible. So turn off the ringer, close the e-mail program, and quit your browser if you cannot focus when you should be writing.

If you've become addicted to social networking sites such as Facebook and Twitter, shut them down so that you're blissfully unaware of the constant stream of distractions and can continue your writing.

And if you find that outside interruptions continue to get in the way of your writing, leave that space and find another, or put up a "Don't Make Me Kill You. Do Not Interrupt Unless There Is Already Blood Involved" sign. Or if all else fails, reschedule your writing time for a specific replacement day — for that day *only* — so it can be productive as opposed to frustrating. And plan ahead if you anticipate similar situations reoccurring.

Interview with Debra Mostow Zakarin, author and editor, www.zoitmedia.com

Successful children's book writer Debra Mostow Zakarin talks about how she keeps focused on writing in the midst of a thousand distractions.

WCBFD: Many new writers think that there is some inspirational Zen-like place you have to get into to write effectively. Is this true for you?

DMZ: After so many years of writing, I find my inspiration from life, from my children, and by just writing, writing, and writing. I've always kind of thought that an actual, physical inspirational place, at least for me, was way too contrived.

WCBFD: Do you have a special place where you do your writing? How is it set up?

DMZ: I have an office set up in my home — a computer, desk, fax, and phone. And, oh, my dog lies at my feet, something that really makes me feel like a writer. The space around my computer must be neat or else I get too distracted and look for reasons to procrastinate. Also, I have learned to turn off my instant messenger so as not to get interrupted. And, I make sure to log OFF from Facebook because that is a total time drain.

WCBFD: Do you have a set schedule for writing? What is it?

DMZ: I try to write in the late morning/early afternoon while my kids are at school; however, if I'm in the middle of writing something that I'm totally into, then I go back to my computer in the late evening, after my kids and husband have gone to bed. My best writing, I have found, is usually done late at night.

WCBFD: Is your schedule strict or flexible? How do you enforce it?

DMZ: If my schedule were strict, I feel that I wouldn't be a "creative" person. I have to be flexible with my time. I try so hard to be strict, but old habits of dawdling are hard to break. If I miss a writing appointment, I try to make it up later that day or the next day.

WCBFD: How do you keep your writing life from intruding into your family life and vice versa?

DMZ: My family is my priority, and I work my writing into my family life. Writing is my creative outlet, time just for me, my escape. I try to make sure the two do not collide by setting times for writing that are inviolate, but knowing that if my family needs me, I'll just have to try again tomorrow.

WCBFD: What advice do you have for new authors who are just getting set up?

DMZ: Join or start a writer's group. The feedback and support you will receive will be invaluable. Also, take writing classes, as they will really help you with structure. Most importantly, write, write, and write.

WCBFD: What pitfalls should new authors watch out for?

DMZ: Feeling frustrated over writer's block or rejection. Just keep on going. Creativity is an ongoing process and you have to be flexible but strict about your commitment when changes occur in your life.

Chapter 5

Starting with a Great Idea

. . . .

In This Chapter

▶ Looking around for inspiration

▶ Brainstorming new ideas

▶ Combating writer's block

. . . .

What are some good ideas for children's books, and how do you come up with them? This chapter is about generating ideas and starting writing. We help you come up with ideas by doing activities and trying to look at the world in different ways. We also help you figure out how to use brainstorming to create additional ideas. And if you get that dreaded disease — writer's block — we help you work through that, too.

Once Upon a Time: Coming Up with an Idea

If you're like many aspiring children's book writers, before you actually begin the writing process you may already have an idea you've always wanted to write about. On the other hand, maybe you have no specific ideas and are looking for a way to address your deep-seated yearning to communicate with children. Or perhaps you've always wanted to be a published writer, and you have this curious notion that because children's picture books are relatively short (how hard can five spreads or 32 pages be to write?), writing for children must be the easiest way to get published.

Whatever moved you to plunk down your hard-earned money to buy this book, having an idea starts you off on the process of actually writing your story. But guess what? Even if you don't have an idea, you can still start writing because ideas and writing go together. Ideas lead to writing, and writing can generate ideas. But writers have to start somewhere, so we start with ideas.

Settling on fiction or nonfiction

You have to decide whether your story is going to be fiction or nonfiction. Fiction is writing that comes from your imagination; it's made up. Nonfiction is writing that is based on a true event or real-life person and verifiable facts. We cover the elements of writing nonfiction in Chapter 12, but be aware that nonfiction writing can certainly benefit from the basics we delve into in this chapter. If you're writing fiction, you must address the basics we cover in this chapter.

An idea is like a seed ready to be planted. With the right soil and fertilizers, it can develop into a strong plant, surviving many seasons and countless generations. In other words, the right idea can lead to a masterpiece of a story — one that brings joy to children for years to come.

A children's book idea is just a seed, a kernel, a morsel. It doesn't need to be complicated or long or even developed. It just has to be a notion of something relating to children that you think you can spend a lot of time and effort working on. And even if you love an idea at first and find out you don't later, don't fret; you never have to stay married to any idea you don't adore. You can just chuck it and move on to a better one.

But how do you come up with an idea that really moves you? One that fills you with the passion you need to skip through the writing process with anticipation and glee? We give you a few tips in the next sections.

Relying on specific ideas rather than big ones

Many new writers figure they have to have a *big* idea to get started writing a children's book. Big ideas are the ones you remember from high school English that involve such grand, overarching concepts as *good versus evil* and *man (or woman) versus nature* — the concepts your teacher assured you were in Shakespeare's mind when he tackled each and every one of his plays. Although most ideas in the universe can indeed be broken down and made as simple as *man versus himself,* where's the fun in those concepts? How many children's books do you think are sold based on the pitch "I've written a sweeping epic poem about child versus nature in iambic pentameter"? None.

So now that you've dumped the big ideas, focus on the more specific and less grand. More specific ideas don't involve the entire universe but a narrower subset of the world. They're carefully defined and can be nailed down in one descriptive sentence, such as

✔ Six-year-old anteaters are having a hard time adjusting to life in anteater kindergarten.

✔ Eight-year-old princesses can't imagine kissing a frog, much less pledging their lives to one.

You may cry, "But that subject/concept/idea has been written about so many times before! Why bother doing it again?" Good question. Nearly every idea you generate has already been written about at least once by someone else. So why bother indeed?

Here's why: You can probably name dozens of books about a young boy's adventures in a magical world filled with witches and warlocks and talking animals. But are any of them quite like J.K. Rowling's Harry Potter series? We don't think so, either. The way to make an "old" idea yours is to research the competition, make sure you don't copy, and write from the heart.

Tapping into your own experiences

You've had experiences in your life that could make great stories. It's all in the way you look at those experiences and memories. Many successful children's book authors rely on personal experiences to provide them with ideas they can develop into fun and compelling books. Dig deep into your childhood; try to recall the events and moments that were so intense the memory can still bring the feelings you had then to the forefront. For example, remember

✔ When your mom told you the family was moving to another part of the city — the day after you finally found a best friend and pinkie swore to be pals forever?

✔ The night your parents came home from a trip to a foreign land carrying twin babies that were now your new brothers?

✔ Feeling small and scared as you hid under the sheet, convinced the monsters hiding in the closet were going to get you?

✔ Feeling like you owned the world as you zoomed across the finish line to take first place?

✔ Feeling overwhelmed and excited as you stepped onto the field in front of a girl you really liked — and promptly slipped in the mud?

Children have very strong feelings about the events of their daily lives. Although an event may seem trivial to an adult, a child — who has little sense of time — can't really reassure himself that "it will be over soon" or "this too shall pass." Children are the center of their universe and live very much in the moment. Everything that happens to them is cause for a reaction, positive or negative — rarely ever neutral, unless they aren't paying attention. If you have an idea based on an experience you had as a child that elicits powerful feelings, you can develop that idea into a story other children can relate to and appreciate.

The heart of your story: Theme

The theme is the subject of the story, its central core, its heart. Most themes can be expressed in a phrase or sentence at most. Common themes for children's books include the old standby, *love*, plus themes of *overcoming problems, dealing with change, getting reassurance, reaching achievements and developmental milestones*, and *becoming independent*. The best themes are simple, easy to understand, and applicable to most children at some time or another in their lives.

When choosing a theme, you need to keep in mind where your target audience is developmentally. To be appropriate, themes for young children have to take into account their emotional growth, their interests, their ability to comprehend increasingly complex issues, and to a certain extent their limited reading ability (depending on format, which we fill you in on in Chapter 2). Themes for older children can still embrace the same issues, but you have to flesh them out with more depth and complexity.

Be sure to choose a theme that really excites you, one you can feel passionate about — no matter how many rewrites you have to go through. It's all well and good to write a story with the theme of *reassurance*, but if you're really more interested in writing about *a child dealing with change*, do the latter! Don't ever write only to please your audience; you also have to please yourself, because you are the one who has to be dedicated to your manuscript for each of the steps in the writing process.

Dig through childhood mementos

Got a diary from when you were little? What about a box of old school papers? Maybe a trunk or dusty suitcase packed with art and class projects? If you can find any one of these, we guarantee you will get ideas for stories as the memories come flooding back. Jot down whatever comes to your mind: bits of information, names of classmates or special friends, field trips or projects you found, trouble you got in — whatever flows into your mind could be developed into a book now or at a later date.

Look at a photo album

Looking at an old photo album can help you come up with good ideas by reminding you of childhood experiences. Your own baby or childhood photo album is best, but anyone's will actually do. The goal of this activity if you aren't in the photo is to see whether you can remember a similar event or time in your own life.

Peruse the photographs until you find one that strikes you as compelling. Then ask yourself some of these questions about the child in the photo, writing the answers as you go:

- ✔ Who is the child? (If you don't know her name, give her one that seems to fit.)

- ✔ When and where do you suppose the photo was taken?

> ✔ What is she doing at that moment? (If the surroundings in the photo don't give you any clues, make up something.)
>
> ✔ How does she feel about what's going on? (Does her body language or her facial expression suggest anything right away?)
>
> ✔ Why is she feeling that way? (Is she scared? Happy? Put off? Proud? Unsure?) What could have caused her reaction?
>
> ✔ Is there someone else in the photo who is affecting her? What did that person do that may have caused the child's expression?

Looking at an old picture of herself, Lisa came up with these answers to the preceding questions:

> That's me! I look about three years old. I'm sitting on a blanket at the beach. I'm holding a bucket up to the camera as if to say, "Look at this!" I seem to be very excited. I don't recall what was in the bucket, but perhaps something alive, like a sand crab. The only other person with me is the one who is taking the picture, and that must have been my dad because my mom detests the beach.

What idea did that photo generate? Lisa can recall when she was young feeling very strongly about protecting all animals, no matter how small, and sensing it was a very important job only she could be trusted with. Perhaps she could use that recalled emotion to write about a child who goes to the beach and discovers a bunch of sea creatures who can speak. They tell her their world is endangered and they need her to save it. They try to get her to follow them to an undersea kingdom only children can see. When she follows them and her feet touch the water, the entire world changes, she develops a fin where her feet used to be, and she finds herself breathing underwater like a fish. Having this new talent allows her to explore where children have never been before — and the story goes on from there. It may not be the most original idea in the world, but it's a totally viable story idea.

Drawing from other children's experiences

Perhaps your memories of childhood are so fuzzy they're practically nonexistent — or you just wish they were. You certainly don't have to limit yourself to *your* childhood experiences. If, as an adult, you've had experiences with children you think are important and interesting, you can use those experiences for ideas. Maybe you're acquainted with a child who's dealing with a particular issue such as the death of a sibling or a divorce, and you're unable to find a book addressing her problem in a way you like — what a great idea for a book! Or maybe you know a child who is a fascinating character and simply must have adventures written around his unique personality.

Pulling ideas from the world around you

Open your eyes. Look around you. Really pay attention to your life. What do you see? What's going on with children today that you find interesting? What have you read or seen about children that grabs your attention?

When you read magazines or newspapers, read with the intent of finding ideas for children's books in the content. When you watch TV, search for stories with kid appeal. (We take you into a child's world and help you figure out what may appeal to children in Chapter 6.) Start looking at the world with writer's eyes — eyes that see everything as an idea or a possible subject.

For example, Lisa once read an article about how researchers believe the teen brain grows and develops. As Lisa read, a thought popped into her head: What if a teenager re-created Mary Shelley's *Frankenstein* monster in robot form from used computer parts? Lisa understands the impulse many teenagers have to gain control of their lives in one way or another, so she likes the idea of a teenage scientist attempting to create a robot monster to wreak havoc on his world. You may say that Lisa's idea has nothing to do with the article and her idea has been done before, but that doesn't matter. One day Lisa may be able to use the idea and write a fresh story based on it. And even if she doesn't, at least she's generating ideas — one of the first critical steps in the writing process.

Stumped? Break through with Brainstorming

Brainstorming is a creative technique in which you freely express random thoughts and ideas on a subject in the hopes of coming up with a creative solution. It's a process of taking your brain's inventive energy, focusing it on a subject, and then opening up and letting ideas flow out of you.

The key to brainstorming is gathering as many ideas as you can in a relatively short amount of time, withholding judgment about their merits until later. When you're brainstorming, focus on the *quantity* of the ideas you're generating, not the *quality*. You want your imagination to be as free as a child's — and children's imaginations are unfettered by judgment because they aren't bound by the constraints adults live by.

The purpose of a brainstorming session, whether you conduct one by yourself or with others, is to amass bits of information you can then cull down into usable ideas at a later time. The best brainstorming sessions are ones in which you allow yourself to think thoughts as crazy, outlandish, far-fetched, and miraculous as possible. When you don't constrain your thinking by what you know or think is plausible, instead allowing yourself to go wild, cross boundaries, and turn the world upside-down, you're using brainstorming for what it can truly offer: interesting information to morph into great ideas somewhere down the road.

The following sections provide helpful brainstorming ideas to get you started.

Going it all by yourself

Do you have a ritual you follow when you want to come up with new ideas? For Peter, the best solo brainstorming occurs when he's in the shower. That's where his very best ideas come to him. Something about hot water pouring over his head — the sound, the heat, the steady pulsing — simultaneously focuses and frees his thoughts, allowing his brain to roam and generate ideas like crazy. Lisa gets ideas while trolling huge gift shows and toy fairs. All those knickknacks somehow get her brain going, and she always fills up a notebook with lots of notes about what she sees and what she imagines creating.

Here's a simple approach to brainstorming by yourself (don't try this in the shower; electronic tablets tend to dislike water):

1. **Find a quiet place where you can be free of distractions for at least 15 minutes.**

2. **Grab a timer plus either a big pad of paper and a writing tool or a tablet with a Notes app and a stylus.**

3. **Set your timer for 15 minutes, and start writing down every story idea you can think of.**

   If you have trouble getting started, picture a child in your head and try to take that child on a trip to experience as many different things as you can think of.

   Your ideas may be similar to stories you're already familiar with, or they may be totally new. Don't judge an idea; just write it down and move on to the next one.

4. **When your 15 minutes are up, stop writing and look at your ideas.**

   Although many of your ideas may not prove usable for stories in the long run, chances are you have a gem or two hidden in the pages generated by your brainstorming session. Pull out these ideas and hold onto them.

When you go back to your lists (we hope you make time to engage in brainstorming every so often in order to have multiple lists), you may find one of the ideas has potential. You'll know an idea is worth pursuing if reviewing it makes you think of lots of ways to expand it, if you can't stop thinking about it, or if it ignites some sort of passion in you. That's when you know you can write about that idea in a heartfelt and sincere manner.

You have to care about an idea to make expanding it into a story fun. No matter how uniquely fabulous an idea may seem, if you don't care about it, it isn't a workable idea for you. It may work for the writer next door, but not for you. At least not at the moment.

Giving free association a whirl

One way to brainstorm about a particular subject is to *free associate,* meaning writing down all the words you can think of that are even randomly associated with a starting word or phrase. Free association works great when you have a *very* vague idea you want to solidify. Say you want to write about a bunny rabbit. To free associate, you write down all the words you can think of related to *bunny rabbit.* You can write them in a column or write *bunny rabbit* in the center of a piece of paper and use arrows to point to the words radiating out from it like spokes on a wheel. There are also apps you can use to do this on your smartphone, tablet, or laptop.

Off the top of our heads, we can free associate the following from *bunny rabbit:* toothy, furry, fluffy tail, fast, lots of sisters and brothers, jumpy, hoppy, long ears, twitchy nose, timid, whiskers, long paws, jackrabbit, hare, white, brown, lop ears, claws. We also find it helpful to list as many opposites to those words as you can think of, because a lot of the drama of a story later comes from conflict, which is often generated from opposites clashing in some way (more on that in Chapter 8). Some opposites we might list would be toothless, bald, tailless, slow, only child (well, only bunny).

The more free associating you do, the more your vague idea forms into a solid idea. Later, when you're ready to write, come back to your lists and see whether any of these words help you with character development (more on that in Chapter 7).

Taking up free-form or structured journaling

Not all solo brainstorming is done in one session. Sometimes, idea brainstorming is done over time. A very popular and common way to record your ideas as they come to you is to engage in journal writing. Why? Because journaling is a great way to free up your mind and create a living record of your life you can go back to again and again to mine for ideas.

Brainstorming in journals falls into two primary categories:

- ✔ **Free-form journaling:** This is writing for the sheer joy (or pain) of writing. No agenda, no exercise, just translating thoughts into words onto screen. Some folks like to begin journaling by writing about whatever prevailing emotion is driving them at the moment. Others like to record dreams and use them as problem-solving devices — attempting to decipher hidden meanings and possible connections to waking life. Others like to use a journal as a listening post. Whatever you decide to write about, free-form journaling helps you develop ideas and get used to writing on a regular basis.

Regardless of your approach or topic, you must follow one rule about free-form journaling: *Thou must not judge thyself, nor even reread what thou hast written, until thou art done for the day.* This writing is intended only for your eyes to help you come up with ideas for your children's books, so feel free to let yourself go. Writing in a journal can be a joyful experience. And before you can discipline yourself as a writer, you need to feel the freedom of writing for the joy of writing.

- ✔ **Structured journaling:** Structured journaling is starting with a theme, an exercise, or a goal, and writing to expand on it. Are you the type of person who prefers structured activities? Some writers like to take a formal approach to journaling. They keep a journal restricted to one set of ideas. For example, they may keep a food journal, a dream journal, a journal written only when it's raining — or a journal of ideas.

Consider buying a bunch of journals and keep them all going at once, each with a different purpose. Or dedicate different folders on your laptop or tablet. Depending on how your mind works, having separate places to hold different ideas can make you feel more productive — or more organized. On the other hand, so many could make you insane. It's your choice.

If you're really brave and have a trustworthy colleague or writing partner, share a journal, leaving a space after each of your entries for commentary or companion entries by your writing partner. If you want to make it really easy, you can keep an online shared journal. With the idea that two heads are better than one, companion journaling is a good way to brainstorm with a friend. At the very least, you may be surprised at what you read.

Aside from helping you get into the habit of writing, structured journaling leaves you with a potential treasure trove of ideas to draw from during your long career in writing children's books. Who knows? One day, a children's book starring a toothsome, slow, only bunny looking for a mother figure may bear your name on its cover.

Your journals don't have to involve "good writing": Simple one-liners can later prove immensely inspiring. Your writing can be as straightforward as this: *No rain today. Feeling parched and dry, much like a reptile bone buried in the sand.*

Buddying up to the buddy system

Brainstorming with writing buddies is a fun way to generate ideas. You and your buddies agree to come to a meeting prepared to discuss current events, trends, changes in the world — whatever you want — with the understanding that these issues should all revolve around the lives of children. Then steer the conversation toward coming up with ideas that may lead to stories or books for children.

In a round-robin fashion, each person gets to bring up his first topic of interest and present it to the group for discussion. So if Peter and Lisa were playing the brainstorming game, it would go something like this:

LISA: I really want to write something about fairies, but I can't think of anything new.

PETER: Will your fairies fly? Will they have magical powers? Will they speak?

LISA: Hmmm. Maybe they've forgotten how to fly. Maybe they're like children who've lost the ability to have fun. Or maybe they're just uncoordinated and can't get their wings to work. Maybe they're like fairy immigrants who have had to adjust to a new culture and in the process have forgotten about their old, magical lives.

PETER: If they're immigrants, where do they hail from? And how exactly are they magical? How're they different in terms of the magic they can do versus what the magic trolls, gnomes, elves, and other creatures of that ilk can do?

LISA: I don't really know. I should find out about all that.

PETER: Maybe there's a battle going on between magical creatures of all sorts.

LISA: Yeah, maybe fairies aren't the only ones who have forgotten their magic. Maybe the entire world of these creatures is in crisis. Okay. I have to do more research about this before we come up with more ideas. But I really like something about getting their magic back — maybe bringing in other creatures. I like gargoyles. I'll add those to my list.

PETER: I had a particular idea in mind. I wanted to write about children who stay in afterschool programs. I wanted to start with a group of kids who're sort of abandoned between the time school closes and the time their parents pick them up, and they go on all sorts of adventures related to learning.

LISA: Be careful not to make the learning part too obvious or preachy. Maybe the adventures involve magic in the sense they can travel to space or to foreign countries or inside an acorn or whatever. But I wonder what they have to do to get there? Is there science involved in the travel part or do they just magically arrive there and then the particular adventure begins?

PETER: I dunno yet. I'll write that down. And maybe they have to solve problems set way back in time, going all the way back to the dinosaurs. Like they could explore age-old questions we all wonder about, like how the dinosaurs disappeared and what made the ice age occur.

LISA: I really like those ideas. Time travel is always intriguing. And maybe you have kids who aren't necessarily the usual stereotypes like the Brain or the Loser or whatever. Maybe these kids each have special powers that help them look at things differently, like scientists do.

PETER: Yeah. I like that. Okay, that's enough for me to start with.

Brainstorming by going back and forth between you and your writing buddies can generate and hone ideas, helping you develop them much faster than most writers can accomplish alone. Also if your writing partners are as brutal as ours are, they tell you when your ideas are lame and underdeveloped and encourage you (or bully you) into going back to the drawing board. After you get an idea that you feel strongly about and your partner(s) think rocks, you can get started writing your children's story — or at least you can go to Chapter 6 and discover what to do next.

Asking the advice of a writing teacher or classmates

Writing classes are great for many reasons, one of which is that you have access to an expert in the field who can tell you if, idea-wise, you're headed off into a place you'd best not go. Writing teachers are great resources.

You can also brainstorm with your classmates to get ideas and then go over them with your teacher, who can help you figure out which ones work better for you. Or you can brainstorm alone with your teacher and have her help you work out which ones have the most promise in terms of uniqueness and interest to you (you're the one investing a lot of energy to make the idea come alive as a story, after all).

Online children's book writing courses attached to major universities can also be a boon, offering individual interaction with a teacher without ever having to leave the comfort of your ergonomic desk chair. But we suggest that you check out these resources before investing any time or effort in them, making sure they offer what you need and involve experts who can really help you reach your goals as a writer.

If you're not taking a class that gives you easy access to a writing teacher, see whether you can pay a professional writing teacher for an hour of her time. Just make sure she knows the specific purpose of the session and come prepared so the meeting is productive, and you get the most for your money.

Seeking help from your audience

Children themselves are a wonderful resource when it comes to ideas. Brainstorming with them, however, needs to be directed, because many kids love every idea you present to them (bless their hearts).

If you're visiting a classroom, consider bringing a list of ideas and generating discussion based on these topics. Brief the teacher beforehand by sharing your list and reiterating the purpose of your brainstorming session. We guarantee that if the children are verbal enough to carry on a conversation, and if you can get the teacher to facilitate based on your list of topics, you'll find out stuff about your topics you never even considered.

A typical session of brainstorming picture book ideas with a group of four-year-olds may sound something like this:

LISA: So I was thinking about writing about little sisters and brothers and how you get along.

CHILDREN: (Silence; no response.)

LISA: Like, if you have a little brother, how you manage to get along with him.

CHILDREN: (Silence; no response.)

LISA: (Getting a little desperate, trying not to let it show.) For example, what would you think if I wrote a story about a little brother who disappeared and had to be found by his older brother?

CHILD 1: You mean his big brother would save him?

CHILD 2: Like a hero?

LISA: (Relieved.) Yes! Exactly. Would save him—

CHILD 1: (Interrupting.) —from a mean fire-breathing dragon? Who would melt the little brother 'cause he took toys from you and broke 'em?

CHILD 2: And you didn't have enough time to save him before he got scared some by the dragon. So he would drop the toys he stole from your room?

LISA: Yes . . . and maybe there would be a princess—

CHILD 3: I like princesses!

CHILD 1: As long as they aren't wearing dresses 'cause you can trip on dresses when you're climbing the tower to save your little brother.

LISA: Then maybe the princess could be a brave one who can help you find your brother. But first you have to find the magic key.

CHILD 3: The key to the castle? Or to mom's car 'cause sometimes my little brother takes the car keys and drools all over them.

CHILDREN: Eeeeew!

Interview with Barney Saltzberg, author/illustrator/performer (Part I)

Whatever exercises you choose to help you generate ideas and get started writing, you need to put pen to paper or fingers to keyboard and just go. Take it from Barney Saltzberg, acclaimed musician as well as successful children's book writer and illustrator, who tells it like it is about ideas and writing.

WCBFD: You have written and illustrated over 25 books for children, not to mention the tons of songs you've written and performed on your CDs. How do you get your best book ideas?

BS: There's no formula. If I had one, every book I write would be a hit! Ideas come to me in many different ways. *Crazy Hair Day* (Candlewick Press) came from seeing a student show up at my son's school, a day early, for Crazy Hair Day. My brain took over from there. Sometimes I'll hear something and say, "That's a great title for a book or a song," and that's how it begins.

WCBFD: Do you think that brainstorming with others is a good way to come up with ideas? Why or why not?

BS: I try to brainstorm with other people from time to time, but personally, I find that I need to sit with whatever I'm working on and brainstorm by myself. It works the best. It's not a bad idea to get someone else's viewpoint, but you really have to trust them to have the same way of thinking as you do, and that's nearly impossible in my case!

WCBFD: Do you use any particular idea-generating exercises to come up with ideas?

BS: No.

WCBFD: Do you start with a format idea that you fit a book idea into, or do you begin with a book idea that you fit to a format?

BS: I begin with an idea and see which format it fits into later.

WCBFD: When an idea comes to you, how do you record it? And how can you tell if it is a good one?

BS: Sometimes I find myself making notes on scraps of papers, napkins, or on my computer. It depends where I am when the idea hits me. I always think they're good ideas. It's only when I've worked on them for a long time that I know if they will truly work or not.

WCBFD: How do you proceed to develop an idea that you feel really good about?

BS: Since I'm a writer and an illustrator, my working habits are different from writers who only write. Sometimes I'll be writing and then find a piece of paper and start drawing the characters I'm writing about. The body language and facial expressions of those characters sometimes color how the written story develops. Mostly, I just force myself to sit with my computer and write and write and write.

WCBFD: Is there such a thing as writer's block?

BS: Unless you're talking about a neighborhood full of writers and that's where you live, "on the writers' block," I personally think there's really no such thing as writer's block. Only a writer who's avoiding writing. I guarantee that if you sit down and just write, things will happen for you! Will everything you write be great? Absolutely not. But you're writing.

WCBFD: Any advice you can offer to new writers trying to come up with great ideas for children's books?

BS: You have to start writing. Write from within yourself, as a child. It sounds corny to say, "Write from your inner child," but that's where the voice is. Don't set out to write an entire book. Just make short sentences, blurting out anything and everything. Eventually, something will pop out. Recess. Homework. Walking home from school. Playing in the yard. The neighbor next door. Something will trigger a flood of memories from which to start a story.

For more sage advice from Barney Saltzberg, see Chapter 6.

Cross our hearts and hope to die, you'll never leave a classroom without at least one great idea that makes your fingers itch to get writing.

Heading back to school

If you haven't recently spent any time around children, why not head back to school? You could be there in an official capacity, perhaps as the coach at a community center or a nearby school, or even as a teacher at your local church or synagogue. Many volunteers give their time and expertise for altruistic reasons, and you can *say* you do, too, while secretly gathering material from children by hanging out with them in a way benefiting both of you. They get an adult to oversee and guide activities, and you get to observe them on the sly, mercilessly using them for the material and ideas they contribute to your idea notebook.

The more time you spend around children, the more your ideas reflect their world — and the more your writing speaks to them.

Or perhaps you prefer to take the *backdoor approach,* meaning that if purposefully trying to generate ideas instantly freeze-dries your brain, some other unrelated but enjoyable creative endeavor may melt down your resistance. Consider taking a class in painting, pottery, drawing, woodwork, beading, gardening — any art or craft class that may interest you. Using your hands and eyes in creative activities other than writing can actually help your creativity, which in turn helps you think of good ideas, which in turn helps your writing — even if you can't make the connection right away. (Bonus: It also relaxes you enough to help you come up with new ideas.)

Fighting Writer's Block

Picture this: You have a great story idea that has kept you writing for days. On the fifth day, you're happily writing when the doorbell rings. You answer it to discover a package delivery. You sign for the package and return to your desk *and realize you've completely lost your train of thought.* Minutes pass. Then a half-hour. Then you notice dust in the corner of the room you hadn't seen before, so you grab the broom. Next you're at the kitchen sink washing dishes. Finally, you return to the computer, but you realize your writing has come to a crashing halt. You're paralyzed in front of a computer monitor that seems to be actively mocking you. And no matter how many times you straighten up your desktop and change the pretty background pictures, you can't seem to write a word.

Getting stuck is something that all writers — no matter how skilled they are or how much practice they've had — experience from time to time. The writer's brain is like a mighty river — usually it flows along smoothly, but sometimes a 40-foot barge sinks right in the middle, causing the river to back up and the words to stop flowing.

If you get stuck long enough, you can experience those two little words guaranteed to strike fear in the heart of anyone who has ever faced a deadline or had to earn a living from his words: *writer's block*.

Based on some research, we found out that not everyone believes in the existence of writer's block. (See "The psychology of writer's block" in the nearby sidebar for the counterargument.) Some blame shiftless Americans who created the so-called phenomenon because they were too lazy to power through the tough times when writing got the best of them.

Other people even think that writer's block is a creation of psychologists who want to take advantage of writers' insecurities and make piles of dough from them. (Hmmm . . . do we sense a lucrative new career path here?)

We think writer's block *does* exist (sort of, but in a way that is immediately resolvable) and is simply a condition requiring one of two remedies:

- ✔ Giving yourself permission to get away from the pressure of writing for a while until the urge to write strikes again — but not indefinitely. If the urge does not strike within a few days, go to the next remedy . . .
- ✔ Using writing exercises to get your writing juices flowing again

If writer's block seems to be plaguing you, flip to the writing exercises in Part III.

You do writing exercises for fun. For laughs. For the sake of doing them. Why is this important? Because the first half of the problem with writer's block is losing the urge to write, and the second half involves being stuck about what to write. So exercise your imagination — a very important muscle in getting over "writer's block" and finding out how to master the process of writing.

The psychology of writer's block

Ever wonder why your brain gets stuck? We have (more than once or twice), so we did some research on writer's block. Much to our surprise, writer's block is not the result of watching soap operas on TV (which is *very* good news for Peter) or of eating too many carbs, or from our enemies sticking pins into twin voodoo dolls crudely designed in our images (though we're still a bit suspicious about that one).

According to the folks in white lab coats who spend their working days and nights researching this phenomenon, writers actually get stuck when a temporary disconnect occurs between the brain's frontal lobes (located behind your forehead) and temporal lobes (located behind your ears). Among other tasks, your frontal lobes act as your writing organizer and editor, while your temporal lobes control your understanding of words and come up with those fabulous ideas sure to capture the interest of your publisher.

When your frontal lobes take charge — pushing aside the ideas set forth by your temporal lobes — you quickly find yourself stuck (bad). When your temporal lobes take charge, the words flow unimpeded, fast, and furious (good). So can you do anything to help your brain move through the occasional slow spots?

Bang your head against the closet door really hard. (Just kidding.)

Pay attention to what kinds of events in your life or environment seem to lead to writer's block — and what kinds of action make it go away. Then do less of the former and more of the latter. (Yeah, yeah, we know that solution sounds ridiculously easy, but remember: Not everyone believes in writer's block anyway. And how much do you want to bet that those who don't believe in it don't suffer from it, either?)

Chapter 6

Researching Your Audience and Subject

• •

In This Chapter

▶ Researching with children

▶ Taking a look at popular culture

▶ Delving into the stacks

▶ Tapping into the experts

• •

*T*he best children's books have some grounding in a child's reality, and the best way to discover what that reality is rather than what you imagine it to be is to get out there and explore. In this chapter, we take a look at some of the best places to find out more about kids and about the people standing between your manuscript and the children you're trying to reach: how they think, how they act, what they like, what they think is gross versus what they think is cool, and what proves perennially popular.

We also touch a bit on researching your topic itself. If your subject falls into the nonfiction realm, you have a lot of facts to get straight. But even if your subject is fictional, you may choose to ground certain aspects of it in reality — a reality about which you are unfamiliar, such as Victorian England — or perhaps one of your characters is a beaver and you have no idea what beavers eat or where they live. Using some of the same strategies you use to dig into the secret lives of children, you must go even further when it comes to presenting the facts. The facts have to be right on target, and this chapter helps you get ready, aim, and fire.

Hanging Out with Kids

If you're writing about kids and the issues that they deal with in everyday life, you want to make sure to write from their perspective. Many new writers make the mistake of writing from a grown-up perspective. As a children's book writer, you need to keep in mind the children you're writing for are looking for entertainment, not parenting. Your job is to capture their imaginations and bring them into your world, not teach them lessons about right and wrong. No one likes a lecture — especially not children, who are probably already getting more than their share of lectures at home and school.

Of course, you also have to remember that children aren't only your target audience but also likely the subjects of the book you're writing, which means the information, the descriptions, and the language have to be accurate. If you want your child characters to be believable, you need to know how children talk, what they wear, what they do, and how they go about doing it. Every detail matters.

If you're panicking right now because the only thing you can remember from your childhood is that you wore smaller clothing or that you used to love peanut butter and jelly sandwiches, never fear. You can gain perspective on kids simply by hanging out with them. The following sections offer a few ideas for how to do just that.

Go back to school

For at least nine months of the year, Monday through Friday in most parts of the world, from approximately 8 a.m. to 3 p.m., children attend (some may claim are held prisoner in) school, which therefore happens to be a great place to go to do your research. Lucky for you, many teachers are open to having writers come into the classroom. Just be sure you check in with the front office before you start wandering the halls. You may need to sign in, and you may be accompanied by a school representative.

Being around children at school is the perfect research venue. You can make the experience active by leading a project or volunteering for an arts and crafts activity or game, or you can simply lurk passively in a corner and watch and listen. How do the kids dress? How do they interact with one another? What do they say to one another? How do they handle conflict? What toys or games do they prefer and is there a difference between how the boys play or act and how the girls do? Is there a time set aside for art? What kind of art do kids create at different ages? What about during lunchtime? Is there gender segregation and if so, why? If there's a rest period, how do the grown-ups make the little beasts adhere to the rules? Do children behave differently upon arrival than they do upon departure? How so?

With older children, do they seem to roam in packs? How are those packs differentiated from one another? Is how someone dresses a big deal? How can you tell? Are the alphas overtly apparent? What do kids have in their lockers? How do they behave with and speak to one another or their teachers?

All this information and more gives you a peek into the lives of real children — the ones you hope will be reading your book after it gets published. And if you're privileged enough to have your work end up in their hands, you best make sure you haven't misrepresented or miscast them. So grab your backpack and your pencil case and head back to class, where you are the student and the students are your teachers.

Get by with a little help from your little friends

Want to observe thinking, busy, creative children in action inside a preschool or kindergarten classroom? Don't just visit a school empty-handed. Take along all the fixin's for a bookmaking session! All you need are:

- Five sheets of white construction paper per child

- One sheet of colored construction paper per child (not too dark of a color that art won't show up on it)

- A single-hole punch

- A ball of yarn

- A children's story, either your own or one whose subject matter is similar to yours but that isn't extremely popular (so the kids are likely to be unfamiliar with it)

- Crayons or markers, one complete set per five children or per table

Have each child fold the five white sheets of construction paper width-wise to create the interior of the book. Then have the children take the colored sheet of construction paper and wrap it around the interior pages. To tie the sheets together (the binding), you are going to punch holes on the left side of the book. Punch the first hole about an inch from the top and ¼-inch in from the outside folded edge, and the second hole about an inch from the bottom and ¼-inch in from the same outside folded edge. Take two pieces of yarn about 8 inches long each and loop one piece through each hole, tying the ends. *Voilà!* You have a blank book.

Next, read your chosen story aloud to the children. Then tell them you need their help to figure out what happens to the characters next or the next day. (Some writers like to leave out the ending in order to fire up their listeners' imaginations.) Together, as a classroom, each child writes the next five spreads (or ten pages) of the book to create the ending or the "sequel" to the story. Every child gets to pick a number out of a hat, and those numbers will be used to solicit answers to the questions you will ask of them to get the story going (the numbers help keep the chaos of many willing participants in check by giving each a turn in order). Tell younger kids not to worry unnecessarily about getting the words just right; they're simply to draw the pictures for the characters.

If you want to go even further, use the numbers again to get the kids answering questions about what words or images should go on the front and back covers to make a kid want to pick up the book — or a parent to buy it.

Become a storyteller

A great way to understand how children in your target age group think is to read a book to them and then have a question-and-answer session. You can do this with children who are as young as three or four years of age, depending on how verbal they are and how accustomed they are to speaking in front of other kids (preschoolers are ideal for this kind of exercise because they love to raise their hands, give their opinions — often in great and meandering detail — and listen to themselves speak to an adult who actually cares to hear what they have to say). Or you can pick older children, such as tweens or teenagers — whoever you think your target audience is, the actual bodies that fall into these age ranges are the ones you need to be getting information from.

Regardless of where you go to get the attention of children, it's important to make sure you're prepared to present a truly captivating read (trust Lisa, there's nothing more humiliating than reading to an audience that could not care less because you are boring and unable to grab their attention or hold onto it once you get it). Don't just read any random old book — make sure it's one that's similar in subject matter or topic to the book you want to write — maybe it's the competition or an out-of-print version of a topic you want to handle. And make sure you know the book pretty well so that you can ask some really good questions afterward.

As well, make sure the kids aren't hungry or tired or waiting to embark on a bus for a field trip to the observatory or zoo — believe us, you cannot compete.

Here's another idea: Don't do the actual reading. Bring someone else to do it. Writers who really want to get the most of the time spent with children turn the time into a partnership of sleuthing. (Peter is Holmes to Lisa's Watson.) When you read out loud, chances are you're so engaged in the act of reading and turning pages and trying to sound interesting to a child that you can't make adequate observations. This is where your partner comes in:

1. **Seat yourself next to your partner, but off to the side a bit so that you can see the faces and bodies of most of the children listening.**

2. **Have your partner read the book aloud while you take notes.**

   Be sure to note the following:

   - How the children respond to the story. At what point in the story do they lean forward in anticipation? Do their faces ever show fear or amazement or sadness?

   - When the children start fidgeting. Perhaps the timing or pacing of the story is lagging, or something about it is not appropriate for your audience.

- Where in the story they interrupt or ask questions? Maybe something isn't clear.

- What their body language is saying. Do they seem interested or bored? Maybe the story is not as great as you thought it was.

After you've written down everything you can, and the book has been read, start asking questions. What did the children think about the main character? Did they like or dislike him or his friends? What did they think about the chosen subject? What do they wish they could have heard more of? Was there anything in the book they did not like? Was there anything they would have changed about the book? Why? The answers to these questions will tell you a lot about how children of that age approach the subject you are interested in and what issues are relevant to them — or not.

To make the most out of any question-and-answer session with children, you want to formulate good questions that will yield the kind of detail you need to use as a writer. For instance, questions that result in yes or no answers with no room for elaboration are sucky ones. For good questions you can start out with the reporter's Trusty Six, detailing them to your particular needs and concerns:

- ✔ **Who:** Ask questions that focus on the main character. Can the children tell you more about this character? Who is he exactly? What kind of person (animal or object) is he? Is he a good person? A bad person? Does he have any problems? What are they? Does he solve them? How? How would they suggest he solve his problem? What about the secondary characters? What are they like? Are they appealing or not? Why?

- ✔ **What:** What is the story really about (that is, what is its core or central theme)? What is the main problem that has to be solved? Does the main character have good ideas about how to handle himself in every situation? Why or why not? What happens to make the story interesting or boring? What do they think happened to the main character or his friends after the story ended? For nonfiction: What did they learn about the subject that they didn't know before? What is most interesting to them about that? What do they want to learn more about?

- ✔ **When:** When does the story take place? If in the past, can that story have happened today? Why or why not?

- ✔ **Where:** Where does the story take place? Is the setting a real place or a pretend place? How can they tell? Can that story have happened where they live? Why or why not?

- ✔ **Why:** Why is the story interesting? Why is the story important for children to read or hear? For nonfiction: Why is the main character or subject important for children to know about?

- ✔ **How:** How does the main character solve his problem? Can readers use the same solution to solve a similar problem? Why or why not? How do the issues brought up in the story affect children today?

Monsters don't touch

Lisa learned one of her most valuable lessons about writing for children of picture book age during a reading. Early on in her career, she had written a story about monsters. These were your run-of-the-mill kind: the ones hanging out under the bed, outside a darkened window, and in the closet. The story's protagonist had to figure out a way to make them all go away so he could get a good night's sleep. The story had been edited by a professional editor friend, vetted by a teacher, and was all ready to submit. But Lisa wanted to see and hear what the children might think about monsters in general. So she brought two stories about monsters with her on the train. One was written by a famous author. The other was hers. While reading her story aloud to a small trio of children on the way from Providence to Boston one morning, Lisa learned that monsters are allowed (even expected) to be scary, mean, smelly, and generally odious, but *they must never, ever actually touch the child protagonist* or someone he loves, because then the story is *too* scary and makes children cry — and worse, that children crying on a train somehow seems to echo in a loud and disturbingly public manner. Now whose story do you suppose made that horrible *faux pas*? (Hint: It wasn't the famous author's.) As you can imagine, Lisa never forgot that particular lesson — and it has helped guide her writing ever since.

The answers to these questions help you as a writer in so many ways. You get to see how children process information. You get an inkling of what they focus on and the issues that are of paramount importance to them (you may be very surprised). You get to hear about the way they deal with fears or excitement. And, if you're very lucky, certain audience members may veer completely off subject and give you some very valuable insider information that you can then use in your writing.

Borrow a friend's child for a day

Think you know how your subject matter really thinks? Consider yourself an expert in children's speech patterns and interests? Unless you work with children on a daily basis or live in captivity with some of your own, you probably don't know how their sinister little minds really work — and you may not be as good at picking up on how they talk as you could be.

Do your writing a favor and make some grateful parent or guardian (very) happy at the same time: Borrow a child for the day to test your theories. Don't just take the kid to a movie, where conversation will be minimal. Take him to a museum, a park, a meal — or all of the above. Engage the child's senses. Then observe and listen.

Interview with Barney Saltzberg, author/illustrator/performer (Part II)

Barney Saltzberg (www.barneysaltzberg.com) is a successful author, illustrator, and children's music performer. Through his varied careers, he's spent plenty of time with children and he continues to discover more about them with each encounter.

WCBFD: As a writer/illustrator/performer who has had success in both books and music, can you tell us what kinds of things you learn from children when you visit them at schools or other venues that help you as a writer?

BS: That life as a child isn't always as fun as I sometimes remember. Traveling around the country, I've seen children going to school hungry and who don't have any books at home. I find that no matter where they come from and how they live, when we sit down together, they want to sing and draw and laugh and that they all have stories they long to tell.

WCBFD: Do you use the Web for researching subject matter for your books? Any clues as to how to start?

BS: I Google a lot. Sometimes for images, when I need to draw something. Other times, I'll Google a title I think up to see if it's out there already. If it is, I'll look up the book or song and make sure I'm not stepping on someone else's toes. If it's not out there, then I run with it. When I finished a book called *Cornelius P. Mud, Are You Ready for Bed?* I found tons of Web sites where parents talked about all the things they do in order to put their children to bed at night. It was very helpful in developing my story.

WCBFD: Your children are in college now, and yet you still write mostly for younger children. With the advent of video games and other media that conflict with books, how do you make sure the topics you choose are still relevant?

BS: People are still people. A good story is a good story. You may be blasting aliens on a handheld device, but if a story has soul and speaks truth, readers will be captivated.

WCBFD: You teach writing and illustrating children's picture books at the UCLA Extension Writer's Program. How do you guide your students when it comes to their own research of their subject matter?

BS: I suggest they go to children's bookstores and libraries, find the picture books, and read and read and read. When they're done reading, read some more!

WCBFD: What do you think about conferences and book conventions for learning about a chosen topic or for researching ideas? Why?

BS: I think any place you can go to gather information is great. You'll never use everything you hear and see, but any way you can get information about publishing and about the writing process can be invaluable. Also, it helps to meet other people who are doing what you are doing so you can learn from the authors and illustrators who have made it. It's also helpful to meet your peers, people at your particular level of writing. People like yourself, who are trying to find their way in this field. You'll have plenty of stories to share.

WCBFD: Have you ever gone to an expert in the field to get some help on any aspect of your writing, illustrating, or performing? What was your experience?

BS: As far as performing for children, the only way I've improved over the years is to continually put myself in front of an audience. I learn something every time I perform. Watching videos of my concerts has helped me improve as well. I see things I like, some things I don't and I try to make adjustments. In terms of my writing, I've read books from other writers on the process of writing, and I have always found some nugget that set off angels singing, "AHA!" and "YES!" I guess that's why they call them experts!

For more words of wisdom from Barney Saltzberg, see Chapter 5.

Getting children to open up isn't always easy, but it shouldn't require hair-pulling on your part. Make your queries seem to be about your needing some information, such as, "I was wondering . . . do you know how a bee makes honey? Want to go to the bookstore and find out?" The goal is to engender discussion, getting children to talk about their lives and their feelings, which will give you more information to write about in your book.

A good trick is to build a comparison between your ridiculous childhood and theirs. For example, "When I was a child, we had to wear orange ties and purple top hats to school every single day. Isn't that silly? What happens at your school that you think is silly?"

When you come home from what we are sure will be an interesting — albeit exhausting — day of research, try to write down everything you can recall about what happened. Then when you go back to developing your idea, you can see how what you learned adds to or changes the direction of your story.

Dipping into Popular Culture

Whatever the latest trend, whether it's related to food, fashion, music, toys, games, cartoon characters — you name it — you can bet that kids and their friends will be the first to know about it, if not actually the ones who create it themselves. Why? Two reasons: First, children have an insatiable curiosity and desire to know about the latest and greatest gadget, toy, trend, and so on; second, advertisers that produce products for children target them mercilessly through television advertising, programming, movies, apps, video games, and more.

Take a dip into pop culture yourself with the information we provide in the following sections. We guarantee your story will be all the richer for your efforts.

No one can spot a faker faster than a kid. Just because you're aware of pop culture and know all the right words, songs, or fashions doesn't mean you can pass for a child. Be sure to not take your pop culture familiarity too far.

Watching kids' TV shows and movies

If there's one quick way to dip your toes into the prevailing popular culture, it's by watching cartoons, specifically the recent hot cartoons. Many of these cartoons — think *SpongeBob SquarePants, Phineas and Ferb,* and *Dragon Ball Z* — have created their own popular culture (and generated millions of dollars in spin-off toy and DVD sales in the process). You can find out all about the latest cool cartoons by scouring entertainment magazines such as *Entertainment Weekly,* perusing online TV guides, or simply turning on the TV Saturday morning (or anytime if you have Disney Channel or Cartoon Network, cable channels that run cartoons 24/7).

Speaking of Disney, there are all those live-action TV shows that have tween audiences — especially girls — mesmerized. What is it about these characters and story lines that prove endlessly entertaining? If you don't know, you should find out.

Don't forget about animated movies. They've evolved way beyond the Disney fare that you grew up on. Although those old favorites are still out there and going strong on DVD and Blu-ray, a plethora of fabulous animated movies and anime (largely imported animated movies and TV characters) are out there for today's kids. These movies spawn toys, which then spawn more films, which then spawn TV shows and apps . . . it's a pop culture wheel that just keeps on spinning.

When you watch children's cartoons or films, pay attention to the lines that generate laughs. Are they verbally subtle, do they bang the audience over the head, or are they largely physical slapstick? In what ways do they suspend reality or bring fantasy into the story line? Which cartoons and films are the most popular? What about them do you think generates this popularity?

Playing kid-focused digital games

The digital age brings kid-friendly games into even the tiniest of hands. In fact, many children growing up today have likely teethed on some electronic handheld device — literally and figuratively. Traditional video game systems that hook up to your TV still exist (think the Wii, Sony PS3, and Xbox 360), but there are also handheld gaming devices such as the Nintendo 3DS and the Sony PSP — plus smartphones and tablets offering hundreds of thousands of apps for kids to play and explore.

When you watch children play these games (or better yet, when you jump on in and play for yourself), pay attention to the worlds created therein: the characters (what they wear, what they do, and what their attitudes are about each other), the setting (real; imagined; outer space; a juxtaposition of all three?), the story lines (it's not all warfare out there), the music, the gaming goal (here's a good one: for what games will your children pay out of their own pocket to buy extras like tokens or coins or virtual currency) — all of these give clues as to what children are really into, how they think, and what they pay attention to.

Reading parenting and family magazines and blogs

Parenting and family magazines and blogs are another great way to dip into pop culture. Within their pages and on their sites, you'll find all sorts of articles and commentaries tackling topics of concern to parents and children. Whether it's how to deal with a teenager who idolizes pop singers (and who wants to bare her belly button at school or wear a dress designed from raw beef just like her idol) or which licensed character piñatas are hot (and which are not), you'll find plenty of thoughtful references to children's issues here.

Major parenting and family magazines (each with an accompanying Web site chock-full of content) include *Family Circle, Parenting, Family Fun, Parents, Working Mother, Today's Parent,* and *Child.* While flipping through these, note the advertisers and the types of products they're selling. Often, you can get good ideas for stories this way, as we discuss in Chapter 5.

But in terms of research, reading parenting and family magazines and blogs allows you to glean details about what parents are really talking about, the issues that concern them, the new objects or trends children are introducing their parents to, and the like. Kids torture their parents daily with all the new information and gadgets they bring home, and if you want to know what those are, reading about parents trying to wrap their brains around all this stuff is pretty interesting — and often hilarious. And then when you go to write your story, the details you choose to include can help you create a more realistic world. Conversely, the details you choose to leave out can also make a big statement about the world you're trying to create, be it reality- or fantasy-based.

Flipping through pop culture magazines

What better place to get instantly steeped in popular culture than by buying and reading a stack of magazines that worship at the altar of all things celebrity and pop? If you want to get a quick course on pop culture, you can't go wrong with *Entertainment Weekly, Paste, Star, Wired, Seventeen, J-14, American Cheerleader,* or *Vanity Fair.* Children are the early adopters of most new technologies, trends, attitudes, and patterns of speech. If you want to see what your tween and teen audience is wearing, read about the music they are listening to, learn about the celebrities they are obsessed about, become familiar with the TV shows and movies they're raving or ranting about, get inundated by the same advertisers that are after their dollars — these magazines are the way to go.

Look for items with relevance to your topic. Are you writing about a main character who is a girl? Research what girls of that age are playing with, wearing, and talking about. Thinking of writing a relationship story for teens?

Look for articles that focus on what relationship issues between modern teens really involve. Those personality and love quizzes in teen magazines are great for clues into this arena, by the way!

Surfing the Web

Whether it's the massive Web site of *Entertainment Weekly* magazine (www.ew.com) or a one-page online sales brochure for an obscure cartoonist who is soon to become a household name, the Web is loaded with pop culture.

There are numerous gaming Web sites targeted to children in different age brackets. Some of the most popular include:

- FunGoPlay (www.fungoplay.com)
- Club Penguin (www.clubpenguin.com)
- PBS Kids (www.pbskids.org)
- Miniclip (www.miniclip.com)
- Steam (www.steampowered.com)

Most of the pop culture magazines listed in the previous section maintain their own Web sites. And there are many more Web sites specifically devoted to popular culture in all its glory:

- Pop Culture Junk Mail (pcjm.blogspot.com)
- NPR Pop Culture (www.npr.org/sections/pop-culture)
- UC Berkeley Pop Culture Database (english.berkeley.edu/Postwar/pop.html)
- PopMatters (www.popmatters.com)

You can also get an authentic feel for what kids really care about by surfing blogs actually written by children, teens, and tweens. Due to the nature of the beast, these blogs come and go at a moment's notice. You need to do some detective work to find ones that are current and up to date. That said, here are some of our current favorites:

- Zoe's Blog (redfish.edublogs.org)
- Jake's Online Journal (mjgds.org/students/jakeg)
- Em's Canvas (emscanvas.blogspot.com)
- Colly's World (www.collyworld.com)
- Teegan's Terrific Blog (teganrm4.edublogs.org)

Last but not least, keep an eye on major pop culture events, such as annual popular arts convention Comic-Con (www.comic-con.org), annual music festival Coachella (www.coachella.com), and others.

Browsing bookstores

Browsing bookstores — particularly independent bookstores devoted to children's books, such as A Whale of a Tale in Irvine, California, (www.awhale ofatale.com), Children's Book World in Los Angeles (www.childrens bookworld.com), and Books of Wonder in New York City (www.booksof wonder.com), or in the often huge and inviting children's book departments in big stores such as Barnes & Noble and Costco — is a great way to find out what's new and exciting in popular culture. Amazon.com (www.amazon.com) and Powell's (www.powells.com) are other great places to browse, but it's far better to be able to hold a children's book in your hand, especially books that are heavy on illustrations or are uniquely packaged.

If you want to know what children are reading, sit down and read. Read books from every section and every shelf — at least a few pages or a chapter. And haunt the section that features the format you are concentrating on so you can know intimately what is out there. A lot has changed in publishing in the last ten years, and you should be aware of what the formats described in Chapter 2 really look, feel, and read like. After you are truly immersed in these formats, you'll find yourself further honing your idea as you come across approaches you like and those you don't.

For instance, if your idea is to write a picture book about pirates, are you going to take the pseudo-real-life approach like the one taken by Melinda Long in *How I Became a Pirate?* (Harcourt Children's Books)? Or are you going to teach children about pirate life in a whimsical, rhymed fashion like Kathy Tucker in *Do Pirates Take Baths?* (Albert Whitman & Company)? Perhaps you prefer to answer questions about pirates in a more encyclopedic (and purposely ridiculous fashion) the way Tom Lichtenheld does in *Everything I Know About Pirates* (Simon & Schuster Children's Publishing). The point is that all of these are fictional picture books about pirates targeting the same audience and all approach the subject in a unique manner. By studying them, you can invent yet another different and exciting approach.

Be careful not to clone your idea directly from the latest smash-hit bestseller — you can bet that as a result of the popularity of that particular book, every publisher has been swamped with hundreds of manuscripts for knockoffs. Be different and stand out from the crowd — regardless of what's currently popular.

Visiting children's stores online or in person

Toymakers are always ready, willing, and able to leverage the latest kids' trends by designing and selling products that are hardwired into them. If it's hot, there's bound to be a doll, action figure, video game, costume, playset, or some other toy devoted to it. Again, although there's nothing quite like wandering the aisles of your local Toys 'R Us or other toy purveyor to steep yourself in a world that's uniquely oriented toward children and their tastes and desires, let your fingers do the walking and visit some of these popular online toy sites:

- ✔ Toys 'R Us (www.toysrus.com)
- ✔ Silly Goose (www.usillygoose.com)
- ✔ Hamleys (www.hamleys.com)

Visiting toy stores and places that cater to children's lives and activities can help you get in the *kid zone*. By that, we mean that when you are surrounded by what kids are surrounded by and get to see what kids like and don't — in other words, when you stand in their shoes — it helps you approach your story more from their perspective. For example, maybe your idea involves writing about a kid who loves to build things. You go to the toy store to see what kinds of building sets are popular today. Surprise! Tons of new building toys and materials have been invented since you were a kid. Does that change what your character does? Maybe!

Studying kids' fashion trends

Clothing and fashion are reflections of the prevailing pop culture. What did today's pop idol wear on last night's MTV Video Music Awards show? You can bet that clothing manufacturers around the world are gearing up production of whatever fashion is hot within hours after the show hits the airwaves. Whatever the trend — from surfing, to hip-hop, to goth, to nerd gear — clothing stores can show you what's hot.

Try Claire's, Tilly's, The Limited Too, or Abercrombie. If you can't find any dedicated children's clothing boutiques in your area, be sure to check out the children's clothing departments in large retailers such as Target, Macy's, Kohl's, Nordstrom, and Dillard's.

Again, standing in children's shoes (or their clothes, for that matter) helps you get a feel for what children appreciate and what they don't. Fashion and clothing trends especially affect tweens and teens, so if they are your target audience, it behooves your writing to develop a familiarity with this part of their world, too. For instance, if you are writing about a tween girl who wants to be just like her bigger sister, who happens to be a completely different type of person than she is, when you have her steal her sister's clothing, what is she going to steal? Chances are it's not the saddle shoes, cashmere pullover, and pleated skirt from some people's childhoods.

Researching Your Nonfiction Topic

Although you can play fast and loose with some facts in a fictional work, you don't have that luxury when you're working on a nonfiction book. To do so not only potentially risks your reputation with publishers and book buyers, but it can lead to disillusioned children who discover that their favorite non-fiction author is a fraud. And you wouldn't want to disappoint all those children, would you?

Also, many educational publishers and publishers of nonfiction require that all information be verifiable and that all attributed dialogue be documented. Your audience is not as savvy and discerning as an adult audience and thus your responsibility for verifying your facts is acute.

So how do you make sure that your "facts" are really true and not just the latest urban legend being passed around the Internet? You research, you research some more, and then you research your research.

Trebling up on your research is known as the *Rule of Three.* If you can find three trustworthy references or resources (go for hardcopy published sources you can hold in your hands and that have been deemed trustworthy by three separate publishers), chances are good that your research is accurate.

Outlining the research process

The amount of research you're going to need to do, where you're going to do it, and the depth of your efforts will be very much determined by the exact genre of nonfiction children's books you're planning to write, how deeply you're going to cover the topic, and the sophistication of your audience. A board book on firetrucks — with fewer than 100 words — requires far less extensive research than a nonfiction middle-grade reader on the life and times of Rosa Parks.

So how do you go about researching your nonfiction children's book?

1. **Choose a topic.**

   The topic you select will have a great impact on where and how you will do your research.

2. Outline your book.

How will you know what research to do if you don't know what topics you'll cover in your book? Here's the short answer: You won't.

3. Create a research plan.

The plan should include the sources you intend to look up (newspaper and magazine articles and books), places you intend to visit (libraries, museums, research institutions, historical sites), and people you intend to interview (experts, researchers, celebrities). If, for example, you are writing a nonfiction book on farm animals, your plan might include visits to a local library, some time on the Internet, time at a 4-H club meeting, interviews with children who live on farms with animals and, of course, a number of visits to real working farms. And don't forget to include in your plan the images you might need to create or acquire permission to use along the way.

4. Put your plan into effect.

Get out there and start researching your topic. For many writers, researching is almost as fun (and in some cases, more fun) than the actual writing process. Peter once wrote a book on New York City's Orpheus Chamber Orchestra, which required him to accompany the orchestra on an all-expenses-paid concert tour through Germany, Italy, Spain, and the Czech Republic to do his research. It was a tough job, but someone had to do it.

5. Organize your results.

Interviews should be transcribed, articles organized, facts compiled, and sources credited. Be sure to triple-check your facts — when in doubt, check it out again and then once more.

To make sure you note all the information you need from each source or reference book — before you place it back in the stacks and forget where you found it — avail yourself of copies of two of the best guides for writers of nonfiction: *The MLA Handbook for Writers of Research Papers* (Modern Language Association) and Kate L. Turabian's *A Manual for Writers of Research Papers, Theses, and Dissertations* (University of Chicago Press). Both of these tiny (but mighty) books can guide you on how to attribute and credit sources properly and completely.

Get around locally

Depending on the topic you're researching, plenty of local resources (and their Web sites) can help with your research. Some of these resources include:

- ✔ Local newspapers
- ✔ Libraries
- ✔ Government offices
- ✔ Company headquarters
- ✔ University research labs
- ✔ Planetariums
- ✔ Museums

Go far afield

You're not limited to doing your research locally: You also have the option of doing your research long distance. Check out these additional resources (and their Web sites) for doing your research:

- ✔ Library of Congress
- ✔ Smithsonian Institution
- ✔ The National Archives
- ✔ National Geographic Society
- ✔ National magazines
- ✔ Out-of-town small newspapers
- ✔ Associations and societies
- ✔ National experts
- ✔ Research institutes
- ✔ Universities and colleges
- ✔ Government offices
- ✔ Foreign embassies
- ✔ Businesses

Using the power of long-distance telephone directories and the Internet, it's pretty easy to track down a phone number or URL for even the most remote resource. Don't be shy — most of these organizations are accustomed to fielding questions like yours. And most experts are happy to help, by guiding you to the next step, foisting you off on someone else, or stepping up and sharing some expertise.

Visit the Web — a lot

The Internet is a great thing — it's entertaining, it's informative, it's immediate, and it's plain fun. But although much of what shows up on the Net is presented as fact, too often these facts are actually fiction.

Sadly, the Internet is chock-full of falsehoods, half-truths, and outright lies. When you're using the Internet to do your research, be particularly careful about so-called experts who really aren't. Anyone can put up a Web site promoting himself as an expert on any topic.

To separate Internet reality from Internet fantasy, keep these tips in mind:

- ✔ If it sounds too good to be true, suspect that it probably *isn't* true.

- ✔ Establish trusted online sources of information on the Internet, such as online encyclopedias or national newspapers and magazines or other long-established, reliable media.

- ✔ Remember that blogs are particularly notorious for playing fast and loose with the truth. Consider them sources of opinion, not necessarily fact.

- ✔ Confirm your information. Use reliable, published sources to confirm what you may have found on a site.

- ✔ Challenge the information mongers by e-mailing them and asking for links to their sources. If they can provide them, great. If not, suspect that they're not telling the truth.

Have an expert look over your work

If you're writing nonfiction and you're incorporating lots of obscure facts that are hard to verify, consider having an expert take a look at your manuscript. There are a number of benefits of taking this approach:

- ✔ If your expert is plugged in and up to date, you'll have the latest and greatest information available anywhere.

- ✔ You'll increase the chances of avoiding a potentially embarrassing factual faux pas.

- ✔ You (and your editors) will be able to sleep better at night knowing that the facts you cited in your book really are facts.

- ✔ You may establish an ongoing relationship with your expert that can be beneficial in your future projects.

- ✔ It's fun hanging out with people who know what the heck they're talking about.

Experts are everywhere. After you decide on a specific topic, do some research to find out who the experts are in the field. Get their names and e-mail addresses and don't hesitate to pop the question when it comes time. Quite often, experts are happy to review short manuscripts for little or no money. It gives them something fun to do while contributing to their communities.

Just ask. The worst that can happen is that your expert may say no. And if you can credit your expert on or in the book, chances are she may just give you a break on the cost of her services, because she, like you, may be able to use the added credibility.

Be careful: Not every expert is truly an expert, and some experts may have been top dog 20 years ago, but today are lagging well behind the pack. Choose your experts carefully — check out their current publications and their reputations within their industry or the academic community before you commit. A little bit of research on your part when selecting experts to work with can save you much heartache down the road.

Part III

Creating a Spellbinding Story

The 5th Wave   By Rich Tennant

FOR WALTER, THE COMPONENTS FOR WRITING GOOD CHILDREN'S BOOKS WERE ALWAYS PLOT, CHARACTER, SETTING, AND MARTINI.

In this part . . .

Writing the first pages of your children's book is exciting — and daunting. You have a basic idea and all these thoughts about it, and now you get to put it all together. But how do you start?

You first need to decide on a few simple but crucial basics as you start writing your story. If you're writing fiction, you need to create and develop characters, figure out the plot, establish the setting, and work on dialogue, point of view, and voice. If you're into nonfiction, you need to do some research and find a way to make the material different from what's already out there and interesting to young readers (and their parents and teachers, too!).

Never fear, dear author! We take on these issues one at a time, simultaneously helping you make the connections between all these topics as you move along in this part.

Chapter 7

Creating Compelling Characters

In This Chapter

▶ Developing memorable main characters

▶ Building supporting characters

▶ Climbing up (and down) a character arc

▶ Keeping your characters real

▶ Doing character building exercises

*Y*our main character is the soul of your story. Flawed or perfect, full of love or temper tantrums, your protagonist must be memorable and must evolve. Think of all those great characters you remember from your childhood —they're great for the very fact you can recall them so many years after reading about them. There must have been something special about them. What exactly is this magic potion you add to a name and a face that makes a character come out so well?

It's not magic at all, actually. In this chapter, we tell you how to create memorable characters. We advise you on how to keep those characters real — not stereotyped or boring — and we show you how a character arc can help you check up on your character to make sure she does the growing and changing she needs to do within the course of your story. At the end, we add in a few character building exercises for practice.

What makes a character great is the way he sees the world and interacts with it. Not just the way he talks (although that is very important), but also the way he walks, the look on his face, the tics he exhibits when nervous — in other words, the manner in which he does everything he does. His actions tell your reader who your main character really is — the narrator does not.

The Secret Formula for an Exceptional Main Character

Kids read children's fiction to encounter characters who are exceptional, not mundane. They want their main characters to be prettier or uglier, more evil or sweeter, nobler or meaner, braver or more fearful than real people. Even if the characters are boring, kids want them to be exceptionally, hilariously, fabulously more boring than the average bore. That doesn't mean the characters should be unrecognizable as human — but they should embody just a tad bit *more* of everything than a child or an adult would in real life — doses of the curious, silly, funny, awkward stuff. Adding a *little extra* highlights the personality quirks important to the story that make the character more memorable.

But here's the catch: Whether they are real people or anthropomorphized creatures, the characters must be believable. No matter how extraordinary they are, they still need to be motivated by the same wants as the readers in your target audience.

So how do you go about creating a character who's three-dimensional and real? You figure out what makes him tick, and you flesh that out. We explain how to do both in the next sections.

Defining your main character's driving desire

Sometime at the beginning of the writing process, you need to ask yourself just what makes your main character move and groove. What does he really want that he simply cannot do without? What is it propelling him to do what he does throughout your story? What burning desire lights him on fire and keeps him motivated from the first time we meet him until we bid adieu? Pretend you had to define your character in one sentence. How would you describe his distinguishing attribute, the one that sets him apart . . . the one that makes him memorable?

Every main character needs to have a goal or something he wants very badly. This is the character's *core;* just as an apple without a core would collapse in on itself, a character without a discernible core is hollow and forgettable. If the term *core* is too obtuse, call it the character's *want.* From the moment you introduce your character to the last page, you focus on what your character wants: how he gets it, what's in his way, how he overcomes those obstacles to get closer to what he wants, how his want changes him in the end — all these driving questions revolve around what your character wants.

A character's want needs to be attainable. It can seem unrealistic, but so are many people's wants — that doesn't mean they stop wanting that one thing. And it also doesn't mean that person won't be able to reach that unrealistic goal; after all, aren't many of the most remarkable achievements those believed impossible until someone made them real?

For example, in *Snow White,* a story everyone's familiar with, the queen wants one thing: to be the most beautiful in the land. When her mirror informs her one day that she's no longer the fairest one of all, she completely loses it. She decides that she wants to be the prettiest so badly she will stop at nothing to make sure her rival is eliminated — not even murder. When all her spectacular efforts fail to make Snow White disappear forever, she hires a hit man (the hunter) to finally realize her dream, her desire — her want.

The entire story of Snow White revolves around the queen's want. It's her want that banishes Snow White from the castle, then from the kingdom. It's her want that makes her dress up like a witch and try to kill the princess herself. It's her want that causes the conflict. And it's her want that nearly drives her to madness. That's true desire, and that's what your character needs.

Fleshing out your main character to show readers her driving desire

So how do you let the reader know about your character's driving desire? Well, continuing with the *Snow White* example from the preceding section, you can spell out this desire in a straightforward, narrated manner by telling the reader: "There was a queen who wanted more than anything to be the fairest in the land." But you shouldn't. After all, where's the drama in that?

What you *should* do is opt for the more subtle approach in which the reader discerns the protagonist's core by observing how she behaves and interacts with others. It's far more captivating for your readers to figure out the protagonist's driving desire for themselves.

In other words, show the queen in action as she flaunts her hatred by arguing in dialogue with the mirror; dresses up like a witch, and hunts down Snow White and then, with gnarled fingers, offers her the poisoned apple. Finally, show the interaction between the queen and the hunter when she orders him to kill Snow White.

Don't *tell* readers the queen is driven by her desire; *show* how she acts in order to fulfill that desire. Have them hear her argue aloud with the mirror. Get them in that bedroom as she transforms herself into a witch. Make them smell the fresh crispiness of the apple she offers Snow White.

You can help your readers discover your main character's desire by going through the *fleshing out* process. Giving your main character a set of physical attributes is important, but what fills out a great character is all the quirks, desires, and emotions that comprise a human being. Literally, fleshing out is taking the want (the skeleton) and adding the muscles, ligaments, skin, and all the rest to bring your character alive on the page.

Fleshing out involves making your character real, just like the Blue Fairy made Pinocchio a real boy. You build a character bit by bit, making him real by planting clues throughout your story about how the character thinks and feels, by letting the reader hear what he says and how he says it, and by allowing the reader to watch as he interacts with other characters to reach his goal.

Fleshing out is all about what your character *does*. The old "what you do shows more about who you are than what you say" adage holds true here more than ever. It's all well and good if your friend says, "I'll be loyal to you forever"; it's quite another to watch her defending you by raising her fists, actively taking your side by stepping over to you, *acting* loyal by the things she does. Readers need to see your characters *doing*. It's what your characters do that makes them memorable.

To flesh out a character, you need to have him lead the way through the basic plot or the action of your story, which we cover in Chapter 8. But if you don't know him well enough to do that yet, you can do one of two things: You can practice having him talk to another character (see the following section and Chapter 9), or you can make a character bible (see the "Making a Character Bible" section later in this chapter).

Getting to Know Your Characters through Dialogue

Using dialogue to get to know your main character better is not the same as having your character talk and talk *ad infinitum* in your story. Instead, dialogue is used between characters to reveal who they are, how they feel, how they think — to flesh them out verbally. For instance, it's one thing for the narrator to write, "Jon was as dumb as a doornail." It's quite another for the reader to be privy to actual dialogue in which what Jon says (or doesn't say) illustrates just how clueless he really is.

Also, each bit of dialogue has to have a purpose. It must either (1) develop a character (flesh him out a bit), (2) move the story forward (add to the plot), or (3) provide a moment of conflict to heighten the drama and quicken the pacing to get readers turning the pages because they simply *must* find out what happens next.

Purposefully using dialogue in your story to develop a character, move the story forward, or heighten the drama does *not* mean including every single "Hello" or "Nice to meet you." The dialogue you write must contribute something meaningful to the story. Do not use dialogue to recap action we have just witnessed in narration or vice versa; that's redundant.

Don't have characters repeat each other's names in dialogue. Names are usually only used when one character is introducing another, when one character wants to get another character's attention, or when someone is upset with someone else — for instance a parent with a child. (Don't you remember your mother using your first and middle names when you were in trouble? And if she used your last name, too, boy, then you were really going to get it.)

Some writers like to have their characters speak to one another in dialogue form just to get a better idea of who they are — to literally write out an exchange between two characters to bring them alive in the writer's mind before the actual story writing begins. Chapter 9 discusses the ins and outs of getting your characters to talk to each other, so we give you only a short preview here of how developing a dialogue between two characters defines them.

Take two characters you're thinking of using in your story, and write a dialogue between them. This can help you jump-start the story from the idea stage to actually writing and developing the main character. Don't worry about how good your dialogue is right now — just let the characters talk to one another.

A good place to have your characters start chatting is to give flesh to your *theme* (the subject of your story; see Chapter 5) and have the characters argue about it. For example, if you're writing about new siblings, perhaps you can have a supporting character challenge your main character on that topic. Like this:

> BUNNY RABBIT: I think my mom is gonna return me for a new bunny.
>
> MOUSE: What do ya mean? You're broken? Sometimes my mom returns broken stuff.
>
> BUNNY RABBIT: No, I don't think so . . . but the other day I heard her say the new bunnies were on their way.
>
> MOUSE: Oh. . . .
>
> BUNNY RABBIT: And when new bunnies come, what happens to old bunnies?
>
> MOUSE: Oh. I see what you mean. What'll she need old bunnies for if she's got new ones? Like shoes. When you grow out of the old ones you give 'em away.
>
> BUNNY RABBIT: Yeah. I wonder who she'll give me away to? You think I'll get recycled or something?

MOUSE: No. Least I don't *think* so. We better come up with a plan to show your mom you're not really broken. And quick!

Notice the use of contractions, truncated sentences, and incomplete sentences? This is the way people speak in real life. If you have a character who doesn't speak this way, that character will sound stilted, wooden, and just plain odd — unless the character is supposed to be a very erudite British professor.

Keep going in this manner until you get a real feeling for who these characters are. Already, you can see here that Bunny is a sweet, sensitive, and naïve little tyke. As well, with the help of his friend, he will become a take-charge sort of bunny. Plot-wise (more on that in Chapter 8), this dialogue shows you that Bunny has misunderstood what he overheard and is in for a big change in his life (although not the one he expects), and that Mouse is going to help him try to solve his problem. This dialogue fleshes out Bunny, Mouse, and their problem. It helps the writer better understand the roles of both characters, their particular personalities, and how they will participate in the plot development so far.

If there are two ways to read the meaning of a bit of dialogue (an unintended double entendre), either rewrite it for clarity or show what the character is doing when he says it. Body language can be very telling. For instance, when a teenager says, "Sure, Mom," it can be taken many different ways:

"Sure, Mom." Her smile lit up her eyes.

versus

"Sure, Mom." She rolled her eyes and stomped off into the living room.

versus

"Sure. Mom?" (answering a question in the affirmative and then getting Mom's attention to ask another question)

Making a Character Bible

A great way to really build a character, attribute by attribute, is to create a blueprint of him, which we refer to as a *character bible*. A character bible is a type of character outline in which everything about your character is laid out in one place so you can find answers to many questions about the character's personality and desires. We suggest starting a separate document from your story, in list or prose form, so that you can refer back to it and amend it as you get more into your writing. It can even include visuals if you are a doodler or illustrator. Some really good questions your character bible can answer include the following:

- ✔ What is his name? Whom was he named after and why?
- ✔ How old is he?
- ✔ What color is his hair, eyes, skin?
- ✔ What is his ethnicity?
- ✔ What does he look like (tall, thin, short, round, gangly)?
- ✔ Where does he live? Where was he born? (If not the same place, when did he move and did it affect him in any way?)
- ✔ How would you describe his personality?
- ✔ What are your character's physical quirks (bites nails, blinks when nervous, brushes hand through his hair, sniffles a lot)?
- ✔ What does he wish for more than anything?
- ✔ What are his character weaknesses or flaws?
- ✔ Does he behave the same way around his friends as he does around adults? Why or why not?
- ✔ Is he smart? Not so bright? In what does he excel? In what does he fail?
- ✔ Is he talkative or more introverted?
- ✔ Is he athletic? If yes, what are his favorite sports? If no, why not?
- ✔ What small details set him apart from others? (Does he wear a special totem hidden under his shirt? Does he speak only in a whisper? Does he always have a headset on in one ear?)
- ✔ Does he have brothers and sisters? What are their names and ages?
- ✔ Does he have a best friend? Name and age, please.
- ✔ What's his big secret that he keeps from everyone?

These questions incorporate the emotional, social, and physical — all aspects that contribute to making each one of us who we are. And because people can answer these questions about every child in the world, you should be able to do so for your main character. The following sections show you an example of what a character bible can look like when modeled off these questions. A character bible can help you achieve consistency throughout the manuscript.

Surveying a sample character bible

Here's an example of a character bible from a middle-grade novel in progress:

- **What is his name? Who was he named after and why?** Barnaby H. Lee. He was named after his granddad, Barnaby Hollis Lee, the man who invented a time machine, performed one public exhibition of how his technology worked, then disappeared three weeks later on the day Barnaby was born. Sometimes, Barnaby's mother looks at him funny, explaining hastily that he reminds her of her dad in many uncanny ways (which is explored later on in the story when Barnaby finds his grand-dad's hidden time-machine blueprints).

- **How old is he?** Barnaby is nine years old, but he seems wiser than his years. Not in a geeky way, but in the way he expresses himself and how he speculates about complicated social and emotional issues.

- **What color are his hair, eyes, skin?** Barnaby has platinum blond hair, big green eyes, and translucent skin. He looks a little otherworldly.

- **What is his ethnicity?** Barnaby's parents are both olive-skinned, of Mediterranean descent. Barnaby looks like no one else in his family — except that he resembles his granddad in a way that is not physical.

- **What does he look like?** He is tall for his age, slender, almost jellylike in his flexibility — it seems as if his limbs kind of flop around when he walks, as if they are attached, but barely.

- **Where does he live? Where was he born?** Barnaby lives in Dead Oak Village, a suburb of a big American city, where he was born and where his family has lived for five generations or more.

- **How would you describe his personality?** Barnaby is a dreamer, but he is also very smart. Unlike most boys his age, he is very sensitive and aware of emotions and feelings. He often has premonitions that turn out to be true, but he has not articulated this to anyone. He likes to be around people, but often seems not present when he is, as if he is listening to a conversation happening in another room. Barnaby is the first to comfort you if you're hurt; he is also the first to defend you if you need it. He has only one enemy: Shark Kittridge, a boy down the street who has been losing first place in the Invention Fair to Barnaby for two years.

- **What are your character's physical quirks?** Barnaby's eyes are weird: Even when they focus on you, you can't really get a fix on what's in them or on his expression. Barnaby's most noticeable characteristic is that he looks up to the left often, as if he is listening to a conversation you can't hear.

✔ **What does he wish for more than anything?** Barnaby wishes he could talk to his granddad. There's something about the old man that niggles at him. He has never met him, of course, but he feels as if there's something important the old man has to say to him, and Barnaby has no idea how he's going to figure out what that is. It is unusual for a boy his age to care about a dead relative this way, so his interest spooks his mom and creeps out everyone in his family.

✔ **What are his character weaknesses or flaws?** Barnaby has the courage of his convictions. He won't ever shove them down your throat, but he won't back down, either. This makes him a great friend to have, and an exasperating one, too. It's as if Barnaby came into this world fully formed, not precocious, but not needing much improvement. For example, his mother never spends time lecturing Barnaby on how to behave; Barnaby came out of the womb knowing right from wrong; however, when Barnaby gets an idea in his head, he will do whatever is necessary to go where he wants, get what he wants. He never means to hurt anyone, but someone always seems to get hurt by accident. This determination imperils his best friend, Phoebe, in a way he may not be able to resolve alone — she's going to disappear, and people are going to assume she was abducted and dead — and Barnaby will have to answer for it. But Barnaby doesn't like to ask for help, so he will make the situation worse for himself and for her.

✔ **Does he behave the same way around his friends as he does around adults? Why or why not?** Barnaby is interested in everyone — from the smallest baby to the elderly. Strangely, Barnaby likes to sit with old people and get them to tell him stories. He even volunteers at a retirement home. And he seems to be able to communicate with infants, who are practically hypnotized by his bulgy green eyes. Barnaby acts the same around everyone (polite, well-mannered, not at all hyperactive or pushy).

✔ **Is he smart? Not so bright? In what does he excel? In what does he fail?** Barnaby is smart and excels at school. He's not so good at group activities because he tends to "disappear" in them; he's not that outgoing.

✔ **Is he talkative or more introverted?** Barnaby can talk up a storm on issues he's interested in, but he's generally more introverted. He's not shy; he just doesn't offer up of himself.

✔ **Is he athletic? If yes, what are his favorite sports? If no, why not?** Barnaby is a great wrestler. Even though he weighs next to nothing, his flexibility allows him to outmaneuver everyone in his weight class, even heavier wrestlers. He's good at track and other solo outdoor pursuits, but he has to be careful in the sun, due to his paleness. He's not good at team sports, because he doesn't seem to be able to pay attention for a long period of time.

✔ **What small details set him apart from others?** Barnaby is set off from others by the way he looks, the way he's so seemingly ethereal, and his maturity. It's not that he's adultlike, precocious, or obnoxious, it's just that he seems to already have been wherever you are going. In a conversation, Barnaby's words seem to precede his thoughts, making him ahead of himself somehow. But he's wistful about it, not a know-it-all, so you don't hate him for it — you're simply perplexed by it.

✔ **Does he have brothers and sisters? What are their names and ages?** Barnaby has a sister and a brother. His sister Natasha is older, age 16, already driving, and moving on into adulthood pretty quickly. She adores Barnaby, but rarely has time for him. His brother Ryan is 14 and also has little time for Barnaby, but he's not mean to him like many older brothers would be.

✔ **Does he have a best friend? Name and age, please.** Barnaby's best friend is a girl named Phoebe. She is 10 and lives next door. Phoebe is also a quiet, strange child who shares with Barnaby an affinity for the paranormal and the ability to stay happily by herself for hours. Barnaby and Phoebe have been best friends since they were three months old.

✔ **What's his big secret that he keeps from everyone?** At the end of the first chapter, Barnaby will find the map of his own house, which will lead him to the blueprints for his granddad's time machine. But he knows he can't tell anyone about it because his granddad died making time travel a reality. Besides that, his mother would completely freak out.

Now not every character will be developed to this extent for every story in every format. But even in a picture book in which your word count is very limited, it can't hurt for you to know lots of details about your characters. Character enrichment is all about adding layers of complexity with bits of description, lots of action, and just the right dialogue. The more you've fleshed out a character, the more real you make him or her (or it) to your reader — and the more memorable.

Creating consistency

Whether a story is real or not, the characters must always be believable and consistent. When you figure out who they are and flesh them out — and be sure to give them enough interesting traits so as not to make them one-dimensional or boring — make sure they stick to who they are. So if you have a character afraid of heights who all of a sudden decides to go mountain climbing, you have a little problem — unless that flip-flop is a ploy to disguise what the character is really doing while he's supposedly out mountain climbing. That doesn't mean your characters can't have qualities that make them seem odd or bizarre — bring them on! — but they need to be *consistently* odd or bizarre.

Every time your character is involved in any sort of action, interaction, or dialogue, think about how you can either add some new fleshing out details or reinforce a character trait you've identified from your character bible.

When you come to a point in your story at which you have to make a plot development decision about something your character is about to do or not do, ask yourself this: Would he really do that? Keep your character bible handy and refer to it when you can't come up with the answer on your own.

How do you know when you've made someone real? If you find yourself referring to him as you would your children, your spouse, your best friend, or your partner, he has become real for you. The challenge is making sure he is just as real to your readers.

Writing Stories with Two or More Main Characters

Many beginning children's book writers are told never to try to write a story with two or more main characters unless they have a lot of experience doing so. Although we think that is sound advice for some writers, we don't think every new writer needs to be constrained by this dictate; however, we do suggest the following to make sure that your characters stay distinct and different from one another:

- **Create a character bible for each main character.** Make sure to flesh out attitudes, manner of speaking, and any other small details that set each character apart from the others.

- **Write out how each of your characters would behave when faced with a choice that compromises the character no matter what he or she chooses — then use this example to continue fleshing out your character.** For example, what if Main Character #1 is caught with a forbidden item in her locker that is not hers, but she knows whose it is? What does she do? If she tells, she will lose her best friend. If she doesn't, she will get expelled. Whichever she chooses, she suffers, but we know more about her. Use the same situation to help define each main character's core.

- **Consider limiting your story to two main characters, perhaps one of each gender.** That helps you to draw differentiations and flesh them out while lessening the chance that they will start sounding or acting alike.

- **Consider making the background of one of your main characters very different from the other.** For example, if Main Character #2 is a recent immigrant from India, his cultural background and experiences will inform not only his actions, but also the way he speaks. Or what if one of your characters is a foster child, raised by many different families, attached to no one? Add something to make her really distinct to differentiate her in your writing.

- **Tape up a picture of each character so that you can really picture him or her in your mind.** If you aren't the best artist, try cutting out photos from magazines or other sources that inspire you. Perhaps assign an actor or a celebrity to each of your characters.

✔ **Use people from real life as inspiration.** Your best friend, a close relative, a co-worker, someone you like or dislike — use that person as the framework for your character. You may even want to use that individual's name in the manuscript until your very last editing, when you change it to protect the innocent — or not so innocent.

✔ **Make sure when each character speaks, he or she doesn't sound like every other character.** For example, if you have one character who is talkative to the point of never coming up for air, make sure your other characters don't possess this particular attribute.

Do not use character names that sound alike or that start with the same letter or phoneme — unless, of course, you're okay with your reader being very confused.

Choosing Supporting Characters

In deciding who else to add to your cast of characters, ask yourself who you need in addition to your main character to tell your story. "Who does my main character need around her to make her believable as well as to help her carry out her destiny?" For example, in 99 percent of stories, the main character needs at least one other character to speak to and interact with (and have conflict with) no matter what your story is or how long it is.

Enter supporting characters. They help to convey the context of the story. For example, if your story takes place 150 years ago, supporting characters could show how life was back then: blacksmiths, butchers, street cops on horseback, one-room schoolhouses filled with children of all ages, and the like.

Additionally, supporting characters can be

✔ **Catalysts in the plot, causing events to occur or information to be shared:** If your story is about a boy like Barnaby (whom we developed a bit in the earlier "Making a Character Bible" section) who is looking for some hidden information, perhaps your supporting character tells him a story about her grandmother, showing Barnaby a photo album that gives him a clue as to its whereabouts. Or maybe your supporting character unwittingly leads the enemy right to your main character's secret hideout.

✔ **So dissimilar to the main character so as to highlight the main character's assets or flaws:** Perhaps your main character is an introvert. His best friend, your supporting character, is an extrovert. The outgoing one puts your main character in a situation causing him extreme discomfort, which in turn leads him to do something completely out of character or perhaps something to totally mess up his life.

Unlike main characters who have to push the story and plot further (more on plot in Chapter 8), supporting characters don't have that limitation and thus can often be colorful, silly, super-brave, or even magical. Literally, they support the main character's journey, whatever that is. Think Tinkerbell in *Peter Pan* and Donkey in the movie *Shrek*. Whomever you choose for your supporting cast, make them three-dimensional and avoid stereotypes.

You develop supporting characters as you need them in your story, and that becomes apparent as your plot calls for someone for the main character to interact with at various points in your plot to pull the story forward. You can ask many of the same questions about the supporting characters as you do about the main character in order to develop them, but you needn't go into quite as much detail.

Here are some steps to help you develop supporting characters:

1. **Decide the function of the supporting character in your story.**

   For example, is the primary reason for including this character so that you have someone who can serve as a foil between your main character and his goal? Or is the supporting character one whose job it is to serve as the conscience of the group, reminding them of the correct path to take, while they insist on going the other way?

2. **Figure out what the function of the supporting character is in relation to your main character.**

   In other words, how does this supporting character support the development of the main character? Children might need parents or adults around them to highlight their uniquely childlike perspectives.

3. **Flesh out the supporting character by adding in details.**

   Create a character bible just as you would for your main character.

4. **After you create the supporting character, figure out how her differences from the other characters help her fulfill her function regarding the plot.**

   If you have an introverted main character like Barnaby from the "Making a Character Bible" section, perhaps the function of his best friend Phoebe is to serve as the one who reaches out to others, who gets things done in the real world while Barnaby is living inside his head.

5. **Step into the supporting character's shoes.**

   When you're writing this supporting character, imagine yourself inside that person's head: What is she thinking right now? What is she seeing? What impulses or emotions is she showing or suppressing? What does she notice while another person is talking? What is her mood? All these markers will help you make her real — which is important, no matter how minor a character she is.

No matter how minor a role, if a supporting character is worth mentioning by name, she is critical enough to warrant your attention. She will have a point of view, an attitude, particular behaviors, a personality — even if we only glimpse a bit of these attributes. Whether she is there to help convey the theme of your story (more on themes in Chapter 5) or move the action forward at a crucial point, she is there to add to your story's flesh and bones.

Calling All Character Arcs

A *character arc* is just a simple visual tool to help you chart out your character's development. Her driving desire must be made clear from the start. The changes your main character makes in her life can be drawn into this arc so you can see how she drives the action as the story starts, then something occurs that requires action, then her plight reaches a climax, and finally she heads toward resolution. You use a character arc by assigning different points of your character's development to the different dots; this helps ensure that your character goes through enough changes and struggles to make her and her story compelling. Here's a summary of the steps that characters tend to face:

When we first meet your main character her driving desire is made clear (ascent begins), she has something happen to rock her world/challenge her reality (steeply ascending), she has to deal with it (ascending further), she fails (peak), she tries some more and fails (dips then peaks even further), she hits a seeming stalemate (flatline, but not for too long), she figures it out (begins descending), she hits a bump but instead of reverting back to old solution(s) tries out new one (further descending), and she ends a changed and ideally better person after all (fully descended).

Take the old-fashioned story of Cinderella and apply it to the arc in Figure 7-1:

1. **You first meet your main character; her driving desire is made clear (ascent begins):** Cinderella is a happy, well-adjusted girl living a privileged life when her father remarries and brings a stepmother and two

sisters into her life — all three of whom detest her. Show Cinderella as sweet and trying to cope, a girl who is confused but still has her father watching her back. Make clear her desire to be considered an equal and equally beloved member of the family.

2. **She has something happen to rock her world/challenge her reality (steeply ascending):** Cinderella's father dies, leaving the poor girl at the mercy of the merciless stepmother and stepsisters, a veritable black sheep. Cinderella tries to stay her course, but fails to move these women whose abuse of her escalates.

3. **She has to deal with it (ascending further):** Cinderella still uses her same old way of coping (being sweet and working hard to avoid the reality of her situation), but the abuse gets worse.

4. **She fails (peak):** Cinderella fails to stand up for herself, and she ends up a scullery maid in her own home. Time for a change, but is she strong enough?

5. **She tries some more and fails (dips, and then peaks even further):** Cinderella and everyone else in the household are all excited over the upcoming ball and is getting ready to attend. Cinderella again resolves to put a happy face on her situation, but she is thwarted and is unable to attend the ball.

6. **She hits a seeming stalemate (flatline, but not for too long):** The fairy godmother helps her attend the ball. Cinderella rises to the occasion, dazzling all attendees, including the prince, but has to run out of the ball at the last minute, leaving a slipper. So she's back to where she started: in rags, with no prospects.

7. **She figures it out (begins descending):** Cinderella decides that she is going to get a chance to try on that slipper no matter what her stepsisters, who may suspect her involvement with the prince, say or do.

8. **She hits a bump but instead of reverting back to old solution(s) tries out new one (further descending):** Cinderella gets locked in the cellar when the prince arrives, but instead of accepting her fate with a smile and cleaning even harder, Cinderella alters her driving desire, gets wise, and fashions a way to break out in time. Eventually, she gets hitched — thus fulfilling her desire to be loved, but creating a chosen family instead of the stinky one she inherited. Wiser and back to her old position and privilege, we have to see how she uses her power.

9. **She ends a changed and ideally better person after all (fully descended):** Although she could have her stepmother and stepsisters thrown into a dungeon from where they would never ascend (or worse), Cinderella opts to take the higher road and allows them to live.

A character arc is just a fancy way of making sure your character has grown and changed throughout the course of the story.

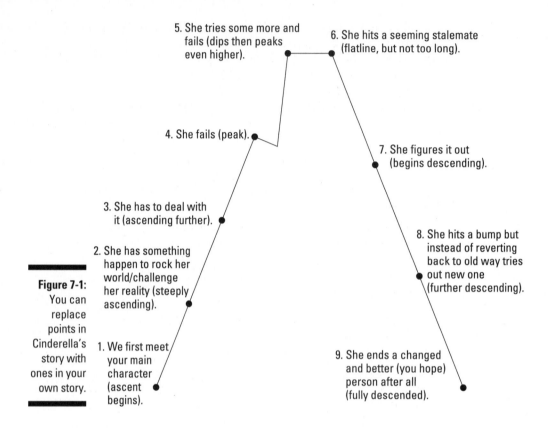

5. She tries some more and fails (dips then peaks even higher).

6. She hits a seeming stalemate (flatline, but not too long).

4. She fails (peak).

7. She figures it out (begins descending).

3. She has to deal with it (ascending further).

8. She hits a bump but instead of reverting back to old way tries out new one (further descending).

2. She has something happen to rock her world/challenge her reality (steeply ascending).

Figure 7-1: You can replace points in Cinderella's story with ones in your own story.

1. We first meet your main character (ascent begins).

9. She ends a changed and better (you hope) person after all (fully descended).

Character Don'ts — and How to Avoid Them

Just as important as what you do with your characters is what you shouldn't do. The following sections take you through some of the most important no-no's and reveal how to avoid making character-killing mistakes.

Steer clear of stereotypes

Stereotyped characters are ones who are too familiar and thus wooden: the smart geek, the airhead cheerleader, the mean beauty queen. When every expectation a reader has about how a character will end up is met, you've created a stereotyped character. When your reader finds no contradictions or surprises related to him throughout the story, your character is in trouble.

One way to avoid stereotyping your characters is to combine traits the reader would not expect to encounter in one character. So if that mean beauty queen turns out to be moonlighting as a janitor at a homeless shelter to pay for her uniforms while conjuring up spells to cure ailing pets at the local animal shelter, then you have a potentially very interesting character.

Another way to avoid stereotyping is using a character bible to spell out unique traits and combinations of traits. (We explain how to create a character bible in the earlier related section.) What exactly makes people unique? Here are steps to creating interesting characters.

1. **List the people you've known in your life who are memorable.**

    Don't just list the ones you know really well who made a difference in your life. Also list the ones who were so quirky and enigmatic you just had to learn more about them and would have been willing to tag along with doing ordinary things like errands all day long — just because they were so different.

2. **Try to identify what makes those people so memorable.**

    Is it the way they act around others, constantly pointing out things about the world and other people that no one else seems to see or care about? Is it how they rarely offer anything up unless they are asked — and then whoa! Do paradoxes in their personality set them apart (such as one who is compassionate about the plight of all animals and insects great and small but who would not share his afternoon snack with another human even if you threatened to rip out his fingernails out one by one)? What is it that identifies this person as truly unique in the world?

3. **Consider whether your character(s) can include one or several of these characteristics.**

    Instead of labeling a character as smart or dumb, athletic or not, get deeper into these labels and decide what they really mean to you. For example, instead of a character developed as smart, how about one whose abilities allow him access to secret and special information others cannot access? Instead of a beautiful character, how about one who is unattractive by choice, choosing to hide her beauty in her quest to find a partner who will appreciate her for more than her looks?

When you think of memorable people, think about the ones who

- ✔ **Really moved you:** The coach who came to a neighbor child's house every day for a week after school to make sure the child mastered skills in a sport, thus allowing her to compete in that week's game.

- ✔ **Made you laugh:** The child in the classroom who had to add her two cents to absolutely everything the teacher said, regardless of what it was, and always had something compelling to add (believe it or not) because of the strange way she looked at the world.

- ✔ **Perplexed you:** The miserable grandma who smiled only when the grandchildren left and she could play with her cats.

Try to take some of the characteristics you have described in these exercises and see whether you can use any of them to build your main character.

If you need an exercise to help you develop interesting, nonstereotypical characters, check out the "Developing Characters through Writing Exercises" section at the end of this chapter.

Show your character in action

Don't underestimate the power of motion. As a matter of fact, it is referred to by a phrase you hear a lot in writing classes and writer's groups: *Show, don't tell.* But what exactly does that mean? *Showing* involves

- ✔ Getting the character actively interacting with another character using dialogue and body language or physicality.
- ✔ Actively going from one place to another.
- ✔ Interacting with the world in some active way.

Telling is narration, describing all the getting, going, and interacting, but never actually demonstrating the character in the act.

Showing (and not telling) equals action and is so important it merits an example. Here is telling:

> Chloe felt bad. She wished she could call up her best friend and tell her how much she wanted to take back what she had said, but by the time she actually did it, it proved too late. The friend had already left. So Chloe sat and pondered what she could do. In the end she called up another friend.

This passage tells us Chloe feels bad, when it should *show* you by dramatizing Chloe expressing her feelings instead. Then it tells you about a phone call to a best friend instead of showing Chloe making the phone call so you can see how she goes about it.

> Chloe wiped the tears from her eyes and picked up the phone. "Is Genevieve there?" she blurted.
>
> "No, she's already gone home for the summer."
>
> "But-but-I never got to tell her —"
>
> "Sorry, hun. She'll be back in September." A dial tone filled Chloe's ear.
>
> Chloe stared at the phone. She punched in a different number. "Hello, Olivia? It's me. I've got an idea. . . ."

We discuss dialogue more in Chapter 9, but suffice it to say here that writing out what a character says instead of telling us about it in narration is a lot more compelling.

When your main character appears in your story, and you do not see him engaged in dialogue or some action within a paragraph or so of his appearance, then you know that you are probably telling, not showing.

Beware of dumping tons of background information in successive paragraphs, known as a *data dump*. Character development must be more subtle and oblique, not hitting the reader over the head with gobs of information all at once. Data dumps can also be referred to as *telling* instead of *showing*. Narration is telling. Action and dialogue are showing. Add character development bit by bit throughout your story.

Toss out passivity and indefinites

Don't overuse the *passive voice* ("to be" verbs). If you want to keep your characters interesting, your plots active (more on plots in Chapter 8), and your writing strong, avoid overusing the passive voice.

- ✔ **Cut out "to be" verbs.** Strong, direct writing eliminates passivity and "to be" verbs. For example, instead of writing *The sound of the shot could be heard from Annabella's house a mile away*, you could write *Annabella heard the shot from a mile away*.

- ✔ **Get rid of the passive voice whenever possible.** Passive voice makes characters and plot boring:

    Passive: There were a lot of people in the square.

    Active: Tons of people packed the square.

    Passive: The reason she felt so bad is that she had a bothersome pain in her leg.

    Active: A sharp pain shot up her leg. "Ouch!"

Search for the phrases *there is, there are,* and *it is* (or their past tenses) in your story. When you find these phrases, cut them out completely and rewrite the sentences. Same with the words *it* and *thing*. Do a universal search of your manuscript and eliminate them mercilessly. And if you can do the same for *that* without destroying your meaning, out it goes!

In the same way, *indefinite prose* (writing that ultimately says nothing and adds nothing useful because it is so nondescript) is colorless, tame, and ultimately timid. Write like you mean it. Instead of meandering into what you want to say, jump right in.

Indefinite: She was not sure that going to that school really made any sense for her life.

Definite: Going to school was a total waste of time.

Indefinite: That story is really not defined in spots. The plot does not have any real climax, the main character seems listless, and the writing could use a little spicing up.

Definite: The plot couldn't be any more lifeless. And does the main character feel anything? I wonder if the writer of this piece is even breathing.

It's hard to stress enough how important positive, strong, direct writing is in character development — as well as in every other aspect of your writing. For more on writing style, see William Strunk, Jr., and E. B. White's classic *The Elements of Style* (MacMillan Publishing).

Don't rely on backstory or flashbacks

Backstory is the account of your character's birth to the day before your story begins. Backstory may include historical references, family connections, allusions to other parts of your story, psychological setup — you name it, but it's basically all the information about how your character came to be the person he is in your story before the action begins. In longer works, dropping in hints of backstory here and there is okay. Even in picture books, allusions to the past are acceptable if they're definitely relevant. But most backstory doesn't belong in your book.

What makes backstory relevant? Backstory should be used only as an immediate and clearly necessary development tool for the character or the plot of your story. If it is important to know your character has lived in foster homes before she gets the scholarship to boarding school, let your readers know, *but only if doing so moves the action forward.* If mentioning her backstory causes you to spend a lot of successive paragraphs explaining the character's past, chances are readers don't need to know all that. It holds up the action of the story. The best way to let out details in a character's backstory is to show it in the way she acts.

A *flashback* is a literary device used to reveal information about some past event by having the character, in her mind, literally flash back to the past, recalling some event so the reader can experience it as well. Flashbacks can interrupt the flow of a story. If you must use a flashback, do so only briefly and only once in a while, and only if you absolutely have to (meaning if you didn't, the reader would be truly lost and wouldn't be able to comprehend what happens next).

Yes, we know *The Catcher in the Rye* by J. D. Salinger (Little, Brown) is arguably one of the most successful children's books in history, found on every high school YA reading list and told almost entirely in flashback; however, this book, like many classics, is an *exception* to the rule — meaning it's something a new writer should almost certainly not attempt. Why? Because a flashback happens entirely in the past and is often referential only, meaning it's told only to explicate something in the present that the story is really about. Most child readers don't care to read about a character who admits he's going to tell you about everything that happened to him prior to his ending up where he is when you find him, because that implies that you're going to have to wait to read about what's going to happen next in the real story. In other words, by using a flashback or a series of flashbacks, you're telling your reader, "Hold your breath for XX pages." You're better off not turning your readers blue and just telling your story in the time it is set.

Developing Characters through Writing Exercises

Children are wild creatures at heart. If they didn't have adults around them to teach them, discipline them, and rein them in, they would naturally grow into wild beasts, experiencing whatever they wanted to and never holding back. That tendency to revel unrestrained in their lives is what allows children to experience events and emotions very deeply. That kind of open emotionality is a good thing to incorporate into children's books.

But we, as adults, have often forgotten what it means to have emotions right at the surface, to care about someone so deeply and unselfconsciously that you notice everything about them and take it all in.

Exercises are great ways to develop and strengthen general and specific writing muscles. Each exercise we introduce here (and in following chapters) can be used not only to get you writing, but also to come up with themes to write about. Writing memorable characters is of the utmost importance — and you can't write memorable characters unless you know them really well.

Describe your first best friend

For a children's book writer, writing memorable characters is the single-most important skill for you to master. But sometimes you may have trouble coming up with a good idea for a character. You can get a head start by writing about your first best friend.

Devote an entire single-spaced page to everything you can remember about your first best friend. Use each of these descriptions to paint her as the substantive character she was:

- ✔ Her appearance
- ✔ Her clothes and style
- ✔ Her favorite color
- ✔ Her family members and what they were like
- ✔ Her favorite food or treat
- ✔ Her favorite activity that you two did together
- ✔ Her favorite activities
- ✔ The secrets you shared
- ✔ The things about her you envied or tried to emulate
- ✔ Her way of walking, talking, or eating that set her apart

Writing about someone you knew well as a child is the perfect way to develop your ability to create good child characters. Ultimately, you'll change a lot of attributes about a character to fit your story (and to protect the innocent), but knowing how to build a unique person out of words on paper is the most important skill you can have as a children's book writer. Long after you forget exactly what happened in Louise Fitzhugh's *Harriet the Spy* (Yearling), you still remember Harriet. Years after reading Roald Dahl's *Charlie and the Chocolate Factory* (Puffin Books), you may not recall the plot, but you do recall Charlie, the Oompa-Loompas, and the inimitable Mr. Wonka (a better childlike adult character has never been written!).

Borrow your favorite children's book characters

Pick up one of your favorite books and write down the names of the main characters, the ones who made you fall in love with the book. Now take those characters and write them a new adventure in your own voice. (Quite a few recently published books have successfully used existing literary characters from books in the public domain.)

This exercise allows you to write using someone else's ideas and characters that you know well (so you don't have to come up with your own) while allowing you to take those characters on a totally different adventure written in your own voice.

Exercises like these may seem unrelated to the task at hand (writing your children's book), but they are *directly* related. They help you hone the skills you need for your writing, allowing you to practice before you commit to the real thing.

Chapter 8

The Plot Thickens: Conflict, Climax, and Resolution

● ●

In This Chapter

▶ Creating a compelling story

▶ Beginning, ending, and everything in between

▶ Building conflict

▶ Designing your plot

▶ Writing your first draft

● ●

*M*ost writers aren't exactly sure what a plot is. Is it the story line itself? Is it the action within the story? Is it the steps the main character takes as he progresses from beginning, to middle, and through to the end? The answer is yes — to all of the above.

Plain and simple, *plot* is what happens. In particular, it's what happens to your main character — all the connected events involving the protagonist leading up to a climax. Your main character is the one driving the plot of the story, directing its forward motion from the very beginning to the very end.

To be convincing, a plot has to unfold in a believable way, regardless of the fact that the characters may be animals or the story may take place in the future. This chapter is all about helping you create believable and engaging plots. Because your main character is so critical to your story's plot, we concentrate on showing you how the events and actions involving the main character make up a plot. We also introduce you to drama and pacing, two important storytelling components that can make or break your plot. And because we're sure you're eager to apply what you're reading, we walk you through the process of outlining your plot and preview some common plot problems (and how to avoid them).

Remembering That It's All about Action

Plot is all about action: what your character does, how she walks the talk, how she interacts with others, and why. In children's books, plot and character are king; stories that children really like are always filled with lots of action and a main character who ends up in a satisfactory place.

Action isn't description. Action is where your character's feet take him and what he literally and figuratively bumps into on his way there.

Action is also showing what happens in the here and now, not relating what happened in the past when the event's already over. Even if you're using the past tense to describe what's already occurred, you should be relating the story by conveying the action in an immediate way.

Here's an example of telling what happened (the action) when it's all over:

> She went to the pet store, but all the monkeys were sold out. So she "liberated" one from the zoo and headed over to the circus tent to meet with the ringmaster. When there, she pretended the monkey and she had an act he had never before seen — but she would not show him the act until he agreed to let them travel with the circus train to the next town.

Try this instead:

> She slipped into the pet store. After searching row after row and finding only empty cages, she walked up to the counter. "Excuse me, but do you have any monkeys?"
>
> "Nope. All sold out." The clerk turned away from the counter, busying himself with paperwork.
>
> Rats! she thought. It's not like I can go to the jungle and invite a monkey to come over and play. Then a wonderful idea occurred to her: Why not liberate one from the zoo? She was sure the monkeys hated it there anyway, all locked up and lonely. . . .

Notice how the second example is still told in the past tense, but the reader is in the main character's shoes, walking where she walks — even listening in to her thoughts. That's how action should be shown.

Kick off your plot with your main character almost immediately in a situation of conflict. In other words, give him a desire to be fulfilled or a challenge to overcome. Then give him something that gets in the way of that desire or makes it difficult to complete that challenge. Your story can detail that problem; add to its complexity; move along to your climax, where the situation gets worse; and then resolve everything.

Centering on the Story

In a successful children's story, the plot and the main character are closely intertwined, which means the way you flesh out your protagonist is by showing readers how he reacts and what he does at each point in your story; however, there's a big difference between a plot that narrates events, and a plot comprising *meaningful* events involving characters who change as a result of their actions. The latter is a *story*.

A plot that narrates a sequence of actions one after another is not meaningful, even if the main character is involved at every step. Consider this basic plot:

> A spoiled young girl's wealthy father remarries a woman with two daughters. The father dies. The stepmother enslaves the girl, treating her badly. The girl grows up as a maid in her own house. A prince holds a ball to find a bride. With a bit of magic, the girl is able to attend, but must leave at midnight. The prince falls in love with the girl. The girl runs from the ball right before she would have been reduced to rags. The prince searches all over the kingdom for her, but can't find her. Many would-be wives scheme to get his attention. He devises a way of ascertaining the girl's true identity. She figures out how to get noticed. At last they are reunited. They marry, and the girl no longer has to be a maid. The princess employs her stepmother and her stepsister in the house, but does not mistreat them as they did her. The prince and the princess live happily ever after.

Even though this is a narration of events, you know instinctively that it isn't a story because you don't care about these characters. You don't see the main characters, the prince and Cinderella, in action. You don't watch Cinderella getting ready for the ball. You don't hear the prince's agitation at her disappearance. As a result, you don't care about them or what happens next.

But if you were to *show* the emotions the characters feel, as revealed through their actions and reactions to events, you would have the beginnings of a real story. And if you were to show the main characters being shaped, changed, and molded by what they do throughout the story — going through conflict and struggling to get to the other side — you'll get your readers' attention.

A good story is one in which at least one main character participates in a series of events, facing and actively overcoming the conflicts that shape him, changing him from the person he was at the beginning.

By taking the basic plot just discussed and adding all the necessary ingredients of character development, conflict, action, and change, you can center in on the *plot* of Cinderella.

Making Sure You Have a Beginning, Middle, and End

Every good story has a beginning, a middle, and an end. The beginning reels you in, the climactic middle keeps you going, and the end satisfies you with resolution.

Keep these pointers in mind, and your plot will be sure to engage readers from start to finish:

- **Hook readers from the get-go.** Your plot must have a beginning in which you introduce your main character and hook readers into the action by introducing the character's driving desire, creating conflict right away. Consider the story of Cinderella. At the beginning of this tale, Cinderella's dad dies, leaving her at the mercy of a cruel stepmother and dreaming of a better life.

- **Direct the conflict to its natural climax.** The conflict must then build to a point where the main character is really in trouble, and the story could go either way. This is your middle in which the conflict reaches a climax. In the middle of Cinderella's story, she has met a partner who can help her escape her terrible life, but he can't seem to find her.

- **Resolve your story with a conquered conflict and a changed character.** You must begin to shape your ending by providing an opportunity for your main character to face the conflict, overcome the worst of it, and become a different — perhaps better — person as a result of all she has gone through by the end of the story. Cinderella's story ends with her decision to escape the cave she's been thrown into and try on the slipper, thus ensuring a better life and fulfills her driving desire to belong to a family — her chosen family and not the one she inherited.

Using Drama and Pacing to Propel Your Story Forward

After you have a beginning, middle, and end, you need to incorporate enough drama into your story, using pacing to keep the reader interested. *Drama* is struggle and conflict, emotionality and turbulence. *Pacing* is keeping the drama at a more heightened note than you would find in real life.

What your character wants (her burning desire, which we help you find in Chapter 7), the actions she uses to achieve her goal (plot), and the conflicts that get in her way (drama), plus the anticipation and uncertainty of her getting to the goal line (pacing), all serve as the elements of a good story and memorable characters. The next sections help you figure out the keys to incorporating drama and pacing in your plot.

A good story, well-fleshed-out characters, and a beginning, middle, and end are only parts of what keep your readers engaged. If you don't have adequate drama incorporated into the action or if your plot plods along from one event to the next, you will lose your readers.

Drama: A reason to turn the page

If your character experiences strong emotions due to the events of the story, you have drama. Likewise, if your character is tossed about by the turbulence of those events, such that his life is changed or his way of life is threatened, you also have drama.

The best way to make sure you have enough drama in your story is to ask yourself whether your character is struggling at each major plot point. Think about the tale of Cinderella. Is she suffering? Is she challenged? Is something threatening what she wants? Are the events in her life turbulent enough to keep people interested? If not, you have work to do.

Pacing: How you keep the pages turning

Pacing is the force that keeps the reader turning the pages, wanting — no, *needing* — to find out what happens next. In your story, each major plot point has to keep readers guessing as to what may happen next.

Because your audience likely has grown up on TV, video games, and smartphone apps with rapidly moving story lines, the action in children's books is quicker and chapters are shorter than in the past. What does that mean for you as a writer? That you need to know when and how to pick up the pace in your story.

Here are some tips for creating good pacing in different types of children's books:

> ✔ In a picture book, you can keep the story going at a good clip by drawing out conflict evenly throughout and writing tightly and well. (For a practical tip on how to check picture book pacing during the editing phase, head to Chapter 13.)

✔ In younger children's chapter books and middle-grade books, you can end the chapters with cliffhangers leaving the reader with a question. Literally, you can end with a question: Would Amanda figure out a way to get enough oxygen before the flooding waters completely engulfed her? Or figuratively: Amanda watched the flood waters rise, wondering when she would be forced to take her last breath. Just beware: Don't do this with every chapter, or you lose the element of suspense.

✔ In young adult novels, you still want to have chapters end on a high note, in the middle of a scene, at a tense moment in order to keep readers turning the pages, but you don't have to be quite as heavy handed about it as you do when writing for younger readers.

Outlining Tools to Structure Your Plot

Structure is simply the bones of your story upon which are laid the skin and organs: drama, pacing, effective transitions, and strong point of view (we cover POV in Chapter 11). You hear a lot of talk about structure in writing circles, and it's true that structure is the key to a good story. To give a story structure means you tie in your story's beginning, middle, and end with characters who move it forward with action and a plot that proceeds apace.

You can turn your story's plot structure into an outline pretty easily. Outlining your story allows you to pinpoint what your main character wants, what she does to get it, and how conflict intermittently challenges her. If other characters become important, you can expand your outline to include them too. Regardless, your outline becomes a repository for the who, what, when, where, why, and how of each of the three parts — beginning, middle, and end — of your story. From there, you can easily flesh out the details. The following sections explain how to create an outline to help you solidify your story's structure.

Plot and character are closely intertwined because the protagonist drives the plot. Character and plot are so connected that they proceed neck and neck on the same schedule. When the plot hits a bump, so does the main character (or vice versa). When the conflict in the plot approaches resolution, so does the main character's desire. And when the ending results in a changed character and a wrapped-up plot, the reader feels like the journey was worth it.

Sometimes visualizing what plot structure looks like is challenging, even with an outline. Fortunately, if you have a character arc created for your main character, you already have a plot visual handy. Refer to the character arc for Cinderella in Chapter 7. Notice how the beginning is illustrated at the bottom left of the arc, the middle/climax is at the top, and the resolution moves on the down slope. If you can take apart your own story and plot it out on an arc like that one, chances are you have your basic plot laid out.

Defend your prose — or let it go

Make sure your entire book's structure works by doing an action outline for every single part.

If you're writing a picture book, for each and every paragraph, ask yourself Lisa's Six Hallowed Action Questions:

1. Is this paragraph moving the plot forward? How?

2. Is this paragraph developing my main character by showing her in action? How?

3. Is this paragraph introducing drama through conflict and thus making the story proceed at a nice pace? How?

If the answer to at least one of these questions is "yes," and you can defend how it is done if you were called in front of a hanging jury, you can keep it in. If the answer is "not really" or simply "no," cut it. If you cannot tell yourself how a paragraph achieves at least one of these aims, cut the paragraph.

For chapter books and longer books, you can ask yourself these very important questions for each chapter. If a chapter has one of these purposes, then it can stay in. If nothing really happens and you cannot point to exactly the sentences that make the answer an affirmative, guess what? OUT IT GOES.

Creating a step sheet

A *step sheet* (also referred to as an *action outline*) is a useful tool for keeping track of plot points. It can also help you keep track of beginning/middle/end, pacing, and character development. You can make your step sheet as detailed or as thinly written as you feel is necessary. The idea is to create a simpler outline to really visualize your story's plot structure. You can follow your step sheet with a detailed outline if you choose.

Here's what the beginning of a step sheet may look like, using the story of Cinderella as an example. We've cut out a lot of the steps in the plot and left just a few key examples for you to look at. Your step sheet, on the other hand, should have a bullet point for every single action that takes place.

> ✔ **The beginning:**
>
> - **Plot point:** A spoiled young girl's wealthy father remarries a woman with two daughters.
>
> - **Character development:** Show Cinderella in action trying to befriend mean stepsisters.
>
> - **Pacing:** Show emotion behind growing dejection she feels.

- ✔ **Also at the beginning:**
  - **Plot point:** The father dies.
  - **Character development:** Show Cinderella's grief.
  - **Pacing:** Show stepmother and sisters plotting to take over house and grounds.
- ✔ **The middle:**
  - **Plot point:** A prince holds a ball to find a bride.
  - **Character development:** Show entire town excited over event, Cinderella depressed at not being able to participate.
  - **Pacing:** Show prince in action as adventurer, romantic — a definite catch.
- ✔ **The end:**
  - **Plot point:** The prince and the princess live happily ever after.
  - **Character development:** Show the rightness of the good guys winning.
  - **Pacing:** Slow down into final ending.

Your main character is the focal point of your step sheet, but you can add secondary characters if they affect the main plotline. Just make sure their fates are also satisfactorily wrapped up at the conclusion of the story.

Fleshing out your outline

A step sheet is a bare bones outline that helps you clearly see your plot structure. Some writers like a more detailed outline so they have a sort of blueprint to write from. A more fleshed out outline can provide a separate place for you to add notes about details you want to remember to incorporate when you get to that point in your story. It can also provide highly left-brained people with a literary to-do list, highlighting specific steps to check off once accomplished.

Outlines are organizing tools. They aren't holy words carved in stone. If, in the course of writing fiction, you find yourself veering away into some interesting but unforeseen place, you're allowed to follow your characters to see where they lead you.

Now suppose you choose to write your Cinderella story as a middle-grade chapter book. Now you can create a full outline of the story, starting with the journalist's trusty six questions:

- ✔ **Who:** Character development
- ✔ **What:** Plot point

- ✔ **When:** Time
- ✔ **Where:** Setting
- ✔ **Why:** Drama, pacing, and character motivation
- ✔ **How:** Plot point

So the start of your outline may look like this:

- ✔ **Chapter 1:**

  - **Setting:** A castle and its grounds.
  - **Time:** Medieval Europe.
  - **Plot point:** A spoiled young girl's wealthy father remarries a woman with two daughters.
  - **Character development:** Show Cinderella in action trying to befriend mean stepsisters.
  - **Supporting characters:** Father, stepmother, stepsisters, house staff.
  - **Pacing:** Show emotion behind Cinderella's growing dejection.

- ✔ **Chapter 2:**

  - **Setting:** Same but widens to include the town and church and burial ceremony.
  - **Time:** A few months later.
  - **Plot point:** The father dies.
  - **Character development:** Show Cinderella's grief.
  - **Supporting characters:** Introduce Cinderella's best friend, Jude.
  - **Pacing:** At end of chapter, show stepmother and sisters plotting to take over house and grounds.

- ✔ **Chapter 3:**

  - **Setting:** Same castle, but show Cinderella going to town.
  - **Time:** A week later.
  - **Plot point:** The stepmother enslaves the girl, treating her badly.
  - **Character development:** Show Cinderella facing up to her tasks with good cheer, determined to survive despite the conditions.
  - **Supporting characters:** Further develop relationship between Cinderella and Jude. Show townspeople watching her demise from upper-class to working class.
  - **Pacing:** Show how stepmother begins plundering Cinderella's father's assets to feed her own vanity and greed.

Interview with Michael Green, president and publisher of Philomel Books

For the real scoop on plotting, pacing, and drama and what they all mean after you get your manuscript to a real-live children's literary publisher, check out what Michael Green has to say. He's president and publisher of Philomel Books, a division of Penguin Young Readers Group.

WCBFD: You've been working in children's publishing for 20 years and have become an expert in what makes a good story work. What is usually the first thing that captures your attention when you pick up a new manuscript and begin to read?

MG: I take an uncommon interest in someone's opening sentence. A weak one doesn't necessarily signal a weak manuscript, but a strong one announces a writer and does tend to bode well for what lies ahead. I also listen for a writer's voice. Before plot or characterization has the chance to take root, voice can take root.

WCBFD: In a similar vein, what is the one thing that when reading a manuscript can cause you to pitch it immediately into your round file?

MG: Nothing earns a rejection slip faster than an overwritten first paragraph. It *never* bodes well. There is a time and a place for character description or exposition, and the story's opening is never it.

WCBFD: How can a new writer tell whether his main character is working? What should he be looking for?

MG: His main character should take life unto itself. It should speak, breathe, and react on its own — that is when an author knows the character comes across as real.

WCBFD: As far as plots are concerned, what are the most important elements in a well-constructed one?

MG: A well-constructed plot is a bit like an open umbrella. It forms an arc that envelopes and reaches out toward all characters and plot points. It unifies and gives purpose to everything that touches that arc.

WCBFD: How important is dramatic pacing to a picture book? A novel?

MG: Picture books and novels are separate beasts. A picture book will always have a sense of pacing, a sense of movement. A good part of that movement is owed to the artwork, though, which needs to move along the story on its own terms. Within the spacious boundaries of a novel, dramatic pacing and characterization are vital. An author needs to be careful, however, of not forcing the issue. Quiet, subtle moments in Chapter 2 might very well be setting up an earthquake in Chapter 5; the contrast between the two will help the tension pop when it finally arrives.

WCBFD: What are some tricks a new writer could use to help him figure out how to accomplish sufficient drama and adequate pacing?

MG: Watch for the unusual when reading other writers' books. Different writers play different games with pacing and drama; be attentive to what works for you as a reader. Also, pay attention to how chapters close. Chapter closing lines should be tiny jewels that close a door on one scene while tempting a reader to tear open that door and burst through the other side to see what happens.

Knowing when to circumvent an outline

When the issue of an outline seems absurd or overkill, chances are it is — for you. For example, it is doubtful that you will need an outline for a board book. Most picture books don't get written with an outline unless the writer gets stuck and needs help figuring out why — applying the advice in the nearby "Defend your prose — or let it go" for every sentence of a picture book always results in a more tight manuscript.

Additionally, some writers simply can't work with an outline at all, preferring to just get writing and work on (and rework) the written pages without an organizational tool to fall back on.

Preventing Plot Problems

Not all plots are the same, but some common plot problems can creep into your story when you're not looking. Fortunately, we can help. Here are a few guidelines about approaches you should avoid so as not to muck up your plot:

- ✔ **Action with no actor:** When you're writing a scene, make it clear who's doing the action. Don't make your reader hunt around previous or successive paragraphs to figure out who is the star of the scene.

- ✔ **Actor with no action:** Don't go on and on about a character — any character — without making sure he does something relevant to the plot. In other words, if you find yourself mired in lots of description or backstory or pages of dialogue in a row, your character and your plot are not moving forward.

- ✔ **Scene it once, scene it twice, but never thrice (or more):** Although some writers like to write from different points of view (POVs) in alternating chapters, it's not a good idea to repeat a scene just so we see it from another character's POV. We got it the first time. Now move on.

    While we're on the topic of multiple POVs, never try this storytelling tactic unless you have character bibles for each character with a POV. You have to know your character very well so you get his or her voice down pat.

- ✔ **Not-so-lovely loose ends:** Remember that character you introduced in the second chapter? The one who was giving your main character a hard enough time for you to mention him by first — and maybe even last — name and spend an entire chapter on him? Make sure you let us know by the end of the story what happened to him. Don't leave any of your plot points without some kind of closure, either. Believe us, there are plenty of readers out there who will notice — and who will hate it. Conversely, don't go on and on belaboring the ending. Make it short and sweet.

Writing Your First Draft

Don't expect to sit down and craft a perfect children's book from start to finish, even if you've fully outlined your characters and plot. Writing is not just about putting your first thoughts on paper and being ready to publish. Instead, writing is about writing, revising, and revising some more.

The only way you're going to be able to write freely is to turn off your inner critic and just get going. Take your character bibles, context bibles (see Chapter 10), and step sheets as far as you can, then just stop. Don't worry about character arcs, plot steps, pacing, or even drama. Just let your main character go. Find yourself blathering on? No problem. Just keep going until you've reached the end. When you do get to the end, pat yourself on the back! You have an official first draft done — which no one is *ever* going to see.

The only element you must make sure of before you start writing is that your character has a burning desire to drive your story. See Chapter 7.

After writing your first draft, you have two choices. You can either go back and work on your second draft using everything you're reading in this chapter, or you can wait until you've finished reading all the chapters in Part III — and then go back and start work on your second draft.

We suggest that in between each draft (or every few drafts, if you're writing a chapter book or longer work), you print out your story and reread it with a pencil, just like many editors do. There is something about reading printed matter on paper that makes it read more "real" than reading it on screen. No one can tell you how many drafts it will take till you are done revising, but you will know. Then you will be ready to edit, covered in Chapter 13.

Chapter 9

Can We Talk? Writing Dialogue

Dialogue is a form of action; it can be used to develop character and plot. It can enhance pacing and drama and increase a book's readability by transmitting necessary information by breaking up passages of narration and description. Writing *good* dialogue isn't the same as writing realistic dialogue. Realistic dialogue is boring as all heck to read if you write it out as it actually occurs. To write good dialogue, you must develop a keen ear and be able to translate what you hear into a wittier, smarter, more meaningful version of itself. Which is to say, in order for your characters to sound good, you need to write the way people actually talk — and then make it better.

In this chapter, we help you figure out when to use dialogue. We also discuss the functions dialogue must serve within your story and your characters' development to make it worth including. We talk about how good dialogue requires drama and tension and how to get in the groove of putting words into children's mouths by listening and paying attention to some actual, living owners of those mouths. We show you how your character bible can help you define each of your characters, making them sound different from one another, and how you can check your dialogue by listening to it read aloud. We also take you through some of the most common dialogue mistakes and help you hone your skills with a couple of handy exercises.

The Fundamentals of Good Dialogue

Writers are like jugglers. They have to keep many elements going at the same time: character development, plot construction, establishing setting — the list goes on. Dialogue can be used to develop everything from characters and plot to setting, drama, and pacing — but only if you know how to incorporate dialogue effectively.

The first step in writing good dialogue is to figure out when to use it at all. Although we cannot give you a rule of thumb about when to use dialogue (mostly because each children's book format differs as does each writer's style), we *can* tell you that you can use it whenever it seems you have a lot of descriptive or narrative paragraphs that need to be broken up. You can also use it if you find yourself *telling* about a character or characters to develop them in your reader's mind rather than *showing* the characters interacting in order to reveal who they really are. Using dialogue also helps when the plot needs to move forward, and you need a character to take the reader to that next part of the story.

Of course, good dialogue also has drama. It creates emotion and inspires action. We tell you more about this, as well as the different functions dialogue can play in your story, in the sections that follow.

If you can't spell out exactly why a piece of dialogue exists, chances are it doesn't belong in your story. For example, small talk or simple greetings between characters don't pass muster if they don't add anything concrete to your story. Dialogue needs to have a true function (like giving information, developing characters, or moving your story forward), and it needs to be interesting to read (in other words, it needs to have drama).

Dialogue has a function

Although it's a great tool for enriching your fiction (and your nonfiction), dialogue is not the same as talking. Talking is two or more people exchanging words, meaningful or not, boring or not. Dialogue has a function, a job to do.

You use dialogue in your story only if it performs at least one of the functions we cover in the following sections.

Giving information

Narration and description, unless they incorporate action, can be static. Dialogue gives information in a direct way, showing us what is going on rather than telling us about it in description. When you use dialogue to convey information, you add spice and emotion, personalization and action, interaction and character development. Consider the following example of how dialogue gives information:

JANE: Didja call him?

NELLY: Yeah. But he wasn't home. Let it ring and ring. Called a bunch of times, too. I think he never came home last night.

JANE: C'mon. I bet I know where he is!

In this exchange, we find out the person the girls are discussing is missing, and they are going to go find him. The narrator could have revealed this information in prose, but it's not as interesting:

Jane called Nelly to find out if Nelly had contacted James. Nelly revealed she had tried, but James had not answered despite repeated attempts. So Jane dragged off Nelly in search of the missing boy.

Developing characters

Instead of describing who a character is and how he behaves in a specific situation, use dialogue. In the following example, dialogue develops characters:

"Do you mean that you think you can find out the answer to it?" said the March Hare.

"Exactly so," said Alice.

"Then you should say what you mean," the March Hare went on.

"I do," Alice hastily replied. "At least — at least I mean what I say — that's the same thing, you know."

"Not the same thing a bit!" said the Hatter. "You might just as well say that 'I see what I eat' is the same thing as 'I eat what I see'!"

"You might just as well say," added the March Hare, "that 'I like what I get' is the same thing as "I get what I like'!"

"You might just as well say," added the Dormouse, which seemed to be talking in its sleep, "that 'I breathe when I sleep' is the same thing as 'I sleep when I breathe'!"

"It *is* the same thing with you," said the Hatter, and here the conversation dropped. . . .

In this exchange from Lewis Carroll's *Alice's Adventures in Wonderland,* we learn that the March Hare and his cohorts are a bunch of semanticists, picky regarding specificity, especially when it comes to their beloved pastime of talking in riddles to Alice, whom they accuse of loose and fast treatment of the language. As the dialogue continues, we also learn that Alice is quite easily puzzled by her companions, by which we take to mean that Alice, as a character, is not as smart or as quick-witted as the others.

We could have accomplished the same character development in prose, but chances are it would not have been half as fun to read, or half as revealing of the characters' personalities, quirks, and thought processes.

Moving the story forward

Dialogue is action through interaction; therefore, good dialogue moves plot points in your story ahead. Check out this example of how dialogue moves the story forward:

> "What's the matter, Mother?" he said.
>
> "Oh, Diamond, my darling! You have been so ill!" she sobbed.
>
> "No, Mother dear. I've only been at the back of the north wind," returned Diamond.
>
> "I thought you were dead," said his mother.
>
> But that moment, the doctor came in.
>
> "Oh! there!" said the doctor with gentle cheerfulness; "we're better to-day, I see."

In this exchange from George MacDonald's *At the Back of the North Wind* between the main character, a boy named Diamond, and his mother, we learn that Diamond does not realize that his journeys with his friend, the North Wind, leave him sicker and sicker. We realize also that Diamond has no idea how long he has been gone or that he leaves his body behind when he travels with her. This dialogue not only moves the story forward to Diamond's recovery in the world inhabited by his family, but it also adds information, characterizing the journeys he goes on as somewhat otherworldly.

Again, this dialogue could easily have been put into straight prose narrative, but it would not have contained the same drama.

Dialogue has drama

Dialogue *needs* to be dramatic. It should create arguments, strong emotions, or conflict between your characters. That conflict should lead to some new action on the character's part (and move the story along). Good dialogue is short, potent, and meaningful.

Let's say you are at a point in your story where you need to move the plot forward. You could do it in narration, or you can accomplish it in dialogue. Often, dialogue conveys more drama and much more emotion, while revealing more about the characters' personalities.

> Jane nearly tripped over Nelly as she approached the train door. There he was. "I don't believe it," she muttered to herself, feeling her heart start to race. He saw her and stopped, causing those behind him to grumble and shove in their hurry to get past him. "I was sure you wouldn't be here," she whispered.

He grinned, raising an eyebrow. "I just lost a bet, too."

"With who?" Jane demanded.

In this short exchange, in which we move the plot forward by discovering James's whereabouts, we also glean important information: that the boy James sought by Jane and Nelly has just come back from a trip somewhere. We learn about Jane that she feels more for James than just platonic concern, based on the depth of her emotion, her heart racing, her speaking in whispered tones, and her instant jealousy at his mention of a bet with an unnamed person, perhaps a rival for his affections. And we also learn that James, a funny, confident boy, shares some of Jane's feelings, because of his happy-go-lucky grin and his raised eyebrow. Plus, all these little actions, expressions, and body language show instead of tell.

This exchange could have proceeded completely differently. James could have stuttered and blushed, indicating that he is not as confident or happy-go-lucky. Jane could have attacked him verbally, demanding to know where he was and why he had not contacted her or Nelly. Written that way, the dialogue would have told us different things about the characters themselves, would have moved the plot forward differently, and would have given us different information about the relationship between Jane and James.

Another way to work in dialogue is at the beginning of a scene. Try writing the entire scene in dialogue, and then just in narrative. Then take the best of the prose parts — those that add to the setting, the actions, the indicators of tone of voice or body language, the expression, the characters' movements, the short descriptions — and merge them together. Between the two versions, you should come up with a scene that is fleshed out, actively moving the plot forward, and sustained by characters who are making it all come alive by what they say and how they speak.

Listening to Real-World Dialogue

Training yourself to listen and really hear is the first step to writing dialogue that sounds like real people speaking to each other and not like a writer trying to simulate real people talking to each other. One time-tested universal tip about dialogue is that children sound very different from adults — and they must do so in your writing as well. Consider the following sections your primer into how kids talk versus how adults talk.

How kids talk

Go to any park or classroom with children the age of your audience. Listen. Chances are you'll encounter the following:

- Contractions (*it's* and *can't* versus *it is* and *cannot*)
- Lots of stuttering and hemming (*uh, yeah, um, well, hmm, like, you know?,* and all their incoherent relatives)
- Incomplete sentences (*If you wanna . . .* versus *If you want to go, you may exit stage right*)
- Nonverbal communication taking the place of actual words (a chin nod or a headshake in reply)
- Body language contradicting words (crossed arms signaling a specific attitude even if the words contradict that attitude — just ask the parent of a teenager if you don't understand this example)
- Communication shortcuts, such as slang

If you write it without at least a few of the above, your dialogue will come out sounding as tedious and wooden as a court transcript. There's no way you can write dialogue exactly the way it's heard in real life, but you can get close. This is how an actual conversation between two teenagers may sound. Notice the shortcuts and the incomplete sentences. Pay attention to how body language must be saying a lot because not much information is actually conveyed here, despite the number of exchanges.

> KID A: Didja hear what happened to Sarina?
>
> KID B: No. What?
>
> KID A: She got totally narced on.
>
> KID B: By who?
>
> KID A: Dunno. Her sister? Maybe that other . . . you know.
>
> KID B: No way.

To make this dialogue really work for you, by developing a character and moving plot forward (see Chapters 8 and 9, respectively), you'd have to rewrite it to make it better.

> KID A: Didja hear what happened to Sarina, that new girl who was, you know, trying to hang with the popular kids?
>
> KID B: No. What?
>
> KID A: She got narced on. Someone told about her shoplifting. You know, stealing to be cool.
>
> KID B: Yeah. But who told?
>
> KID A: I dunno. Maybe her sister; you know she's gotta be jealous . . . being all smart and stuff. . . .

This version tells us a lot more about who the players are, what happened, and what's really at stake in terms of the plot. It's not much changed, only blown out to make it better than it was, while still retaining the tone of the teenagers' original speech.

How grown-ups talk

Grown-ups, for the most part, speak like children do in terms of shorter sentences mixed in with longer ones, interruptions, crossing over each other's speech, incomplete sentences, contractions, and more. The major difference is that in their dialogue exchanges, grown-ups are allowed (depending the situation) to swear, use big vocabulary words (sparingly and in context), use less slang, and generally sound more mature.

Yes, we all know adults who sound like kids (makes them appear as if they are trying too hard to be cool, right?) and kids who sound like adults (read: Poindexter alert!), but unless you have a definable purpose for these two instances, try to avoid them. Otherwise, you'll be like a person pretending to be a writer who can actually write good dialogue. Cannot have that. We want you to write the real thing — the good stuff!

Adding a Speech Section to Your Character Bible

In Chapter 7, we discuss creating a character bible that really lays out who your character is in terms of personality, looks, history, family, quirks — all the elements that contribute to making a person who he or she really is. A character bible functions to help you get to know who your character is and to help you differentiate between characters.

A great addition to a character bible is a speech section where you identify how your character speaks. Consider the following characteristics of speech and lay out where each of your characters falls where these attributes are concerned:

- ✔ How articulate is she? (We're referring to characters who are old enough to be articulate here.) Is she educated, and is it reflected in her speech?

- ✔ Is she not a native speaker? What is her native tongue? Does her English sound like she got it from a book? Or is your character a younger child apt to make grammatical mistakes such as mistaking one word for another?

- ✔ What is the quality of her voice? Is it hoarse? Loud? Soft? Squeaky? High? Low?

- ✔ Does she have any verbal anomalies such as lisping or stuttering?

✔ Is she direct in her speech or shyer, more obtuse?

✔ Does she use swear words or slang, jargon, or street talk?

✔ Is she loquacious or terse? Abrupt or apt to talk your head off?

✔ Does she answer every question with another question?

Though not all of the preceding questions can (or should) be answered where every character is concerned, they can be very helpful in finding your character's particular voice and keeping that voice consistent and differentiated from the other characters in your book. Plus it helps you avoid the problem of having your teenage protagonist sound the same as his mother.

Reading It Out Loud

The best test of whether or not your dialogue is working is to listen to someone else read it back to you. When you hear your dialogue read aloud, pay attention and ask yourself:

✔ **Do the child characters sound like children?** If they consistently speak in complete sentences or use strings of huge words, you probably have your English professor in mind and not a child. Shorten sentences. Add a mild stutter. Fill in some blanks between speech with brief descriptions of telling body language and facial expressions.

✔ **Do the characters sound different from one another?** If not, you need to listen to how various people speak and try to capture those differences. And revisit that character's speech section in her character bible to see if you are remaining true to your original idea of how she actually speaks.

✔ **Is the speech wordy or to the point?** If wordy, chances are you have too many adjectives and are describing too much. Shorten. Hone. Tighten. Make better, more precise word choices.

✔ **Is the emotion clear from the words chosen?** If not, try to be more precise with your choice of words, making each one count; keep your thesaurus within reach. Go back to your character bible. Between important speakers' lines, add occasional, brief descriptions of their revealing facial expressions or body movements.

✔ **Does your main character have a strong voice? Does he sound interesting and unique?** If not, you may want to reexamine his personality and see what special speech patterns or tone of voice may make him more compelling. Perhaps you do not know him well enough. Try some of the exercises described at the end of this chapter.

✔ **How does each piece of dialogue move the story forward or further embellish a character?** If it doesn't, *sayonara,* baby!

Dialogue is never easy for a new writer. But you can write much better dialogue with practice and determination. And when in doubt about a particular piece, leave it out.

 The great thing about writing dialogue is that on paper you have time to craft the ultimate witty comebacks, astute questions, and on-target answers (unlike in real life). On paper, you can make your characters sound better than the rest of us lug heads. So, for all those times you went home cursing yourself for failing to deliver that perfect retort — the one that came to you on your way home — consider writing books as your revenge and make those characters talk pretty.

Divulging Common Dialogue Mistakes

People really do speak in fits and starts, but that doesn't mean your characters should — it simply takes up too much valuable space to include all those hems and haws and pauses and incomplete sentences — unless you can fill them with meaning, and that takes practice. A big difference between speech that you hear and speech that you read is that all the nonverbal communication, nuance, and inflection of real dialogue is lost when it's written down, so your words have to work extra hard.

It takes practice listening, writing, and editing to become a good writer of dialogue. It also takes being willing to make some mistakes, at least in your drafts. Of course, some mistakes have been so commonly made that there's no need for you to make them yourself. Check out the next sections for the scoop on these mistakes and how to avoid them. These sections feature scenes with Jane, James, and Nelly, whom you may have met in the earlier "Dialogue has drama" section.

Failing to have conflict or tension

Dialogue that just delivers information or develops a character without, in itself, containing any hint of drama or tension is not very interesting. That doesn't mean your characters have to get into a fight or speak meanly to one another. But they should actively move the story forward. For example, here's our short scene from earlier in this chapter with Jane, James, and Nelly without any tension:

> Jane and Nelly approached the train door. James appeared a moment later. "There he is," she said. He saw her and stopped, causing those behind him to mutter and shove in their hurry to get past him. "Good, you're here," she told him.
>
> James hefted his backpack over his shoulder. "Yep, I'm here."
>
> "OK, let's go then," Jane said.

Repeating information

Many beginning writers feel they have to introduce the dialogue with an explanation of what's to follow (or conversely, to follow up the dialogue with a recap), essentially repeating the same information. Don't waste the reader's time. Choose one or the other, not both. And remember to choose *showing* (actual dialogue) rather than *telling* (recapping) whenever possible.

The following scene illustrates just how silly it is when your dialogue repeats information you've already given readers in the narrative:

> As they made their way out of the train station, Nelly wanted to find out where James had been, so she asked him. He told her he had been to visit his uncle, the murderer. She was so shocked, she could hardly let him finish his sentences. Jane had to get her to quiet down so they could hear James speak.
>
> "Where'd you go?" Nelly asked, trying to act casual now that they had left the bustle of the station.
>
> "I went to see my uncle," James replied. "And he told me . . ."
>
> Nelly interrupted him in a rush. "The one in prison? The . . . the murderer?"
>
> "Yep. And boy did I find out . . ."
>
> "You went to visit a murderer? Are you crazy?" Nelly nearly shouted.
>
> "Will you please shut it?" demanded Jane. "I want to hear what he found out."
>
> Nelly sniffed, looking at the ground. "Fine. But I still think it was dumb of him."

Describing dialogue

Some beginning writers forget that dialogue is an option and describe verbal exchanges between characters instead of just giving us the exchange in dialogue. Case in point:

> Once they had steered clear of the train station, Nelly casually asked James where he had gone. He told her that he had gone to see his uncle. Nelly, shocked, interrupted him, demanding to know if he is talking about his uncle the murderer. James admitted that that was indeed the uncle that he saw and tried to explain, but Nelly interrupted him again. Finally, Jane had to tell Nelly to be quiet so James could tell them all about what he found out.

Putting this exchange into dialogue instead of reporting about it would have been so much more interesting.

Using too many speaker references and attributions

Believe it or not, you do not need to have your characters use each other's names in each leg of your dialogue. Nor do you need to identify each speaker by name each time with an attribution *(he said, she replied, he asked),* though when there are three or more speakers in one exchange, you might choose to for clarity. See for yourself how unrealistic dialogue can sound when you use too many references and attributions.

> "Hi, Nelly," said James.
>
> "Hi, James," replied Nelly.
>
> "How are you, Nelly?" asked James.
>
> "Oh, doing fine, doing fine, James," said Nelly.
>
> "Hey, Nelly, how is Jane?" asked James.
>
> "Jane is fine, James," replied Nelly. "How is your Uncle Bob?"

People just don't talk that way, whether they know each other or not. Notice also the lack of contractions *(How is* instead of *How's),* which is also unrealistic.

Real conversations never have people repeating each other's names every other line — or even every once in a while. As a matter of fact, only when a character cannot hear and has to be summoned in a louder voice do we hear his name; or if he is being introduced to someone new his name might be mentioned. Using a person's name over and over suggests the following:

- ✔ The person using the name over and over looks down on the other person or has to speak slowly to get his attention.

- ✔ The person mentioning the name is in a position of power over him: for example, "Peter Michael Economy! Get your butt over here before I — ," said Mrs. Economy. You get the gist.

Creating heavy-handed and unrealistic dialogue

People talk in shorthand, using contractions and body language to convey meaning. So don't load up your dialogue with a lot of information that would not ordinarily be found in dialogue. For example:

> "Your uncle is in prison for a reason. He stole all that money from your grandfather with that no-good best friend of his in 2004, killing that poor nurse from Kentucky in the process. The bullet went straight through her heart, which we all considered symbolic, considering he broke your grandmother's heart, not to mention ruining the family name when your family history was dragged through the papers, revealing your illegitimate birth and your grandfather's sketchy past," said Jane.

> "Yes," agreed James, "he is in prison for a reason. But that reason is not what you think. That reason is wrong. He was wrongly convicted because he was not holding the gun when it went off and he did not even want to go into that bank in the first place! And . . ."

As you can see, this is narrative disguised as dialogue. These words do not belong in young people's mouths, especially the way they are written. The amount of detail is unrealistic for the context in which it is given. There is too much information packed into each speaker's turn. Dialogue needs to be simple and to the point, not encumbered by tons of background information and backstory or flashback (more on those in Chapter 7).

Filling space with unnecessary dialogue

Dialogue shouldn't be used to fill up space on the page or accomplish things that are best left up to a sentence of narrative. For example, when characters are being introduced to one another, chances are you do not need to do it in dialogue, not unless something else important happens during the introduction that gives it a clear function in the story.

> "Hello, Mr. Sloan," said Nelly.

> "Hello, Nelly," said Mr. Sloan. "And who have we here?"

> "Mr. Sloan, I'd like to introduce you to my friends, Jane and James," said Nelly.

> "Hello, Mr. Sloan," said James, extending his hand to Mr. Sloan.

> "Hi, nice to meet you, Mr. Sloan," said Jane, smiling at Mr. Sloan.

This exchange is much better off in narrative, where it is short and to the point:

> Nelly walked into the office of Mr. Sloan, her father's lawyer, and introduced her friends.

Nit-picky dialogue problems

Some of the mistakes people make when writing dialogue seem pretty minor. But when you see them again and again, particularly in a short children's book, they only get more annoying. Sure, the following list may read like pet peeves to you, but now that we mention them we bet they'll start sticking out to you, too (if they haven't already!):

✔ **Writing long speeches, lectures, or monologues:** These are passages where one character goes on and on, uninterrupted, for paragraphs. Yaaaaaaaawn.

✔ **Using said tags:** Writing action or body language into the dialogue can move things along. *Dialogue tags (he said, she said, she muttered, he interjected,* and so on) slow things down. Use them sparingly when you have to, but when you do, use them only with one character in the spoken exchange.

✔ **Relying on adjectives and adverbs:** The words of dialogue that you put in the character's mouth should be specific and well-chosen enough to convey the emotion without requiring clarifying phrases or adverbs (such as happily, sadly, tearfully, and angrily).

✔ **Using semicolons:** Semicolons aren't recommended in dialogue.

✔ **Indicating a pause in conversation with a comma:** Use an ellipsis in dialogue to signal speech trailing off and an em dash (—) to signal an interruption.

✔ **Using phonetic spellings of dialects:** Use dialect or regional accents in dialogue only if you're *very* familiar with the dialects. Do it flawlessly and consistently — or don't do it at all.

Improving Dialogue by Using Writing Exercises

Writing dialogue well takes developing a good ear and lots of practicing. But you may be better at it than you think. The writing exercises in the following sections are part of getting in the practice of regular writing and can help you rehearse writing dialogue without the pressure of having to make it good.

Talking on paper

One of the aspects of letter-writing (or e-mails, texts, and instant messages) is it can be as free-form as you want. You can write like you speak. You can be trivial and funny and even use bad words. And you can write ungrammatically, in truncated sentences, using shorthand and even emoticons or Internet slang (think LOL or IMHO) to get your meaning across. So sit down, fire up the old laptop, and start talking on paper.

Write letters to anyone, about anything. Got a friend you owe a call to? Surprise her instead with a handwritten page or two about what's been going on in your life. Haven't been in touch with that friend from college? Pretend she's on the phone and carry on a conversation. And to get some practice with dialogue, instead of writing it all in narrative, relay some conversations you've had recently with others (or overheard others having) — and feel free to make your replies more witty and to the point than they really were.

And if you really want to increase the usefulness of this exercise, write a letter to a child whom you know: your own child, your friend's child. Keep the subject matter appropriate, but write whatever comes into your head. Kids love to get mail; really little ones can't even tell if it's well-written or not — and won't care.

Being yourself and being relaxed on paper, not worrying too much about how you sound, is a good way to get comfortable with writing. Then when it comes to writing the "real thing," you won't feel as if you're embarking on a scary journey.

Introducing your first best friend to the love of your life

Want to try a tactic that can really bring characters to life through dialogue? Simply choose two people you know (such as your first best friend and your significant other — see the exercises at the end of Chapter 7) and begin a dialogue between them on paper, just as you'd imagine them talking with one another face-to-face.

A famous writing teacher who guided many aspiring novelists to fame and fortune, always had her writers begin her workshops with this exercise. Now that Lisa runs her own workshops, she also has new writers try it. She always tells them that if nothing else happens, they are holding in their hands some interesting character studies to auction off on eBay when they become rich and famous children's book writers.

Chapter 10

Setting the Scene

· ·

In This Chapter

▶ Establishing setting, context, environment

▶ Understanding when you need context and why

▶ Including the right amount of setting and context

▶ Exercising your memory with a smellography

· ·

Many books about writing don't talk about setting, but whether you're writing fiction or nonfiction, your characters need to do whatever they do *somewhere,* right? And that particular somewhere needs to be set up for the reader almost the same way you would set up a character, only much more subtly and much more briefly, so the reader gets a picture in his or her head about the places all the action in the story occurs.

In this chapter, we show you how to set up scenery to give your stories and characters context, creating a much more interesting and believable children's book in the process. We share exactly when to include scenery and context and how much of it to include before giving you a demonstration of how to use one of your senses to create context.

Giving Context to Your Story and Its Characters with Scenery

The most important reason for setting up scenery is to give your story and characters a context to do what they do. For example, when your adventurous main character comes from a house in a city, it's not enough to just name a city, real or imagined, and leave it at that. You need to give that city *character,* imbue it with a sense of uniqueness so that it adds to who your protagonist is when he or she is in that place. Why? Because you are shaped positively or negatively by the places where you live. These places contribute to who you are.

How many times do you hear about people who left home and never looked back? That's indeed interesting, but we need to know more: What's the character's hometown like that made him want never to return? Describe the aspects of the town that create emotions in your character. It follows that your characters are shaped in turn by these contexts. In addition, a well-established context gives us a starting point from which to dive into the action.

Context, environment, venue, place, somewhere — we use all these words pretty much interchangeably in this chapter. And the most important contexts to get right are the ones in which the main character — and the characters who get in her way — spends the majority of her time.

Creating a Context Bible

Every story needs to be grounded. That grounding or foundation is created when a context is developed. A context gives a character a place to begin, a place to set her feet and then jump into or away from when the action indicates. Although it's always advisable to begin a story right away with the main character in action (as we explain in Chapter 8), sooner or later that character is going to need to go somewhere. Where is that somewhere? And is that somewhere important? The amount of context developed in the story answers those questions for the reader. And to help you figure that out, you need to develop a context bible.

Creating a context bible isn't much different from creating a character bible (which we show you how to do in Chapter 7). Its purpose is pretty much the same: to help you develop, know, and evocatively describe all the different places where the action occurs. A context bible keeps all the location information in one spot.

To create your context bible, you need to ask some fundamental questions about the environment where you want to place your character. The purpose to these questions is to make a place come alive, much like a well-developed character does. The context should be so well created that a reader can place herself there and actually imagine what it looks like, how it feels to live in or visit that place, what different parts of the city smell or feel like, and what characterizes its tone, style, and inhabitants.

Here are some questions you can ask to develop an environment for your story:

- What is the place called? Where did that name come from?
- What part of the world is it in? Is it near water? Mountains? Plains? How does this location establish a tone to the place?
- What is the ethnic makeup? If mixed, is it blended or segregated?

✔ Is there a central area where people congregate, tourists visit, or the place is known for?

✔ What does it smell like?

✔ What different noises or sounds do you hear when walking down a street?

✔ What is the place known for? How does that affect its character?

✔ What is the first thing newcomers notice when they arrive?

Creating and developing a context does not necessarily mean including paragraph upon paragraph of description in your finished story. Exactly the opposite: It means knowing a place well enough that a few well-chosen sentences can evoke a feeling or tone for the place for the reader.

Often, you read books starring characters that come from real cities. The author drops the name of the city and leaves it at that. What a rip-off. The reader may not know what he is missing — and that is the writer's fault. For example, Lisa comes from Los Angeles, California, which isn't just a huge city, but is a huge county with many different cities inside it, each with its own character. People who live in each of these cities are assumed to share in the character of the place they have chosen to live. For example, people who live in Venice, California, have chosen to inhabit an artsy, youthful beach community packed with pedestrians, culturally mixed, and impossible to drive through on sunny summer weekends. There are lots of restaurants and funky shops, with the decrepit right next door to the brand-spanking new. If you're familiar with Venice, you know that people who choose to live there accept and even embrace what Venice has to offer — both good and bad. So a character who comes from Venice will be assumed to possess an artistic and accepting attitude or to enjoy being surrounded by others who do — but only if you're familiar with that area can you know enough to assume that about the character. If you're not familiar with that area, you need the writer to let you in on its secrets so that you can better understand the character inhabiting or visiting that place.

Knowing When to Include Scenery and Context

A reader who is not getting enough information about a main character's whereabouts won't necessarily be able to tell you that's the reason he's not enjoying your book. But he will feel a certain lack of connection to the character — which is the kiss of death. If a main character isn't engaging, children will put down the book and never pick it up again. If you don't explore contexts at all, your reader may feel lost, as if the characters are floating around, homeless, groundless, foundationless — for even a character on the run from home has to come from somewhere, pass through somewhere else, and be headed somewhere.

With middle-grade novels and longer books involving many different scenes and chapters in which the main character moves from place to place, you need to make sure your readers know something about where the characters are. When your story begins, make sure it takes place somewhere and that you give the somewhere at least one fabulously descriptive sentence within the first few paragraphs of the book. As your book progresses and the main character moves from place to place in each scene, make sure you have at least one descriptive sentence about each new context.

Board books, picture books, and other formats for the youngest readers don't necessarily require descriptive sentences establishing context because the illustrations usually do that job for you. In these cases, identifying home, school, or the park as such is sufficient. You can include scene-building sentences or phrases, but what you don't need to do is go into great detail. If you do go into great detail regarding scenery when writing a shorter format book, you just use up your word count and then a lot of those words will get axed when the illustrator is hired. So although you *can* establish scenery and context in picture books by using words, don't go on and on about what the reader sees — it's the illustrator's job to do that.

Here's an example of a middle-grade setting that works:

> Barden Woods was haunted. Everyone knew the story about Barden, the famous wood carver. He had spent his days among the giant redwoods, surrounded by children, whittling toys, tiny furniture, even treehouses. One day, not long after The Great Fire destroyed part of the woods, Barden disappeared. The villagers whispered that he had been carried off by wood spirits. Barden Woods became a place forbidden to children, a scary, dangerous place. It still was.

How do you know when a scene needs scenery description or contextual establishment? The next sections help you out.

If there are no pictures to tell readers where they are, and if you can say yes to any of the seven examples in the following sections, you need to describe the scenery.

When place figures prominently

Every story needs living, breathing characters — people, animals, or anthropomorphized objects such as the dancing teapot and candelabra in Disney's *Beauty and the Beast* — to create reader interest and move the action forward. But sometimes, the place in which a story occurs can be almost as important as the characters that inhabit it — and therefore deserving of a level of description sufficient to provide complete context and scenery.

For example, a mystery story involving the inhabitants of a haunted house requires the description of the house. In the same way, a story involving a character who is an explorer means you need at least a brief description of each place explored. Consider the important role that context and scenery play in historical fiction, such as the American Girls Collection series of books (American Girl Publications), which are set in specific years and places. For example, *Meet Kirsten: An American Girl* by Janet Shaw, opens with Kirsten's first view of the United States from the vantage point of a ship in the ocean, moving — along with the main character — to New York City and finally to Minnesota. Or consider the elaborate descriptions of Master Stevens's plantation in *Meet Addy: An American Girl* by Connie Porter, which is about a girl who moves from slavery to freedom in 19th-century America.

When the place isn't just incidental

The setting of your story is far from incidental when it's not just a starting place for the character or an ending place in the action. In the following passage, notice how the setting isn't nearly as important to the plot as the character's personality:

> Nina left for school every morning at seven o'clock. And she returned home promptly at three in the afternoon. At noon sharp, she sat down for lunch and after school she allowed herself a snack at 3:15 on the button. Nina was a very punctual person. So when Nina did not show up for her first class right on time, Mrs. Feinstein knew something was wrong.

Nina's punctuality is the subject of the passage, and to describe her school would both interrupt the flow of the prose and fail to add anything interesting that readers need to know. If however, the passage reads like the following, a description of the school is warranted:

> Nina left for school every morning at seven o'clock, dragging her feet the entire way. With each step, she thought of recess at ten, lunch at noon, and, best of all, the end of classes at three. With her shoulders slumped, Nina barely managed to get to her first class on time, no matter how hard she tried. Today was no exception. As she heard the first bell, signaling three minutes left to get to class, Nina lifted her eyes and increased her pace. The tall, red-brick facade soon came into view, its disheveled eaves and broken windows looking like a face that had barely survived a car accident. She slipped into Mrs. Feinstein's room just as the last bell rang.

Here, the main character's reluctance to go to school is the subject of the passage, because she is reluctant about the specific place she has to go to. As such, we are interested in the reason; we need to see that reason.

When description of place doesn't interrupt flow of action

Sometimes, tossing in a description of the place where the action is occurring can interrupt the flow of the story you are meticulously crafting. When that happens, your reader may become momentarily confused or disoriented or may simply lose interest in your story — outcomes you do not want as an author.

Suppose your main character is plummeting down a mineshaft, mere seconds away from certain disaster. This is probably not a good time to describe what California in the year 1849 looked like. It is, however, a good time to describe the thoughts going through your character's head as the bottom of the shaft fast approaches.

Or suppose a giant squirrel is chasing your knight in shining armor through the woods, teeth bared and saliva dripping from its furry mouth. Stopping the action to describe the verdant soil, the softly swaying flowers, and the gentle pollen-filled breeze would certainly interrupt the story — distracting the reader and ruining the moment.

 How do you know whether your description of a place interrupts the flow of your story? A sure sign is if you feel like putting it in parentheses — or if you find yourself moving it around because you are not sure where it really should go. Our advice? When in doubt, leave it out.

When description of context adds something measurable

Sometimes, adding a description of place or context in a story isn't absolutely essential in and of itself, but it adds something measurable to the mood or power of the scene or to the main character. In cases such as this, you may very well want to include the description.

What do we mean by measurable? If it moves the plot forward by providing information that causes the character to move his feet. Or if the description creates the mood you want to set for the scene. Or if it adds flavor and spice that really set the tone for the scene.

Consider the example of a witch's house deep in an ancient, dark woods, with a huge, black, bubbling cauldron over a raging fire in the center of a decrepit, dusty, cobwebby kitchen. The tendrils of steam flowing from the cauldron add to the foreboding mood of the setting, and the character is moved forward and given power as she reaches for ingredients — an eye of newt here, a lock of a young child's hair there — to add to her evil soup.

When you must mention an exotic locale

We don't mean to sound America-centric or xenophobic, but the great preponderance of readers of books written in English do come from North America, Great Britain, Ireland, Australia, and New Zealand. It's important to consider your probable audience when dropping a reference to an exotic locale. If, for example, you're writing in English and you mention a place like Borneo or Tierra del Fuego, consider it exotic to most of your readership and let us in on what it's like there. For an example of a children's picture book that does a great job of describing a foreign country — in this case, Kenya — for an English-speaking audience, see *Ndito Runs* by Laurie Halse Anderson and Anita Van Der Merwe (Henry Holt & Company).

When beginning a novel and a specific place is mentioned

Chances are you've read a zillion books that start off with a lovely description of a place in the first paragraph or two and then plunge right into the action. There are a couple of good reasons for that. First, when your reader encounters your reference to a specific place, his curiosity will be piqued — he'll want to know more about it. Second, setting the scenery and context at the very beginning of a longer story quickly transports the reader out of the day-to-day reality of his current environment and into the fantasy world created by the book's author. Indeed, this is part of the magic of any well-written book — to transport readers to new places, to meet new people, to see new environments.

Consider the first words of L. Frank Baum's book *The Wonderful Wizard of Oz*:

> Dorothy lived in the midst of the great Kansas prairies, with Uncle Henry, who was a farmer, and Aunt Em, who was the farmer's wife. Their house was small, for the lumber to build it had to be carried by wagon many miles. There were four walls, a floor and a roof, which made one room; and this room contained a rusty looking cookstove, a cupboard for the dishes, a table, three or four chairs, and the beds. Uncle Henry and Aunt Em had a big bed in one corner, and Dorothy a little bed in another corner. There was no garret at all, and no cellar — except a small hole dug in the ground, called a cyclone cellar, where the family could go in case one of those great whirlwinds arose, mighty enough to crush any building in its path. It was reached by a trap door in the middle of the floor, from which a ladder led down into the small, dark hole.

Can you picture Dorothy's home in your mind? Did you forget where you are right now because you moved to a different place? Although it isn't always going to be the case that your book will *begin* with a description of the scenery or context (your book may, for example, focus on an action scene starring your main character), it's an approach that merits your serious consideration.

In a new scene where place is used to transition

Not every story stays in the same place for the duration of a children's book. In fact, more than a few stories start in one place and then move to one or more other places during the course of the action. When you end a chapter or scene in one place and start the next one in a new place, you need to tell readers where they've gone. If you don't, they'll feel lost and frustrated.

The following description from Lewis Carroll's *Alice's Adventures in Wonderland* ends a chapter and marks Alice's arrival at a new scene — at the March Hare's house (which happens to be the location of the Mad Tea-Party, which commences at the beginning of this new chapter):

> She had not gone much farther before she came in sight of the house of the March Hare: she thought it must be the right house, because the chimneys were shaped like ears and the roof was thatched with fur. It was so large a house that she did not like to go nearer till she had nibbled some more of the left-hand bit of mushroom, and raised herself to about two feet high: even then she walked up towards it rather timidly, saying to herself, "Suppose it should be raving mad after all! I almost wish I'd gone to see the Hatter instead!"

Be sure to describe new scenes as your characters encounter them — your readers will appreciate it.

Providing the Right Amount of Setting

Knowing how much to write to describe scenery or context is a skill that you develop as you become a more experienced writer. But in the meantime, here's a simple rule for how long or involved a description should be in a children's book without pictures: One sentence per new place is enough, except where to write more adds significantly to plot or character development.

When writing an early chapter book, a middle-grade novel, or YA, don't think that just because you have more space and higher word count, you should feel free to devote entire pages to scenery or place descriptions. Keep it short. Make your words work hard for you. More than a paragraph for the most important place/context in your novel should be considered long — perhaps too long in many cases.

Consider the description of the workhouse that opens Charles Dickens's classic story *Oliver Twist*. It manages to provide enough information in one sentence — albeit a *long* sentence — for the reader to develop a picture of the building in her mind, but not so much as to begin to distract from the overall flow of the story:

> Among other public buildings in a certain town, which for many reasons it will be prudent to refrain from mentioning, and to which I will assign no fictitious name, there is one anciently common to most towns, great or small: to wit, a workhouse; and in this workhouse was born; on a day and date which I need not trouble myself to repeat, inasmuch as it can be of no possible consequence to the reader, in this stage of the business at all events; the item of mortality whose name is prefixed to the head of this chapter.

Or consider this brief mention of the town of Cardiff Hill early in Mark Twain's *The Adventures of Tom Sawyer*. Is there reason to say any more about Cardiff Hill? (We think not!)

> Cardiff Hill, beyond the village and above it, was green with vegetation and it lay just far enough away to seem a Delectable Land, dreamy, reposeful, and inviting.

Engaging Your Readers' Senses

What constitutes a good sentence or description of scenery, of place, of context? One that evokes a strong image in the reader's mind. Getting someone to read words and see what you want her to see requires careful writing. One way to help you create a vision for your readers is to engage their senses. You engage their sight when they are reading your words, but to engage the mind's eye, you need to help them use their imagination. The best contextualizations about a place describe

- The way it tastes
- The way it feels on the skin or to the touch
- The way it sounds
- The way it smells
- The way it looks

Don't spend too much time on the way a place *looks*. We may need to be able to see it in our mind's eye, to imagine how it looks, but it's better to show us using words that develop a sensory experience focusing more on the other senses. That way, you won't get too caught up in *telling* (a no-no) versus *showing* (a yes-yes).

Most of these make sense, but how can a place taste? The following example uses the reader's sense of taste to evoke an image in her mind's eye:

> The house reminded her of a sour lemon on a hot day, both refreshing and surprising. Flanked by traditional white houses with blue trim, it was light yellow with screaming purple trim and an enormous orange front door.

This description uses the reader's sense of sound to convey the terror the main character feels:

> From somewhere deep within the school came screams of fright, groans of pain. Staring at the dark windows and boarded-up doors, Roxy could not move a muscle.

For real examples of how the senses can be engaged, check out C. S. Lewis's *The Lion, the Witch and the Wardrobe* (Harper Trophy) for the tastes of Turkish delight, the bitter coldness of Narnia, and the sounds of footsteps and carriages approaching. Also read Natalie Babbit's *Tuck Everlasting* (Farrar, Straus and Giroux) for the bristly, itchy grass; the heat of the noon-time sun; and the deep, damp mattress of leaves on the ground. Finally, read Frances Hodgson Burnett's *The Secret Garden* (HarperCollins) for the wailing of cholera victims and the sweet taste of wine.

The best writing gets the reader's senses fired up alongside the heart and mind. Whenever we experience an event, our senses record it right along with our hearts and our minds. As a result, most people have years and years of stored experiences trapped inside them that can be accessed by reawakening those sense memories. Engaging your senses, your emotions, and your fertile imagination brings you closer to a child's world.

Knowing When Not to Make a Scene

There are lots of reasons to include scene development or description of scenery. There are also reasons why you should not. Often writers will decide to include a context description that fails to add anything measurable or meaningful to the story. How do you tell whether something is meaningful or measurable? Ask yourself whether it has a purpose that you can articulate if called upon to do so. The following list reveals scenarios when setting the scene can do more harm to your story than good.

> ✔ **When you have scenes with no characters:** Does the sentence or paragraph you are including involve your main character or an important character? Does it provide a place in which you will see that character do something or experience something meaningful to the story? If you can't answer yes *and explain it to your reader,* then out it goes!

- ✔ **When the scenes don't advance the plot:** Does the piece you are including provide a setting that is intrinsic to action occurring in or around that place? Does it move the story forward by taking us somewhere involving conflict or drama? Is the place related to the main character's compelling desire or want? If you can't answer yes *and explain it to your reader,* then it's not worth adding.

- ✔ **When scenes tell rather than show:** It's fun and easy to write narrative description. And writing scenery often falls into that category. But it's really, really, really (did we mention really?) easy to end up *telling* and not *showing. Telling* involves readers in events occurring in the past as opposed to the present (even if the entire book is written in the past tense), removes immediacy from the story, slows down the pacing, and bores the reader in many cases. *Showing* is writing that moves the character's feet, propels the story forward, increases conflict or drama, and focuses on action. Does your text show rather than tell? If not, then rewrite it!

Exercising Your Nose with a Smellography

Setting the scene for readers can be scary to some new writers. It often requires research and if it's based on a real place, authenticity and detail are musts or readers familiar with the place will dismiss you as a writer outright. As we note in the earlier "Engaging Your Readers' Senses" section, in order to create a meaningful context, a foundation from which your character will start, go to, or end up in, you need to make readers feel, smell, taste, hear, *experience* the place you are developing. How do you do that? Engage their senses.

The sense of smell is one of the easiest senses to engage. It's also one of the most powerful senses. Have you ever found an old tub of delicious-smelling cocoa-butter sunscreen or a vial of flowery, fragrant perfume and been instantly transported back to that precise moment where you smelled it before — years or perhaps even decades ago? Smells often lead to memories and emotions that you can translate into great ideas and powerful writing.

To uncover memories you may have forgotten, give the following exercise a try. It's so easy that you won't even feel as if you're working on your context-giving skills.

1. **Set a timer for 15 minutes, think of the first smell you can remember, and start writing a simple *smellography* — an autobiographical record of your smell memories — filled with as many smell memories as you can think of until you reach the present day.**

Set aside enough time to really think back deep into your past. For example, here are some of the smell memories from the beginning of Lisa's smellography, starting with her very first memories and working toward the present day:

- My hands after playing with modeling clay

- Toe jam from tube socks

- My wet dog at the lake

- My grandparents' freshly mowed lawn

- Freshly ground coffee for the grown-ups and hot cinnamon rolls after dinner

2. **Choose one or more of the smell memories, and write a short story about it/them.**

You can turn each of your smell memories into an idea for a children's book if you do three things:

1. **Take the memory and recall the emotion behind it.**

2. **Take that emotion and attach it to a character.**

3. **Start writing from that character's point of view (more about point of view in Chapter 11).**

The exercise is working if it gets you writing. Don't worry right now about the shape the writing takes or how the story is unfolding or which particular words you are choosing. This is a free-flowing, stream-of-consciousness exercise. Just write.

Chapter 11

Finding Your Voice: Point of View and Tone

. . . .

In This Chapter

▶ Taking a look at point of view

▶ Playing with words

▶ Having fun and making it funny

▶ Digging into voice, style, and tone

. . . .

*E*very story is told from some point of view, or POV for short, and that POV indicates who's telling the story and what limitations he or she has to contend with. When you write, you must do so from a consistent point of view. In this chapter, we help you choose a POV and figure out how to keep it consistent.

Choosing a point of view is just one of the decisions a writer has to make when developing a writing style best suited to the tale at hand. Along the way, you're also choosing which words you use to convey your own style and the tone of the story. Words, the basic building blocks of a story, help to draw pictures in the reader's mind, bringing the reader into your make-believe world. Words give a character a voice, develop a point of view, and elaborate on a plot.

But words serve other purposes besides providing a basic foundation; they also give life to your writing. By using words in creative and innovative ways, writers can evoke all kinds of emotions in readers, from wistful nostalgia to wild hilarity to bite-your-fingernails suspense.

In this chapter, we also explore the nuances of how to use words to make your prose come alive, to evoke strong emotions in your readers, and to give your writing a tone of its own.

Building a Solid Point of View

Point of view (POV) is the perspective from which a book is narrated. It is the position or vantage point from which the story is presented to the reader. Point of view is used to show readers in *whose mind* and through *whose eyes* they are seeing the world of the story. In the following sections, you find out what the different types of POVs are, how to pick the right POV for your story, and how to choose the tense that best supports your chosen POV.

Reviewing POV options

The primary POV decision you have to make before you can write even one sentence is *person*. Third-person stories are told by a narrator who isn't part of the story, whereas first- (and usually second-) person stories are told by a narrator who's also a character.

✔ **First person:** First person entails the author outright telling a story, perhaps his own, by being the main character of the story, narrating the book using the pronoun *I*. Your character (usually the protagonist) is telling the story through his own eyes. First-person POV means the teller of the story cannot be *omniscient* (all-knowing), because regular people cannot be omniscient; as such, the teller of the story can report only what he or she can realistically know. For example, she can't know someone else's private thoughts or what will happen in the future. Here's an example:

> I could not believe my eyes. There she was. Standing there in the outfit that we both admired yesterday at the mall. She hadn't had the money to buy it then, so how had she come to be wearing it now? That was when I remembered the strange bulk in her shopping bag after we had left the department store. "My jacket," she had said, noticing my look.

> "Hi," she now said, all cheerful and bright. "Like it?" She shimmied a little and laid a big smile on me, oblivious.

> It was clear to me now. In this new school, I was clueless about the rules of right and wrong. I'd learn soon enough.

First-person POV is tough for a new writer to tackle because it requires truly establishing a unique voice and not getting caught up in your personal reality. Although it's fun to experiment with various voices, most writers try to get plenty of experience writing in the third person before moving to first.

✔ **Second person:** This perspective allows the writer to address the reader directly, using the pronoun *you.* Second-person POV is used when the writer wants to distance himself from his own involvement in the story and uses the word *you* in place of I.

Second-person POV is rare in published novels. In fact, Jay McInerney's *Bright Lights, Big City* (Vintage) and *The Missing Girl* by Norma Fox Mazer (HarperTeen) are two of the few successful examples we can think of. Stories told in second person require an extremely skillful facility with voice and language; it's a hard sell if it isn't nearly perfect. You may feel your story warrants it, but we suggest waiting until you've had a lot of practice writing before you tackle this particular beast.

✔ **Third person:** Third-person POV is the author telling the story using the pronouns *he, she,* or *they.* Three types of third-person POV exist:

- **Third-person limited POV:** In this type, the author gets to read the thoughts of only one main character.

- **Third-person multiple POV:** Although this type allows you to tell the story through multiple characters' viewpoints, most of the main action viewpoint is still reserved for the main character. E. L. Konigsburg's *The View from Saturday* (Aladdin) is told in third-person multiple POV, with quite a few main characters (Noah, Nadia, Ethan, and Julian) all contributing to the telling of the story.

- **Third-person omniscient POV:** This type is writing told from the viewpoint of a narrator who knows all and sees all — kind of like God. As a totally omniscient author, you are God. You can go into the mind of any character; report on *anything* that's happening *anywhere* with *anyone* in the story at *any time* (even the future!); interpret any character's actions or thoughts; reflect, judge, and reveal truths.

The main difference between the three types of third person is the amount of *omniscience,* or all-knowingness, the author chooses. For the record, most children's books use the third-person limited POV; it's also the easiest to master.

Picking your POV

So how do you know which POV to pick for your story? There are so many variations of the nuances that go into every story that it would be impossible for us to tell you in which situation you should choose which POV. What goes into the choice is often personal. But here are some general situations in which the choice becomes more transparent.

✔ **If you're an in-your-face type of writer and you know your main character as well as you know yourself, then the first-person POV may be for you.** Just know that its limitations are the same facing us real-life characters: When writing about the other characters besides the *I* character, you can only reveal their motives, thoughts, and feelings through dialogue. You get to play God, but only with half a deck of cards.

When writing in the first person, your main character has to be involved in the story from beginning to end and everything in between — but cannot read other people's minds or foretell the future. As well, do not fall prey to writing long, descriptive passages in which your protagonist is mainly an observer (that's not only boring for the reader, but it's also probably engaging in more *telling* than *showing*). If you do, you may find that writing in the third person might actually work better for you because it allows you to narrate from more than one character.

✔ **If you're an experimental person who likes to put himself to the test when trying new things and you think you want to make yourself, the writer/narrator, an actor in the drama, the second-person POV may be the ticket for you.**

In the days when oral storytelling was all the rage (before books were common household possessions), the storyteller would often interrupt his tale and directly address the listener, asking questions or making personal commentary and then going back to his tale. Talking directly to the reader is also known as *editorializing* or *authorial intrusion*. Unless you're writing an instructional book, talking directly to the reader isn't something we recommend. It's disruptive to the narrative, not to mention annoying to the reader who gets thrown off track and jolted back to plain old reality.

✔ **If you like to take the path well traveled, try writing in a third-person POV — also known as the most common way of telling a story.** You need to determine how much omniscience you need with how many characters in order to choose between third-person limited, third-person multiple, and third-person omniscient, but we can help you with that.

- If your story is about one main character, such as in Ian Falconer's *Olivia* and *Olivia Saves the Circus* (Atheneum/Anne Schwartz Books), choose third-person limited, because you need to get into the head of only one character.

- If your story involves two or more main characters, all of whom have a different take on the story and contribute equally to the telling of that story, third-person multiple POV will probably work best for you.

- If you're writing an epic story in which you cover many generations or many characters over an expanded period of time, and you feel that you may need to be able to read every character's mind (telling the reader everything about everyone), third-person omniscient is the way to go.

The only real way to figure out which POV you feel comfortable writing in is to try out all the POVs. The one that best suits you, your writing style, and your story becomes apparent as you write. For example, if you try writing in one POV and find yourself straining to write or sounding completely off, chances are you're not comfortable writing in that viewpoint.

If you aren't sure which character's viewpoint should rule, ask yourself these questions:

- ✔ Can this character be present at all the main events?
- ✔ Can this character be actively involved and not just an observer?
- ✔ Does this character have a stake in the outcome of the story?

If you can answer yes to all of these questions, your character is worthy of having the first-person POV in your story.

After you choose a viewpoint, you have to stick to it. When writing short books, such as board books or picture books, it's especially important to stay with one POV. Changing the POV in books this short is generally a big fat no-no.

If you're writing a longer book with chapters, you may choose to write one chapter from one character's POV and the next from another's POV, like Natalie Babbitt does in *Tuck Everlasting* (Farrar, Straus & Giroux Books for Young Readers). However you choose to organize the narrative, don't change POV within a scene or chapter. And be consistent; if you choose to alternate POV in every other chapter, stick to the rhythm and don't deviate.

Matching tense with POV

Part of choosing a POV includes choosing a tense to write in. When writing a kids' book, you have two main tenses to choose from:

- ✔ **Present tense:** I write, you write, he writes, they write, we write
- ✔ **Past tense:** I wrote, you wrote, he wrote, they wrote, we wrote

Present tense is the tense of choice for stories told from a first-person POV due to its immediacy, its intimacy, and its now-ness. Putting a first-person POV in the past tense simply is not emphasizing the *now*. Second-person POVs also benefit from the present tense, which allows you to more directly address your reader as you take him through your story.

Past tense works best if you plan to tell your story using any of the third-person POVs. In fact, most classic children's stories are told in the past tense, using a narrator whose job it is to describe what transpired.

Story*telling* versus story*showing*

We think story*telling* should be called story*showing*. Why? Because story*telling* is a throwback to the oral tradition of passing on tales face to face around a campfire or through the grapevine. Today's stories have to be active, focusing on what happens where with the main characters, *showing* all the aspects of the story in the here and now (even if it takes place in the past or future tense) through action and dialogue and to a much lesser extent, narrative description. Story*telling* implies a relaying of information or events that happened long ago and often includes authorial intrusion (as in *The Canterbury Tales,* written in the late 14th century, in which the narrator often jumps in to comment on and interrupt the story she is relating); it's simply not done anymore.

Having Fun with Words through Wordplay, Rhyming, and Rhythm

For many writers of children's books, having fun with words is the best part of the writing process. Getting the opportunity to play with words, create word pictures in your readers' minds, and build rhymes out of thin air can be more fun than a barrel of monkeys. In the sections that follow, we take a closer look at the many different ways you can play with words, including rhyming and rhythm.

Engaging in wordplay

Words are fun. And what better way to have fun with words than to write a children's book? You have far more freedom to play around with words when writing children's books than you do when writing other kinds of books. The sky is truly the limit.

Use some of these common methods to have fun with words:

- ✔ **Alliteration:** The initial consonant sounds of words two or more times in a line or sentence creates a rhythmic component to the writing. For example, "She stewed in her soft and simple shoes."

  Assonance is similar to alliteration, but uses vowel sounds instead of consonant sounds.

  New writers often fall into the trap of using alliteration or assonance in naming characters, which is amateurish and displays a lack of skill in properly developing a character. It also screams: "I am new at this and think it's so cute!" For example, Billy Bully. If Billy is a bully, you should be showing him bullying and not just giving him a label to make your reader "get" that he is a bully. In other words, alliterative names are annoying as all get-out. Just say no.

✔ **Parallelism:** Repeating similar thoughts in two different phrasings. There are variations on the theme:

- **Antithetical:** When the second phrasing is the exact opposite of the first: "The good boy did his homework and cleaned his room; the bad boy threw his homework in the trash and dumped his dinner on the floor."

- **Synonymous:** When the second phrasing is almost identical to the first. "The warm sun warmed the faces of the children at play; the children's faces glowed with the first rays of the sun."

Be careful not to use parallelism to repeat yourself or insert redundancies into your writing. For example, "The good boy did his homework on time, completing all his tasks in a timely manner." This is unnecessary repetition as both sides of the comma relay the exact same information. That is not fun; that is verbosity that needs to get cut. Choose one and lose one.

✔ **Refrain:** A line or group of lines are repeated throughout a story. Consider the following lines, repeated throughout Dr. Seuss's *Green Eggs and Ham:* "I do not like green eggs and ham. I do not like them, Sam-I-am."

✔ **Polyptoton:** The same word is repeated in different forms. "The ogre was strong, and he revealed his full strength as he toppled tree after tree in the forest, headstrong to the very end."

✔ **Metaphor:** Comparing two unlike things using any form of the verb *to be.* "The color blue is a cold, winter's day — snow forming drifts on the sides of the road and icicles hanging from the roof of the house."

✔ **Simile:** Comparing two unlike things using *like* or *as.* "His anger was like a summer's storm — arriving quickly and without warning, then soon passing without a trace."

✔ **Anthropomorphism:** Human motivations, characteristics, or behavior appear in inanimate objects, animals, or natural phenomena. For example, Thomas the Tank Engine (from *The Railway Series* by Rev. W. Awdry) is an anthropomorphized train with a human face, feelings, and emotions. He's always getting into all sorts of trouble.

✔ **Personification:** Human qualities appear in an animal or object. "Flowers danced in the field."

Some children's book writers make up words. Dr. Seuss (whose real name was Theodor Geisel) was a master at this; his made-up words were understood because of what was happening in the story. Lewis Carroll, author of *Alice's Adventures in Wonderland* and other stories and poems, ranks up there with the very best, making up words that could be evocative because they were told in a particular context, allowing the reader to envision what they meant.

We used to advocate making up words, but we've found 90 percent of the time this tactic does not work for beginning writers. Usually, made-up words are a sign of laziness (unwillingness to find the right *real* word or combination of words) or an attempt to insert humor that ends up feeling forced (as in your idea of a funny, made-up word does not necessarily jibe with a child's). So steer clear of wordplay that involves making up words. Your readers will be glad you did.

Taking different approaches to rhyming

Rhyming is an essential tool in many children's books, especially those written for younger readers. In general terms, words *rhyme* when the last stressed vowel and the sounds that follow it are the same — for example, *blue* and *zoo,* or *horse* and *Norse.* The effect of rhyming is to introduce a repetition of sound patterns that makes your words more interesting to listen to or read — and easier to remember. Rhyming, when done well, also gives words a rhythm that can approximate music when read aloud. You can rhyme with sounds or create rhyming patterns, as you discover in the next sections.

Rhyming sounds

When playing with rhymes, sounds are the usual place to start. Take a look at these different rhyming schemes based on sound:

- ✔ **Perfect rhyme:** When the vowel and final consonant match exactly, as in *mute* and *pursuit.*

- ✔ **Partial rhyme:** When a rhyme is close, but not perfect, as in *fought* and *fault.* Also known as *near rhyme* or *off rhyme.*

- ✔ **Half rhyme:** When the final consonants match exactly, but not the vowels, as in *rats* and *hits.*

- ✔ **Eye rhyme:** When words rhyme in sight, but not in sound, as in *cough* and *tough.*

- ✔ **Masculine rhyme:** A one-syllable rhyme, such as *pop* and *stop* or *soak* and *poke.*

- ✔ **Feminine rhyme:** A rhyme of two or more syllables, as in *jeepers* and *creepers* or *torrid* and *horrid.*

Young, beginning readers (not those who are still solely read *to*) may not be sophisticated enough as readers to "get" or even properly sound out partial, half, or eye rhymes. Eye rhymes in particular aren't a good idea in children's books because this particular rhyming technique may tend to confuse young readers who are still working out the right and wrong ways to spell and pronounce words.

Rhyming patterns

When it comes to rhyming, sound is important, but so are the patterns of the rhymes you use. Two of the most common rhyming patterns are

- ✔ **End rhyme:** When words at the end of successive lines or sentences rhyme, such as

   "The more she ate the more she grew,

   until she reached five foot two."

- ✔ **Internal rhyme:** When words rhyme within a line or sentence, such as "The old man on the moon sang his weary tune."

Keeping your story moving with rhythm

Just as music depends on *rhythm* — a recurring pattern of notes or beats — to propel it forward, so too can the written word depend on rhythm. This rhythm in the written word is often called *meter.* When you read your story aloud and something doesn't sound quite right, chances are your meter is off; that is, it is not consistent. To check meter, you actually have to count the syllables and keep the same rising and falling tone and the same accented words in the same place for each line.

As a writer, you can select the rhythm for your story that sounds best to you, mixing different ones to provide variety and the occasional surprise or maintaining the same rhythm throughout. Different approaches to rhythm and meter affect how your story is received by your readers. The choice is yours.

The most basic unit of rhythm is the syllable. A *foot* (plural is *feet*) is a unit of stressed and unstressed syllables. You can build a rhythm throughout your work by repeating any of the five most common feet:

- ✔ **Iamb:** One unstressed syllable, then one stressed syllable (da DUM), as in, "I *do* not *like* greens *eggs* and *ham.*"
- ✔ **Trochee:** One stressed syllable, then one unstressed syllable (DA dum), as in, "*Pe*ter, *Pe*ter *pump*kin *eat*er."
- ✔ **Anapest:** Two unstressed syllables, then one stressed syllable (da da DUM), as in, "'Twas the *night* before *Christ*mas and *all* through the *house.*"
- ✔ **Dactyl:** One stressed syllable, then two unstressed syllables (DA da dum), as in, "*Hick*ory, *dick*ory, *dock.*"
- ✔ **Spondee:** Two stressed syllables (DA DUM), as in, "One fish, two fish, red fish, blue fish."

To figure out whether your rhymes work, find someone who rhymes well (like a poetry teacher or a published writer of rhyming poetry or even a songwriter) and have her look over your work. If you don't have access to these talented individuals, then try the method we like to call "pounding on the table." Identify your rhythm, and pound it out to your words to make sure your meter is even and consistent. Better yet, have someone who isn't familiar with your rhyme read it out loud and record him speaking. Listen to your story being read, and notice where the reader stumbles over the meter. Also, don't force the meter by assuming the reader will stress a normally non-stressed syllable to make it fit into the meter of the surrounding lines. If you can't keep up the same rhythm throughout the manuscript, then the meter is off, and you need to fix it.

Thou art not allowed to torture, mangle, or otherwise beat up proper English in an attempt to make your rhyme work. Your lines need to be comprehensible as regular, unrhymed prose *before* you attempt to rhyme them. If you are in doubt: Just say them aloud. If you've never heard anyone in this century speak like that, chances are your English is all wrong. Precisely 99 percent of editors will agree that nothing's worse than writing that sacrifices understandable English simply to force a rhyme to work. Just because Seuss did it well does not mean you can. And on that note, do not use Seussian meter. Seuss did it over and over and his books continue to sell. Seussian meter is Seuss's. Leave it be. Make up your own. Being a derivative writer is like crying out, "I am not imaginative enough to come up with my own meter so I'm just going to copycat." Believe us, Dr. Seuss is not flattered from the great beyond.

A final caution about writing in rhyme: The rhyme must be incidental to the story. The text still needs well-developed characters, a plot with a beginning, middle, and end, no unnecessary words, good pacing, and so on. The rhyme should be the last consideration, simply adding another level of whimsy to the book, which is not your first priority as a writer. In other words, don't manipulate the characters and events of the story or add unnecessary words, just because they make the rhyme flow.

Using Humor to Your Advantage

Perhaps the quickest way to a child's heart is through humor. Children love to laugh, and after you get them laughing, you've truly captured their hearts (and their minds, for that matter). In the following sections, we take a close look at what kinds of things kids find humorous and share how to incorporate outrageous (and even gross) ideas into your writing.

Figuring out what kids consider funny

Before you can start writing funny children's books, you need to understand the kinds of things that kids tend to consider funny. And although there may seem to be no rhyme or reason for exactly what children find humorous, research shows that children go through different stages of humor development.

According to humor researcher (no, we didn't make that up) Paul E. McGhee, Ph.D., you can expect the following developmental changes in preschool children's humor:

- **Stage 0 (Age 0 to 6 months):** Laughs, no humor. During the first six months of life, children laugh not because they find something funny, but because something physically arouses them — like bouncing the little tykes on your knee or tickling them. To tickle this age group's fancy, write your story in a way that requires the actual reader (parent, sibling, or care provider) to do something funny, like read in a funny voice or make unexpected physical movements or gestures. The content doesn't matter — how it's presented does.

- **Stage 1 (Age 6 to 12 months or so):** Laughs with or at parent or caregiver. During this period, children begin to find humor in the behavior of a parent or other significant people in their lives. Making silly faces or odd sounds can get a laugh from kids in this age bracket, as will a funny game of peek-a-boo. Write these kinds of actions into your story so that the parent or caregiver can act them out.

- **Stage 2 (Age 12 months or so up to 5 years):** Pretends that a particular object is something it's not. If you've ever seen a child sit in a big, cardboard box, making noises like a gasoline engine (pretending the box is a race car) or inviting her favorite dolls to an elaborate tea party (pretending they are real, live people), or turning a folded-up piece of paper into a jet airplane (pretending it is coming in for a landing), then you've witnessed the power of pretend. Use the power of pretend in your stories to tap into this source of humor.

- **Stage 3a (2 to 3 or 4 years):** Plays with the names of common objects or actions. At this age, as language skills improve, kids begin to find humor in misnaming common objects. You can plumb this source of humor by calling a shoe a boat, turning a dog into a cat, a father into a mother, and so forth.

- **Stage 3b (2 to 3 or 4 years):** Misnames with opposites. This form of misnaming — particularly attractive to many children — involves stating the exact opposite of a particular word. Cold is hot, up is down, over is under, fast is slow, wet is dry. Every adjective has an opposite — consider the possibilities!

✔ **Stage 4a (3 to 5 years):** Plays with the sounds of words. At about three years of age, children begin to play not just with word meanings, but with their sounds. A common word such as *turkey* springs forth any number of variations including *lurky, wurky, perky,* and so on. Children alter words for the humor of doing so and begin to create their own nonsense words to be funny. Use word sounds to create humor in your story.

✔ **Stage 4b (3 to 5 years):** Uses nonsense word combinations. Most three-year-olds also begin to put real words together in combinations that make no sense. Examples of these kinds of humorous combinations include "I want some monkey juice" or "Give me that mushroom spoon." What nonsense word combinations can you insert into your story?

✔ **Stage 4c (3 to 5 years):** Distorts features. As children increase their command over the real names of objects, people, or animals, they find humor in distorting some aspect of them. They do this by adding features that don't belong (putting a fish's head on a dog's body), by removing features that do belong (a house with no doors), by changing the shape, size, location, color, and length of familiar things (a person with a grapefruit head), and by ascribing impossible behavior to people or animals (a cat that talks).

✔ **Pre-riddle stage (5 to 7 years or so):** Discovers riddles and jokes. Sometime during this period, most kids discover the joy of jokes and riddles, and the verbal humor shared by older children around them. The ubiquitous knock-knock joke is an example of this kind of humor. ("Knock knock." "Who's there?" "Orange." "Orange who?" "Orange you glad I didn't say 'knock knock' again?")

If, however, you want to aim your writing more toward older kids, it helps to understand their unique sense of humor. Children in early elementary grades love broad physical humor, such as pie in the face, pants falling down to expose underwear, slipping on a banana peel, and so on. William Kotzwinkle and Glenn Murray's *Walter the Farting Dog* (North Atlantic Books) is the perfect example of poo-poo humor in a picture book. It's especially funny if a "serious" character (such as a parent or teacher) unwittingly does these things. Witness the popularity of the *Captain Underpants* chapter books for ages 7 to 10 by Dav Pilkey (Blue Sky Press/Scholastic). From about second grade on, kids begin to appreciate verbal humor (witty banter, sarcasm, irony, and so on in dialogue) and have the patience to allow a joke to be set up over several scenes.

As you get more experienced incorporating humor in your writing, you can try branching out beyond specific humor stages. Tons of books achieve many levels of humor, thus appealing to many different ages — even adults enjoy reading them again and again (imagine that!). Dr. Seuss books fall into this category, as does Sandra Boynton's Little Pookie series (Robin Corey Books/Random House). In particular, *What's Wrong, Little Pookie* so brilliantly and unexpectedly captures a child's sensibility that it's hilarious, destined to become an evergreen.

Interview with Leslie McGuire, children's book author

Leslie McGuire, author of hundreds of children's books ranging from board books to picture books, from easy-to-reads to middle-grade novels, is a talented writer with a very quirky outlook on life that often finds its way into her prose.

WCBFD: What role does humor play in your books?

LM: I don't always use humor, but when I do, it's usually a way to make children think. After all, laughter is really a shock reaction. Something unexpected gets said or done, and it's enough to get your diaphragm in your chest fibrillating — and that's what a laugh is — physically at least. That's what makes a good joke. The punch line is quite unexpected.

WCBFD: How do you use words to engage children in your books?

LM: Again, I use the unexpected, especially in descriptions of things. In one book — which wasn't funny—I described a baby owl's view of a Luna moth as "A delicious, pale green moth." That makes children think about the eating habits of owls, and what may seem yucky to you might actually be gourmet-style wonderful to an owl. You could always describe a fancy sweater that has a feather boa trim around the neck and sleeves as "A bicycle accident with an ostrich." Language is so very powerful, it's a true shame that most writers for children (and everyone else, I might add) tend to rely on clichés or just boring exchanges. That's dreadful, especially when you consider that in a children's book most of the descriptions are in the picture, so unless you have something interesting to say, you really should avoid saying anything at all.

WCBFD: How do you make sure your rhyming works, such as meter-wise, rhyming-wise, and in terms of making sense? What's the trick?

LM: Although this isn't as pompous as it sounds, I like to fall back on Gustave Flaubert at times like those. It took him seven years to write *Madame Bovary* because he yelled every sentence out loud until the music of it was correct. I don't yell it, but I say each sentence or sing it rhythmically until it has the correct meter. Not all that easy, I must say. Even worse, considering what I write, Flaubert would probably be horrified.

WCBFD: What are your tried-and-true ways for making your books fun to read?

LM: The trick is just to avoid overblown words — and when you must use one, define it in the very next sentence. Not only does that upgrade their vocabulary, it's a comprehension thing. Part of using humor is injecting an engaging way to make children think about what they just heard or read, and that's an opening for reading comprehension that's actually fun.

WCBFD: How do you vary your writing style for different age levels of readers?

LM: When writing for each age group, you have to see the world through their eyes, not through your own. Become a 5-year-old. Become an 11-year-old. If that's too hard, then pick a child of the age you're supposed to be writing for, one that you know, and tell that child the story as if that child were sitting right there with you.

WCBFD: What pitfalls should would-be authors watch out for?

LM: Low self-esteem. That's the worst. Don't let it get to you. If you love what you wrote, then someone else will, too.

Turning to the outrageous and the gross

Would it surprise you to learn that kids love ideas and concepts that are either outrageous, gross, or both at the same time? Well, it's true. A number of books — including *Oh, Yuck: The Encyclopedia of Everything Nasty* by Joy Masoff (Workman) and *Grossology* by Sylvia Branzei and Jack Keely (Price Stern Sloan) — have tackled a wide variety of formerly taboo topics, much to the delight of young readers everywhere. Some of these topics include

- Barf, burps, boogers, poop, and farts
- Internal animal parts: eyeballs, hearts, and brains
- Acne or other itchy red spots
- Leeches and worms

These topics tap deeply into the spirit of young people for the following reasons:

- Kids haven't yet been fully conditioned to pretend that these everyday things and events don't exist.
- These topics get a rise out of adults whenever they're mentioned.
- They're just plain fun to read about.

If your story merits their inclusion, then by all means don't hesitate.

Adults continue to debate about whether using gross and outrageous topics and words is bad form or whether they should be acknowledged and celebrated. The message from kids, however, remains loud and clear: Bring it on!

The Mojo of Good Writing: Voice, Style, and Tone

After you figure out how to set your scenes (see Chapter 10), write scintillating dialogue (see Chapter 9), and inject so much humor that even *you* can't stop laughing (see the earlier "Using Humor to Your Advantage" section), you still need to be aware of a few more aspects of good writing. And these are the ones that, unfortunately for writers everywhere, nearly defy instruction.

For example, when you read a particular author and are drawn in by everything you're reading, so much so that you savor every last page and hate for the book to end, then you have fallen for the writer's *mojo* (magic). Instantly addicted, you search frantically for other books by the same author. You even order her books in advance so that you can get them the second they're released. That is falling prey to mojo. And as you know in your every cell, every nerve ending, mojo is pretty heady stuff.

So where can you get some? Well, we don't know any dealers, and wouldn't pass them on if we did, so you're just going to have to develop your own mojo as a writer, just as your favorite writers have, and they do it with three things, which they keep consistent throughout a story:

- ✔ **Voice:** The communicative and cumulative effect created by the author's way of writing. The best books are always written with a voice that's strong enough to make the protagonist — and the book as a whole — memorable.

- ✔ **Style:** The panache with which the writer manipulates the conventions of modern language. In other words, style is the way the author adds his own particular twist to *diction* (word choice), dialogue, sentence structure, phrasing, and other aspects of the language. Like trends in fashion, style can be sparing and minimalist, outrageous and flowery, terse and evocative, or crisp and formal.

- ✔ **Tone:** The attitude the story conveys toward its subject matter. For example, a story may convey an attitude of humor or sarcasm toward its characters and events, signaling to the reader that the material is to be taken with a grain of salt. Then again, it may convey an attitude of sincerity and earnestness through subtle content and language manipulation, thereby telling the reader to take the story seriously.

Capturing your mojo and suffusing your words with your particular tone, style, and voice takes a lot of practice. Beginning writers have so many aspects of writing to ingest and master that developing these other qualities in their writing doesn't always come easily. As you write more and more, becoming increasingly comfortable with your abilities and skills, you will most likely find that your mojo starts sneaking into your writing without you knowing it. As time goes on, you may even find that others begin to recognize your style before you do.

Regardless of what you experience, promise yourself to never try to copy someone else's style or self-consciously force a voice on your writing — that would be cheating the world of the unique voice buried deep within you, just waiting to come out.

The next sections explore the elements of voice, style, and tone in more detail so that you can begin to create your own.

Finding your story's voice

To determine your voice, start by identifying the voice of your favorite authors. While you're reading, ask yourself this question: What kind of person does the narrator sound like? Search the narrative, and pay attention to the dialogue for the answer.

Voice can be expressed strongly in dialogue, when the way the characters speak and express themselves is so unique as to conjure up portraits of what the characters would look like if they suddenly appeared in the room. We give you tips for creating stellar dialogue in Chapter 9.

Although we can't excerpt huge passages from other books to demonstrate what a strong voice is, anything you read in the Olivia series by Ian Falconer (Atheneum Books for Young Readers) or the Llama Llama books by Anna Dewdney (Viking Juvenile), both picture book series, are great examples. So too for the early chapter book series of Ivy and Bean books by Annie Barrows and Sophie Blackall (Chronicle Books) or the middle-grade Diary of a Wimpy Kid series by Jeff Kinney (Amulet Books). In young adult (YA), the Hunger Games series by Suzanne Collins (Scholastic Press) illustrates voice in a memorable way. And another particularly fine example of a strong and recognizable voice in a recent YA dystopian novel is Mike Mullins' *Ashfall* (Tanglewood Books).

Some older titles you may recognize that offer up a powerful writerly voice include books by S. E. Hinton — *Rumble Fish* (Laurel Leaf), *The Outsiders* (Puffin Books), *That Was Then, This Is Now* (Penguin Books for Young Readers) — and E. L. Konigsburg — *Silent to the Bone* and *The View from Saturday* (both Atheneum).

In the aforementioned books, the author's voice calls to you from the first page, drawing you into the main character, into the setting, and into the drama. The only way to develop a unique voice and improve upon it over time is to write from your heart, to develop an attitude and a worldview that permeates your writing.

Voice embodies the writer's quirks, her good ear for subtle differences in dialect and accent, her ability to observe a person and steal that person's unique mannerisms, the way she expresses her sense of humor — in other words, her personality and the way she interjects it into the narrative. Voice can be serious and calm, harsh and judgmental, incredibly funny and wry — you name it.

For additional help finding your voice, see the "Helping Your Voice Emerge by Playing Pretend" section later in this chapter.

Writing with style

Somewhat indefinable, style involves the unique way talented writers put together their words. You need to read writers with style to really get how they achieve it. One stylist extraordinaire is Francesca Lia Block, the writer who burst upon the YA scene with her Weetzie Bat books (HarperTrophy). Read any of her books and you will immediately feel as if this airy personage, half real, half fairy, has invaded your consciousness and drawn you into a world that you recognize but that has somehow become expanded to include magical possibilities. Now, that's style!

The cool thing about style, just like with clothing, is that you get to choose it and present it however you want in your writing. All this freedom sounds great, right? Well, you have to choose a style you can stick with and feel comfortable with before you can pull it off successfully in each manuscript. Sure, blending plaids and polka dots makes a statement that others may not soon forget, but can you wear it consistently for six months or a year? Will you still believe in the statement you were trying to make a year from now? That's what you have to ask yourself before you choose your voice and attempt to make it real in your writing.

Have you found your style yet? If not, then experiment and have fun!

Taking the right tone

Think of how you use tone of voice to convey your real meaning when speaking with a friend. Tone can change the meaning of the declaration "That was so moving I nearly cried" in many different ways. Depending on the way you say something, the inflection you place on certain words and the vocal range you use, not to mention your body language or facial expressions, that sentence can be taken seriously, sarcastically, hysterically — it all depends on tone. The same goes for writing. How you present your words changes your tone.

The tone of Ian Falconer's Olivia picture books is very matter of fact: Olivia is a crazy little pig, but make no bones about it, she is who she is and she ain't ashamed of it. The tone of Barney Saltzberg's picture book *The Problem with Pumpkins* (Gulliver Books/Harcourt) is juvenile, getting right at the level of its preschool participants and helping them deal with their problem in a straightforward manner. The tone of Robert Munsch's *Love You Forever* (Firefly Books) is tooth-achingly sentimental from start to finish — which is the secret to its bestselling success.

There are many tones you can take with your words and toward your characters, but the right ones will seal the meaning of your story and make your writing memorable. And, for any writer, there's not much better than making a lasting impression on your reader. Experiment! Enjoy your writing!

You Know You Need a Voice Makeover When . . .

If your story is suffering from blandness, if one character blends into the next, or if your protagonist seems like every other character in your story, chances are you need a voice makeover. The following sections reveal some other clues as to when your voice needs work.

. . . you have more than one POV in a scene

A changing, inconsistent POV is confusing to the reader. In one sentence we are in one person's head. and in the next sentence we are in another's. How do readers know you've changed POV? They figure it out because something is off. Even if you indicate you've made the POV change with a dialogue tag — such as "thought Harry" — right after you've gotten into Dana's head, your reader's still going to pause. That nanosecond pause is jarring and can make your reader fall out of his suspension of disbelief. And then you may lose them for good.

It's best to not change the POV in a scene, or in the same chapter if you're writing a chapter book for any reading level. But if you *must* change POV, use a new chapter or a clearly delineated scene to get the job done.

. . . you experience the anxiety of influence

The *anxiety of influence* is when a writer worries that in immersing herself in someone else's writing, she will begin to write in a way that sounds just like the other writer. You can succumb to it easily if you're not careful.

So if you choose to read ten Dr. Seuss books in order to get in the mood for rhyming, or the entire Hunger Games series to spark your imagination as you write your YA novel, be careful that what you write immediately afterward does not mimic the other writer's style.

Developing your own voice is the best way to avoid the anxiety of influence. Refer to the earlier "Finding your story's voice" section for help.

. . . you find your omniscient narrator battling one (or more) star

If you choose to write from the POV of the omniscient narrator and find that one or more of your main characters seems to keep butting in and taking over the story with his or her voice, pay attention. Perhaps this character (or characters) is strong enough to carry the story in his voice. Try putting your story in the first-person POV with that character doing the narrating.

If one or more of your characters keep jumping up and down to get your attention, give it to him. He may just turn out to be the star of your story.

. . . your story sounds monotonal

If your story sounds like the droning of a finely tuned engine, no sputtering or stuttering, you're in trouble. This problem occurs most often when every single one of your sentences is about the same length, has the same rhythm, carries the same structure (for example, subject + verb + object), or repeats the same words in too close proximity (such as in the same or a nearby sentence).

Fix a monotonal voice by varying sentence structure and length, word usage, rhythm, and word choice.

Helping Your Voice Emerge by Playing Pretend

Ever wonder what it's like for a child to experience something for the first time? When the boundary between fantasy and reality is transparent — as it is for most young children — the possibility of magic occurring as one walks down a street is high. This is what is so amazing about being a child — and what most adults seem to forget. You don't need to spend any time explaining in a picture book why something magical has happened, because it's not so far-fetched for a child to imagine. As a matter of fact, much of what is explainable in the "real" world may appear to be magical to a child. Getting into this mindset is important for you as a writer of children's fiction.

In the following sections, we give you a few different writing exercises. These are designed to help you find your voice and fire up your imagination by getting you into the place where children spend most of their free time: their minds.

Pretending to be someone else

Pretend that you're someone you know intimately, like your significant other or best friend. Write for 15 minutes in that person's voice. Don't judge, just write.

What is your subject's morning routine? Coffee? What kind — homegrown, Starbucks, or McDonald's? Newspaper? Which one — *New York Times* or online? Does your subject go to work, or does he have a secret rendezvous scheduled in a local shopping mall? How does he get there? Carpool? Bus? Train? Who does he meet when he gets there? What do they do together? Let your mind wander freely.

This exercise helps you get a handle on how writing in your book character's POV feels.

Pretending you swallowed a magic potion that makes you only three feet tall

Remember when Alice in *Alice's Adventures in Wonderland* by Lewis Carroll finds the bottle with the words DRINK ME on it and she does, suddenly finding herself only ten inches tall? Well, this exercise requires you to get down to about four times that height, but we don't have any more potion left to give you. You have to exercise your imagination for this task.

Spend an hour on your knees, shuffling around your house while you try to accomplish your normal tasks. Really pay attention to what you see at that level, what you smell, what you can reach, and what you struggle with. Then write about your experiences.

After ten minutes of this exercise, which happens to be one of Lisa's favorites, you may have sore knees, but you'll also have a better perspective on the child characters you're writing about. This exercise can also help you think about things a child experiences from down there so you can come up with new story ideas.

Chapter 12

Writing Creative Nonfiction Books

● ●

In This Chapter

▶ Stepping into the nonfiction world

▶ Deciding on a topic

▶ Using an outline to get organized

● ●

As any writer who writes both fiction and nonfiction can tell you, writing nonfiction books is quite different from writing fiction. Although fiction allows you to pick any topic and create a unique universe around it, that's not the case when writing nonfiction, which must be factually correct. If you're writing nonfiction about Thomas Jefferson, for example, you can't ascribe superpowers to him. Although he may have been fit and strong, it's unlikely that he possessed X-ray vision or the ability to fly.

With that thought in mind, we dedicate this chapter to discussing everything you need to know about writing nonfiction children's books. We talk about some major similarities and differences between writing nonfiction and fiction. We consider how to choose fun and fascinating topics, and we take a look at why outlining your nonfiction story is a good idea. We also share some common mistakes when it comes to children's nonfiction (and how to avoid them, of course) as well as a couple writing exercises you can try to hone your nonfiction chops.

The Nonfiction Children's Book World at a Glance

A nonfiction book is one based on facts. It can be historical, focusing on an event (such as the Civil War) or a person (think Susan B. Anthony), or it can hone in on a topic such as dinosaurs, insects, or mammals. Biographies are nonfiction, as are autobiographies and how-to books. The available subjects and topics for nonfiction are nearly endless, which is why we help you find a topic that inspires you in the later "Choosing a Great Topic" section.

Nonfiction for the fiction lover

A nonfiction style that's written in a way that makes it read like fiction is called *narrative nonfiction*. It uses fiction techniques such as narrative, dialogue, and a story structure with a beginning, middle, and end — but everything that happens in the book is true. Biographies can be narrative nonfiction, as can books about events in history, or memoirs. Books with narratives focusing on the main character's diary entries fall into this genre, as do epistolary books, in which the narrative consists of protagonists who wrote letters back and forth to one another. All the letters and correspondences in these books must be real documents — though verifying whether the writers of these documents were telling the truth about their lives would probably constitute a completely different book on the topic. Examples would be *Heads or Tails: Stories from the Sixth Grade* by Jack Gantos (middle-grade memoir; Farrar Straus & Giroux Books for Young Readers) or *The Boys' War: Confederate and Union Soldiers Talk About the Civil War* by Jim Murphy (young adult history; Clarion Books).

The different elements that go into nonfiction books are often the same as in fiction, only the contents are different. For instance, nonfiction books often use *photorealistic illustrations* (illustrations done in a style that approximates photographs), photographs, line drawings, and simple diagrams, maps, and charts for the visuals. The ratio of text and visuals must be very well balanced, so that the text does not overshadow the images, cluttering up the page with too many words. (A pet peeve of many book buyers — see Chapter 3). The design of a nonfiction book may have to juggle many more elements per spread than a book of fiction; for instance, if there are main text, main visuals, charts, factoid boxes, text bubbles, and other visually stimulating graphics, all must be laid out to encourage the reader to peruse all the content without feeling overwhelmed.

Nonfiction plays a very important part in the spectrum of children books. Teachers use nonfiction books in their curricula from preschool to high school. You can find nonfiction in board books, Young Adult (YA) books, and everything in between. And nonfiction lends itself perfectly well to the parameters of all the formats you can read about in Chapter 2. The only major difference is that although fictional picture books target ages 3 through 8 and max out at a word count of 1,500, nonfiction picture books can be aimed at audiences up to age 12, and the text can run up to 2,500 words or more.

A great example of a nonfiction series that is appropriate for ages 9 through 12 and so beautifully balances many different visual elements with the right amount of text is Dorling Kindersley Publishing's Eyewitness Books series. Each title, written by a different author or team of authors, offers an in-depth look at one subject — say pirates, or horses, or insects — and spends about

56 to 72 pages really digging into the aspects of the chosen topic that kids really care about. (For more about idea development and what your audience wants, see Chapters 5 and 6.) Instead of reading like dry reference books, these are like mini encyclopedias — fascinating and packed with information.

Children love to read nonfiction, too, and their teachers often build nonfiction reading into the curriculum. That means your easy reader about horses or your middle-grade book about pirates can be used in schools. So if you are into a topic and have always wanted to learn more and share it with others, writing nonfiction may be just the ticket for you.

Writing a Nonfiction Masterpiece

Writing nonfiction is different from writing fiction in a few ways. Although you may not have a main character (unless you are writing a biography or autobiography) or a plot tied to that main character, you will still have to make some decisions early on:

- **Theme or subject:** This refers to the book's main idea or concept. What's your subject? See the "Choosing a Great Topic" section later in this chapter.

- **Characters:** Will you have a main character? What about supporting characters? (If your book is not about a particular person or group of people, or if you're writing a how-to book, the answer to this is usually no.) See Chapter 7.

- **Plot:** A plot is what happens in your book. You may not have a plot in nonfiction, but you still need to set up your work with a series of intertwined actions that progress from a beginning, through a middle, to an end in order to keep it moving and interesting to your young reader. Your outline will help you track and accomplish this, as we explain in the later "Outlining Your Creative Nonfiction" section.

- **Setting:** Where does the subject take place or is the place your subject? Many nonfiction books explore many settings. (Flip to Chapter 10 for more on setting.)

- **Point of view:** Except for many biographies and, of course, autobiographies, nonfiction, and how-to books are usually written in the third person. (To find out more about point of view, see Chapter 11.)

- **Format and target audience:** Although not absolutely necessary for you to begin writing, it can be helpful to know what format and what audience you think you might like to write for. (We cover formats and audience in Chapters 2 and 3 and researching your audience in Chapter 6.)

Adding "extra" info to your nonfiction children's book

Librarians and booksellers tell us that the design and layout of a nonfiction book are paramount to their buying decisions. Chances are good they won't buy books with too much text and not enough pictures, or books in which the design is cluttered, illogical, or hard to follow. Although the publisher will design the interior of a nonfiction book, you can do much to encourage good design.

✔ Research well-designed nonfiction books and note the elements they use to add extra information to the primary text. For example, if little, interesting factoids are interspersed throughout the book using talk bubbles and cartoons that are different from the photorealistic illustrations you want to use, you can write text for these and include them in your manuscript. Or in this book, note the sidebars, tips, warnings, and interviews. These metatexts are not strictly *necessary* to convey the basics, but they add interesting

and beneficial information to the main body of the text.

✔ If you have lots of terms to define on each page, write them out separately as an addendum with page references so the designer can figure out a cool way to incorporate them into the overall design.

✔ If text blocks seem to work better in your mind's eye (and in the competition), then create actual text blocks in your manuscript. (**Warning:** Some publishers will prefer that you simply add an addendum if the manuscript is a submission; any extra formatting can be viewed askance.)

✔ When you sell your masterpiece, you can even try to negotiate input in the design phase of the book, though unless you've had other titles under your belt, this might be an uphill battle.

After you make these decisions and begin your writing, you have to make other choices that you do not have to when writing fiction. For example, in nonfiction, all dialogue must be factual and verifiable — many publishers require complete and documented accuracy. Will your book be long enough to need a table of contents? What about an index? How are you going to keep track of and credit those from whom you borrow information? (The two classic reference books for researchers are Kate L. Turabian's *A Manual for Writers* [The University of Chicago Press] and *The MLA Handbook for Writers of Research Papers, Theses, and Dissertations* by Joseph Gibaldi and Walter S. Achtert [Modern Language Association].) What illustrations or other graphics will you seek to keep your text engaging? You have to get legal permission to use existing images from the originators — publishers will require copies of these signed legal documents. (Go to www.nolo.com for permissions information, books, and forms.) Or you may choose to create some of the visuals yourself or pay someone else to design them for you.

Aside from the visuals, how are you going to keep your text engaging? If you are writing about an event in history and do not have a single historical figure you'd like to use as a main character, how are you going to keep readers engaged? Suspense, humor, and romance all still have places in nonfiction, and you still are the one who must provide them. (Chapter 8 gives ample tips about pacing and drama that you can easily apply to nonfiction writing.)

From here on out, the actual process of writing nonfiction is no different from that of writing fiction— until you hit the researching part. For instance, after you come up with a great topic and nail down the basics, you need to go out and make sure your topic is relevant and up-to-date and interesting enough for kids today— same as fiction. But then you jump into researching what your topic is all about — not necessary for all fiction, absolutely necessary for nonfiction. And the vast majority of nonfiction writers, unlike most fiction writers, use outlines to organize their thoughts and help them flesh out their ideas. Then once you have written your first draft, your rewrites and your edits will involve the same sort of painstaking and careful attention to detail — if not more.

A great majority of nonfiction books, even the short ones, are sold via a proposal. We cover the basics of writing a nonfiction book proposal in Chapter 17.

Choosing a Great Topic

Writing a great nonfiction children's book begins with finding a great topic. You have an almost infinite variety of topics to work with. Of course, some topics will interest your audience — and you as a writer — more than others, so you must be selective when choosing the one on which to focus your creative efforts.

In the sections that follow, we consider how to choose a topic to both delight the children who read it and excite you during the writing process. We also take a look at sources for nonfiction book ideas and great places to test your ideas before you spend all your time and energy developing them.

Looking at topics that get kids' attention

When it comes to fictional topics, you probably already have a pretty good idea of what gets children interested in reading: stories about wizards, flatulent canines, heroes with superpowers, princes and princesses, talking fish, cats with hats, Martians, girls from Kansas with ruby slippers, and many more. But what about ideas for nonfiction children's books? What topics float kids' boats? Here are just a few:

- Pets
- How bodies work
- Sports

- History and culture
- Dinosaurs
- Biographies
- Backyard nature
- Science
- Strange, terrible, gross, interesting facts

Choose a slant to the topic that will be unique and interesting to the intended audience. Younger kids (preschool through first grade) like topics presented as they apply to the kids' lives. For example, how to find and study bugs in your backyard. Kids in second grade and up often use nonfiction books to write reports at school or do research, so tie the topics into the curriculum. And it's always good to add humor whenever possible, through the text, illustrations, or both. Consider the example of a nonfiction book in the picture book format for kids up to age 10 called *It's Disgusting and We Ate It! True Food Facts from Around the World and Throughout History* by James Solheim (Simon & Schuster Children's Publishing). It combines history and social studies, and it even includes recipes.

Finding topics that interest you

When we say you should choose a subject that floats your boat, we mean choosing a subject that you have a strong personal interest in. Although it is ultimately of critical importance that your reader be interested in the topic you choose (otherwise, why buy it?), you have to be interested in it first. If you're not, it will show in your writing. To decide which topics float your boat, use the following indicators as a guide:

- **Choose a topic you know a lot about.** If you know a *lot* about a particular topic, not only is that an indication you probably like it, but it also means you likely have plenty of background knowledge to get you off to a smooth start.

- **Choose a topic you're curious about.** Perhaps there's a topic you've been wondering about for a long time — maybe years — but it has never made the top of your list of things to learn more about. You may, for example, have a fascination with tornadoes — a topic about which you know little beyond what you learned from watching the film *Twister* years ago. This fascination may drive you to research the topic thoroughly — to the point that you become expert at it.

- **Choose a topic you're passionate about.** Passion for something — an idea, a thing, a person — can really motivate you to achieve great things, including writing a great story. Tap into the emotion, energy, and inspiration your passion releases by choosing a topic that you're passionate about.

✔ **Choose a topic with personal meaning to you.** If you, your parents, or your grandparents immigrated to this country from, say, China or Mexico, why not choose a topic that allows you to further explore your own roots and your cultural heritage? Maybe a book based on Chinese New Year or Mexican Day of the Dead festivities.

Life is too short to waste your time writing books for which you have no passion or feeling of connection. Leave those books to someone else while you focus on finding the topics that work best for you.

Branching out into the real world

Beyond finding topics that interest your potential readers — and that interest you personally — it's a good idea to branch out and look at the real world and real topics that are going on today or that have happened in history. Perhaps it should come as no surprise that a glance through the pages of most any newspaper or magazine can reveal a wide variety of topics for you to consider.

Honing in on the hot topics of the day

Kids are connoisseurs of all things current and hot. If there's something new out there, chances are that kids will already know about it. Whether it's the latest hot singer, the edgiest fashions and trends, or the coolest electronic gizmo — kids are likely already way ahead of you. Be sure to check out Chapter 6, where we devote an entire section to dipping into the popular culture for ideas on what's hot.

Delving into broad topics that need more coverage

It's unlikely that topics such as dinosaurs or firetrucks are lacking coverage in the children's book market; however, other topics — such as the plight of American citizens of Japanese descent who had to abandon their homes and land when the U.S. government herded them into forced relocation camps during World War II, or great women astronomers, or the impact of population growth on fragile ecosystems — very well may have been overlooked. Consider asking the following questions as you search for a subject that needs more coverage:

✔ Is the person, event, or thing historically significant?

✔ Is the person, event, or thing relatively obscure?

✔ Would a book based on the topic have a measurable and positive impact on its young readers?

✔ Are there other books on the topic? Do they leave certain issues unaddressed (that you can address in your book)?

✔ Is this a story that simply *must* be told because in your view it is particularly unique, timely, or compelling?

If you answer a number of these questions in the affirmative, you've created a compelling case for writing about the topic you have chosen. So don't just think about doing it, do it already!

Testing your topic

After you have a nonfiction topic picked out, how can you be sure it's a good one? By testing it. And who should test your ideas? We suggest getting feedback from kids, teachers, and librarians.

Seeking feedback from kids

What better place to get feedback about your idea than straight from the horse's mouth, right? Kids can help you quickly determine whether your idea is a winner or something that belongs on the back burner. Here are some questions to ask to get the feedback flowing and to ascertain whether you're on the right track:

- Do you like this idea?
- What about this idea do you like?
- What about this idea do you dislike?
- What would you do to make this idea more interesting?
- What idea would you like better than this one?

Be sure to check out Chapter 5, in which we discuss going to kids to generate ideas for your stories. Many of the same ideas we discuss apply here, too.

Seeking feedback from teachers and librarians

After you select your topic, get a second opinion. And why not get that second opinion from people who spend more time with eager young readers than most anyone else on the planet: — librarians and teachers?

Librarians and teachers are on the front lines of every youthquake and megatrend that passes through their libraries and classrooms. If the kids like something, librarians and teachers probably know about it weeks — perhaps even months — before you do.

Another way of finding out whether a topic is good is to look at the public school curriculum for different grades, or for specific grades of the age for which you want to write. There are state and federal educational guidelines and curricula online — even word lists for each grade. Most school districts have their curriculums on the Web. Then you can go ask teachers who teach that grade if they see a need for more books on certain topics for use in the classroom.

The one nonfiction children's book not worth writing: Your memoir

Write about what you know is an old adage. And what do you know better than yourself and the details of your life? So why not write a *memoir* (a nonfiction book written by a person about his or her own life experiences or a portion thereof). Here's the problem: Why should anyone read your memoir? We know *you* think your life is endlessly fascinating and so do all your closest friends. But how do you tell if anyone outside your circle of BFFs and family would be interested in buying and reading your memoir?

Unless you've lived through a known event or series of events in a wondrous, courageous, or heretofore unheard of fashion so incredible as to be almost unbelievable (but verifiable, of course), then the answer is you should probably keep your life to yourself. Think of it this way: Remember being a small child held unwillingly captive at the knees of an aged relative who went on and on about his childhood, boring you to tears? Do you really want to be that person to some poor, innocent child?

But you just *have* to tell the world about how you survived your impoverished, abusive [fill in the blank] childhood to become the upstanding citizen you are today. Just because you've been possessed by the writing bug and have compiled 300 pages about your life and all its gory details does not a great read make. Sometimes you have to write it all down to get it out of your system and move on. Most memoirs serve this cathartic purpose for the writer, the paper or laptop screen being the perfect outlet for lifelong unspoken frustrations, grudges, unhealed wounds, family dramas, [fill in the blank here, too] — kind of like the best shrink you've ever been to. The problem is this: A nonfiction book for children is not the same as an outlet for your life's problem issues. Consider writing a blog first and then see where it takes you. If enough people are interested in your story, you may very well have the makings for a decent memoir, but odds are your target audience still won't be children.

Outlining Your Creative Nonfiction

After you figure out what kind of nonfiction book you want to write, choose your topic, test it out on kids, and conduct further research on your topic (flip to Chapter 6 for research pointers), now it's time to turn your fully researched topic into an outline.

Many nonfiction writers rely on outlines to help develop and organize their stories. A good outline displays, at a glance, all the topics needing to be covered, in the order they should be covered, and it helps avoid chronological or topical holes. Because an outline must cover the selected topic from beginning to end in a logical and sequential way, it essentially serves as an author's road map, telling her where she's at right now, where she's been, and where she's going.

Also, because the outline is written down and planned out in advance, the author can see whether the story moves smoothly and can make minor (or major) adjustments as necessary. Not only that, but an outline provides the author with a detailed template of what she'll write. After preparing a fully developed outline, the actual writing falls right into place.

We help you develop an outline for your nonfiction book in the following sections.

Starting simple

An outline's primary purpose is to guide an author's writing, which, ultimately, helps with the planning process. A simple outline has three main parts:

- ✔ **Title:** This is the title of your book.

- ✔ **Headings:** Headings are the major points you plan to address in your book. In the finished book, they may become separate chapter titles, or they may remain headings.

- ✔ **Content:** This is the text that elaborates on the topic named by each heading (or chapter title).

Say you decide to write a children's book on megalodons, those gigantic, ancient sharks that roamed the seas from about 1.6 to 25 million years ago. Your outline for this topic may look something like the following, where the title is in bold italics at the top:

***Megalodons: The Real Story* (Outline)**

- ✔ What is a megalodon?

  - Ancient shark (name means *big teeth*)

  - Existed from 1.6 to 25 million years ago (Miocene and Pliocene epochs)

  - Looked like present-day great white shark

- ✔ How big were megalodons?

  - Estimated at 40 to 100 feet long

  - At least three times larger than present-day great white shark

  - Jaws could open 6 feet wide and 7 feet high

- ✔ What did megalodons eat?

  - Mostly ate whales

  - Squid

  - Sushi

✔ What about those big teeth?

- Largest fossilized teeth discovered to date are 6 inches long

- Had three to five rows of teeth in mouth

- Megalodon didn't chew its food, gulped it down whole or in large chunks

Working through the outlining process helps you avoid potential problems by ensuring your book progresses logically from topic to topic. Without an outline to help you keep your facts straight and in order, you may decide to go into details about what megalodons ate before you tell your readers what a megalodon was, which clearly doesn't make much sense.

A number of different approaches work when it comes time to create your outline. You can type it out on your computer or write it out by hand. Or you can write each of your headings on an index card and write out a paragraph describing its content underneath. The great thing about using index cards is that you can lay them out on a table and easily rearrange them, allowing you to try out a variety of different organizational options. You can also use sticky notes on a blank wall (just keep the windows closed; wind is not your friend).

Whatever approach you take, the time you put into creating an outline for your nonfiction book will be paid back many times over when it comes time to write your manuscript.

Fleshing out your ideas

After you've drafted an outline, you have a choice: Either start writing your book from the outline as it stands, or continue to refine the outline, adding more material to flesh it out. Why bother with that? Because the more fleshing out you do, the closer you actually bring yourself to the finished product. And every step closer to the finished product brings you closer to accomplishing your goal: creating a children's book you can be proud of.

You can flesh out the ideas in your outline in a couple of different ways: either starting at the beginning and strictly working your way to the end or jumping back and forth between different sections of the outline, working first on what interests you most and dealing with more challenging sections later. The exact approach you take to filling out your outline isn't so important; what is important is adopting the approach that works best for you.

In the case of a nonfiction children's book, fleshing out your outline likely requires you to do more research. (For more details on conducting research, see Chapter 6.)

Here's an example of what a fleshed-out, researched outline may look (if you're writing about megalodons, that is):

Megalodons: The Real Story **(Outline)**

✔ What is a megalodon?

- A megalodon was an ancient shark that may have been an ancestor of the present-day great white shark. Megalodons churned widely through the oceans, off the coasts of large parts of the earth — North America, Europe, South America, India, Oceania, and more. The name megalodon means *big teeth* — the largest megalodon teeth found to date are about 6 inches long.

- Megalodons glided through the world from 1.6 to 25 million years ago, and they are now extinct. Megalodons lived during the Miocene and Pliocene epochs.

- Megalodons looked like a present-day great white shark. They had many of the same features as modern-day sharks, including gill slits, front and rear dorsal fins, pectoral fin, pelvic fin, mouth, nostrils, and so forth. Their skin was rough and gray in color with sharp scales.

Enhancing your outline with visual aids

As the old saying goes, a picture is worth a thousand words. Some people are simply better and more creative thinkers when they see ideas presented visually rather than via the written word. If this is the case for you, it's a good idea to draw out your outline so that it can be visualized.

A *storyboard,* for example, is simply a series of drawings that represent events occurring in sequence. You can use a storyboard to outline a single chapter or an entire book. If you're an extremely visual person, a storyboard may be helpful. Some writers buy cue cards, put their salient plot points on them, and arrange them on a corkboard. Others who are writing picture books or board books paste the outline points on actual pages to help them visualize the progress the book must take and the word count they must keep in mind. Still others draw pictures, making dummies with illustrations or sketches in place of the action to show on the page what the words must express.

Other visual aids can be quite useful, too, including presentation software or even a simple paper-based flip chart that flips through the action as it's expected to happen.

Presenting Common Creative Nonfiction Mistakes (And Fixes)

As you can imagine, a variety of mistakes can occur when you're writing a creative nonfiction children's book. Here are some of the most common mistakes, along with some quick fixes for them:

- **You don't know your stuff.** Remember, you have to have your facts straight when you write nonfiction. If you're not sure about something, then look it up!

- **The book is out of date.** Many nonfiction books — especially about fast-moving topics like technology — are timely today, and out of date tomorrow. Keep up with the latest-and-greatest news on your topic, and make sure your book reflects it.

- **The story is boring.** Because creative nonfiction is by nature nonfictional, it can sometimes be a challenge for authors to push the creativity button hard enough to avoid writing a boring book. You can avoid this trap by having fun with your writing — be creative!

Writing Exercises for Creative Nonfiction

Yes, writing nonfiction children's books means you have to get your facts straight, but it doesn't mean you can't have fun doing it. At its heart, writing creative nonfiction is all about presenting factual information to your readers in a way they will enjoy. The following writing exercises will help you develop the nonfiction chops you'll need to make your work shine.

Pretend you're a newspaper reporter

Newspaper reporters are masters of presenting factual information in an engaging, concise, and accurate way. The best newspaper articles draw you in with a captivating title and opening first sentence or two (what news organizations call the *lede*), and then they tell you five important things about the story:

- Who
- What
- When
- Where
- Why

So, what better way to practice writing creative nonfiction than to pretend you're a newspaper reporter? To begin this exercise, first imagine that you are a newspaper reporter and that your editor has just given you an assignment to write a short article on some person, thing, or event. The assignment can be local in nature — perhaps a construction crew recently uncovered an intact wooly mammoth skeleton at a building site — or it can be national or even international. Research the story to gather the facts; then write your article.

Don't forget that your article shouldn't just be factual, it should be engaging and fun — *creative*. Keep an eye out for the unusual — facts that your readers will find interesting and entertaining. If the subject of your article has a large collection of bugs in her garage, organized by size, color, and wingspan, then by all means report that. If the new Ferris wheel in your city is the tallest in the tri-state area, then make sure you write about that, and about any interesting factoids that you uncovered in your research. Like how many boxes of popcorn stacked one on top of the other it would take to reach the top of the wheel.

Try writing at least three newspaper articles — more if you are particularly inspired by this exercise.

Create a funny five-step procedure to wash a dog

A large segment of nonfiction writing is what is known as *how-to,* that is, explaining to the reader how to do something. The book you are holding in your hands right now is a proud member of that segment of nonfiction writing — it shows you how to write a children's book and get it published. Whether or not the creative nonfiction children's book you plan to write is a how-to book, writing a how-to procedure can help you sharpen your creative nonfiction writing skills. And it can be a lot of fun.

In this exercise, you will write a five-step procedure for washing a dog. Now, we don't want you to write just any five-step procedure. We want you to write one that is as factual as can be, but that is also as funny as can be. As you detail each of your five steps, think about at least one funny thing to help you illustrate the step. For example, if you've decided one of your steps is to place your dog in a bathtub in your home and lather him up with doggie shampoo, then what happens to your bathroom walls (and you!) when the dog suddenly decides to vigorously shake off all the soap suds? You get the idea.

Interview with Susan Goldman Rubin, author

Susan Goldman Rubin, a children's book author extraordinaire, has regularly wowed her readers with well-researched and captivating nonfiction books. (See Chapter 2.)

WCBFD: How did you get started writing children's books, and how was it that nonfiction became your strongest suit?

SGR: I started writing because I was an illustrator and had nothing to illustrate. So I wrote a little story about my kids sleeping over at their grandmother's house. I eventually illustrated that picture book and published it (after five years of trying). But I found that my writing won more interest from editors than my artwork. I turned to nonfiction because I loved art and wanted to share my enthusiasm with young people. My first nonfiction book was a biography of architect Frank Lloyd Wright. It came about when my husband and I were going to take our kids on an outing to Hollyhock House, one of Wright's buildings in Los Angeles. When we told the kids where we were going, my 10-year-old stepson (who had visited many museums) said, "Frank Lloyd Who?" That's when I knew I had to do the book. I published it with Abrams, a house known for their splendid art books. One project led to another. Sometimes my editor invited me to do a book for young readers in conjunction with an upcoming exhibition. Along the way, I began to write about Holocaust themes. This, too, came from the heart.

WCBFD: Many would-be children's book authors ignore the nonfiction genre — why is this a mistake?

SGR: When I teach or speak at a writers' conference, I strongly encourage would-be children's book authors to try nonfiction. I urge them to choose a subject that greatly interests them and find an approach suitable for a particular age group. About half of all published children's books are nonfiction, and there is a real need for fresh, new material. Chances for breaking into the market are greater with nonfiction.

WCBFD: What is it about writing nonfiction children's books that excites you?

SGR: I love research. Finding out secrets and gathering information about real people and actual events thrills me. The process is like a treasure hunt. One clue leads to another whether I'm looking for text information or for photos and art to use as illustrations. When I wrote *Toilets, Toasters and Telephones: The How and Why of Everyday Objects,* for instance, I spent hours on the phone looking for a photo of an early Egyptian toilet seat dating from 1370 b.c. I called Cairo and wound up on a first-name basis with an Arabic-speaking phone operator as I searched for The Egypt Exploration Society. Finally I found that it was located in England and the society provided me with the picture I needed — gratis!

WCBFD: How do you select a topic to write about?

SGR: I select a topic from the heart. Something that I feel passionately about, that I must do even if I think it may have limited sales. Perhaps the subject has never before been presented to children and I feel compelled to write about it. This happened when I stumbled upon the story of artist Friedl Dicker-Brandeis, an unsung heroine of the Holocaust. The true story gripped me. I put aside another book project under contract and with the permission of my understanding editor, focused on *Fireflies in the Dark: The Story of Friedl Dicker-Brandeis and the Children of Terezin.*

WCBFD: In what ways is writing a nonfiction children's book more challenging than writing a fictional children's book?

SGR: The challenge of writing nonfiction is to show, not tell, and use narrative techniques

(continued)

(continued)

of dramatization with action and dialogue. However, scenes have to be based on reliable sources. A nonfiction writer has the responsibility of being accurate and truthful. Quotes can't be made up. Finding words that were actually spoken that will be clear and meaningful to young readers presents a difficult challenge.

WCBFD: Please describe the process of research you undertake when working on a typical project.

SGR: When I begin a project, I read everything I can get hold of on the subject. I read books and articles geared for adults as well as those written for children. I especially want to know what the competition is so that I can come up with something fresh. I watch videos on the subject. I interview people who can give me new information and quotes. When I was working on *L'Chaim! To Jewish Life in America!* I found out that Professor Jonathan Sarna, the eminent scholar in the field, was soon to publish a book for adults called *American Judaism.* I did some research to find out his e-mail address, wrote to him, and asked him if I could possibly read some of his book before it was published to be sure I was on the right track. Professor Sarna generously sent me his entire manuscript via e-mail and even agreed to check mine for accuracy before it went into print. Research also often involves music. When I was writing *Degas and the Dance: The Painter and the Petits Rats Perfecting Their Art,* I listened to Degas's favorite ballet music to immerse myself in his world.

I went behind the scenes as Degas did and observed classes at the School of American Ballet in New York. Travel gives authenticity to nonfiction writing. When I wrote the book about Friedl Dicker-Brandeis, I managed to go to Terezin, the ghetto/concentration camp near Prague where she had been imprisoned. If I've taped interviews as I did for that book, I play them back at home, transcribe the words, then incorporate the best quotes for my purposes into the narrative. I write the book chapter by chapter, getting feedback from my supportive but critical writers' group. I keep going over the manuscript, "tightening and brightening," until it's ready to show to my agent and editor as a first draft. Even then, there's more research to be done when my editor and the copy editor give me their comments and queries.

WCBFD: What advice do you have for prospective nonfiction children's book authors?

SGR: My advice for prospective nonfiction children's book authors is to follow your hearts. Write about subjects that truly excite you. See what else has been published and how recently. Maybe it's time for a fresh look at an old topic. Or perhaps in today's world it's appropriate to introduce very young readers to a subject formerly offered only to older children. Come up with a catchy working title. Find a unique angle. One of my editors says, "If you've got the hook, you've got the book."

Part IV
Making Your Story Sparkle

The 5th Wave   By Rich Tennant

"This morning I was reading the baby my latest manuscript, and she signed the words for 'fresh,' 'insightful,' and 'poignant.'"

In this part . . .

To turn your rough stone into a polished diamond, you first need a vision for what your children's book will look like when it's finished and then shine it and buff it until it sparkles. In this part, we explore how to rewrite and edit your book. We also take a look at how to format it, whether or not to illustrate it, and how to get feedback — and encouragement — from others.

Chapter 13

Editing and Formatting Your Way to a Happy Ending

*E*ven the best, most professional, writing-for-a-living type of writers can't create books or stories that are absolutely perfect the first time around. In the real world (that place where we hope most of you live), writing is a repetitive process during which you first input some words, then you make some changes, and some more changes, add and delete a word or paragraph or section or chapter or two here or there, and correct some misspellings or grammar issues — then start all over again. In short, you revise and edit and polish again and again. Revising and editing are very much a part of the writing process, and a good revise and edit can turn a lackluster manuscript into a compelling, award-winning book.

Sometimes editing and revising are considered the same process. But for our purposes, we separate them as follows:

> ✔ *Revising* is the fixing process you do when you go back to check whether all the major parts of your book are working (as in the parts we cover in Part III).

> ✔ *Editing* is the fixing you do after you're pretty sure the major parts are complete, and you're working on fine tuning.

We, therefore, dedicate this chapter to arguably two of the most important parts of the process of writing a children's book: revising and editing.

Your Revising Checklist

The revising phase is all about making sure the major elements of your story are in order — specifically theme, characters, plot, pacing and drama, setting and context, and point of view. The following sections walk you through how to examine each of these major elements in the course of revising your book.

When revising with major issues in mind, we have a way to make it easier to keep track. Each time you go through the manuscript from start to finish, attempt to tackle only one issue at a time. So if you're ready to revise your characters to make sure they're properly fleshed out, take one character at a time from start to finish of the manuscript. Then go back to the beginning, and do the other characters one by one. When you're finished, go on to the next issue. This way you won't go crazy wondering where you are as you work your way through.

We would argue that a lot of the points you need to check for in a revision of fiction also apply to nonfiction. Perhaps the correlation isn't exact, but the major issues are more similar than not. The one main difference is that in nonfiction, you have to check and recheck facts while making sure to provide for a balance in the text and other ways of conveying information (such as sidebars, marginal factoids, illustrations or graphics, accuracy in headings, and the like).

Theme

Is there a clearly defined theme? If another reader (like a friend or someone in your writing group) is unable to tell you in a word or two (maybe a sentence) what your theme is, perhaps you've not homed in on one. If that's the case, you might need to revise your story with theme in mind.

To do that, make the theme apparent at the start of the story in the type of problem the character is going to have to solve. For example, if your story's theme is reassurance, you need to put your protagonist in a situation in which the solution leads to his *finding* reassurance. Then you need to insert reminders to the theme throughout the story in the form of foils — issues that get in the way of your character's desire or need. Furthering the example, you would need to show your character feeling insecure. You might even want to show other characters playing upon his insecurity to create conflict. And in the end, you have to make sure that character finds the reassurance he has sought — or achieves an equally valuable replacement.

Only you can tell what the essence of your story is. What is its heart? Find the answer, and keep it in mind while you revise your draft.

Characters

Your primary goal as a writer is to create unforgettable characters. Why? Because if your characters are dishrags, your manuscript may as well be, too. In 99.9 percent of children's books, character is what makes or breaks a single title versus a book with series potential. If the character is poorly developed in the text, no amount of magnificent writing or perfectly crafted plotting will save you. (In board books, so few words are used you may conclude the characters are made memorable by the illustrations alone — and in most cases you would be correct.) But a memorable character mostly comes from the marriage of complementary illustrations (when appropriate to the format) and an active story line.

What makes a good character great is the way he sees the world and interacts with it. The character's quirks and preferences, the way he talks, the way he moves, the actions he takes, the way he deals with conflict, the reactions he demonstrates — all the characteristics that bring the written character alive make him seem like he exists in real life — as a human or otherwise. Seeing characters in action shows the reader who they are.

Your main character and his supporting cast must be fleshed out and made interesting. They also need to sound their age. Additionally, throughout the book, your main character must actively change from who he was at the start of the story — preferably as the result of his own actions and choices. If you're writing a picture book, make sure the main character appears in every important scene. If you're writing a longer book, make sure the main character is further developed in some way, no matter how small, in each chapter, whether through plot events, dialogue, conflict, or interaction with another character.

To determine whether your characters are relatable, go back through your book and check each character from start to finish. Make sure each one is active and has a definable core and burning desire driving the story, making us want to tag along with him no matter where he goes just to see what he does next. In a chapter book, identify at least a few places for each character where a *plot point* (a place where the action moves forward in time) or dialogue contributes to developing that character beyond a name or a convenient one-time description.

Plot

Plot is the action that drives a story forward. Every story has a beginning, middle, and end, and when these plot elements are handled clumsily, the resulting work exhibits major problems. Although huge surprises and plot reversals or twists can work well in children's books, you may be left with a disjointed mess unless you tie up loose ends very carefully.

Ask yourself these questions about your plot:

- ✔ Is what happens in the story from start to finish pretty clear?
- ✔ Can you point out the beginning, middle/climax, and end/resolution?
- ✔ Is there enough conflict between your main character and the primary issue he has to resolve?

If you haven't created an action outline (also known as a step sheet; see Chapter 8) to help you determine answers to these questions and give you something concrete to check off, now might be the time to do this to help you revise. If you need to reconfigure your plot for more dramatic, engaging impact, the action outline is a great way to keep track of what action leads to what reaction, which conflict leads to which consequence.

Pacing and drama

Pacing and drama are intrinsic to a well-written plot, particularly when you're writing for children — an audience not known for its patience. To maintain the interest of your reader, your story needs to move along briskly. When your pace lags, you'll quickly lose your reader to other pursuits (like a more engaging electronic device or a TV show.)

To judge the pacing in your book, simply ask yourself whether the rate at which the action is moving is fast enough to keep the reader wanting to turn the pages. In older children's books, make sure each chapter ends with a cliffhanger or an unresolved conflict. To check the pacing of a picture book, break your manuscript into about 26 separate book pages for a 32-page book or 36 pages for a 40-page book (leaving 1 page for the title page, the back of that page for the copyright information, and 2 pages for endpapers). Then put each page of text onto a separate sheet of paper, staple together along the spine like a book (you'll have to staple pages back to back as well), and read them. The first page of text should be a right-hand page, the last a left-hand page. See whether there's a different action on each pair of facing pages (also known as a *spread*) so the illustrations differ from spread to spread. And make sure something happens on the right-hand page of each spread to make the reader want to turn the page to see what happens next. ***Note:*** This division of the text is for your benefit only — don't send your picture book to an editor like this. (For proper submission formatting, see "Formatting: First Impressions Matter," later in this chapter.)

To gauge the drama of your story, ask whether there are enough OMG! or Oh, no! moments to keep the story compelling — and whether you can verbalize why.

Setting and context

When an author writes about a particular place, the reader should be able to picture it, meaning she should feel the wind blow, smell the pine trees and cedar on a high mountain peak, or sense the grainy sand under her soles and between her toes. If the reader can't picture a particular setting after reading about it, the author hasn't done a good job of describing it.

In any format other than a board or picture book, you must identify the place or the particular context in which the story takes place. This doesn't mean cheating the reader by simply stating that it takes place in a city called Los Angeles. What if someone has never been there? You have to describe a bit of its flavor: The pedestrians passing in front of the house, what the main character sees, how the trees grow haphazardly and break through the sidewalk. Don't just include the run-of-the-mill details — write about the interesting tidbits that color the environment and develop its character, making a place more special than Anyplace, USA.

Developing a simple context that's interesting and different does *not* mean that you write a *data dump* (running on and on) about a place, describing every little leaf and crack in the sidewalk. It means you ground your story in a place so readers know where the character is coming from or going to and can quickly understand what sets this place apart from all of the rest — and you do it little by little as you proceed from place to place.

During revising, ask yourself whether the reader knows immediately where he is at the start of the story. Have you made apparent any contextual information, setting the story apart from real life (meaning, if the story takes place in a mining town in 1849, do we know that right off the bat)? Are the setting and contextual clues elegantly intertwined in the action, or is the reader having to slog through long descriptive passages to get the information? Go through and check each instance the place and/or time changes, making sure the setting is clearly drawn without wordiness. (For more pointers on setting and context, see Chapter 10.)

Point of view

The point of view, or POV, you choose is how your reader experiences your story. Have you chosen a POV and stuck to it consistently? If you're writing a picture book, your story should have only one POV — period. If you're writing a chapter book for older children or a YA novel, you may choose to alternate POVs, but you shouldn't alternate them within a scene or a chapter.

You can check whether your POV is consistent by reading your story and paying attention to how you're seeing the events. If you get confused, chances are your reader is, too.

Concise, consistent, and compelling writing

As any English major can tell you, there are enough rules for writing well to fill more than a book or two. But all you really have to do is keep the Three C's in mind:

✔ **Be concise.** Never use 50 words when just 5 will accomplish the same goal. Your publisher isn't measuring the value of your book by how many words you write; your book is much more powerful when your message is clear and unfettered by flowery, vague, or otherwise superfluous language. Pare your story to its barest essence.

✔ **Be consistent.** Plots, characters, chronologies, and story lines must be consistent and develop logically from page to page and from chapter to chapter if you want your reader to be able to follow along. Take time to look at the big picture to ensure consistency throughout your work; you may even want to chart plots, chronologies, and the like to be sure that your story hangs together. (We explain how to chart your story's plotline in Chapter 8.)

✔ **Be compelling.** The best stories are ones that seem driven from within, that pick you up and move you along on an exciting journey to some new place you've never been before. Use action words to draw your reader into your story and to keep his interest after you've got it.

Recognizing the Power of a Good Edit

Pros know good writing takes a lot of work. Every time you make a *pass* through your story (revising or editing your work from beginning to end), your story will improve — sometimes in small ways and sometimes in very big ways.

Editing can fix some of the common writing problems we've mentioned here. Don't believe us? Take a look at this example and you soon will:

> The rabbit went back at a not so fast pace and acted kind of anxious as he did. He looked at the ground and all around him like he had lost something. He wondered how his whiskers and paws would fare if the Duchess made him pay for the lost objects with his life. The little girl who was watching him figured out that he must be looking for the fan and the white pair of gloves and she started looking for them to help him out but she could not find them. No matter where she looked everything she had seen the first time she had been there was gone and replaced by something else.

What's happening here? It's clear we have a frightened rabbit who has lost his possessions and a little girl who is trying to help him. But the writing is boring, passive, and vague: What's the rabbit's name? What has he lost? Who is the girl? What exactly changed from the first time she had been in the place?

Here is the passage as Lewis Carroll wrote it in *Alice's Adventures in Wonderland*:

> It was the White Rabbit, trotting slowly back again, and looking anxiously about as he went, as if he had lost something; and she heard him muttering to himself "The Duchess! The Duchess! Oh my dear paws! Oh my fur and whiskers! She'll get me executed, as sure as ferrets are ferrets! Where can I have dropped them, I wonder?" Alice guessed in a minute that he was looking for the fan and the white pair of kid-gloves, and she very good-naturedly began hunting about for them, but they were nowhere to be seen — everything seemed to have changed since her swim in the pool; and the great hall, with the glass table and the little door, had vanished completely.

Notice the difference between our butchered passage and Carroll's. Carroll names both characters, instantly giving them some personality. In the single word *anxious* he conveys the tone of the passage, whereas ours is toneless, boring, replete with run-ons, and has no rhythm. By giving us dialogue instead of reported speech, Carroll brings the White Rabbit alive, further fleshing out his character as forgetful, nervous, and slightly harebrained. The sentences about Alice further develop her as a good-natured girl who wants to help. And the scene detail lets us know we are in a place that was formerly quite grand.

Seasoned writers know that the revision process is just as important to the final result as completing that first draft. In fact, good revises and edits are often *more* important than the first draft. So don't fear the revise, embrace it. Look forward to it. Trust us: A good revision is every writer's best friend.

Editing Out Common Writing Traps

Sometimes there is something wrong with your manuscript, and you simply can't identify what it is. When you're editing your work, you need to know not only how to recognize the problem, but also what to do to fix it. Most likely, if you've addressed the major issues in your revise, what's off will be one of the smaller (yet still mighty important) issues we describe in the following sections. (Don't worry. In addition to outlining some of the most common problems writers face, we also hand over tips from professional editors for conquering them.)

Always take a break after completing a pass through your work. Each time you check an issue from start to finish, take a breather of at least a few minutes, even a day if you can. If you go back to it the next day and it seems you have ceased to improve your work or, worse, that you are only creating more problems for yourself, then it's time to stop revising. At this point, you are ready for some serious feedback. We help you find resources in Chapter 15.

Strengthening your opening

You need a strong opening sentence. This may sound like a no-brainer, but it's really quite important. It's just like when you are watching a movie on TV: If the plot or characters don't grab you right away — click! — you're on to the next channel, looking for something that can hold your attention.

To hook your reader right away, your opening lines should contain some suggestion of conflict, apprehension, suspense, or at least a promise of such. Tricks for creating good opening lines include starting off with a bit of dialogue or a conversation, piquing the reader's curiosity with a glimpse into some very dramatic event, then pulling away before its conclusion to set the mood of the story, or describing the main character and her problem in one short sentence:

> Now Kathryn Camille had a big, fat problem, and if she didn't solve it by eight o'clock that night she was dead meat.

With a chapter book, you can spend an entire paragraph setting a scene. In a picture book, you have to jump into the action ASAP. Don't worry if it takes a while for a strong opening sentence to come to you. Many writers leave that task until the very end.

Keeping your dialogue tight and on target

Are your characters' personalities reflected in their speech pattern, tone, or the content of their dialogue — or do you have a five-year-old character who speaks like a teenager or a mad scientist who has trouble articulating even basic scientific concepts? Dialogue that doesn't match the characters as you've drawn them makes your writing seem implausible and confusing, or wooden and lifeless. For example, here's a kindergartener whose dialogue sounds like a teenager's: "Yo, dude! I gotta majorly big news. She's hot. Smokin'." Pretty ridiculous, huh?

Go through all your dialogue and make sure each character sounds appropriate for his age and what he's in your story to accomplish plot wise. Also check that the characters sound different from one another.

Another issue is excessive use of dialogue. Ever hear someone talking and instead of finishing what they are saying, they end their sentence with, ". . . and blah, blah, blah"? In general, blah times three is used as shorthand to indicate that whatever followed in the dialogue isn't worthy of the time it takes to say it. When too much dialogue is used in children's books, the readers' minds automatically switch into blah-times-three mode. They start skipping what's on the page to get past all the blah-blah-blah.

Dialogue is a great way to get information across to your reader through an interesting source: the character. But a character (just like a real person) who just blabs on and on can be boring. Don't write a character you wouldn't want to spend any time with in real life.

Characters who talk to themselves or spend too much time wondering aloud are not effective characters. Dialogue must involve interaction that moves the plot forward in a meaningful, measurable way.

Check out the discussion about writing realistic dialogue in Chapter 9 and then pass through your manuscript, reading your dialogue aloud to see if it rings true for each character, further develops that character, moves the plot forward, heightens drama or pacing — or if it's just plain blah-times-infinity.

Transitioning effectively

When you're having a conversation with your best friend, you can jump from subject to subject without confusing him. Your hand gestures, body language, and tone of voice can all add to your story, allowing your friend to follow you without getting lost. But in a book you must help the reader move from scene to scene, from place to place, from character to character. How do you do that? Simple! You use transitions effectively.

Transitions are passages that connect one bit to another. They move you forward in time without getting you lost and are necessary when your character changes locations, activities, conversations, or time frames, or when your story alters its focus. They can be as brief as one word or as long as a sentence.

Here's a trick: Use one word from the last sentence of a paragraph in an obvious way in the first sentence of the next paragraph to indicate change while promoting continuity. For example:

> Mary was trying on a pair of glittery pink shoes when the ceiling fell in. *Miraculously,* she escaped unscathed. Her favorite purse was not that lucky. Brushing herself off, Mary left a twenty to pay for the shoes and scooted out of the rubble.
>
> "Speaking of *miracles,*" Mary said into her cellphone as she left the store, hopped on her scooter, and headed for home, "can you believe . . ."

Notice the one word that allows Mary to change venues without leaving the reader confused about the fact that one minute she's trying on shoes, then disaster occurs, and the next minute she's motoring around town with bits of plaster in her hair? That's a sneaky but effective transition.

When you have managed to put together all the little pieces into the coherent whole that make for a great story, check that all your transitions are present, accounted for, and effective.

Trimming wordiness

Many would-be writers think that because children's books are short, they must be really easy to write. We wish! It's actually *more* difficult to write shorter works. When you have a lot of words to work with, you can be lazier. You can beat around the bush, decorating your words with popcorn strings and colorful lights and butterfly wings — all manner of ornamentation. What's an extra word here or there when you've got *thousands* to work with, right? When you have a limited word count to work with, though, every single word counts.

But even if you're writing a novel for children, that doesn't mean your words should work any less hard. For example, instead of writing your paragraph like this:

> The orphanage was a gray place, with gray walls, a gray ceiling, water-stained gray floors, gray furniture, and even a sort of grayishness floating in the air. The children themselves, possessing a gray pallor, seemed to emanate an unhappy gray mood.

You may consider instead:

> The orphanage and its inhabitants were gray as rain. The floors, the furniture, even the children seemed muted and colorless.

Although the first example explains the dismal context, setting a mood and letting readers know that the even the orphans themselves (the characters) are unhappy, it is too wordy, using 41 words to say and accomplish what half do just as well. Why does the writer get to keep that rewritten, tightened sentence in the book? Because it sets up the context where much of the plot takes place; therefore, it contributes to plot development. The writer can defend it because there's a specific, defensible reason for it — so it gets to stay.

Children's books have typical word counts for each format. Because of these word-count expectations, the shorter the work, the more carefully you have to build your plot and your characters. Whatever excess verbiage you have *must go.* Here's a trick we use: If you find yourself overwriting because you are having trouble expressing exactly what you mean, sit back, say what you mean aloud to yourself, then try writing it again. Another trick is to read your work aloud; often this will help you tell if the writing really works.

Additionally, check overuse of adjectives and adverbs, and eliminate long, descriptive passages. Go through every sentence of your book with a fine-toothed comb, always seeking to tighten, to replace a weak word with a more evocative one, to eliminate redundancies. It's hard work, but it's so worth it!

Here is Lisa's trio of Rules for Revisions: A sentence or paragraph doesn't deserve to stay on the page if doesn't:

- ✔ Flesh out a character
- ✔ Build a plot through action
- ✔ Develop a context

Out it goes. Goodbye.

Keeping your chronologies in order

Time is a constant. But when sequential timelines are violated with no clear and apparent milestones, or when time becomes unclear or loses its grounding in reality, then readers get lost. And a lost reader is not a happy reader.

For example, if you had your main character bunny speaking to his teacher before he goes to school that day, you have your chronology of events out of order. We don't mean to sound like a broken record, but an action outline like the one we describe in Chapter 8 is a great way to make sure your beginning, middle, and end (and all the important plot events in between) are in order.

Removing assumptions

Often writers assume their readers understand what they're writing about, without really thinking about whether that's likely to be the case. Perhaps they use jargon or refer to a lesser-known historical event. The end result? Your reader feels left out in the cold.

Make sure you clarify any subjects that by their nature might be confusing or obscure just as soon as you mention them in your text. For instance, any subject too advanced for a three- to eight-year-old child in a picture book has to be treated with kid gloves and made abundantly clear.

Here's an example: If you're writing about a child who turns into a plant during the day because he's exposed to sunlight, and you throw in the word *photosynthesis,* make sure to define it in context with simple words that do not create any more confusion by adding more complex words into the definition. "As the sun beat down upon his head, Shane could feel photosynthesis happening in his body as the leaves pushing their way out of his skin reached toward the nourishing light to feed them and make them grow."

Need to know vocabulary lists or your state's core curriculum to know what subjects kids are familiar with at each grade level? Just search the Internet for "[state] core curriculum K–12." For lists of national reading vocabulary words for grades 1–5, e-mail Lisa at `EditorialServicesofLA@gmail.com`.

Formatting: First Impressions Matter

If you don't make a good first impression, your manuscript will likely get sent right back to you accompanied by one of those dreaded rejection letters. (See Chapter 17 for advice on dealing with that nasty but inevitable part of a writer's life.) The key to a good first-millisecond impression? A well-formatted manuscript. Editors see a gazillion manuscripts every day, and the sight of certain common errors makes them sigh with impatience. With so many resources available to writers of children's books, it seems crazy to submit anything other than a clean and well-edited manuscript.

Although all publishers and agents have submission guidelines, some more detailed and specific than others, there is generally accepted formatting that is expected. We walk you through this standard formatting in the following sections.

Some additional tricks to impressing editors? You may think it goes without saying, but you'd be surprised: Never send something that shows the signs of an argument you had — and lost — with your printer's ink cartridge. And for goodness' sake, don't forget your complete contact information on your manuscript *and* in your query or cover letter.

One surefire way to irritate editors — and sentence your submission to the scrap pile — is to use fancy fonts or typesetting. Avoid colors, bigger letters (known as drop caps) on the first words of a new chapter — all that fun stuff you see in finished books. These are decisions made by page designers and art directors at a later stage. Right now, all they do is distract from the story you're trying to tell.

Including the proper information on the first page

Every manuscript you send must go out with complete contact information on the first page, as well as the title of your book and the word count (see Figure 13-1). The number of words, combined with the information in your query letter (which we explain how to craft in Chapter 16), will immediately indicate to the editor or agent whether you are submitting an entire picture book or the first three chapters of an epic YA.

Lisa Rojany Buccieri
1234 Some Street West
Some City, California 90000
310.555.1212
Editorialservicesofla@gmail.com

Words: 10,000

THE VAMPIRE HARE THAT ATE ROOM 35

Chapter One

Blah blahdeb lahblah blahdeblahblah blahdeb lahblah blahdebl ahbl ah blahdebl ahblah blahdeb lahblah blahdebla hblah blahdebl ahblah blahde bla hblah bla hde blahb lah.
        "Say what?"
        "Ditto that. Huh?"
        Yet more blahdeblahblah blahdeblahblah blahdeblahblah blahdeblahblah blahde blah blah blahdeblahblah blahdeblahblah blahdeblahblah blahdeblahblah blahdeblahblah blahd eblah blah blahdeblahblah blahdeblahblah blahd eblahblah blahdeblahbla blahdeblahblah blahdeblahblah blahdeblahblah blahdeblahblah blahdeblahblah blahdeblahbla blahdeblahblah.

Figure 13-1:
A sample first page of a manuscript submission.

Whether you're writing a board book, a picture book, or a chapter book, the title of your book needs to be centered and in all caps, and you need to have two line spaces (or one double space) between it and the first line of text. And speaking of the first line of text, it must always be flush left. The only difference between a board book or picture book submission and a chapter book submission is that you add a centered chapter header under the title on the first manuscript page, and on the first page of every subsequent chapter.

Neither repeat your name under the title with a "by" line, *nor* do you need to indicate what kind of manuscript it is (for example, "A graphic novel by . . .").

Printing your manuscript

Although your local printing and office supply store likely now offers a rainbow of textured and fluorescent paper to choose from, along with a dozen different bindings, embossing, debossing, and sparkly calligraphic glitter pens, just say no! All these embellishments do is distract from your work. Let your manuscript wow editors, not your attempt to blind them with fluorescent paper. Your submission may look plain — perhaps even homely — to you, but your unadorned, fully edited, and deftly polished manuscript will look simply beautiful to the publishing pro who receives it. This goes for electronic submissions as well. If your agent or editor allows electronic submissions (many still do not), you still need to format the document you attach to your e-mail according to these conventions.

Following children's book formatting conventions

Ready to become a formatting pro? Then be sure to pay close attention to the following children's book manuscript conventions. (Your agent and editor will appreciate that you did!)

- ✔ Print your manuscript on 8.5-inch × 11-inch regular 20-lb. printer paper in black ink only.

- ✔ Use 12-point Times New Roman or Arial font (unless the publisher's submission guidelines indicate otherwise).

- ✔ Double space.

- ✔ Turn off the function that takes an entire paragraph at the bottom of the page to the following page if the paragraph is split between two pages.

- ✔ Make sure the *first line only* of story text on the first page — and of every new chapter or scene break — is flush left, *not* indented. Every new paragraph thereafter gets indented ten spaces or one hit on a tab. Do not use your space bar to make the spaces. Publishers also prefer that you *not* use the Document Ruler in Word, instead letting the Word program indent the document those five spaces internally so the entire document is consistent.

- ✔ Your text area page margins should be formatted with one-inch margins all around (top, bottom, right, left).

- ✔ Make sure your headers begin on page two by choosing "different first page" in your document layout.

- ✔ Make sure your pagination is continuous by creating automatic page headers starting at the top of page 2. Do not use your footers for any content whatsoever.

Your header starting at the top of page 2 should look like this. Choose the same font as you use for the manuscript for both the text *and* the numeral — with the following content filled in and your page numeral flush right by tabbing after your last name till you reach the right margin and then clicking on the # icon in your Formatting Palette:

BOOK TITLE/Your last name only 2

For example:

THE VAMPIRE HARE THAT ATE ROOM 35/Rojany Buccieri 2

Notice the title is in caps, the slash closed up, followed by your last name starting with an uppercase and then all lowercase, finally the page numeral flush right.

✔ Now make sure you have a line space after your header *inside your header* so that there is extra room after the header so it's not sitting right on top of your story text. Now close the header space. You're on your text area again and ready for the next step.

Headers are important because they allow you and others to keep track of your pages. If the editor loses a page on her desk and finds it later, she'll know where it belongs because the header identifies your book's title and you as the creator. Also, if you are having a conversation with her, you can reference the page number in the header to make sure you are both on the same page.

✔ Do not justify your text. This is only done in finished books, not manuscripts.

✔ Don't add art directions to your text unless you're illustrating your own book. (*Art directions* are notes to the illustrator indicating what image should be illustrated and where it should be placed in relation to the text.) Your words need to stand on their own, evoking strong images in the reader's mind without any prompting. If you need to explain what the editor or agent should be seeing in his mind, then your words aren't working.

Wondering whether you should include images in your board or picture book submission so editors get the meaning of your text? We help you figure that out in Chapter 14.

Presenting Your Pre-Submission Basic Grammar and Style Primer

Although many publishing houses have their own in-house style or grammar guides stipulating how to treat serial commas or ellipses or em dashes (don't panic yet, we cover them), the following primer will guarantee you a manuscript that's clean enough to impress any nit-picking editor — even if she later changes it to reflect the publishing house's style choices.

For more detailed advice on writing style and grammar, check out the short (but absolutely right on) classic, *The Elements of Style* by William Strunk, Jr., and E. B. White (MacMillan Publishing Company). Hey! Did you notice that the second author of this seminal work is the very same one who wrote the children's classics *Charlotte's Web, Stuart Little,* and *The Trumpet of the Swan?* See? You can be both a very creative writer *and* a formatting and grammar pro.

Punctuation

Punctuation consists of periods, commas, apostrophes, question marks, quotation marks, plus dots, dashes, and all manner of little doohickeys too numerous to list here. We're just going to throw in a few of the most common errors of punctuation:

- ✔ **Watch your commas.** Use a comma only to separate two sentences joined into one, which is called a compound sentence, or for making meaning clear when you cannot rewrite to do so. Commas aren't used just because you paused in your typing or because you feel like it. There are lots of specific rules for commas, but the most important is that you use a comma to separate two sentences that could be complete sentences on their own. A complete sentence's structure looks like this: subject + verb + object. Notice how this sentence separates two complete sentences from each other: Little Bear ate a lot of honey, and he went to sleep soon after.

- ✔ **Put ending punctuation inside quotation marks.** Whether it's a question mark, an exclamation point, or a period, they all fall inside the ending quotation mark when writing dialogue. One of the only exceptions is when you're quoting a quote and exclaiming about it or questioning it. For example: "Did you hear her ask, 'Does Little Bear deserve any honey after that temper tantrum?'? She actually asked him a rhetorical question! A two-year-old bear!"

- ✔ **Use single quotes only inside double quotes.** For example: "Did you hear her say, 'Little Bear is never, ever, ever getting any more honey?'"

- ✔ **Use the correct ellipses.** *Ellipses* are used to indicate pauses, usually in dialogue. An ellipsis should look like this: . . . with spaces evenly throughout. The period, exclamation point, or question mark at the end of a complete sentences is not part of the ellipsis. Here's an example of an ellipsis in action: *"She couldn't have . . ." he said, surprise rendering him speechless.*

Style

Style is simply how *you* write. Style involves issues in which you have choices in both your approach and your execution.

- ✔ **Stick with closed-up em dashes.** *Em dashes,* which are the length of two dashes, indicate interruption and lists. Keep your em dashes close to the text instead of adding spaces. For example, say *Rabbits, guinea pigs, mice, hamsters, fish, turtles, dogs—all the domestic animals you can imagine lived in Chloe's house* rather than *Rabbits, guinea pigs, mice, hamsters, fish, turtles, dogs — all the domestic animals you can imagine lived in Chloe's house.*

  Even though it's more common *not* to use spaces, each publishing house's style guide is different, including our book's publisher, John Wiley & Son, Inc., which is why you see spaces surrounding em dashes throughout this book.

- ✔ **Indicate a range of numbers with en dashes.** An en dash is longer than a dash and shorter than an em dash. Here's an example of it in use: *Everyone who would ever matter on Planet V was born 1964–1970.*

- ✔ **Turn off word breaks.** *Word breaks* — which is using a dash to break up a word at the end of a line of text like this: manu-script — should not appear in a children's book manuscript. Let the page designer worry about breaking words at the ends of lines.

- ✔ **Stick to hard text breaks in a chapter book manuscript.** Hard text breaks are actual page breaks from one chapter to another. You have to manually insert them according to your word-processing software's specifications. Don't rely on hitting the Enter or Return key until you cross over into the next page to get the job done. Additionally, if you don't have hard text breaks, revising means reformatting your manuscript every time you make changes — a huge time-waster.

- ✔ **Follow the rules for numbers.** Spell out numbers under and inclusive of ten and use numerals for 11 and up. Don't mix both in one sentence. And if you have a bunch of numbers in a sentence, remember that the majority wins: If more of the numbers are under ten, spell 'em all out; if more of them are 11 and over, use numerals. The exception is dialogue. Always spell out numbers in dialogue, no matter how large or small they are. And never start a sentence with a numeral.

- ✔ **Pay attention to hyphenation rules.** Only hyphenate numbers that modify a following word (as in, one hundred *not* one-hundred *unless* one-hundred feet). Similarly, time isn't hyphenated unless the numeral is hyphenated (so that's two thirty *not* two-thirty *unless* two thirty-five). Last but not least, don't hyphenate someone's age unless it modifies a noun (so seventeen year old *is not* seventeen-year-old *but rather* seventeen-year-old girl).

✔ **Use serial commas.** A *serial comma* is the comma that appears before the word *and* or *or* in a string of three or more verbs, adverbs, adjectives, nouns, or parallel phrases. For clarity in children's books, we use serial commas to separate more than two objects in a list and to help children keep things straight. For example: *Mrs. Bornhoeft leaned over Genevieve's desk, picked up the pencil, tapped it on the desk until the child awoke, then turned away in a huff.*

In this section, the main thing to take away is that consistency is king. If you choose to put spaces before and after em dashes, do so throughout the entire manuscript. Same goes for spelling out numbers and using serial commas. With so many differences in style guides and house styles across publishers, there's no one correct way to style a manuscript — though Lisa would insist otherwise!

Miscellaneous

Here are some additional common mistakes:

✔ **Don't mix up *which* and *that*.** *Which* is used for a sentence with a modifying phrase that could be deleted and still leave the sentence's meaning intact. If you can take away the modifying phrase and still give the same amount of information you were trying to get across, use *which* (and put a comma before it). Otherwise, use *that* — but only if you have to. Using *that* too often can sound clunky.

✔ **Eliminate lazy words and passive words.** Vague words such as *it* and *thing* don't really do much for your story. Neither do "to be" verbs. Get rid of as many of them as you can.

✔ **Delete said tags.** *Said tags,* such as *she said* and *he said,* tell the reader who said what. You may think you need them, but you really don't unless there are more than two speakers in a scene of dialogue. Trust us.

✔ **Don't start every other sentence with *But* or *And* or *However*.** Old-school editors still hate that, and doing so has not been a regular part of American English usage for long enough to gain acceptance among the literati — or at least those who fancy themselves as such. Once in a while is okay.

✔ **Indent for a new paragraph each time you switch speakers when writing dialogue.** Each speaker gets her own indent, no matter how short or long her speech. And if you have to use a speech tag or body language, join it up with the speaker's dialogue.

✔ **Always spell check your document.** Be sure to run your word-processing software's spell check feature — even though it isn't always correct. When in doubt, find a good online dictionary or thesaurus. Never wing it if you aren't sure. That's just plain silly and makes you look like a bear of very little brain.

✔ **Use contractions in dialogue but not the narrative.** Contractions are and should be used in dialogue, because that's just how people speak; however, in children's books it is preferable not to use contractions in the narrative. The only exception is when you are writing in the first-person point of view in a very conversational style or when to eliminate a contraction would unnaturally torture the English language.

✔ **Vary the rhythm and length of your sentences.** Mix up long and short ones. Break up description with dialogue. If you use the same monotonic pattern — *First I did this. Then I did that. Then she did this. Then we did that.* — your manuscript reader will start to get bored and turned off by the lack of spark and variation.

✔ **Address parents and other adults with Mr., Dr., Ms., Miss, or Mrs., as appropriate to their elevated station above children — at least in age.** To do otherwise is to put parents and children on the same level, which is inaccurate in children's books. When referring to parents in particular, use a capital letter when the relationship is used in lieu of a name and a lowercase letter when preceded by a pronoun. For example: *Mom is an expert quilter. Everyone knows my mom spends her weekends quilting up a storm.*

In kids' books, children are the stars, the main characters, the ones we are supposed to get to know on a first-name basis. It will be confusing to the reader if you throw out first names for adults like you do with children. Adults can speak to each other using first names, but kids should not use an adult's first name — and neither should your narrative.

✔ **Don't rely on shortcuts for emphasis.** If you find yourself **bolding,** *italicizing,* USING CAPITAL LETTERS, or lots of punctuation!!!!, then your words aren't doing their job. You need to choose your words more carefully so that any emphasis is indicated in your word choice, NOT *these* **amateurish** shortcuts!!!!

✔ **Do not have names that sound alike in one manuscript.** As a matter of fact, do not use names that start with the same letter, letter sound, or diphthong. And don't switch from a proper name to a nickname and back again willy-nilly. Readers get easily confused — more importantly, so do editors.

✔ **Don't just jump from one scene to the next without a transition indicating a change in place or time.** Put it this way: How would you feel if someone you were engaged in a deep conversation with at work on Wednesday were to simply disappear (Poof! Gone!) in the middle of speaking — and show up three days later in your bedroom to continue where she left off? Don't treat your reader this way, either.

✔ **Watch tense changes.** If you are telling a story in the past tense, stay there. You cannot switch tenses in books for readers 12 and under and only do so at your peril for young adult readers. It requires significant skill to alternate different points of view in different time frames. If you're a first timer, leave the tricky stuff for your sophomore effort.

Hiring an Editor or Editorial Service

After you've rewritten your story and edited it, you may need a professional editor or editorial service to check overall large elements of your story — such as plot, character, structure — or to address final smaller (but no less important) issues — such as word choice, grammar, and formatting — to ensure you're ready to submit your manuscript to an agent or publisher.

An *editor* is someone who corrects, finesses, and polishes a work at different levels of complexity to prepare it for publication. An *editorial service* can simply constitute one editor's business, especially if she offers many different services (such as proofreading, line editing, and ghostwriting), or it can be a business composed of several editors with expertise in different areas.

Before you can choose someone to work with, you need to know exactly what kind of service you are seeking. Following are the different types of services you may be interested in:

✔ **Book doctoring:** Rewriting, editing, and fixing a manuscript that has already been written. Usually done digitally.

✔ **Line editing:** Going through a manuscript from start to finish and editing every line for every issue from grammar, spelling, and style to drama, pacing, characterization, and anything in between. Usually done on a hard copy of the manuscript or using a track changes tool for a digital document.

✔ **Copyediting:** Type of editing that involves mostly fact and grammar checking; usually used for nonfiction books.

✔ **Read-through and evaluation:** A general, overall reading of the work for its literary merits (or lack thereof) that points out the major flaws needing to be addressed without necessarily telling the writer how to go about executing them in detail.

✔ **Ghostwriting:** When an editor or writer writes or thoroughly revises an original manuscript from start to finish and isn't credited on the book, but does get paid and often shares in the royalties — or gets a nice flat fee.

✔ **Proofreading:** Checking one printed version of a book against another printed proof of the book to make sure it doesn't have misspellings, nothing is missing, images correspond to text, and all the edits were performed as indicated. Side by side, the two proofs should mirror one another after a proofread.

✔ **Literary consultations:** Consultations between a seasoned writer and an editor can determine the literary merits of a work in progress. These can range from a read-through of the work and a citing of general impressions to more involved editing for character development to complete line editing. Before the manuscript is ready for submission, the editor and writer exchange it back and forth a few times so that the editor can check that the author has executed the feedback. Sometimes the author even involves the editor during the publication process to help with the edits mandated by the publisher.

✔ **Writing coach:** Service offered by an editor who acts as editor, teacher, and mentor to the writer throughout the entire publishing process. A writing coach may work one on one with the author or may lead a writing workshop. Unlike a critique group in which every member participates equally, the workshop leader may do most of the critiquing.

Choose line editing if you aren't sure what kind of editing you need. Line editing covers every type of editing your manuscript might possibly need to make it the best it can be — and it usually comes with a detailed critique letter to help you accomplish what the editor suggests.

The following sections help you find potential editors or editorial services to work with and help you narrow down that field with the right questions.

Ultimately, your experience with an editor or an editorial service should be fun and informative. You should walk away from the process with specific ideas and methods for making your manuscript the best it can be and the secure knowledge the money was well spent — regardless of whether the manuscript ultimately sells. A good edit will avail you of the type of information about writing and editing you can use again and again.

Finding a good editor or editorial service

When you are in the market for a professional editor, you need to do some homework before you hire someone. This may be a labor of love for you first and *then* a business transaction, but no matter how much the editor ends up loving your work, editing is a business for her. And just like financiers do their due diligence on companies they want to buy or invest in, you need to do yours regarding your choice of editors.

These are the issues we think you ought to consider to get the most out of your experience:

- ✔ **Find a professional children's book editor.** Children's books have different requirements than adult books. You want someone who has at least ten years under her belt as a children's book editor at a reputable children's book publishing house with published books containing Library of Congress numbers, books that have been sold in bricks-and-mortar bookstores, and can be located in a walk-in library.

  Children's book writers can find a list of freelance editors who have been verified for professionalism at www.scbwi.org.

- ✔ **Ask whether your editor published her own children's book or two.** If so, you can assume that she's had experience on both sides of the line: editing and being edited. An editor who is also a published writer knows what it's like having words critiqued and may carry this sensitivity into her work with you.

- ✔ **Find out what the editor's clients and colleagues say about her.** Look for quoted accolades or awards on her Web site or on the Internet. You want someone who is spoken of highly by at least a few industry professionals who can be reached by e-mail for verification. (For more on referrals, see the next section.)

- ✔ **Inquire about your editor's education.** Although university education shouldn't make or break your decision (a few editors are self-taught or may have been mentored by the best in the business), knowing your editor has a passing familiarity with quality written material through the ages is a comforting feeling.

- ✔ **Find out how much the editor charges.** Some charge a per-page rate of $2.50 to $5.00 or more, and some charge by the hour. Others charge a flat-rate minimum to start and then more money depending on how many pages there are in the manuscript. Some charge a per-project fee, specific to the length of the manuscript and the stage of writing or editing it is currently in. Some offer professional discounts for repeat customers, published authors, or members of certain organizations. Only you can determine the kind of editing you need, how much you can afford, and what price is fair.

  To avoid any price surprises later, give your manuscript to the editor before she quotes you a rate. Not all manuscripts are alike, even if their word count is similar. The writer's writing style, previous experience, and formatting all affect how much time is needed to edit a manuscript. So it's important for the editor to peruse your manuscript before giving you an accurate price quote.

Most editors don't require contracts, but they do require up-front payment in full with the understanding that they return any *underages* (money not used) with the manuscript. You can expect to be called or e-mailed to approve any *overages* (more money required to complete the job because of an unintended miscalculation on the part of the editor regarding how much time would be involved or the writer's decision to add more services to the tab).

Some editorial services list one editor's credentials to bring in business and then send out the work to some other editor. Check to make sure you're getting the services from the person whose credentials are listed and that your work isn't being farmed out to a subcontracting editor without your knowledge. Or if it must be subcontracted out, make sure you have the right to approve the subcontractor.

Asking the right questions

Asking the right questions before you hire an editor or editorial service helps ensure that your experience goes more smoothly and that there are no misunderstandings about the work that is to be done. Following are some essential questions to ask the editor or editorial service you're about to hire. (Whether the answers please you depends on the services you've decided you need.)

- ✔ Do I get a written evaluation or critique letter along with manuscript comments? (These are very helpful because they offer guidance as to how to go about making the changes suggested by the editor on the manuscript itself, but critique letters also add to the cost.)

- ✔ If I have questions, do I get to talk with you for free after you send back my edited manuscript? (Usually the answer is no.) If not, can I e-mail you questions (preferably in bulk as opposed to one e-mail at a time) regarding issues I may be unclear on?

- ✔ Do we correspond by e-mail or phone? (Mostly likely e-mail is faster than the dreaded game of phone tag.)

- ✔ Do you charge for a pre-editing phone consultation or a face-to-face meeting? How much?

- ✔ Are you willing to work digitally with a track-changes edit and commentary? Or do you edit on a hardcopy printout?

- ✔ How much do you charge for editing or reviewing my revisions? (Two separate processes, by the way.)

✔ Can you provide a client list or a few referrals that I may contact by
e-mail or phone? (A must when a writer is performing his due diligence
on an editor.)

✔ Do you give any discounts for members of professional writing organizations, published writers, need-based clients, or repeat customers?

The editor should also specify what *formats* (types) of children's books he
has been paid to edit. (Refer to Chapter 2 for more on formats.) If an editor
indicates a preference or a predilection for editing a particular format, such
as middle-grade books or picture books, consider that information in your
decision-making process.

Whatever you do, do *not* send out an NDA (non-disclosure agreement) to an
editor to sign before you send your manuscript for an estimate. Professional,
credited, respected book editors do not steal ideas; they help articulate those
ideas and make them better. If you are worried about copyright protection,
see Chapter 17. If you have done your homework on your editor, you should
trust that she is trustworthy. Chances are she doesn't have the time much less
the inclination to steal ideas because what would she do with them? Submit
them and risk getting caught and destroying her reputation and thus her
entire business? Seriously, it's like using a nanny cam: If you sense you need
to set them up all over the house, you have not found the person trustworthy
enough to leave your children with. So move on.

Digital versus hardcopy edit

Did you know that in most cases it takes much longer to line edit a book via
the Track Changes feature in a Word document — and is, therefore, more
expensive while not necessarily benefitting a writer who wants to learn how
to write well?

Hardcopy line editing (actually printing out a manuscript and working on
actual paper) is often preferable for a writer compared to a digital edit for
quite a few reasons:

✔ With a hardcopy edit, the editor can focus on the words as they appear
in sequence and in context, meaning that the big picture is always visible and not broken up with a lot of distracting editorial commentary on
the pages on the screen.

✔ A page of a printed manuscript is not riddled with the changed colors
or marginal notes that result in a document edited using track changes,
which in turn can disrupt a writer's understanding and absorbing the
process of a linear edit. And isn't the purpose of getting an edit in the
first place for the writer to learn more about how to write well — and
ultimately edit himself?

✔ With a printout and the suggested edits marked on a hard copy, a writer must make changes to the manuscript himself. On a digital edit, the editor likely makes the change or does the revise. Do writers read all the little track changes comments and learn from them? From what Lisa has discovered, not so much — the writer is too interested in getting the fixes made and moving on to the next step: submission. As well, the error may be corrected, but the writer has not learned *why* and will likely repeat that mistake.

✔ When the writer has to make the changes himself, he ensures the manuscript stays in *his voice,* not the editor's. It's too easy to just accept a digital change that reads well; it's much harder for a writer to discipline himself to go in and think about the editor's suggested edits (because *all* meaningful content edits are *suggestions*) to make sure the voice remains consistent — and many beginning writers may not yet even recognize the change in voice or writing style.

✔ Sometimes, on a digital document, an editor can get carried away, revising or editing in a way that the writer does not like or decides does not feel right. What if the writer likes part of the suggestion and not all? It's much faster for a writer to decide what to accept and input the change as he likes it as opposed to cutting and pasting bits and pieces in a digital document, highlighting separate pieces to accept, and deleting multiple unacceptable changes, or accepting all and then re-editing. (We get tired and frustrated just thinking about it.)

✔ With a printed copy, the writer always has a document with all those brilliant suggestions that can be referred to again should the need arise. For instance, what if you lose your hard drive and have no backup, silly? Or the disc to which you copied your manuscript gets damaged? Or the cloud that automatically backs up your computer goes mysteriously offline or "loses" your digital documents backup in cyberspace? Or that latte gets dumped on your keyboard, sneaking in and shorting out your motherboard? (Lisa has an entire list of Doomsday scenarios she can share, but she does not want to scare you back into using a pen and paper — which has its own list of potential Doomsday scenarios.)

✔ Printed books still represent the reading experience most people grew up with and are accustomed to. Reading on a tablet, computer, or phone provides a different experience than reading an old-fashioned hardcover or paperback. And while many folks do both, most authors aspire to printed copies of their book to establish perceived "legitimacy" as published authors. Note, however, that with the proliferation of e-books and self-publishing (see Chapter 18), this statistic will change within this generation as electronics assume increased saturation of the market. Besides, your actual children's book target audience has likely had electronic devices at their fingertips since birth, which is why most publishers now release the e-book version simultaneously with the printed version of a book.

Editors don't agent, and agents don't edit

One piece of misinformation shared by many new writers is that their professional editors should *agent* them (represent or sell their book to publishers) after the editing process or refer them to a particular agent or publisher.

In our opinion, charging a client for an edit with the promise of a referral to an agent or publisher is unethical. If an agent charges a client for an edit prior to or as part of representation, this practice is also unethical. Although many editors may have a list of professional agents they refer clients to, and agents may choose to refer new clients to certain respected editors, no money should change hands between the agent and editor — it's called *double dipping* and it's largely frowned upon. (See Chapter 16 for more about agents.)

An independent editor and an agent are two separate but equally important parts of a writer's life — and should remain separate. Use The Society of Children's Book Writers and Illustrators (www.scbwi.org) to research agents. Membership in this organization allows writers access to a list of agents willing to take on new clients. Again, be sure to do your homework, because some agents don't accept all formats, may be on hiatus regarding new clients, or may specialize in a format different from yours (fiction versus nonfiction, young adult novels versus picture books). The Association of Authors' Representatives (www.aar-online.org), to which your agent should belong, provides a canon of ethics for all its members.

Chapter 14

Creating Pictures from Your Words: The World of Illustrations

● ●

In This Chapter

▶ Looking at the pros and cons of illustrating your own work

▶ Getting your art in front of the right people

▶ Understanding an illustrator's process in creating art

▶ Paying someone to illustrate your book if you're self-publishing

● ●

As an author, how do you get your book illustrated? Should you get illustrations before sending the book to an agent or publisher? If you're not an illustrator, how do you find the right one for your book? And if you're an illustrator, how do you get considered for illustrating jobs?

This chapter gives you answers to those questions, even providing a detailed interview with an experienced art director and book designer, but here's the bottom line: If you aren't an illustrator, you shouldn't illustrate your book. Simply said, bad or amateurish illustrations turn off editors and agents in a big way. And turned off editors and agents aren't in the mood to represent you or buy your story. Even if a story is well written and may very well be the Greatest Children's Story Ever, there is a chance it will get rejected solely because of the recipient's reaction to subpar art.

In this chapter, we talk about illustrating or not illustrating, the steps of illustrating from sketch to final color art, and hiring someone to illustrate your book if you are self-publishing.

To Illustrate or Not to Illustrate

Nothing surprises new writers more than this: Unless you're an artist with lots of artistic talent, you shouldn't be illustrating your own manuscript. Nor should you bother paying or contracting with someone else to do it. Period.

Seriously. We're not joking. Amateurish illustrations make your manuscript look unprofessional. They also distract from the words. And if the editor likes the words but absolutely hates the illustrations (or vice versa), he's likely to reject both because the assumption is that the writer and illustrator are already connected and to rip them apart would invite a host of complications best avoided.

If you're a talented illustrator as well as a writer, congratulations, you're a rare breed indeed. But are you really as talented an illustrator as you think you are?

It's tough for a writer trying to break into illustrating, too, to determine whether he has the requisite talent and skill. If you're already agented, you can get feedback from your agent — trust us, if you *are* indeed good, the agent stands to make just that much more money off of your endeavors and thus should give you an honest, experienced opinion. But if you're not agented, how do you figure out whether you're good enough to risk submitting your art with your manuscript?

Three words: Get. Professional. Feedback. Why? Because you can't answer this question on your own. Professional feedback doesn't mean paying someone to pat your back or run away screaming in horror. It means getting your work in front of art directors and designers and editors at children's book houses via portfolio reviews at book conferences *before* submission. (For more on this tactic, see the later "Getting Your Art Seen by the Right Folks" section.)

Recognizing Why You Should NOT Hire an Illustrator

Editors like to pair up authors with their own choice of illustrators. They choose someone they believe can add yet another dimension to your words with images, truly complementing and completing your work. Your editor may choose to pair you, an unknown writer, with a known and recognized name illustrator to help sell the book. Or perhaps she wants to pair you with a newbie illustrator who has just created a style she thinks will take the world by storm. Maybe she has been waiting for just the perfect writer to pair up with her most favored and beloved illustrator. Whatever her decision, it's hers to make.

Chances are you, the writer, will never even meet the illustrator during the publishing process unless you two decide to reach out and make the effort to communicate on your own. After you and your editor have worked together to make your words the best they can be and your manuscript goes into the process of being turned into a book at a publishing house, you will most likely not see your words again until they appear in print. We discuss more about this process in Chapter 17. But suffice to say that editors tend to keep their authors separate from their illustrators.

Leave the art to someone else

Glenn Murray is co-author, with William Kotzwinkle, of the bestselling *Walter the Farting Dog* (North Atlantic Books), a book that took a lot of detours before it finally found a publishing house. Glenn recommends that you leave the illustrations to the publisher if you aren't an artist yourself. Read on and see why.

WCBFD: Your collaboration with an illustrator, prior to finding a publisher, on your bestselling book, *Walter the Farting Dog,* was an exception. What have you learned since then about how most publishers work?

GM: One thing I notice is that many writers of children's stories are unaware that most publishers don't want you worrying about the artwork. Publishers have editors and art directors and designers in house to handle the images and do not necessarily want or need your input as the writer. Publishers also often choose experienced illustrators who understand the process as well as page design, formatting, and all that. I have found that most authors and illustrators have never met or talked — all arrangements were made through the publisher's art department and the editor in charge of the project. Editors seem to like it this way, but most novice writers don't understand this. Novice writers feel they need to submit a whole package [text and art] and don't realize that they are making unnecessary work for themselves and possibly limiting the potential acceptance of the manuscript.

WCBFD: What else have you learned since you wrote that first *Walter* book?

GM: I've also learned an awful lot about the legal relationship between authors and illustrators [who pair themselves up prior to submission] that most people don't realize — why, for instance, if you insist on submitting art with your story that you might want to simply contract an illustrator with a flat fee rather than offer them a percentage. And I've met a few other children's authors who've had hassles later on from contractual arrangements they made early on with wide-open but ill-informed eyes. On the other hand, there are some author/illustrator partnerships that bring themselves together before submission that last happily for decades. So go figure.

WCBFD: So what would you tell a writer if she is considering finding an illustrator prior to submission?

GM: You just need to write a good story and get that story to an editor to read. If the editor likes it, she'll know what to do with it.

We know you have images in your mind of how to bring your characters to life. Unless you're a professional illustrator, though, keep them to yourself. Board books and picture books (formats that always come with pictures) are really half the job of the author and half that of the illustrator. An illustrator can't be restricted by the author's ideas of what the pictures should be. You may be surprised what professional artists will come up with.

Word people (as opposed to picture people) often assume no one will ever be able to create images as unique and creative as their written stories. But artists often see the world in a slightly different way (how could they not — they even favor the opposite side of the brain from word people). And these differences often interpret words in the most astonishing and gorgeous manner — one a word person might never have envisioned.

Walking through the Illustration Process

So the publisher has accepted your manuscript for publication. Congratulations! Your picture book is slated for publication about 18 months in the future. Why so long out? Because it needs illustrations, design, and pre-production work — all before it goes to the printer, gets checked and corrected a few times, and makes its way back as a bound book.

Illustrations! Great! Yet another skill for you to master, you think. But you would be wrong. Unless you're an author and illustrator in one, whose self-illustrated manuscript has been purchased; or a powerhouse oft-published writer, then you, the writer, are pretty much out of the process for now.

After your manuscript is in house at the publishing company, the art director takes over. She and the editor in charge of the project get together and discuss possible directions for the art. Artists are considered, agents of the shortlist of preferred illustrators are contacted, and a decision is made. After an illustrator is hired, he follows a specific process to deliver the art to the publisher. First, if requested by the art director, he draws some concept sketches — quick drawings that demonstrate where the illustrator sees the project going. Next come the black-and-white pencil drawings, followed by the finished color art and completing the various bits and pieces the publisher might require. Often, the cover is left for last.

Tim Bowers is a multitalented, award-winning, *New York Times* and *Publishers Weekly* bestselling illustrator with more than 30 children's books to his name. Illustrating in styles as diverse as those found in *Memoirs of a Goldfish* written by Devin Scillian (Sleeping Bear Press) to *Fun Dog, Sun Dog* written by Deborah Heiligman (Amazon Children's Books), Tim Bowers agreed to share with us his particular process for illustrating the picture book *It's a Big World, Little Pig* written by Kristi Yamaguchi (Sourcebooks Jabberwocky).

Starting with black-and-white pencil sketches

Tim Bowers, like most illustrators, has a three-prong process with pencil sketches. He starts with black-and-white pencil sketches. Figure 14-1 shows a spread in *It's a Big World, Little Pig* in which the main character, Poppy, has just arrived at a new place and is feeling very nervous.

Depending on the art director and editor's reaction to the sketch, Tim may be given the go-ahead, or he may be given change notes and then allowed to proceed to step two: pencils.

Figure 14-1:
Sketch from
*It's a
Big World,
Little Pig.*

Written by Kristi Yamaguchi, illustrated by Tim Bowers. Reprinted courtesy of the illustrator © 2012 Tim Bowers.

On the publisher's end, after the artist has started sketches, the book designer usually starts putting together a preliminary design of the book's pages. She lays down the text for each page in a size and font and *leading* (space between the lines) appropriate to the readership (though it might change, it serves as a space holder for now). Then she places the sketches on the pages as they come in so the editor can start to envision what the final book might look like when the color art is in. The benefit of starting page design early is that if changes in the images are necessary, they will become apparent right away, *before* color art has been created, saving everyone time, money, and the inevitable headache of crunching right up to the edge of a deadline — or missing it altogether.

Moving on to finished pencils

After he completes sketching out the entire book, Tim proceeds to the second step: pencil drawings, also known as "pencils." Although he prefers to create one, cohesive piece of art at every stage, his publisher with *It's a Big World, Little Pig* asked that he create the foregrounds and backgrounds separately at both pencils and final art stages in order to allow for repurposing and splicing of the illustrations in animation sequences and apps for tablets and smartphones. Figures 14-2 and 14-3 show the background and foreground of one spread in *It's a Big World, Little Pig.*

Figure 14-2:
Background
finished
pencil from
*It's a
Big World,
Little Pig.*

Written by Kristi Yamaguchi, illustrated by Tim Bowers. Reprinted courtesy of the illustrator © 2012 Tim Bowers.

Figure 14-3:
Foreground
finished
pencil from
*It's a
Big World,
Little Pig.*

Written by Kristi Yamaguchi, illustrated by Tim Bowers. Reprinted courtesy of the illustrator © 2012 Tim Bowers.

Creating color art

The final prong of the illustration process is creating the color art. In *It's a Big World, Little Pig,* Tim works with acrylic washes on Bristolboard. In other words, he paints with very thin washes of acrylic paint, adding layers of color and saturation as he goes, leaving the opaque areas last. As he renders with more layers and more color, the object being illustrated is given more dimension and depth.

Tim creates distance and contrast between the foreground and the background in his drawings by muting the value contrast of the background (lighter lines, less saturated color, less definition) to allow the foreground to take center stage.

Recognizing the importance of the right cover

If a picture's worth a thousand words, then a cover is worth all your advance and royalty put together and multiplied — if it's done right. We don't care what anyone says: *Everyone judges books by their covers and makes his or her buying choices accordingly.*

The cover of a picture book is a free for all with the most important job of all: selling the book in the space of a nanosecond. Sometimes some portion of the lettering on the cover is hand drawn to marvelous effect. Text can swirl or curve, animate or morph. It can set the tone for the whole book. In the first book in his series, *Dream Big, Little Pig,* the publisher, Sourcebooks, created hand-drawn lettering for the final cover instead of choosing a pre-existing font. As Tim Bowers observed, this choice was made "to soften and feminize the cover."

If a children's book cover doesn't grab a customer's attention in a microsecond and hold onto it long enough for her to pick up the book, then it has failed in its job. A good cover is

- ✔ Full of personality — especially of its main character, if shown
- ✔ Representative of the interior both visually and emotionally
- ✔ Surprising
- ✔ A teaser, making you want to either open the book or at least turn it over to read the *sell copy* (an incredibly seductive paragraph, usually on the back cover, that captures the essence of what the book is about without giving away the ending)
- ✔ Unusual enough to stand out from the crowd

Figure 14-4 is Tim's final cover art, featuring the book's main character in *It's a Big World, Little Pig*. Notice how much personality, movement, and verve are encapsulated in this one piece of spot art. In Figure 14-5, notice how the hand-drawn lettering, the ample white space, and the other elements come together to sell the book in the final cover. And yes, the celebrity author's name is prominently placed.

Although beginning writers almost never get cover approval written into their contracts with publishers, getting to have input early on in the development of a cover is a gift. Take it if it is offered; but never insist on it unless you are contractually entitled.

Figure 14-4:
Cover art prior to design from *It's a Big World, Little Pig.*

Written by Kristi Yamaguchi, illustrated by Tim Bowers. Reprinted courtesy of the illustrator © 2012 Tim Bowers.

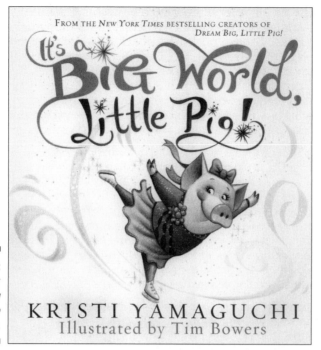

Figure 14-5:
Final cover
of *It's a Big
World, Little
Pig.*

*Written by Kristi Yamaguchi, illustrated by Tim Bowers.
Reprinted courtesy of the illustrator © 2012 Tim Bowers.*

Getting Your Art Seen by the Right Folks

Making sure your art gets in front of the right people — namely, the art directors in publishing houses and the in-house book designers who actually put together all the pieces of a book — is pretty easy if you're already signed by a literary agent who also represents artists or an *artist's rep* (an agent who specializes in representing illustrators). In this case, you will likely be asked early on to create samples of your work for the agent or rep to send around to all her contacts.

If you don't have an agent or an artist's rep, you need to do a little more work to get your artwork seen by the children's-book-powers-that-be. Fortunately, you have a few options:

- **You can arrange face-to-face meetings.** If you happen to live in New York City, perhaps you can make appointments with every person who will answer your call so you can set up a face-to-face portfolio review. Good luck with that.

✔ **You can send out full-color portfolio postcards.** Unlike a complete portfolio containing everything you've ever illustrated, a portfolio postcard is a two-sided full-color postcard highlighting a style or two at which you excel. In other words, it's a sample percolating with all the personality and skill you infuse into your work. You can then do the research to get these directly to all the art directors and designers at publishing imprints around the world. Believe us, they are just as interested in discovering new talent as you are interested in being discovered — and hired.

Many art directors use shortcuts to determine whether an illustrator can handle the usual objects assigned to create art in a children's book. Some of these include having the illustrator draw a child's face, a child's body, an infant (in its entirety), or a domestic animal (think puppies or kitties). Include samples of these in your portfolio postcard. And if you can send images from different perspectives (from the front, at a three-quarter angle, from the character's height-challenged perspective), then you're even more ahead of the game. When the art director or book designer sees your postcard, he'll be focusing on your skills rather than questioning whether you can deliver.

✔ **You can attend writers and illustrators conferences and sign up for portfolio reviews.** You may have to pay a small fee, but an art director or book designer will sit down with you, go over your work, and discuss it in detail with you. This kind of face-to-face feedback with a professional is absolutely worth every cent — assuming you've vetted the venue and the participants, making sure they provide the professional, experienced audience you seek. (For pointers on picking worthwhile conferences and workshops, see Chapter 15.)

In any meeting with someone who is there to give you specific feedback on your work, *listening is key.* Listen to hear which pieces of your work stand out and ought to be considered calling cards. Listen when an art director suggests your work might be less derivative if you went instead in this direction or more on trend if you went in that direction. Listen to the criticisms that will constructively aid you in bettering your work and your chances of being hired.

✔ **You can add some additional information about you as an artist to your query letter.** We explain how to craft a creative query letter in Chapter 16. Here, we focus on what you can include about yourself:

• Has your art ever been published? Where?

• Do you have a formal art background? From which school(s) or super-famous mentor(s)? If you mention someone non-artist types may not know, supply enough information so the unknown schools or mentors can be researched online. Name dropping should be used judiciously.

• Are you flexible and open to art and text suggestions, both minor and major?

- Do you take art direction well?

- Are you open to having someone else illustrate your text or to illustrating someone else's words? This can double your chances of getting a contract from a publisher who likes your art and will keep the text from being rejected if the editor likes the words but not the pictures.

You need to try your best to keep your query letter to one page; sometimes; however, you must exceed that limit by an extra sentence or two listing your illustrating credentials. But as with writing well, *showing* is always more effective than *telling.* Maybe leave out some of the verbiage and *show* your talent with fabulous portfolio postcards we mention earlier in this chapter.

Book dummying for the author/illustrator

A book *dummy* is a booklike sample of what your book pages look like with text and illustrations in place. Its purpose is threefold: to showcase both your story and your art; to demonstrate that your text can support different illustrations on each page or spread; and to pull together the entire vision you have for your book. Author/illustrators sometimes submit color photocopies of a book dummy to accompany their manuscripts (never send out the original or only copy). Although art directors generally find book dummies to be overkill (color art samples from the artist's portfolio normally suffice to represent the artist's style or styles), sometimes an editor may ask for a book dummy if she thinks the manuscript and illustration samples together show promise.

We're in the green camp when it comes to book dummies. Submitting hard copies of your manuscript along with a few color samples of your art is enough to give an editor and her art director an idea of where you are headed. If an editor asks for more samples or a book dummy, then feel free to comply. Why waste more trees for the initial submissions process?

However, just in case you're asked to provide a book dummy, we don't want to leave you hanging.

A complete picture book dummy would consist of all 26 pages and a front cover suggestion — or if you are good at designing the entire page, then endpapers and the titles and copyright pages, too, to take it up to 32 pages. Not all pages have to be full color; some can just be black-and-white pencils or sketches to show where you are going. Make sure to include your contact information on the dummy itself in case the query letter gets lost or misplaced. And *paginate* (put page numbers somewhere on each page) no matter what.

The cleaner and more professional your work looks, the more likely you are to get taken seriously. Make sure the dummy is complete and doesn't look rushed — even pencil illustrations can look finished and well thought-out. If you can put together a book dummy on your computer, you'll probably save yourself lots of time regarding multiple submissions. If you are creating one by hand, make sure your pages are clean and no paste-up glue remains; no smudges or corrections are obvious; and copies of your art are clean, cut evenly, and on sturdy paper that doesn't wrinkle or rip easily.

Handling Art When You're Self-Publishing

Lots of writers and writer/illustrators these days are opting to self-publish instead of going the traditional route of submitting directly to agents, publishers, or art directors. Although we cover the ins and outs of self-publishing in Chapter 18, there are some special considerations when it comes to self-publishing an illustrated book. If you've taken on the role of the self-publisher and are working on an illustrated children's book, consider the following tips:

✔ **Find an illustration style to match your story.** There are as many ways to illustrate a book as there are to write it. Look at already published books and see how various illustrators realize their styles. Decide on a few that you like.

✔ **Find an illustrator.** If you have ample resources, you can track down the exact illustrator whose style you like and inquire as to her interest, price, and availability. In the event your funds aren't overflowing, you can take the example of a style you love and use it to find other, hungrier illustrators who create art in a similar style.

✔ **Research.** Go to both online and real-world venues where children's book artists hang out and promote their wares. If you can't find anyone through the Society of Children's Book Writers and Illustrators (www. scbwi.org), you can check out art colleges, book conferences, or the annual comic book convention in San Diego. In addition, artist's reps are listed in sources such as *Children's Writer's and Illustrator's Markets* by Alice Pope (Writer's Digest Books) and *Literary Market Place: The Directory of the American Book Publishing Industry* (Information Today) and usually have online artist portfolios you can peruse.

✔ **Put together a written agreement.** Before contacting the illustrator, decide whether you want to pay the illustrator a flat fee or partner with him, sharing in the proceeds (and hope that he is amenable or willing to negotiate). After you agree on fees and basic scheduling, you both should sign and date a contract, which usually involves hiring an entertainment or publishing attorney and should cover, at minimum, the scope and quantity of illustrations to be produced (how many sketches, pencils, pieces of color art, and corrections will be considered reasonable); formatting instructions, including size, black-and-white versus color, and so on; any pre-production preparation of art; the book design and layout fee (if both parties are splitting the cost, irrelevant if not); the total amount to be paid the illustrator (for example, a flat fee or an advance against a portion of the book's royalties); a schedule for payment; whether the illustrator will transfer or retain rights to the illustrations — and be specific regarding which rights; and a schedule for delivery of sketches, pencil illustrations , final color art, and any corrections.

Although we aren't sure what to call it, an element that's just as important as a contractual agreement is the *feel-good mojo* between you and anyone you work with — especially someone with whom you partner to realize your lifelong dream in book form. We have heard too many nightmare stories of authors and illustrators partnering with each other in the heat of the moment without getting a feel for each other, or establishing clarity on the items just delineated, or really taking the time to consider a project before jumping in. Get references and ask pertinent questions about working with that person *before* you hire him or her.

✔ **Establish open communication.** Open communication between the two of you about what you both expect in terms of your involvement in the illustration process and its details ensures you start off on the right foot — and stay there. One way to make sure you're on the same page is to create a sample page together — another reason spending time on sketches up front will save time and heartache later in the illustrating process.

✔ **Pay attention to the details.** Here's a checklist for what makes good art great:

• The images not only complement the text, but also provide spark and personality, earning their space on the page. Some illustrations may replace text; others may add an all-important layer of deeper meaning. Regardless, each page or spread has to come alive with an exceptional interpretation of an active part of the story.

• The images employ different perspectives from page to page, focusing on different aspects of the main character and taking place in different parts of the scene or context of the story.

• There's consistency from page to page, spread to spread, regarding characters and backgrounds (if a shoelace is untied on the first page, it should remain so throughout; if your main character's eyes are hazel, better make sure they don't turn blue all of a sudden).

• The images also incorporate variety. There is nothing more boring than viewing inherently the same illustrations throughout an entire book. Intersperse spot art against a white background with a spread of full-bleed art here and there. Give us the world as it appears from a short person's point of view (POV) looking up instead of always *us* looking at *them.* Give us three-quarter views and aerial perspectives instead of just front and side views.

Although different illustration styles require different focal characteristics, all must have that little something that appeals to children — be it charm, personality, simplicity, sweetness, humor, quirkiness, or plain old goofiness. Good illustrators (and good publishers) pay attention to all of these issues as well as to each and every minuscule detail.

Interview with Allison Higa, art director and children's book designer

Allison Higa is an art director and designer of children's books with experience in novelty books, as well. She has worked in house at Intervisual Books/Piggy Toes Press and Golden Books, and now manages a flourishing free-lance business at Allison Higa Design. She can be contacted at www.allisonhigadesign.com or ahigadesign@gmail.com.

WCBFD: OK. So the editorial team of the publishing house has agreed to acquire a manuscript for publication. When do you come into the process?

AH: For a printed publication, the editor will contact me with a brief description of the project and a time line to determine my availability. In many cases, the projected release date is barely a year from the current publishing season (either fall or spring), which means turnaround times for the design stages are fast and furious!

WCBFD: What does the designer do, exactly? Aren't the story and illustrations the substance of the book?

AH: Yes, absolutely; however, if you look at any book, even a traditional, flat children's book, you'll be amazed to discover any number of elements which neither the writer nor the illustrator wants or needs to deal with. Take the front cover, spine, and back cover. They often require elements such as a series title, a "burst" treatment such as, "Over 10 Million Sold Worldwide!", the age suggestion, credits, and sell copy, not to mention the very important publisher's logo, price, and ISBN numbers and barcodes.

WCBFD: The editor supplies this information to you?

AH: Yes. But one element the illustrator might have a hand in (with the editor's direction) is the title type treatment. The editor might decide the title would be fabulous in a hand-drawn style unique to the book or series. All of these elements, whether hand-drawn or not, must be designed into an eye-catching cover to stand out among hundreds of others in the racks of bookstores or online.

WCBFD: That's the cover design, then. What about the interior pages?

AH: A designer does that all. She may also need to lay out the endpapers if there are any and compile all of the pages into a digital paste-up for the printer, using consistent fonts, page numbers, spot art, and so on. In these days of digital paste-up, it's often the designer who doubles as the production artist, spending long hours at crunch time — when the files are due at the printer — checking art file placements, making any last-minute copy revisions, and uploading the files to the printer's server. The designer is usually involved at the proof stages as well, as he/she can spot technical or artistic issues.

WCBFD: Is that process any different for a novelty book?

AH: I would estimate, from my experience, that as much as a designer is involved in a flat book, his/her involvement is doubled for a novelty book. This is because a novelty book generally has 3-D elements. Even a flat book packaged with add-ons (bottle caps, face paint, stickers, and so on) usually needs a box to house those add-ons. Therefore, the box needs a 3-D template from the printer or production house because, hopefully, all of these specs have been figured out long beforehand, given the high cost of paper and manual labor. And that box template needs art and text, even if it's just a flat color picked by the designer. If it's art the illustrator will do, then he/she needs that template sent to them with art direction. And believe me, those little pieces of art are SUPER tedious for the illustrator to do after creating multiple, full-page, creativity infused pages under a time crunch. Therefore, some hand-holding and extensive encouragement are often useful at this point. Novelty books are definitely a collaborative effort among art director and designer and illustrator!

WCBFD: What's the process for a client who comes to you for art direction *and* design with a manuscript for self-publication? Can you tell us how that works?

AH: If the client does not have an illustrator in mind, or even if he/she DOES but doesn't know how to go about hiring this person, then I would also take on the role of art director. I would try to source that illustrator or one with a similar style, working within the client's budget and the illustrator's output schedule.

Sometimes an illustrator will agree to do one illustration first, perhaps Spread 1, for approval before being hired for the entire book, and if so, it should be outlined in the contract. I should mention that although I empathize with new writers and self-publishers, I discourage any artistic endeavor done "on spec" — shorthand for "on speculation," which means that a creative person does something for free with the understanding they will be hired for the entire job if it goes through. Designing on spec is also frowned upon by AIGA, the professional association for design. Spec work hurts everyone, really. As a client, you want to work with someone who values his/her own work and has pride of ownership.

Art directing aside, for me the design process is not really different between a self-published project and a publisher-backed one. But the work ethic is. I personally work better under stress and timelines — don't we all surprise ourselves with how much we accomplish when we're forced to? I would say, if you're going to be a publisher, then act like one. Have a budget in mind to offer to your designer and illustrator. If you're thinking of offering a

percentage of sales (just like a publisher would offer a royalty), then outline this clearly in your signed agreement. Have a timeline with defined endpoints, so that everyone can collaborate on their schedules.

In my design career, I've done my share of *pro bono* projects and projects at the "friend rate." But there's a difference between a designer doing volunteer time at his child's school by designing a library logo, and a designer working for months on a book design as it goes through several stages and revisions. You have a great manuscript idea? Awesome! Build your business with professional, mutually respectful relationships and you may soar.

WCBFD: What about design and art direction for an e-book? Which platforms, beyond giving a template for the cover art and design, allow the introduction of creative page design and illustrations throughout the manuscript?

AH: Currently, it appears that most e-books suffer from an inability to easily display large illustrations along with text, especially text overlapping the illustrations. More often than not, you may end up with a squared-off illustration with text flowing above and below it — and its text that wrapped over from the previous page and no longer matches the illustration. (This is often a function of font sizing options in certain electronic devices.) Also, it is difficult to get type to show on curves or in any other whimsical manner. In other words, at the moment, e-books are great for 400-page novels in ePub; not so great for illustrated children's books.

WCBFD: What is ePub?

AH: ePub is an open standard of e-book used by Apple (iOS), Barnes & Noble (Nook), and many other makers of e-book readers. (**Note:** At the time this was written, Amazon has decided NOT to support ePub in the next version of their Kindle; however, ePub files can be converted for use on the Kindle.)

(continued)

(continued)

WCBFD: So a beautifully illustrated children's e-book is not possible yet?

AH: It IS possible to create what are called "fixed layouts," which means the spread ends up looking very similar to what you'd expect it to. The best current formats of this are simple board books with full-bleed illustrations and text kept in traditional rectangular paragraphs in a consistent area of the spreads; however, even this simple layout involves a learning curve: coding.

WCBFD: A fixed layout page sounds like a PDF. Why not just create a PDF? Why learn to code? This will add time and cost to an e-book.

AH: A fixed layout ePub is much smaller in file size than a PDF. When dealing with rich content like children's book illustrations, loading and refresh rates are dramatically faster and storage requirements are greatly reduced with a fixed layout ePub.

WCBFD: Ugh, HTML coding to format correctly for the web. Writers want to create inspirational words and magical settings. This is a big enough undertaking just by itself! They don't want to bother with dry, boring numbers and symbols.

AH: If the writer doesn't want to learn to code, there are companies like Lulu that will take their Word document and turn it into an e-book for a fee. But this is for text-only books. For illustrated books, keep an eye on `www.smashingmagazine.com` for a heads up on when the format limitations are eventually overcome. Then they'll be able to pay someone a lot of money to make the children's e-book they envision.

Vook will translate your files across formats — and they will also take a percentage of sales — but how they handle images is another question.

But if a self-publisher can accept the challenge of learning to code, then a whole new creative experience could await. Can you imagine? Links to real-life maps are hidden inside fantastical ones. Audio and video files can be embedded into pages so that characters "speak" when double-tapped. (Maybe in Mandarin!) These enhanced e-books exist already, but it's important to remember the content has to be truly germane to the reading experience and not just bells and whistles for the sake of bells and whistles.

Perhaps the best design direction I can give is this: Don't try to force the flat book page into the e-format. Instead, use the e-format to take readers to a *different* visual and instructive place.

WCBFD: Do you recommend writers illustrate their own books?

AH: Writers should illustrate their own books only if they are already artists. I've seen hundreds of samples from amateur illustrators — even from ones with agents. Some of them are not technically proficient, some of them are obviously copied from other illustrations, and most of them don't fit the children's books prerequisite of being beautiful, cute, funny, whimsical, and/or sometimes-gross-but-not-too-offensive. Tim Bowers's illustrations DO fit that prerequisite (except the gross part). His illustrations are evocative, humorous, a visual delight — and exhibit a level of skill no amateur can duplicate. Art directors can recognize this full-scale talent in an artist's portfolio right away; editors know just as well what the real thing looks like.

Chapter 15

Finding Feedback and Encouragement

*A*lthough the words *practice makes perfect* certainly ring true in the writing profession, *every* writer can benefit from candid feedback and constructive criticism from others. Most writers do plenty of rewriting and editing before their stories ever make it to an agent or an editor at a publishing company. (Chapter 13 discusses the revising and editing processes in detail.) But even producing multiple manuscripts doesn't change the fact that having someone else take a look at your work brings a fresh perspective that can lead to invaluable improvements in the manuscript.

So where's the best place to get feedback? When should you get it? And from whom? In this chapter, we answer all these questions and more by focusing first on the most common source of outside feedback — friends and relatives — and then moving on to writing conferences, workshops, and writing groups.

Feedback is the breakfast of champions, and good, timely feedback can make the difference between a story that is merely so-so and one that knocks the socks off everyone who reads it. And guess what? Good feedback can make the difference in whether your children's book ever finds its way to a bookstore shelf.

Recognizing When to Seek Feedback

We writers get very close to our work. How can we not? We become enamored with the words we write. We pour our feelings, research, desires, and dreams (not to mention our neuroses and ignorance) into our work. And after the manuscript is printed out, it *feels* so final, so hard copied, so finished. But it's not. Skipping out on feedback can mislead you into thinking that a less-than-perfect manuscript is ready when it's not.

Feedback is a very powerful tool, but because it introduces the possibility of being criticized for personal failings or shortcomings in the writing skills department, many people do everything they can to avoid it. Keep in mind that criticism, when given constructively, is a very good thing. The right feedback can help you hone your story, making it more compelling and powerful (and sellable) in the process.

Using different sources for feedback as you revise exposes you to a variety of perspectives. We suggest where to go for feedback throughout the rest of this chapter. Here, we give you our suggestions for when to get feedback throughout the writing process:

- ✔ **In the beginning:** You may not have any words down on paper, but in the beginning you have an idea — an idea of what your story is about, where it will take place, who (or what) will be in it, how it will progress, and how it will end. Before you've written a word, you can get feedback on your idea from others to find out whether it is derivative or novel, intriguing or limp. This early feedback lets you know whether you need to develop your idea further — or toss it aside and move on.

- ✔ **After you've written a few pages:** Getting feedback after you've written a chapter or five can help you identify major story flaws before you go too far down the wrong path. Trust us. You don't want to be that writer who's so turned on by a particular idea, so convinced of its inherent greatness, that he huffs, and he puffs, and he knocks out a complete book manuscript in several days or weeks of nonstop, caffeine-fueled laptop love — only to receive a response that's on the low end of the Richter scale after showing his manuscript to his agent.

  An alternative to getting feedback on your first few chapters is to take your outline and character bibles to a group feedback session and spend some time discussing their merits. There are pointers on finding and working with writing groups later in this chapter.

✔ **When you're stuck or uncertain:** If you're unsure about whether a particular scene, dialogue, and so on is really working, get some feedback on it. If something doesn't feel right to you, chances are it won't feel right to others, and it's good to get that confirmation. Then again, you may just be overthinking the matter. The only way to get some perspective is to ask for it!

✔ **After you've completed the manuscript:** Before you send your manuscript to an agent or publisher, get it critiqued. As the other old saying goes, you only have one chance to make a first impression; getting feedback on your manuscript before it gets to an agent or publisher is the best way to ensure that the first impression you make is the best one.

What questions should you ask to get the feedback you need? If you have a complete manuscript, check out Chapter 13, where we talk about the most important issues to check on while revising and editing. And even if you're just at the idea stage, you might still ask questions, such as

✔ Is this an interesting idea, or has it been done to death recently? If so, how can I develop a hook and take a fresh approach?

✔ Can children relate to it, or is this an idea only grown-ups will be interested in? How can I make it relevant to kids and not preachy or didactic?

✔ Is it a current or timeless topic? If it's current, how do I make sure it's not built on a trend that's on its way out or that will disappear soon from pop culture?

Do be sure to tell the person you seek feedback from exactly what kind of feedback you're looking for *before* she provides you with the feedback, not after. For instance, if you want your chosen feedback provider to critique only your dialogue, don't wait until she's line edited your entire manuscript to tell her so. Your guidance helps her focus her efforts in the direction that provide you with the feedback you seek. You have no reason to play hit-and-miss when you can clearly describe the target to the other party.

If you're the type of creator who is likely to get thrown off track if you receive feedback *before* you've had a chance to really develop your story, go ahead and use those character bibles, develop your action outline, write out a complete draft, and *then* reach out for feedback. There is no right or wrong process; there are simply elements of the process that work for many but not all writers. If you've experienced some success or are intimately familiar with your creative process through other writing endeavors, feel free to pick and choose among methods of creation (for example, hop on those character bibles after you've met your characters through some dialogue practice and toss outlining right out the window). Just be sure never to skip the feedback part of the creative process. Obtaining feedback is *never* a part of the process you can skip. And we mean *never*. (Did we emphasize *never*?)

The pitfalls of writing to trends

Trends in publishing are predictable and common. Say a book or series of books hits at the right time and the right place, is written well and tightly polished, and soars to the top of the bestseller charts. It's 95 percent likely that the idea or topic or theme isn't a new one, per se. Rather, this particular author has managed to package and present her idea in a fresh manner and hit a vein in her target audience. (Need we remind you what the Harry Potter series did for upper-middle-grade and YA fantasy or what the Twilight series did for the YA vampire and paranormal fantasy genres? A flood of riding-in-your-wake titles, that's what.)

The next first thing that happens is that every publisher dives headfirst into her pile of hidden manuscripts, contacts all the agents with whom she has a close relationship, or calls up every reliable author she's worked with in this general genre to find the next big seller just like *Bestseller X* or *Bestseller X Meets Something*

Slightly New . . . and we're off to the races to see who else can jump on that bandwagon and share in the bounty while the public is still eating up the subject. This approach works for publishers for a while — until the next big thing hits. Then the cycle begins anew.

What this means for you as a writer is . . . precisely nothing. If you try to write to a super-hot trend, chances are likely that you will not be sufficiently inspired by it to do a good job (unless you are already happily and coincidentally finishing one). If you are not, by the time you are, the wave will be over and suffering from a glut in the marketplace as well as reader exhaustion from overexposure.

The moral of the story? Be true to yourself, your interests, your creativity, your passions. Write what you will love to immerse yourself in for months or even years, and ignore the trends. They'll flit away as quickly as they came.

Getting Help from Friends and Relatives (or Not)

Many writers feel most comfortable testing their work on the people closest to them. They sit down with their children, their significant other, or their best friend's dog, and they read their manuscript aloud. And — almost invariably — they're showered with kudos and accolades (or dog licks).

After a response filled with praise, how could a writer *not* believe that he's destined for great things? But getting help from friends and relatives has its pluses and its minuses. Do the most honest critiques really come from the people who know you and care most about your success or failure as a writer? Well, unless these people are professional, published children's book writers with experience in the genre you've chosen to tackle, chances are . . . not really. The following sections present the pluses and minuses of getting reviews from family and friends, and answer the age-old question, "Should I send this manuscript to my old college pal who's now a big name in the children's book biz?"

Delving into the pros and cons of friendly advice

The good thing about having friends and relatives read or listen to your manuscript is that you get some initial feedback that's most likely going to be very enthusiastic. It's important to be appreciated and to feel that you're doing a good job, and friends and family are great at providing that kind of support. Also, if someone within that close circle is an avid enthusiast of children's literature (or has children he reads to a lot), then you may get some helpful criticism as well.

The bad thing about soliciting help from friends and family is that although they are usually a willing audience, they aren't always the most discriminating. Or objective. Or professional. Or knowledgeable. According to editors we've interviewed, the one item that leads to an almost immediate rejection of a submission is hearing the writer gush about how much the spouse, grandkids, students, or very own children loved it. Of course they did! Would any kid say he or she *didn't* like what Mom or Dad wrote? Think about that for a second.

Truth be told, pretty much every editor in the universe feels this way. Do yourself a favor: Get your material in front of a real writing group where you receive some honest and pointed criticism, or find a professional editor who can do the job. A familiar audience is fun, and you can get great initial feedback from children regarding certain parts of your story and its pacing and drama, but neither audience can give you a critique you can feel confident will pass muster at a publishing house. When in doubt, farm it out.

Having a friend in the business

If you have a friend in the children's book business, do you approach him with your manuscript? Do you take advantage of this connection for yourself or your other writer friends?

The simple answer is: Of course you do! But if you want that person to respect you, show him respect by doing a few things before you go to him for feedback:

> ✔ **Have your manuscript carefully (perhaps professionally) edited beforehand.** Yes, we know this person is your friend; but that does not mean you should not put your very best effort forward. Although you'll have to shell out some dough if you choose to hire an editorial service (see Chapter 13), making a positive first impression by presenting professionalism in your work is particularly important at this stage of the game. Would you really show up at a job interview unwashed and wrinkled? Of course not. Your manuscript shouldn't either.

✔ **Do your homework.** Research what *imprint* (publishing division) in the company your manuscript fits best with, plus the name of the editor in charge of that unit.

✔ **Ask whether you can submit a query letter and/or manuscript to the editor you found because you've done some research and think your work may prove a good fit with that editor's imprint.** When your friend's eyes widen or you hear a "Hmmmm" of intrigued consideration of your idea — not to mention a newfound respect for your brilliant sleuthing — you'll know you're halfway there. Then whip out the manuscript and the query letter from behind your back, and present them to your friend (complete with self-addressed, stamped envelope, of course). You can then turn tail and run like heck, yelling out thank-you's over your shoulder before he changes his mind. If you're super-super lucky, the stars are aligned in your favor, Mercury retrograde is not in force, Murphy's Law has failed to pass your state legislature, and your horoscope does not warn you to shut down all communications before self-immolating, your friend may even offer to present your material to the editor himself.

Granted, this approach assumes your friend in the children's book business has a few years under his belt and isn't the newly hired editorial assistant. (Yes, there's most definitely a hierarchy in publishing houses.) And even if your friend is new to the company, you owe him as much respect as you owe the veteran.

Attending Conferences or Retreats

Writing conferences and retreats are great places to go to get support from fellow writers and immerse yourself in the world of children's publishing. You can learn so much just by listening to the speakers, attending the gatherings, even lunching next to someone new. Writers, editors, illustrators, librarians, agents — it's great to be surrounded by a lot of people who all share a love and respect for children's books. But first you need to figure out what kind of feedback you're seeking and then choose a conference or workshop that can deliver just what you want. We help you determine what to get feedback on and when in the earlier "Recognizing When to Seek Feedback" section. The following sections get you acquainted with the world of writing conferences and retreats.

Exploring the conference scene

If you're turned on by the idea of writing children's books now, you can't imagine how pumped up you'll be after attending a well-run conference. Particularly for an aspiring author, being immersed in a total children's book writing experience for one exhilaratingly packed day or several days and nights can be a very heady brew indeed. We highly recommend taking a gulp or three!

Although different conferences have different aims, most children's book conferences are similar in structure in that they usually

✔ Offer presentations and workshops conducted by published authors, illustrators, or industry professionals (such as editors, art directors, public relations experts, or literary agents)

✔ Have cocktail parties and group luncheons or dinners to allow attendees to meet other writers and industry professionals

✔ Offer critique groups, portfolio reviews, or manuscript reading services — usually for a nominal fee and usually requiring submission well ahead of the conference date.

If a conference doesn't offer specific workshop sessions, manuscript reviews, or individual face-to-face critiques, you *won't* get specific feedback at the venue.

The Society of Children's Book Writers and Illustrators (SCBWI) is the largest organization of its kind, so you can find chapters of it almost anywhere in the world. SCBWI puts on a couple different kinds of conferences:

✔ **Large-scale biannual conferences in Los Angeles and New York City:** The summer conference in L.A. and the winter conference in New York are chock-full of presentations and workshops (including sessions such as "Bunny Eat Bunny: Surviving the Kid-Lit Jungle," "Drawing Words and Writing Pictures: The Art and Craft of Picture Books," and "Creating Your Author Platform Through Social Networking" — all led by top industry pros). Critique groups and opportunities for individual manuscript readings, portfolio reviews, and consultation services are a very popular part of SCBWI conferences. Early registration is available at a discount to SCBWI members. To find out about SCBWI membership and conferences, check out www.scbwi.org.

✔ **Smaller-scale regional conferences:** Each regional area of SCBWI hosts at least one major annual event. Usually these chapters cover a certain geographical area (say, Ventura and Santa Barbara, adjacent counties in Southern California). They're open to members and nonmembers — the latter may have to pay a nominally higher entry fee. Often these are day-long or afternoon events focusing on a single aspect of children's book writing and publishing, such as "Illustrators' Day" or "The Art of the Picture Book."

Conferences for the more experienced writer

As you advance in your children's book writing career, you may find it beneficial to attend industry conferences. Here are two of the big ones:

✔ **Book Expo America:** Also known as BEA, this is the biggest annual book trade fair in the United States. It's usually held in a major city in late May or early June, and is composed of nearly all the major publishers, small presses, agents, subrights buyers and sellers, service providers, licensors, even toy manufacturers and more from the United States (with quite a few international companies represented as well).

The Children's Book & Author Breakfast is a fun and interesting event to attend — if you can get in, as it sells out nearly every year. Visit www.bookexpoamerica.com/ for more information.

✔ **The American Library Association Annual Conference:** Although authors and illustrators attend this conference and even have events like book signings or presentations, it's really a trade conference in the purest sense. Its primary purpose is to give publishers and librarians an environment in which to connect. Visit http://www.ala.org/conferencesevents/ for more information.

You can find other conferences by asking around for recommendations or by typing "children's book conferences" into an Internet search engine. Just be sure to check out any conference thoroughly before you spend your hard-earned money on a registration fee. Find out the answers to these questions before committing to attend any conference:

✔ What are the credentials of the people running it?

✔ Why are they qualified to put it on?

✔ Are the headlining presenters noteworthy?

✔ Has the conference garnered lots of positive reviews?

✔ Can past attendees be contacted for their candid feedback?

Getting away with retreats

Writers' or illustrators' retreats offer another incredibly satisfying opportunity for children's book creators. Imagine spending a weekend, a week, or even a month or more away from the phone and your job and focusing on just your craft. Nirvana? To many, a writers' or illustrators' retreat can provide a setting in which creativity can absolutely flourish. Whether stimulatingly urban or country idyllic or somewhere in between, writers' retreats offer a place and time for the children's book creator to hone in on manifesting the passion you have for children's books in a meaningful and productive fashion.

As opposed to providing a zillion interesting events all competing for your attention, the purpose of a retreat is to provide a welcoming space conducive to creativity. As such, the atmosphere is calm and allows for hours of writing, contemplation, or group readings. In a retreat, you are literally and figuratively moving away from your usual life to focus on your craft. As everyone else will be doing the same, retreat organizers often set up times in which you can choose to get feedback from those willing to give it.

Consult the ShawGuides (`www.writing.shawguides.com`), or visit SmartWriters.com to find a writer's retreat that suits your tastes, budget, and time constraints.

You might also consider a retreat focusing on yoga, personal growth, spa services, or any number of themes. As long as there is time and space set aside for writing or illustrating or both, a retreat can be as simple as going away for the weekend. You can lock yourself up in a hotel room somewhere pleasant and order room service, or borrow a friend's beach house for an extended weekend, clearing your mind of clutter, and focusing on your craft without interruption.

Participating in a Workshop

A *workshop* is just a fancy name for a class or course about some aspect of the children's book writing process, usually lead by a writing teacher or publishing pro. Depending on the particular workshop you enroll in and the way it's structured, a workshop may or may not be a good source of feedback for you.

To ensure that you get the feedback you seek, consider the following when signing up for a workshop:

- ✔ **Quality of workshop leader(s):** Who is leading the workshop? If your instructor is a current bestselling children's book author or an acquisitions editor at the children's book imprint of a large publisher or an art director with dozens of books under his belt, you're likely to get much better feedback than if your instructor has only shopped around a couple of book proposals and has yet to be published.

- ✔ **Quality of presenters:** Many workshops offer informational or inspirational speakers. Are the workshop's speakers experienced or professional enough for you to spend time on your butt listening when you could be writing? If the speaker is a current bestselling children's book author or the acquisitions editor at a vibrant children's book imprint, chances are the answer is yes.

- ✔ **Length:** You're much more likely to get the quality feedback you seek in a workshop that lasts at least a day or more.

✔ **Number of attendees:** If you're jockeying for your instructor's attention along with 100 other eager children's book writers- and illustrators- to-be, your chances of getting any sort of useful feedback are greatly reduced. Small workshops of, say, five to ten people, are much more conducive to getting you the feedback you seek than the let's-see-how-many-people-we-can-pack-into-this-room variety.

✔ **Structure:** Some workshops specifically set aside time for critique and feedback of attendees' work; some don't. Be sure to take a look at the workshop schedule to find out whether feedback is a part of the plan. If it's not, you should pass.

With a plethora of workshops available around the country, we don't list any specific ones. Ask other children's book writers for their recommendations or type "children's book workshops" into any search engine.

In general, workshops are smaller and more intimate than the large national or regional writing conferences. Consequently, they offer you a much better chance of getting direct feedback on your writing from the person(s) running the workshop.

Working with a Writing (or Illustrating) Group

Have you ever read a book by an established writer, and the story seems like a good idea, but the execution is poor or the length excessive? Although an editor is ultimately to blame (for not brandishing the editorial whip no matter how famous and influential the writer), so is the writer who probably failed to get adequate feedback during the writing and revising process.

If you join or create your own writing group, chances are your fellow members will not let you get away with such sins. A *writing group* is a gathering of committed writers — typically composed of at least two members, but often more — who get together on a regular basis to critique one another's work and make it the best it can be.

Some writing groups have stuck together for years with the same participants year in and year out — insular, protective, and productive for its members. Some writing groups have members joining and then quitting every few months. Your ideal is somewhere in between.

So what better way to get feedback during the writing process than by joining a weekly, biweekly, or monthly writing group? A good writing group can shave years off the time required to refine your writing skills. A bad writing group can really set you back or derail your writing career altogether. The following sections help you find a good group to join, assuming there's one in your area; if there isn't, we help you prepare to start your own. We also explain what to do with all that feedback you receive from your chosen group.

Finding the right group

Before you can hop into the ideal writing group, you need to *find* it, which leads to the $64,000 question: How in the heck do you go about doing that?

First, try contacting local community colleges or universities that offer writing programs. These programs often have bulletin boards that list writers who are looking for other writers interested in forming a group.

 You can also check out your local chapter of the Society of Children's Book Writers and Illustrators (SCBWI). You can find the chapter nearest your home and contact the regional advisor about joining a writing group through SCBWI's Web site, www.scbwi.org.

Other resources that can help you find a writing group that's right for you include the following:

- ✔ **Writing classes:** Take a class in writing, and join up with some of the people you meet in the class.

- ✔ **Word of mouth:** If you personally know writers in your area and are friendly with them, ask whether they know of any writing groups.

- ✔ **Online writing discussion groups:** Functioning like a group chat, online discussion groups consist of writers who get together online to share ideas and offer feedback. Manuscripts are sent as e-mail attachments or posted on a Web site. The manuscripts are read by a certain deadline, and members get together online to discuss the chosen manuscript. We have certain issues with the public nature of this option, given that anyone could *potentially* steal your manuscript (unlikely scenario), but if the only time you have to yourself is during the middle of the night, participating in an online writing discussion group is better than nothing. Besides, these sites can always get password protected by the Webmaster before the event(s) take place.

 Tons of online resources can help in your search for a writing group or online writing class. But again, we urge caution: Make sure the Web site is a reputable one before committing yourself and your precious creative energies.

Take discriminating notes

In Lisa's very first writing class, being a diligent, apple-polishing, A+ student, she wrote down every darn thing everyone, including the teacher, said about her writing. And she didn't separate one comment from the other. She took notes this way throughout the ten-week class, even though she began to figure out about halfway through that perhaps not everyone's comments were as educated or on the mark as the teacher's. Alas, when the class was over, and Lisa tried to apply what she had learned, she was extremely confused as to whose advice and commentary to pay attention to — and whose not to. She had no way of distinguishing the teacher's comments from the yahoos', so she had to put aside the rewrite of her story for a good year until she forgot most of the remarks and could start from scratch. The subject matter was timely the first time around, but unfortunately, by the time she got back to her story it wasn't. So let Lisa's mistake be a lesson for you: Always take discriminating notes when you're receiving feedback in a group setting!

Starting your own group

Having a hard time finding the right feedback group? Why not start your own? All you need to form a group is one friend who wants to write (or a friend focused on children's book illustration) and is serious enough to commit to producing meaningful content and meeting on a regular basis. If you're in a class, choose a few people who impress you and seem tolerable and ask them if they're interested.

We recommend recruiting more than two members, but definitely no more than eight. In our experience, everyone eventually has something to read and wants time to share. If your group has ten members, and they each get a half-hour, your meeting lasts five hours — that's way too much time for people who are likely juggling busy careers, families, and extracurricular pursuits. A group of three to eight people ensures that enough people — and not too many — have new or revised material for consideration at every meeting.

After you have your members selected, establish some ground rules to help avert problems later on. Here are some good rules to consider:

- ✔ **Size of submission:** Limit the length of submissions covered in each session to one picture book manuscript (or its equivalent of 1,500 words max), one middle-grade chapter, or a limited number of illustrations or black-and-white sketches.

- ✔ **Type of critiquing:** Does each member read aloud and get verbal feedback? Or does each member submit a written manuscript and get written feedback? Or a combination of both? If your members do not like the idea of "homework," they may prefer simply to listen to the writer read aloud during the workshop while they take notes, offering a verbal critique at the end of the reading. If they like to read in peace and quiet, take notes, and then offer their critique aloud during the next workshop, that's also a possible approach. What's important is that all your group's members decide together how they want to conduct the critiques.

- ✔ **Required critiquing:** Does each member have to critique each submission? How long does she get to critique her peers? In most groups, everyone can participate in critiquing if they have something productive to add to the discussion. And the time taken to offer a critique is totally up to what the members consider appropriate. If a written critique is required, everyone who gets a hard copy should offer at least some comments.

- ✔ **Participant behavior:** Certain behaviors shouldn't be tolerated and should lead to dismissal from the group. For example, if a member misses a certain number of meetings in a row, the group should require that he drop out, opening up a place for a replacement. Also, there's always a member who tries to get more from the group than the others, which can cause resentment and, ultimately, dissolution of the group. Speak up (nicely) if you notice this happening.

Mean-spirited criticism, sarcasm, and *ad hominem* comments are not acceptable and do not help create a forum for open and creative discussion. Make this a basic ground rule for your group.

- ✔ **Meeting location:** If the meetings take place at the same private home, you need to decide how to deal with refreshments. Does everyone contribute a sum of money to be applied every month toward coffee and donuts? Is it BYOM (bring your own munchies)? If the group alternates between different members' homes each week, should the weekly host provide the refreshments?

- ✔ **Structure of readings:** You also need to decide whether the participants' readings or critique times will be timed in order to keep a big group from running overtime each week. How much time is allowed?

Print out the preceding list of rules and considerations and hand them out at the first meeting. Open up the floor to discussion so you can decide together how your group will work. Taking this approach allows you to get rule making out of the way quickly so feedback takes precedence. The group host or leader can create a member roster — always appreciated by members of any committed group to allow for easy group and individual communication.

Sifting through the feedback you receive

The major benefit of writing groups is that you get free feedback from the many different writers participating. The biggest potential drawback inherent in writing groups is that the feedback you receive comes primarily from other new writers who may not know any more than you do and may not steer you in the right direction. So how do you get the right feedback from the right people?

Interview with Stephen Mooser, SCBWI president

Stephen Mooser is an author and the president of the Society of Children's Book Writers and Illustrators (SCBWI). A founder of SCBWI, he knows a lot about how writers and illustrators obtain feedback. Although he runs SCBWI's biannual international conferences with Lin Oliver, the other SCBWI cofounder, requiring writers' and illustrators' physical attendance, he's also familiar with the online world of information expertise and sharing in children's books.

WCBFD: The only way to get feedback and input on your writing or your illustrating used to be by physically going somewhere, sitting down, and interacting with other children's book creators face-to-face. Is that still the case?

SM: Hardly. The Internet, of course, has made it possible to form a critique group with other writers whether a street away or a continent. But you still need to find a group you are compatible with and whose opinions you respect. I've discovered the best groups are made of people generally at the same stage of their careers and wrestling with the same problems. Sometimes putting together a group like that takes time and comes from at least initially getting to know someone face-to-face, even if just for a few days at a conference.

WCBFD: What do you know about online writing or illustrating workshops?

SM: With any online commercial business, do plenty of research before handing over any money. Look for backup information online and, if possible, talk to one or more former students. Besides online sites like Writer Beware and Preditors and Editors, I always advise people to type in the name of the business and such key words as scam, trouble, and disappointed. Finally, research any listed instructors. Well-published and respected authors are unlikely to lend their name to an institution they don't believe is honorable.

WCBFD: Are authors' or illustrators' own Web sites good places to try to get feedback if you are new at all of this?

SM: It depends. Most writers and illustrators probably don't have the time to critique your manuscript. Think, instead, about attending a local workshop or conference. Ones sponsored by SCBWI often offer critiques at a reasonable price as well as opportunities to meet fellow authors and illustrators who may be interested in participating with you in a critique group.

WCBFD: Are blogs good places to try to get feedback?

SM: Yes — I think blogs are excellent places to get in on the conversation. Spend a few hours checking out blogs by authors and illustrators whose work you admire. Links leading from these blogs can often take you to all kinds of places where you can learn about everything from the latest industry gossip to the hottest trends in young adult fiction.

WCBFD: What about online classes? How might they offer unique value to a newbie?

SM: What I like best about online classes is that they enforce discipline. Most schools, such as The Institute for Children's Literature, have top-notch faculty, but just as importantly give out weekly or monthly assignments forcing you to sit down and write. If you want to be a success at writing or illustrating, you have to be disciplined. Going to school is a good way to get in the habit of writing every day.

WCBFD: How do you judge if online feedback is good or bad?

SM: That's a hard question. It is why you need to find someone you respect, someone honest, but also someone who sees the positive and is constructive. It also means you may need to have more than one person (again, whose opinion you respect) look at your writing. Illustrators ought to attend events such as SCBWI portfolio displays to discern how their work stacks up — particularly against portfolios that tend to win prizes.

WCBFD: I know of one very motivated person who is self-taught in many different approaches and styles of art creation entirely by watching instruction videos on YouTube. Her name is Michelle and when she got Parkinson's at 37, she finally pursued her artistic dreams. While I understand this may be an extreme and unique situation, do you believe this is a viable option for beginning illustrators?

SM: Different approaches work for different people. I do know the one thing that every illustrator says is that before you can really hope to create that unique style everyone is looking for,

you must be able to draw. That probably means getting some kind of formal art education.

WCBFD: Any closing comments?

SM: No matter whether you are using online resources, reading books on writing and illustrating (illustrators should check out *Writing with Pictures* by Uri Shulevitz), or taking classes at a university, two things matter most: (1) Come up with something unique that no one has seen before, whether a character, a plot, or an art style; and (2) Be persistent. There's generally not a lot of money in children's books, but those who work at their craft and are persistent will almost always end up selling a book to a publisher — even if that takes 5, 10, or sometimes 20 years.

If you're in a writing class in which everyone takes turns reading aloud, and everyone else is allowed to comment, your best bet is to listen carefully to the teacher's comments and to take into consideration the participants in the class who consistently make solid observations. Whom you decide to listen to is a strictly subjective choice, so consider everything, but choose only what seems to make sense to you.

The difference between critiquing and criticizing is very important. When you give a *critique,* you offer well-reasoned, pointed, clear criticism with an eye to possible solutions. When you *criticize,* on the other hand, you offer a judgment about why something is bad. Writers tend to be a sensitive lot, and a critical, mean-spirited evaluation isn't helpful to the writer's creative process. So watch your tongue. You could be the one on the other end someday.

A great way to ensure you get clear feedback is to ask pointed questions when you finish reading your piece aloud to the members of your writing group. Here are some good questions for writers to make sure you get useful feedback:

- ✔ Is my main character believable here? Why or why not?
- ✔ How can I improve the secondary character(s)?
- ✔ Is my story exciting or interesting to you? Do you want to learn more or find out what happens next? If not, why?
- ✔ Is the action well paced or did you feel the story lag?
- ✔ Is my point of view consistent?
- ✔ What do you think about what the characters said to one another? Does the dialogue ring true?

✔ Does anything in particular bother you about my story/chapter/scene? Something you'd like to see improved? (Only the brave of heart need apply here.)

✔ Do you think the humor worked? (Usually the audience's response during your reading lets you know whether your humor is effective, but asking is a nice way to find out how to make something funnier if the response fell flat.)

If you're a writer-illustrator, following are some good questions for you to consider asking to make sure you get the type of feedback you need:

✔ Do my illustrations complement the text or merely compliment it? In other words, do the images add a layer of meaning, development, or humor to the text? Or are they merely representative, failing to add your (the illustrator's) personality?

✔ Are my representations of the character(s) on target?

✔ Do the beings illustrated show personality? How exactly?

✔ Are my images derivative; does my style and execution feel original?

✔ Do my backgrounds add a layer of dimensionality to the book, or are they mere clutter or settings?

✔ Do I offer different perspectives for the eye to feast on? For instance, would an aerial view or three-quarter perspective add insight and excitement? What about spot art versus full-bleed pieces interspersed for interest throughout?

✔ Are the faces of my beings — human or animal or otherwise — expressive and do their emotions register in a way that is subtle enough to be detected easily, or do I slam the reader over the head with a screaming termagant of a mother every time she is shown?

✔ Do I follow through consistently with the details of each character, place, setting? For example, same color shoelaces on the same day, same color curtains in the window of the front view of the school, and so on.

✔ Are my backgrounds competing for attention with the characters?

✔ Are there enough details in my illustrations so that a writer can delete some descriptive parts of the textual narrative?

Questions like these and others tailored specifically to your work elicit answers that you can use as opposed to criticisms that you can't. And although you aren't usually allotted the time to ask all your questions at one group meeting, asking the right ones can make all the difference when revising.

Ask people to be specific in response to your questions. This way, when your time is limited in a group meeting, you can quickly get to the heart of what someone thinks about your work.

Part V
Getting Published and Promoting Your Book

The 5th Wave   By Rich Tennant

"The margins on your book proposal are sooo even, Ms. Holly, and the type so black and crisp. I'm sure whatever the book's about is also good, but with centered headlines and flush left columns like this, we'd be fools not to publish it!"

In this part . . .

Despite its fun leanings, publishing children's books is ultimately a business, and the key players — agents, publishers, and even (many, if not all) authors — are in the business to make money. This part sets you off on the right foot in your search for an agent or attorney to help you deal with the paperwork and other legal mumbo jumbo such as publishing agreements, financial concerns, and contractual conditions.

It also gives you an overview of the publishing process and helps you find the right publisher, if that's your ultimate goal. Or you may decide to forge your own path to self-publishing success. If so, we help you explore the pros and cons of self-publishing. We also tackle the most effective ways to promote your book and get it noticed using social media (such as Facebook, Twitter, and YouTube) to spread the word.

Chapter 16

Getting an Agent to Represent You

*B*elieve it or not, children's books usually don't sell themselves to prospective publishers — you have to get your manuscript in front of the right person at the right time if you hope to sell it. There are two time-honored ways to accomplish this. One, you can engage a literary agent to sell the manuscript for you, or two, you can try sending off your manuscript yourself to acquisitions editors at every appropriate publisher you can find.

In this chapter, we cover what you need to do if you go with the first option: finding an agent. We explain where to find an agent, what to look for in one, how to get his interest in your book, and what to expect after you've hired him. We also tell you what to do if you decide to part ways with your agent. (Want to have a go at selling your manuscript to a publisher yourself? You find a bit of information on that approach in Chapter 17.)

Defining the Perfect Agent — and His Not-So-Perfect Counterpart

An *agent* (or an *artist's rep* for illustrators only) is someone who works to sell your work to a publisher. Agents may own their own businesses — working solo, or perhaps with another agent or two — or they may work for a larger agency among many other agents. Regardless, agents work on commission. They receive a percentage (usually a flat 15 percent) of the advances and royalties stipulated in your publishing contract. (If the agent has to engage the services of a subagent in order to sell foreign or other specialized rights, sometimes the commission percentage is increased up to 25 percent.)

Although you might not be too happy about giving away 15 percent or more of your hard-won publishing deal to someone else, many authors consider the price to be well worth it. Agents can work magic because they're in much better contact with publishing companies than unpublished authors are. Publishers rely on good agents to filter out the riffraff — the vast number of manuscripts that just don't make the grade and have little or no chance of being published — and present them with the cream of the crop. The best agents know exactly what children's book editors at different publishing houses are looking for, and they do their best to provide it.

In addition to a commission, your agent will probably bill you for costs that are out of the ordinary, such as extensive copying, manuscript retyping, long-distance or overseas phone calls, and overnight delivery, but you should be clear on these charges and agree on them in advance. Most legitimate literary agencies include in their regular cost of doing business (that's the 15 percent agency fee) items such as reading your manuscript; providing you with general advice on the publishing process and tips on improving your manuscript; local phone calls, fax, and computer time; and routine photocopy and mailing costs.

Your agent can be your best friend and advisor, your teacher, and your literary confidant. The relationship you form with him or her can play an extremely important role in your success as a children's book author and can last the rest of your life. If you decide to work with an agent to sell your work, be sure to get a good one. We reveal the qualities of both good agents and bad agents in the next sections.

Many of the big children's book publishers (as well as many of the smaller ones) deal *only* with agents or artist's reps. They won't even *look* at unagented manuscripts submitted directly by prospective authors.

Recognizing what good agents can do

Agents provide a vital service to authors, and a good one is well worth the fee. From advice, to hand-holding, to negotiating, good agents do a lot of work for their authors:

- ✔ Help you shape up your manuscript by offering free editorial advice or by referring you to a professional editor or *book doctor* (someone who fixes manuscripts for a living).

   That said, note that the Association of Authors' Representatives (AAR) rules stipulate that it is unethical for an agent to charge you for editing your manuscript as well as selling it; it's double dipping. If you suspect any collusion (such as kickbacks or a referral fee) between the editor your agent refers you to and your agent, we'd advise you to find more scrupulous partners in publishing.

✔ Help you find a publisher for your work by sending your manuscript to one or more selected editors, *pitching* your idea by assertively touting the general wonderfulness of your manuscript, following up to gauge interest, and then negotiating and closing the deal. An agent may also sell or license your work in other markets, such as foreign or television and film.

✔ Hold your hand through the publishing process, from manuscript to finished book and beyond. There are a variety of things to consider after a book is published, such as getting the author's rights back if a book goes out of print, or selling foreign, film, electronic, and other rights that may have been excluded from the primary publishing contract.

✔ Negotiate the terms and conditions of your publishing contract, including such things as advances, royalty rates, submission and payment schedules, rights, and much more. (We help you get a feel for contract terms and conditions in Chapter 17.)

✔ May be contractually empowered (in your agency agreement and in the publishing contract) to receive your advance and royalty payments, take their cut, and then send you a check for your portion of the earnings. In this case, they also monitor publisher royalty statements and keep accounting records of your earnings and payments.

✔ If your work is licensed to other parties, the agent may monitor how they use your work to ensure that such use complies with the terms and conditions of your licensing agreements.

✔ Advise you on standard industry practice and on new trends in the publishing industry.

Watching out for bad agents

Although we wish the world of literary agents was all fluffy bunnies, sweetness, and light, we're here to tell you that it can sometimes be ugly. Although many children's book agents and agencies are completely reputable, ethical, and honest, there are some whose primary goal is to devise efficient and effective ways to separate you from your hard-earned cash.

Real agents are paid out of the proceeds (the advance and royalties or flat fees) of your publishing agreement and the sale of any other rights. Bogus agents will want you to pay them out of your own pocket (often because they have no intention of actually selling your book to a publisher).

Definitely watch out for the following when investigating agents (and agencies):

✔ Agents who ask for money up front, before they do anything

✔ Agents who ask for a fee just to read your manuscript

✔ Agents who have little or no publishing industry experience

✔ Agencies that have been in business for only a very short time

✔ Agents who are unwilling to give you names of clients they have handled or recent sales

✔ Agents who offer to make your work saleable by editing it for a fee before the agent will consider or commit to handling it

For a general discussion of potential pitfalls with agents (and publishers, too), be sure to check out the warnings and cautions at the Writer Beware blog: http://accrispin.blogspot.com.

Finding an Agent

So you've decided you want to work with an agent. Now what? The next step is to find a great one who will not just sell your book to a publisher, but who is ethical, who will take the time necessary to properly develop your work and present it in the best light, and with whom you can develop a long-term working relationship.

Keep in mind that agents are in business to make money. This means that they're very selective about the authors they choose to work with. Many agencies receive thousands of queries, proposals, and manuscripts from prospective authors each year; of necessity they reject far more authors than they accept. If an agent turns you down, don't let that rejection slow you down, too — submit to another agent or consider submitting your manuscript directly to a publisher (a process we cover in Chapter 17).

The following sections walk you through the process of finding your ideal agent.

Obtaining referrals

Authors who are happy with their agents are usually very willing to refer you to them. So the next time you're chatting with a children's book author, be sure to ask him who his agent is, whether he's happy with her, and whether he can make an introduction for you. (Or if you've already found an agent you like, ask for a list of clients you can contact for feedback before signing any sort of contract.)

If you don't know any children's book authors, consider other avenues for obtaining referrals. Do you have a friend, relative, or acquaintance who already works with a good literary agency? Or do you frequent Internet forums where people share stories about their children's book publishing experiences? Or do you ever enroll in writing workshops led by successful children's book authors? If so, approach the people you meet who already have an agent they're using.

Literary agencies are businesses, but few advertise in a traditional way. Although they might run a small advertisement in the back of a writer's magazine, it's unlikely that you'll see an agent's face on a highway billboard or in a television commercial. Instead, agencies rely on word-of-mouth advertising as well as their own recruiting efforts to bring them new authors.

Researching your heart out

If you don't know any agents personally, or if you can't get referrals to agents, then you'll need to do some research using online agency listings or print resources.

These directories provide you with agent and agency names, addresses, phone numbers, and detailed information about what kinds of books the agency specializes in representing. Find an agency that looks like it meets your criteria, get the contact information, make sure they are accepting unsolicited (unrequested) submissions, and if they are, get in touch.

As you look through agent directories, be sure to focus only on agencies that specialize in children's books. Why waste postage? And yes, lots of agencies still prefer snail-mail submissions.

Use an online agent directory

If you have a computer or tablet handy, you may find the following online agent directories to be helpful:

- ✔ The Association of Authors' Representatives (www.aaronline.org)
- ✔ Association of Authors' Agents (Great Britain — www.agentsassoc.co.uk)
- ✔ Publishers Marketplace (www.publishersmarketplace.com)
- ✔ Agent Research and Evaluation (www.agentresearch.com)
- ✔ WritersNet (www.writers.net)

Note: The Society of Children's Book Writers and Illustrators (www.scbwi.org) provides a list of agents to its members.

Use a hard-copy agent directory

There are a number of terrific hard-copy directories for finding literary agents and agencies, including these industry standards:

- ✔ *Children's Writer's and Illustrator's Market* (Writer's Digest Books)
- ✔ *Guide to Literary Agents* (Writer's Digest Books)
- ✔ *Writer's Market* (Writer's Digest Books)

You can find these online or in most general bookstores.

Attending conferences

Agents sometimes participate in conferences and workshops to find promising new talent — some agencies even sponsor them. Because the promising new talent may very well be *you,* you should consider attending writers' conferences for the express purpose of hooking up with an agent. Here's how to increase your chances of finding a great agent at a conference:

- ✔ Check out writers' conference or workshop agendas and participant lists to see whether agents will be attending.
- ✔ Be sure to memorize your pitch and bring a few copies of your manuscript. Although it's highly unlikely an agent at the conference or workshop will ask for a copy then and there (unless you paid for a manuscript or portfolio consultation in advance), you never know.

Agents attending conferences and workshops are often very popular people, so it may be hard to corner one to make your pitch. They may be leading roundtable discussions or making presentations, plus getting pitched by other prospective authors. Get a jump on the competition by making contact with the agent via e-mail before the conference to let her know you're hoping for a minute of her time to introduce yourself. Be patient, be polite, but be persistent — eventually, you'll have an opportunity to make your pitch.

Submitting Your Ideas to an Agency

So, you've decided to try to enlist the services of an agent to sell your children's book. What next? You need to get your ideas in front of an agent. Here's how to do that in a way that will increase your probability of success.

Self-addressed stamped envelopes say a lot

Although many agents now allow e-mailed submissions, some still prefer the printed page. When you submit an idea to an agency in hard copy, send along a self-addressed, stamped envelope (SASE) as a courtesy so that the material can be returned to you if it is rejected. To save on mailing costs, you *may* consider sending SASP (a self-addressed stamped postcard — yes, we made that up) for an acceptance or rejection and tell the recipient to simply recycle the manuscript if it's rejected. On the other side of the SASP, include these five checkboxes:

✔ Loved it — let's e-mail. Here's mine: _____
_____

✔ Not my taste/area of interest — contact this agent instead:_____

✔ Needs a good edit. Try again. ___

✔ Not so much. Please lose my name and address. ___

✔ Any additional comments? _____
_____

Following submission guidelines

The number-one mistake that many prospective authors and illustrators make when submitting to an agency is that they don't first find out what the agency's submission guidelines are. Instead, they create an epic work that violates every rule the agency lays down for prospective authors — landing their work in the trash can. Don't let this happen to you. Check the agency's Web site or give a call and ask for a copy of its guidelines.

Depending on the agency's preferences, you may be asked to submit your book in a variety of different forms:

✔ A query letter (which contains a short synopsis of your idea as well as your contact information and brief biography — see the sample in the later "Perfecting the query letter" section)

✔ A complete manuscript (you have one of those, right?)

✔ Sample chapters and an outline (especially if you're pitching a nonfiction book, a young adult novel, or another longer work)

✔ A proposal (which contains a synopsis of your idea, a proposed table of contents, marketing and biographical information, analysis of competitive works, and perhaps a sample chapter or two)

After you have the agency's guidelines, make sure to follow them to the letter! And illustrators: Artists' reps also have guidelines for portfolio submissions. Find out what they are before sending out your materials.

Standing out from the pack

How can you stand out from the pack of hungry authors beating down agents' doors? Here are a few tried-and-true tips:

- ✔ **Choose the right agent for the job.** Make sure you have the agent who specializes in the type of children's book you wrote.

- ✔ **Follow the agency's guidelines.** Just following the agency's guidelines automatically makes you stand out from the rest of the competition. Visit their Web site or ask for the guidelines before you do anything else.

- ✔ **Be sure your manuscript is complete and polished to a shine before you submit it.** Either get feedback from a writer's group or a writing class or engage the services of a professional children's book editor or book doctor (see Chapter 13 for more on this topic).

Perfecting the query letter

A good query letter is short and sweet; one page should do the trick. Why? Because the point of a query letter is to give the agent (or publisher) a quick rundown on your idea, describe how it fits into the marketplace, and show some indication of your ability to write the book and help promote it. A query letter is also the first chance you have to wow an agent or publisher after you've completed your research and are sure this is the person or entity you simply must make contact with.

Lisa has a tried-and-true approach to writing query letters, and she shares this approach with everyone who asks. Here's what you need to put into your one-page query letter:

- ✔ **Greeting:** You know, "Dear . . ." then two lines down you start. Your greeting should use the respectful Mr. or Ms. prefix before the first then last name. If you've actually met the agent or editor at a conference, then, and only then, can you start the query letter with a more person-alized greeting acknowledging where and when you met and reference that person's *expressed* desire to consider manuscripts from attendees.

Never ever send group messages with the generic "To Whom It May Concern"! You don't have the time to send a personal e-mail? Guaranteed you'll not get a personal reply — if any at all.

✔ **Hook:** This is one powerful, attention-grabbing pitch sentence or two that will make the reader *want* to read the book. For instance: What would you do if your older sister was the famous, glamorous, legendary Tooth Fairy and you were just the pesky little sister no one cared about? Would you hang onto her coattails (or gossamer wings) hoping just a bit of attention will rub off on you? Or would you get inventive? Meet *Switch Witch,* a 964-word picture book about a little sister named Esme who decides enough is enough. (Yes, this is a real pitch.)

✔ **Overview:** A bit more about the book, including audience, age, format, and word count (this is not a book report or a plot summary; it is an overview of the main character(s), setting, and dramatic conflict written in the same style and tone of your captivating manuscript). It should also briefly reference why your book is different from other similar books. A sentence telling why you chose this particular agent/publisher might score major brownie points by showing you did your homework. Try to keep it under 75 words.

✔ **Biography:** This is where you convince the reader you're the best person to write the story you've summarized above. (Published writers always list their most recent books first; if you haven't been published, then *relevant* professional experience will do.)

✔ **Closing sentence:** Brief, but powerful! Just make sure you don't plead to be published. After all, they know why you're writing them.

✔ **Contact information:** Provide your phone number, e-mail, and physical mailing address.

A query letter going to an agent versus one that goes to a publisher will differ only in the research you indicate you've done that led you to choose submitting to this particular person.

Figure 16-1 shows what a query letter looks like, but be careful to tailor your letter to a prospective agency or publisher's guidelines. (You can find these guidelines on the agency or publisher's Web site or in writing if you request them from the company).

Your Name
Address
City, State Zip
Phone
E-mail

Date

Agent's Name
Agency Name
Address
City, State Zip

Dear Ms. _____:

What would you do if your older sister was the famous, glamorous, legendary Tooth Fairy and you were just the pesky little sister no one cared about? Would you hang onto her coattails (or gossamer wings) hoping just a bit of attention will rub off on you? Or would you get inventive?

Meet *Switch Witch*, a 964-word picture book about a little sister named Esme who decides enough is enough.

I have selected your agency because of your success in placing humorous, high concept, picture books, most notably your recent sale of *Tutusaurus Rex* by Ima Big Author to Chronicle Books.

Switch Witch is the story of how Esme, jobless and aimless (and not a little jealous), gets to work trying to find a purpose in life. She goes through all the other major events and holidays in a kid's life (Easter? Nope. Bunny's got that covered. Christmas? Nope. Santa and a whole lotta small guys are already up and running the toy factory.) Finally, one Halloween night, Esme realizes she could do some real good. She turns herself into the Switch Witch, the one who takes all the extra candy kids don't really need and swaps it out for an alternative after all the trick-or-treating is over. And of course she does something virtuous with all those leftover sweets!

I have been writing for 20 years. I've had three picture books published over the last five years: *Doggone!* (2012), *You Can't Pet a Pet Fish* (2011), and *Stinkerbella* (2010). All three have sold over 5,000 copies in hardcover over the first year and have been reprinted in paperback picture books for the book clubs and book fairs.

I'm a member of SCBWI, and I was a finalist this year in the SCMMWWSMW (Southern California Misguided Mommies Writing While Simultaneously Mud Wrestling) Contest.

Please let me know if you are interested in switching out this query letter for the entire, thrilling manuscript of *Switch Witch*. I have enclosed a SASP for your convenient reply — as well as a piece of leftover Halloween candy as a friendly bribe.

Thanks for taking the time to consider this query.

Sincerely,

Your Name

Figure 16-1:
A sample
query letter.

When communicating with agents or publishers in a query letter (see more on going directly to a publisher without working with an agent in Chapter 17), always make sure to identify the format of your book (we tell you all about formats in Chapter 2). In the preceding query letter, the format is identified as a picture book, allowing the agent or publisher to immediately understand your intended audience as well as the approximate page count and size of the book. It also assures that the right in-house editor will receive your submission if it gets past the first reader. And perhaps most important, it shows you have done your research and separates your submission from those of the wannabes who refer to their work only as a "children's book" (and who most likely will receive only a rejection letter in return for their limited efforts).

Managing multiple submissions

When you're first looking for an agent, it's generally okay to send your query or manuscript to multiple agents all at the same time. Just be sure you check the agent's policies if you decide to take this course. Some agents get touchy when they find out they are competing against other agents. If you send out multiple submissions, set up a computer spreadsheet listing the name of each agent, contact information, exactly what you sent, and the date you sent it. As you get responses (or not), note them on your spreadsheet.

If you don't hear from a particular agent after about two months, you can safely assume there is no interest in your submission. Go ahead and move on to the next agent.

Asking the Right Questions before Signing an Agency Contract

After you've found an agent you want to work with (and who wants to work with you), the Association of Authors' Representatives (www.aaronline. org) suggests you ask questions like these to help ensure the agent you've selected is the right one for you:

- ✔ How long have you been in business as an agent?
- ✔ Do you have specialists at your agency who handle movie and television rights?
- ✔ Do you have subagents or corresponding agents in Hollywood and overseas?
- ✔ Will you handle my work personally?
- ✔ Do you issue a standard agent-author agreement?

✔ How do you keep your clients informed of your activities on their behalf?

✔ Do you consult with your clients on any and all offers?

✔ When you issue 1099 tax forms at the end of each year, do you also furnish clients with a detailed account of their financial activity — such as gross income, commissions and other deductions, and net income — for the past year upon request?

✔ In the event of your death or disability, what provisions exist for my continued representation?

✔ If we should part company, what is your policy about handling any unsold subsidiary rights in my work?

Different agents will answer these questions in different ways, and answering one question in the negative shouldn't necessarily disqualify an agent from your consideration. But use their answers to help you make the very important decision of who will represent you and your work. And don't forget to ask other authors what they know about the agent, do a search for information — good or bad — about the agent or his agency on the Internet, or check with the Better Business Bureau (www.bbb.org).

Understanding Typical Agency Agreements

Depending on the literary agency you select, you may or may not be required to sign a written agency agreement before an agent will represent your work to publishers. Although a handshake agreement may work out fine for you and your agent, our preference is for agency agreements to be in writing. Life is complicated enough; it's always better to get it in writing. The following sections describe the standard terms and conditions that go into most agency agreements and give you tips on how to negotiate your end of the deal.

Sizing up the standard terms and conditions

A variety of terms can make their way into a typical agency agreement, including some of the following:

✔ **Scope of the agreement:** This part of the agreement spells out exactly what the agency is going to do (represent your work), where the agency is going to do the work (within your country or throughout the world), and whether the relationship with you the writer is exclusive or for a specific project (see the next section for more details on this distinction).

✔ **Duration of the agreement:** Many agreements last for the duration of a specific project — from the initial pitch to publishers until the book eventually goes out of print. Other agreements are for a minimum of one year and apply to all projects sent out during that year; after the one year it may be assumed the relationship will continue until either party decides, at will, to pull out.

Suppose you've been with an agent for over a year and really feel she's not the right fit for you. Your contract may allow you to terminate the agreement from that point on, but any project the agent has submitted to publishers and that is accepted after you terminate the agreement will still be covered under the old agreement. In other words, for any work that she's done for you on any particular book that you gave to her during the time of your agreement, your contract applies in perpetuity.

✔ **Handling of funds:** This part of the agreement spells out how funds will be handled. Typically, the agency will receive payments from publishers, disburse your portion to you within a certain amount of time, and keep an accurate accounting of all financial transactions.

✔ **Commission rate:** The amount of each publisher check the agency gets to keep for doing its job is typically 15 percent (or 20 to 25 percent for sales of foreign and other rights involving subagents) off the top before any monies get to you.

✔ **Authorization to sign on your behalf:** The agreement may contain a provision that allows the agent to sign contracts or checks on your behalf. We are personally uncomfortable with turning over that much control to an agent — we want to review publishing agreements and sign them ourselves. But as far as payments, if your agent disburses funds to you after taking his cut (typical in the industry), then it's fine for him to sign checks.

✔ **Expenses:** The agreement may spell out exactly what expenses the agency will bear as a part of its standard commission (typically, routine overhead items such as local phone calls, small copying jobs, computer, fax, employee time spent editing your manuscript and presenting it to publishers, and so forth) and what expenses will be billed against the author's royalties (typically extraordinary expenses such as overnight shipping, messengers, large copying jobs, long-distance phone calls, and the like). Avoid agents that charge reading fees. These border on being unethical and are expressly prohibited by the Association of Authors' Representatives' Canon of Ethics.

✔ **Indemnification:** Some agencies may want the author to *indemnify* (protect) them against legal claims resulting from acts or omissions on the part of the author that exposes the agency to legal claims. Such provisions are generally not in your interests, and you should consider trying to negotiate them out.

✔ **Termination:** This part of the agreement spells out the conditions that each party must undertake to end the agreement. It usually involves waiting a specific amount of time from signing, typically a year, and then allows either party to bow out, at will, in writing.

Make sure your agency agreements contain a specific mechanism for termination. It's better to have these understandings spelled out in advance — when you and your agent are cool, calm, and collected — than trying to sort out a big, bloody mess when emotions are running high.

Distinguishing between exclusive and by-project services

One question you may face when working with an agency is the issue of whether your relationship is going to be exclusive or by project. The difference between the two is major and can have a significant effect on your writing career:

✔ **Exclusive agreement:** When you enter into an exclusive agreement with an agent or literary agency, you're turning over representation for all of your work for as long as the agreement is in effect. Although this may make your life easier because someone else is worrying about placing your projects with publishers, on the other hand, your flexibility in being able to try different avenues to getting published is greatly reduced — perhaps for many, many years. On the other hand, an agent who handles all your creative work is more likely to be invested in your career in the long run and will have more incentive to sell all your projects as opposed to just one.

✔ **By-project agreement:** This kind of agreement is for one project only, including any sequels or derivative works that may spin off of the original work. Although your agent takes full responsibility for selling a particular work to publishers, you can take your other projects to other agents, or submit them directly to publishers yourself — whichever approach makes the most sense to you.

A by-project agreement can be looked at as kind of like going steady or getting engaged before you tie the knot. But to make the up-front investment in building your career from the ground up and then keeping it simmering between sales, most agents won't even offer this option. It's mostly for already-published writers who are changing directions in their writing and may not have contacts in this new area, or who have publishing agreements they already set up on their own and just want an agent to handle all the negotiations so they can get back to writing, or who are already active in the industry and for some reason have gotten to the point at which they need an agent to step in and take over the selling portion of the job.

Negotiating like a pro

As is often the case with business deals in other industries, you may find the terms and conditions of your agency agreement are negotiable. Of course, you will also find that agents will be more flexible with the terms and conditions when they really, really want you to sign up as a client.

In the mood to negotiate? Here are some tips guaranteed to turn you into a negotiating pro (okay, maybe an advanced intermediate) in no time:

- ✔ **Be prepared.** Being prepared gives you a definite advantage in *any* negotiating situation.

- ✔ **Leave plenty of room to maneuver.** When you develop your negotiation goals and positions, build in enough flexibility so that your agent can achieve his goals, *while* you achieve yours.

- ✔ **Have lots of alternatives in mind.** For every possible reason your agent gives for *not* agreeing to one of your positions, you should have one or more alternatives ready to go. For example, if your agent-to-be insists on an exclusive agreement in perpetuity, but you don't want to be locked in for more than a year, then be ready with an alternative that gives your agent the exclusivity she seeks but only for a year.

- ✔ **Keep your word.** Your word should be your bond. Good relationships are built on a foundation of trust and mutual respect. If you aren't willing to keep your word, then you'll quickly lose both respect and trust. It's okay to make an honest mistake, though — that's something that most anyone can understand and deal with.

- ✔ **Listen more than you talk.** One of the most important negotiating skills is an ability to listen — *really* listen — to the other party. If you ask the right questions and then let your counterpart talk about the answers, you'll usually find out exactly what it will take to successfully negotiate and close a deal. Don't forget — if you're talking, you're not listening.

- ✔ **Don't give up too much too soon.** In our experience, it pays not to give up too much too quickly when you're dealing with a tough negotiator. Not only will you appear weak and perhaps a bit desperate, but you'll miss out on getting any significant concessions from the other party. Take your time when you're negotiating. It's much better for *them* to be in a big rush to close the deal than for *you* to.

- ✔ **Be able to say no.** Telling someone no is a very difficult skill to acquire. Everyone wants to tell business partners yes and encourage positive relationships. However, when you're negotiating a deal, sometimes you must say no to achieve your own goals. So, if you're not happy with the terms and conditions of a proposed deal, just say *no*.

> ✓ **Pay attention to your gut.** If you can meet face-to-face with your agent during negotiations, think seriously about exploring that option. After listening, paying attention is a most important skill. How you *feel* about this person can give you an idea about your future relationship.

If you're uncertain what terms and conditions you should accept or reject, or if you're uncomfortable negotiating the agreement yourself, seriously consider engaging the services of an attorney who specializes in the practice of publishing law. Although such representation isn't cheap, you may find that hiring a lawyer will put you way ahead money-wise in the long run.

Terminating Your Agency Relationship

Entering into a long-term relationship with an agent can be like getting married — there are a lot of expectations on both sides of the aisle, and when things go wrong, breaking up can be rather like getting a divorce. But sometimes you have no choice, and breaking up isn't just the right thing to do — it's the *only* thing.

When things go from bad to worse, don't hesitate to terminate your relationship, invoking the termination provisions in your agency agreement. Typically, this would involve simply mailing a letter to the agency stating you are terminating the agreement. Your particular agreement may or may not require a certain number of days prior notice before the termination becomes effective (usually 30 to 60 days). Be sure to send the letter via certified mail, return receipt requested, so that you have a record of the mailing.

Before you break up with your agent, make sure both of you have been on the same page about the particular problem. If you have an issue to address with your agent, always try talking about it first, hammering out the details between the both of you. But if you have tried to work through whatever your issues are and truly have reached the end of your rope, then take the high road and behave like a perfect gentleperson. Get your divorce agreement in writing and then move on. Above all, be professional, be polite, and do whatever you can to avoid burning bridges along the way. The children's book industry really is a small world, and the relationship you save today may be one that will serve you well years down the road.

Chapter 17

Finding the Perfect Publisher and Signing a Contract

*B*efore you can get your children's book published, guess what? You have to find someone to publish it. In these days of self-publishing, e-publishing, and print-on-demand, you have more options than ever before to get your children's book into print. But to truly *get published* — to have a real live publisher pay you an advance and royalties, promote and market your book on its own dime, distribute your book to all the bookstores, and hire salespeople to sell your book — is truly something special. It's so special that each year thousands of aspiring children's book authors send manuscripts to agents and publishers, all hoping to be one of the lucky ones chosen to get a publishing contract.

There's no reason that you can't be a lucky one. It's all about getting the right book to the right publisher at the right time. In this chapter, we focus on identifying and approaching the right publisher to sell your book.

Identifying the Right Publisher

There are many, many publishers out there in this wide and wonderful literary world. Some are small — publishing only a book or two a year — whereas others are relative giants — publishing houses with many different *imprints* (smaller publishing divisions within the publishing house), each with its own publishing director, churning out catalogs full of books and other book-related products. Not only that, but each publisher and imprint has its own distinct personality. Some are buttoned-down and corporate, whereas others are impetuous and quirky. Some love to make a big splash in the marketplace; others cater to a distinct niche of readers.

We suggest you make a chart of the publishers you are considering, listing the imprint name, the acquiring editor's name, and the formats, genres, and subject matter (even comparative titles) they specialize in. You can expand this same chart when you are ready to submit to help you keep track of where your manuscript is, when you sent it, and what the response was.

Interview with Doug Whiteman, former president of Penguin Books for Young Readers

Doug Whiteman, former president of Penguin Books for Young Readers (and current executive vice president of business operations for Penguin Group (USA), has some pointers for writers submitting books for consideration at any publishing house.

WCBFD: You started out in the publishing business as a book salesperson and now you're running one of the top three children's publishing companies, so you know your stuff. Tell us what in a submission identifies a children's book writer as a pro who knows her stuff?

DW: That's actually pretty simple: It's all about the homework. The writer who has gone out to the stores to see what her potential competition is and who has presented her submission in a way that distinguishes it from the rest of the field gets my attention immediately. And you really have to go to the stores; simply looking things up on Amazon or going to the library doesn't do it because you need to see the space stores are giving to the various genres; you need to see the jackets against each other; and you need to see what is drawing the customers' attention.

WCBFD: In your experience, what is one of the most common mistakes new writers make?

DW: Not listening: To your editor, your publicist, your booksellers, and your readership. It's really imperative that you soak up everything you can about our business and the way things

work if you're going to succeed over the long term. And that includes advice, particularly in the editorial area.

WCBFD: Anything you'd like to rant/rave about?

DW: I wish you'd asked me this one first! I'm always willing to rant. I think the thing that annoys me most is the new writer (or veteran adult writer) who assumes that writing for children is easy, and gives me a half-hearted, half-baked submission that they'd never do for an adult book. One should come to children's writing with at least as much respect as you would for an adult project, and many would argue that it takes even more effort to connect with children. It's not easy for an adult to communicate with kids via the printed word, and all prospective writers need to remember that!

WCBFD: Do you have any pet peeves when it comes to the book business?

DW: I'd like to leave new writers with this quote from Barbara Kingsolver: "This manuscript of yours that has just come back from an editor is a precious package. Don't consider it rejected. Consider that you've addressed it 'To the editor who can appreciate my work,' and it simply came back stamped 'Not at this address.'" While submitting your work, keeping looking for the right address . . . or let someone like me do it for you!

Gathering information from the marketplace

Checking out bookstores, libraries, and online booksellers can help you gather more information about the publishers you should pursue. Hit the stores and walk the aisles to find children's books organized by overall category — fiction and nonfiction, series and award winners. Not only that, but board books have their own area, as do chapter books, young adult novels, and everything in between. Then check out the back covers or copyright pages to see who is publishing what. Doing this can help in a number of ways:

- ✔ You can compare your book to published books to see where yours fits. Then when you submit, you can mention how your book trumps the competition.

- ✔ You can find out which publishers are publishing books like yours so you can target them during the submission process (write down editor names, often found in the acknowledgements, and then hunt down their contact information online).

- ✔ You can see whether any other books approach your topic in the same way you do so you can make sure yours is different.

Perusing writer's guides and directories

Writer's guides and directories — both printed and online versions — can be terrific aids in identifying the right publisher for you *and* in giving you all the information you need in order to determine what kinds of communications the publisher prefers, along with editors' names and mailing addresses (many editors and agents still prefer snail mail).

Here are a couple of our favorite printed directories:

- ✔ *Children's Writer's & Illustrator's Market* **(Writer's Digest Books):** This book is a great tool for figuring out the best publishers to approach and how to reach them. It also includes lists of literary agents and art reps. Remember: It is updated annually, so you'll want to get ahold of the latest version.

- ✔ *Writer's & Illustrator's Guide to Children's Book Publishers and Agents* **by Ellen Shapiro (Three Rivers Press):** Another solid reference book for finding the right publisher for your work.

We also like the following online guides and directories:

- **Children's Book Council** (www.cbcbooks.org): This Web site includes a comprehensive list of all members of the Children's Book Council, a trade group representing children's book publishers. Contains publisher names, contact information, publishing interests, and brief submission guidelines.

- **Literary Market Place** (www.literarymarketplace.com): Lists publishers by subject and type of publication; sorts by specific city, state, or zip code; can help you find an editor's or literary agent's name and title; and can even help you produce mailing labels.

- **Publishers Marketplace** (www.publishersmarketplace.com): An online hub for writers, agents, jobseekers, and anyone who wants to know what's going on in the publishing trade, such as which publisher acquired what title and for how much, publishing companies in the news, and agents on the hunt for new material. Writer members can even post information about their books, offering the rights to acquiring editors.

- **Society of Children's Book Writers and Illustrators** (www.scbwi.org): Aside from offering its members an annually updated SCBWI market survey listing the names of all the major acquiring editors at all the publishing houses that choose to participate and all their contact information, SCBWI also offers a resource guide entitled "Ideas to Execution" in which it lists directories, online resources, and more.

- **Canadian Children's Book Centre** (www.bookcentre.ca): A national not-for-profit organization and registered charity, the Canadian Children's Book Centre (CCBC) was founded in 1976 to promote, support, and encourage the reading, writing, and illustrating of Canadian books for children and teens.

- **U.K. Children's Books** (www.ukchildrensbooks.co.uk/pubs.html): A detailed listing of children's book publisher Web sites with an emphasis on publishers in Great Britain.

Drafting Query Letters and Proposals

Publishers don't have time to review mountains of complete manuscripts. Instead, they require prospective authors to submit either a *query letter* (a one-page letter of introduction inviting the publisher to ask for more details about your project) or a *proposal* (a longer document providing additional editorial and marketing information about your book).

Most publishers have guidelines for how they want your material to arrive, regardless of whether you're sending a query letter or a full proposal. Always find out the guidelines and follow them to the letter. Ignore them at your own risk.

Take one of these three easy routes to getting a publisher's guidelines:

- ✔ Visit the publisher's Web site. (This is probably the best option of the three because you're guaranteed to get up-to-date information quickly.)

- ✔ Write a letter to the publisher requesting its submission guidelines (and include a self-addressed stamped envelope).

- ✔ Consult a written or online guide to children's book publishers. (We list several in the earlier "Perusing writer's guides and directories" section.)

After you know how your chosen publisher wants your materials submitted, you're ready to pull together your query letter and/or proposal. We explain how to write a query letter in Chapter 16; for guidance on crafting a proposal, read on.

A proposal is generally appropriate only for longer nonfiction books. You would never do a proposal for a board book, for example — unless for some strange reason that's how the publisher you're targeting wants board books submitted.

A nonfiction book proposal most often contains some form of the following, although many publishers (and agents) have specific guidelines for submitting nonfiction proposals. If you are submitting a requested proposal for fiction (also unusual), you may use the same elements:

- ✔ **Contents:** A guide to the contents of your proposal, not your actual manuscript. This part, like a table of contents, should just list all the other parts of your proposal — such as marketing plan, target audience, author biography, and so on — as well as the page on which each part begins.

- ✔ **Summary:** Write the sexiest, most engaging, intriguing teaser about the book without giving away the ending, much like the copy on a hardcover book jacket or the back cover of a trade paperback. Aim for no more than two pages of summary material.

- ✔ **Author bio:** This is the part about you, often written in the third person, that indicates why you are the best possible person to write this book. What are your special qualifications? What else have you published, and were any of these publications critical or commercial successes? Do you appear a lot on TV? Have a blog with tons of visitors? Have a million Twitter followers already? Don't be afraid about bragging here — but don't do it in more than one page.

✔ **Audience:** Who is your target audience? (And no, "children of all ages" is not a target audience — see formats and ages in Chapter 2.) And why will the audience you are targeting buy, keep, download, talk about, and share your book with others? What does your book offer that others of its specific ilk do not? What about it will get the Twitterverse tweeting like mad on the day of its release? You should describe your audience as specifically as possible — in one page.

✔ **Competition:** What other books out there like yours have been successful? How is yours different and unique in comparison? Be sure to identify the exact title, author, publisher, and year of release for all competitive titles you list. This part can be up to two pages long.

✔ **Marketing plan (if any):** How does your standing in the universe or in your profession or in your social life afford you — and thus your publisher — any advantages when it comes to advertising, promoting, or marketing your book? Famous friends? How can your publishers legally use those relationships? Blog with 10,000 hits a day? Have a contact in the Department of Education who can get your book in front of book adoption committees for school curricula in various states? Is this topic appropriate for foreign sales? Be specific and realistic, don't overpromise and underdeliver upon closer scrutiny, and keep this section of your proposal to one page. (See Chapters 19 and 20.)

✔ **Manuscript specifications:** This is where you note the nitty-gritty details of your proposed book: Word count or amount of pages based on a specific existing format. Number of illustrations, photographs, images, charts, and so on, will you have? Will you take care of obtaining them in the proper form and getting legal permission to use them? (The answer is usually yes and yes.) Anything special about the format you are proposing that makes it out of the ordinary (for example, if you are writing a nonfiction book about how to build miniature Victorian dollhouses and you want to include the materials to make a miniature rag doll; or if most books like this come with color photos and you want to use graphics imitating comics for the majority of the images) — make sure to mention that. Finally, is the manuscript complete?

✔ **Outline:** Tell the publisher what she can expect to find in the guts of your book, starting with the table of contents and adding a paragraph about each specific chapter's contents. Imagine a screenshot of how the entire book is organized. You don't have to marry this outline — often content and plans change — but your outline must be as thorough as you intend your book to be. It should contain section and chapter headings; beneath each heading, give one to three paragraphs explaining what the chapter contains and how the content moves the book forward.

✔ **Sample chapter(s):** Three complete sample chapters is the norm here. You don't have to include the first three chapters, but three *great* chapters well representative of your style, approach, voice, and ability to deliver what your proposal proposes.

Not counting the introduction and sample chapters, a proposal typically runs 10 to 15 pages. It should be unbound, double-spaced throughout, and have 1-inch margins all around.

Copyright: Protecting Your Work Before You Send Anything

You may think of your children's story as a wonderful beam of heart-warming light in an otherwise dark and cloudy world. That's all well and good, but your story is really something a bit less ethereal. In actuality, it's property and like any other property it needs to be protected.

But why would anyone want to steal your story, you ask? Although your children's book-to-be may never turn into a full-blown, raging bestseller, there's always a possibility it may. And guess what? Full-blown, raging bestsellers can be worth a lot of money, especially if your characters are turned into licensed products (to be used on T-shirts, lunchboxes, smartphone apps, or action figures) or your story becomes a Saturday morning television cartoon or major motion picture. And if your rights aren't fully secured from the very beginning, then you can kiss all that money (and fame and glory) goodbye.

Drawing inspiration from public domain works

A story falls into *public domain* if it is a creative work or intellectual property that is no longer protected by copyright and can be used by anyone. This includes many fairy tales and works such as *Alice in Wonderland* by Lewis Carroll or *A Little Princess* by Frances Hodgson Burnett. What do you do if you want to use a story that's in the public domain as a starting point for your own story? You first have to find out if you can.

To find out whether anyone owns a story and whether you can retell it in your words without getting in trouble, use this fairly reliable test: If you can find at least three different and separately copyrighted and recent adaptations or retellings, then you can fairly assume the story is up for grabs. For instance, the Old Testament Bible and the musical works of Beethoven are in the public domain, but translations of, adaptations

of, or performances of these works could be copyright protected. Make sure to actually get your hands on the book the story comes from, checking the copyright and permissions pages, and ascertaining that the author has not obtained permission from someone to use the story — because if he did, he would have to credit it, and if the credit is in the book, he may have had to pay for the privilege of using it or adapting it — something you may not want to do.

A word of caution: If you choose fairy tales, make sure to go back to the originals and not to the Disney adaptations, because certain additions to the Disney tales are not public domain, such as Disney's addition of the characters Flounder (a fish) and Sebastian (a Jamaican-accented crab) to Hans Christian Andersen's classic tale *The Little Mermaid*.

The most commonly used — and perhaps most commonly misunderstood — way of protecting a literary work is by a copyright. A *copyright* is simply a legal protection of an original work. This includes literary, dramatic, musical, artistic, and other intellectual works. Only the owner of the copyright (or someone the copyright owner expressly authorizes) may reproduce the work, prepare derivative works based on the work, perform the work publicly, and display the copyrighted work publicly.

You're probably familiar with the famous mark that signifies an item is copyrighted: ©. The copyright symbol is one-third of what is known as a copyright notice. A complete *copyright notice* consists of the copyright symbol (©), the year of first publication of the work, and the name of the owner of the copyright, like this: © 2015 Lisa Rojany Buccieri.

Legally, you aren't required to place a copyright notice on your work for it to be protected under copyright laws, and our advice is not to. A little © on every page or on a cover is a sign of an amateur who doesn't know that the moment you save a file with the contents of your story with its date and time stamp, you are protected by copyright law. Having a dated document does not mean that someone else cannot use the same idea — no copyright can protect you from that (besides, most stories have been told before). What a dated file *does* do is protect your unique voice and the particular way you developed the story you wanted to tell. It also never hurts to e-mail yourself a copy of your first draft or to snail mail yourself a copy so you have a dated record in case your original digital file gets changed in any way.

Ideas, procedures, methods, systems, processes, concepts, principles, discoveries, or devices, as distinguished from a description, explanation, or illustration, can't be copyrighted (but, boy, you can sure patent and trademark the heck out of some of these things; visit the U.S. Patent and Trademark Office at `www.uspto.gov` for more details). What does this mean to you in practical terms? It means that even though you have an idea, you can't protect it until you develop and write that idea into an actual story.

A common misconception about copyrights is that you need to fill out a form, hire an attorney, or pay a fee to copyright your work. Although any number of attorneys would love to have you spend big bucks hiring them to secure a copyright for your work, you don't have to. According to U.S. copyright law, your work is automatically copyrighted the moment it is created in fixed form (meaning that it is tangible — such as a published story or written song or a printed photograph — or if not directly perceptible, that it can be communicated with the aid of a machine or device), and the copyright immediately becomes your property as the person who created the work.

Say you submit a query letter to a bunch of publishers about your idea for a story about a girl who finds a lost puppy. You get rejected everywhere.

Then months (or years) after that rejection, three different books with the exact same premise are released from three different publishers. Have they stolen your idea? They can't! Ideas are not protected; therefore, they cannot be stolen in the first place. Regardless of copyright law, the chances of three book publishers — or really even one — taking an idea from a query letter or manuscript they've rejected and going out and soliciting the story from another writer are slim to none.

Although copyrights don't protect your work forever, they do last a pretty long time. In the United States, for works created on or after January 1, 1978, the copyright lasts for the author's entire life *plus* 70 years after her death. When the work is a "joint work prepared by two or more authors who did not work for hire," the copyright lasts for 70 years after the death of the last surviving author.

So what happens to ownership of your work after the copyright expires? When your copyright expires, your book enters the *public domain* (see the nearby "Works in the public domain" sidebar); that is, no person or organization has an exclusive right of ownership in the work, and anyone can then use the words you wrote in any way he or she sees fit. Eventually, all copyrighted children's books meet this fate.

Success! Reviewing Your Publishing Contract

One of the greatest moments of a writer's life comes when you get the news a publishing company wants to publish your book. Quite quickly following that wonderful moment comes the (very) scary part: signing the *publishing agreement* — the legal contract spelling out the terms and conditions under which the publisher will publish your book, including important considerations such as payment, schedule, and copyright. Never fear. In the next sections, we arm you with the information you need to distinguish between the types of agreements and ensure you get what you want in yours.

Surveying the two types of publishing agreements

There are generally two types of publishing agreements: a *work-for-hire* or *flat-fee* agreement and the traditional *advance against royalties* agreement. For our purposes here, the terms *contract* and *agreement* refer to the same thing. Here are the two main types of agreements:

✔ **Royalty agreements:** The traditional form of a publishing agreement has long been the standard *royalty agreement. Royalties* are a percentage of the proceeds from the sale of each book, minus the *advance* (which is the money the publisher pays you upfront).

✔ **Work-for-hire agreements:** When a publisher engages an author under a *work-for-hire agreement,* the publisher pays the author a fixed amount of money for a specific piece of work. When the work is delivered, the publisher pays the money and takes all rights to the work with no residual payments, such as royalties due the author.

In contrast to a royalty agreement, which has a life long after a manuscript is delivered, a typical work-for-hire agreement ends upon delivery of the manuscript. If the book becomes a bestseller, the author won't see a single dime more than what was already paid (unless the author has negotiated some sort of bonus provisions based on number of units sold).

Publishing agreements usually contain all kinds of provisions, including grant of rights, payment, reversion of rights, and more. Check out *Getting Your Book Published For Dummies* by Sara Parsons Zackheim with Adrian Zackheim (John Wiley & Sons, Inc.) for more details and specifics on contract pitfalls or, if the entire process gives you hives, just go and consult with an attorney who has demonstrable experience in publishing agreements.

Getting what you want in the contract

Publishing contracts are drafted by the publisher and written to minimize the publisher's risk and maximize the publisher's financial return, not the author's. You must decide for yourself the degree to which you'll give up provisions (such as getting a net royalty rate versus a gross royalty rate) in order to secure the publishing contract for your book.

Although new authors often give in on a lot of issues because they're so excited to have their first book published, take a look at some of the aspects of a contract about which you should try to have a say:

✔ **Front cover byline:** New authors especially should require that their name appear on the front cover and the spine of the book in a font size that is large enough to be read without difficulty, and that it's as big as the illustrator's name.

✔ **Digital or electronic rights:** Many agents complain nowadays that they spend the majority of their contract negotiating hours with publishers haggling over *digital rights* (rights including those for e-books, apps, podcasts, video trailers, and multimedia formats we haven't yet invented). That's because there's a lot of profit to be made — and a lot of unknowns to consider — in this arena. If you're negotiating by yourself, do some research. Or to play it safe, if the publisher suggests 25 percent of net receipts goes to you for digital rights, double 25 to 50 percent, make it *gross* not *net,* and negotiate from there.

✓ **Free copies:** Make sure you get enough free copies to give away to your family and friends, as well as to hand out as promotional copies to noted bloggers, reviewers, your local cozy cafe, and so on.

Many publishers will send out promotional copies, including an introductory letter at no cost to the author, to important media contacts provided by the author. Find out their publicity department's standard practice and see if you can negotiate more free copies if necessary.

✓ **Additional copies:** Make sure the price at which you can purchase additional copies is at a deep discount, typically the publisher's cost or 50 percent of the suggested retail price, which is what publishers sell the book at to most retailers (though in some cases the discount to retailers may be even steeper).

✓ **Option to purchase:** Just before it's about to go out of print, your book may be remaindered (sent off to discount retailers at a price significantly lower than the suggested retail price). Make sure your contract states that you'll be notified first so you have the option to purchase those copies at a certain (low) price per unit before they're sent away.

✓ **Royalty rates:** Royalties are specific to the format and geographic territory, generally 10 percent total on hardcover sales and 5 to 8 percent total on trade paperback sales. The royalty rates for electronic versions of your book can range from a few percentage points to 50 percent or more.

On the print version, push for a *gross royalty rate* (royalty based on the suggested retail price without the publisher's cost subtracted from the price) versus the *net royalty rate* (royalties based on the retail price minus the publisher's costs). Why? Because it's often hard to quantify ahead of time what the publisher considers fair, fixed costs to charge against the royalty monies owed to you, often resulting in a lower net royalty rate than you may have expected when you negotiated your contract. It's always best to go for the gross royalties.

Even if you self-publish an electronic version of your book, you will likely be using some company's template to format it and someone else's Web site (in addition to your own) to sell it. There are fees associated with both. Check them out before you commit. For example, Kindle e-books are created using a particular template, and there are lots of different ways to structure how you sell your book and the fees you have to pay Amazon. Same goes for Apple iBooks, e-books for B&N's NOOK tablet, and every other creation and delivery system. Do your research. See Chapter 18.

✓ **Escalating royalty rates:** This means that the more books you sell, the more royalties you get paid. While first-time authors often won't get the option to push for this, you can always try. Why? Because you only make more if the publisher makes more — a win-win situation as far as we're concerned. And be sure that sales for a revision to your book are counted in as additional sales for the initial edition (instead of being counted as a new book for which you have to earn out the new and usually lower advance before earning royalties).

✔ **Royalties from other countries:** *Subrights* (generally rights concerning other countries, languages, and formats) are very specific in publishing agreements. Although you cannot predict what subrights will sell where, make sure your negotiated royalty rates are specific. Do you get the same amount of royalty for World Rights as you do for North American Rights as you do for World All Languages? For instance, do you get the same amount of royalty for books printed in the United States in English (American English) and sold in Britain (as opposed to British versions with British English) as you do for those same books sold in the United States? Or are Britain and Canada considered foreign sales with applicable royalty rates. Here's a simple tip: If the publisher suggests a subrights split of 50/50, why not push for 75/25 — your favor?

✔ **Copyrights:** Make sure that the agreement provides that the copyright will be in your name, not in the publisher's name. (You will not have this option in a work-for-hire agreement or an agreement in which you are contributing to an already established series like this one.) For more on copyright, see the earlier "Copyright: Protecting Your Work Before You Send Anything" section.

✔ **Schedule for manuscript delivery and acceptance of manuscript (timeline and format):** Give yourself a reasonable amount of time to complete the manuscript *well.* Don't rush to try to please the publisher; he is already pleased, that's why you're in contract negotiations. If you are so new you cannot define *reasonable,* the publisher will provide a suggested date; if that date gives you hives, chances are you're allergic to it and need more time.

Also, if when you deliver the final manuscript the work is not accepted, the publisher should explain, in writing, why this is so and allow for good faith changes within a designated period of time. Assuming the work has been rejected or there has been a failure of timely delivery, negotiate a kill fee in your contract that allows you to retain a portion of the advance. In the case of termination, negotiate a *first proceeds clause,* which allows for the repayment of any amounts advanced by the publisher. Make sure that it shall be from — and not greater than — the first proceeds (or the first money) paid to the writer from the work by another publisher. In the event of advance recoupment, make sure to delete the term "other payments" to ensure that the advance is repayable only from your royalties and not from your split on the licenses for the various subrights. To be clear, add language like: "in no event shall an unearned advance be considered an overpayment."

- **Accounting statements (annual, semiannual, or quarterly):** Make sure that the publisher is not using *cross accounting* (sometimes called *cross collateralization* or *joint accounting*), meaning that this agreement is for this book only and won't be tied into the royalty accounting for subsequent titles that may or may not earn out their advance.

- **Indemnity/insurance:** It's highly unlikely that you'll be able to obtain any concessions in the indemnity clause, but you should try nonetheless. If the publisher has the ability to settle claims without the prior approval of the author, make sure there is a dollar amount limitation. Furthermore, the withholding of legal expenses should be held in an interest-bearing account. Query as to whether the author might be included as an additional insured on the publisher's insurance policy.

- **Right to audit:** Every publishing contract should give the author the right to audit the publisher's accounting records for that book.

- **Publisher bankruptcy:** Some authors try to include a clause in their contract stating that if a publisher goes bankrupt, the rights to the book will revert immediately to the author — *regardless of whether the publisher's assets are subsequently sold to another entity.* We think that's a fair request: If they aren't doing anything anymore with your work, why can't you get the rights back to try to exploit them instead of letting a total stranger sit on it for the next century while he figures out what if anything to do with it?

- **Out-of-print:** Which brings up our next suggestion: If the book is not printed on the contractually promised date or within 18 months of it, you have a right to ask for the rights to revert back to you. Also, if no print copies remain of your book and the publisher has not sold one in 18 months, it can be considered out of print, and you have the right to ask for the rights back. But understand that all a publisher has to do is sell *one* copy for this clause to remain unenforceable.

In our experience, newbies often have to accept 90 percent of the original terms in a publishing contract — but that doesn't mean you cannot get some concessions here and there. If it's your first book and you've been offered a contract with a reputable publisher, ask yourself this: Do I want to be published more than I want X? If the answer is yes, suck it up. You'll have more clout with your second book.

Whatever you may find in your publishing contract, be sure the contract is carefully reviewed before you sign it — either by your agent, by you if you're sufficiently qualified, or by an attorney if you're not. And don't sign the contract until you understand exactly what you're signing and are in full agreement.

Dealing with Rejection

A *rejection letter* is notification from someone you sent your manuscript to — usually a literary agent whom you hope will represent your work to publishers or an editor who acquires new titles for a children's book publisher — that your manuscript isn't being accepted for publication. If you sent along an appropriately sized, self-addressed, stamped envelope (SASE), then your original manuscript may also accompany the rejection letter, or your manuscript may have simply ended up in someone's round file (otherwise known as the wastebasket).

The bad news: You are going to get a lot of rejection letters as you travel along the path to getting published — from literary agents, editors, and publishers.

Interview with Glenn Murray, author

Glenn Murray, co-author of the Walter the Farting Dog series (North Atlantic Books), knows all too well what it feels like to be rejected. No one wanted Murray and Kotzwinkle's first story of a farting dog. Until one dark and windy night . . .

WCBFD: Tell that great story about how your book, the bestselling *Walter the Farting Dog,* finally came to be published after ten years of solid rejection.

GM: I've had a lot of requests to read manuscripts since Walter's rise to success — as if I have anything to offer! My co-author was the guy who wrote the novel *ET: The Extra-Terrestrial* (Putnam), and that still wasn't enough to get our book published. Walter's story of getting published shows that even when you try to cover all the bases, and you have an agent, it's not always enough. There's a certain amount of luck, of being in the right place, and of timing. It's amazing the difference a little time can make, especially in matters of taste or propriety. The problem was that we used the F-word [farting] in the title and throughout the book. We went out on the edge a little before the publishing world was ready for

us. What's acceptable today was not acceptable 10 years ago.

WCBFD: Where did the idea for *Walter the Farting Dog* come from?

GM: One night, when we were working on this kids' adventure screenplay, my co-author, Bill Kotzwinkle, was reminiscing about this dog he had met in an office supply store in town. This dog had a prodigious capacity to produce gaseous emissions. The dog was famous for this. When he let go, the entire store would clear out, it was that bad. I asked Bill if he remembered the dog's name and he said, "Yeah, it was Walter." Immediately, I could see it, the title — *Walter the Farting Dog* — blazing across the skies. "Gee, that would be a great title for a children's book!" And we sort of let it go, like a joke. Then circumstances changed, and we had to put our children's adventure screenplay away for a while. As a consolation to ourselves, I said, "Let's write that farting dog story." And we did. We laughed all day long and had a pretty good time. We wrote about a dog who was making the best of a bad situation, turning his liabilities into assets, which was what we, as writers, were trying to do as well. It was a simple, but satisfying, story, and I knew, having spent a great deal of time reading to kids in the school system, what kids like and what would grab their attention. Little did we know that we would have such a hard time selling it.

WCBFD: So what happened next?

GM: Bill has been published a bunch of times, so we sent it to his longtime agent as well as to the illustrator he had been paired with on previous books. And before we even got the agent's reaction, we got rejected by the illustrator, who was not interested. But we still had high hopes. And it didn't take long before a lot of responses came in.

WCBFD: What were those responses?

GM: We laughed and laughed, but we cannot publish this. No one wanted poor Walter. Then after five years had gone by, we sat down again and tried to soften up the manuscript a little by changing a bunch of F-words to "and he did it" and the title to *Get That Dog Outta Here!* — a change that made me pretty unhappy. But we wanted to get published and we thought it would help. It didn't; the rejections kept coming. Then, in 2001, Bill was at a dinner party, and the host asked him to get the dog story out and read it to everyone as sort of an after-dinner

mint. So he did, and the entire room fell off their seats roaring with laughter. One of the guests was a publisher who said he had to publish it, even though he didn't publish children's books. That's how it all started.

WCBFD: What advice would you give fledgling writers regarding rejection?

GM: You can't be too sensitive at the beginning. The people at the other end have their guidelines about what their company wants to publish, and they have their own idea of what they are looking for. There is not much that we can do about it. But they are not out to get us. So as soon as the manuscript comes back, send it out again. If you have a manuscript in the mail, you have hope. If you don't, you are just sitting around kicking yourself in the head and no way anything will ever happen. Remember Ted Geisel. His first manuscript was rejected 26 times. That was *To Think That I Saw It on Mulberry Street*. And he, as Dr. Seuss, is the most loved children's book writer in America today. Do you think we would know about him if he were easily discouraged? Rejection is all about tenacity. As I tell the children I speak with: If you are gonna give up the second time you fall off a bicycle, you are never going to learn to ride a bicycle.

So what should you do when you receive a rejection letter? After having a quick cry (always keep a box of tissues handy when you open letters from publishers), you can do a number of things to turn this particular lemon into lemonade and grow from the experience:

- ✔ **Take some time to cool down.** A rejection can bring your dream of getting published to a screeching halt, and it can be a very emotional event. If you find yourself upset by the rejection, take some time to cool down before you do anything related to your manuscript. Relax. Take a deep breath. Don't throw your manuscript in the fireplace.

- ✔ **Look for clues.** Is the rejection letter one of those form letters where someone wrote in your name after the typed-in "Dear . . . ," or is it an actual personal letter in which the editor offers advice or encouragement? If advice specific to your book is included in the letter, read it closely! These bits of info — like how to improve your manuscript or where you can find a more appropriate publisher for your book — can help you create a better book (while giving you a greater chance for eventual publishing success).

✔ **Revise your manuscript.** If the person who sent you the rejection letter took the time to give you specific advice on how to improve your manuscript, by all means take it and revise your manuscript accordingly. Editors and agents know what books will sell. Sure, they make mistakes from time to time — launching books that sink in the marketplace faster than you can spell *Titanic* and rejecting books that another publisher picks up and turns into a raging success — but their advice is as straight from the horse's mouth as you'll ever get, and most of the time it's dead-on accurate, as painful as it may be. Not only that, but the advice costs you nothing.

Someone who takes the time to write a real reply with suggestions on improvement may be willing to take a second look once those suggestions have been implemented. Consider it a slightly opened door. You may be able to revisit the contact if you agree that the suggested changes make your work better — and you make them well enough to substantially alter the manuscript. Our advice? Make the changes.

✔ **Redo your research.** Did you send your manuscript to the right agent or publisher? Different agents and publishers specialize in different genres and types of children's books (see our extensive coverage on these topics in Chapter 2). Does your manuscript conform to the common publishing standards for that type of book? If not, then your manuscript may be rejected for that reason alone. Do your research and double-check that you sent the right manuscript to the right agent or publisher.

✔ **Remember that it's not personal; it's just business.** Book publishing is a business. If your manuscript was rejected, the editor didn't believe the book would sell enough copies to be a profitable venture for that publisher. It's that simple. Move on and keep looking for the right publishing home for your baby.

Chapter 18

So You Want to Self-Publish?

. . . .

In This Chapter

▶ Understanding the good and the bad of self-publishing

▶ Exploring your self-publishing options

▶ Setting a price for your book

▶ Getting your book into the hands of your readers

. . . .

For an increasing number of people, self-publishing is not the only way for them to get their books into print — it's the preferred way. Not too many years ago — before the proliferation of blogs, e-books, print on demand, Kindles, Nooks, iPads, and all the rest — self-publishing was considered by many to be the province of losers, the last resort of those rejected by traditional publishing houses. This is definitely no longer the case.

Today more than ever before, authors — including children's book authors — are choosing to self-publish their books. According to Bowker, the world's leading provider of bibliographic information, while the number of traditional U.S. print titles increased only 5 percent from 2009 to 2010 — from 302,410 to 316,480 — the nontraditional sector experienced explosive growth. This sector, which includes self-published and print-on-demand titles, grew a phenomenal 169 percent — from 1,033,065 in 2009 to 2,776,260 in 2010.

There are lots of good reasons to self-publish your children's book, as well as more than a few reasons you might want to avoid it. In this chapter, we explore both the good and the bad and consider the best options for becoming your own publisher. In addition, we take a look at what price to set for your book and then how to get it into the hands of children. We consider self-publishing a printed book first and then we approach e-books.

The Good and Bad News about Self-Publishing

So why self-publish? Maybe you've huffed and puffed and you still can't get an agent or publisher interested in your book. Maybe you want complete creative control, and the only way to get that is to do everything yourself. Or maybe you just want to keep all the proceeds from selling your printed book. Here are some of the best reasons for taking the self-publishing road in print:

- ✔ **It provides you a viable (and perhaps the only) alternative for getting your book into print.** Most children's book publishers reject 95 percent or more of the manuscripts they receive. Self-publishing offers rejected authors a path to being published that traditional publishers may not be willing to provide.

- ✔ **Self-publishing is way faster.** It can take 18 months or more to go from pitching your idea to an agent or traditional publisher to finally seeing your book in print. With self-publishing, you can go from final, edited manuscript to e-book (or even hardcopy) in just weeks. And with the advent of self-publishing platforms such as iBook Author and Vook, this time can be reduced to days.

- ✔ **You're the boss!** When you print and publish your own book, you keep the rights to your work, you decide what words and illustrations lay between the covers, and you set your own writing and production schedule.

- ✔ **You get to keep most of the profits.** Traditional publishers and agents take a big cut of the proceeds from your book sales. If you're organized, willing to learn about the business, and have a knack for marketing, you can make just as much money — or more! — self-publishing as you would if your book were published by a traditional publisher.

- ✔ **Some books actually are better off self-published.** If you've written something for a small, niche audience that you have direct access to, it may be the best way to get your book to that audience and keep the largest portion of profits. Part of what a large publishing house offers is broad distribution, a sales force, and a marketing and publicity team, but if your book doesn't need that, self-publishing may be a good way to go.

- ✔ **You may be able to turn your successful self-published children's book into a successful, traditionally published children's book.** Sometimes self-published books that sell a lot of copies attract the interest of a traditional publisher, which can be your golden ticket to success as a children's book author. Although this is rare, a few self-published authors have managed to sell a ton of books on their own and/or ended up on a bestsellers list. Although bucket loads of books sold are probably a prerequisite for the few instances in which this happens, the sidebar example of self-publisher Amanda Hocking's success in traditional publishing reads like a virtual fairy tale.

Just as you may have plenty of good reasons to put your own printed book on the market, you're going to run across a number of reasons to pass on this option. Here are just a few:

- ✔ **Self-published books are still taken less seriously than traditionally published books.** Unfortunately, few legitimate and credentialed reviewers, reviewing sites, or reviewing venues bother reviewing self-published books, and few bricks-and-mortar bookstores carry them. This can be a problem because those sites, publications, and venues are where many people find out about books they choose to buy.

- ✔ **Self-publishing is hard work.** Writing, illustrating, laying out text and art, and arranging for printing, distribution, and promotion of a print book is no small task. That's why the first choice of many authors is to approach a publisher or agent when they have a manuscript they want to turn into a printed book.

- ✔ **Self-publishing isn't necessarily cheap.** Some authors who have selected the self-publishing path spend upward of $25,000 or more to create, print, and bind a couple thousand copies to hand out to family, friends, clients, and associates.

- ✔ **You don't get to keep *all* the money.** Most print-on-demand (POD) publishing platform providers will want a piece of your proceeds, as will your distributors (Amazon.com, Barnes & Noble, and so on). If you go directly to a printer, you will have to pay them in advance of selling a single copy.

- ✔ **You can get scammed.** A number of shady operators know some people will do most anything to get their books into print, and these folks know what buttons to push to separate you from your hard-earned money. Be careful with self-publishing promises that seem too good to be true — they may be just that.

To self-publish often requires a renegade's personality: a willingness to go against the grain, push huge boulders uphill, scoff off rejections as misguided, and simply forge ahead. Ready to give it a try? Then check out the rest of the sections in this chapter, which serve as your self-publishing primer. (For a more detailed discussion of the ins and outs of self-publishing, we recommend *Self-Publishing For Dummies,* by Jason Rich [John Wiley & Sons, Inc.].)

Amanda Hocking's path to self-publishing success

So can you really find success through self-publishing — enough to create a sizable fan following and maybe even make some serious money in the process? Ultimately, it depends on the quality of your work and whether or not you are able to get the word out effectively to your waiting horde of potential fanboys and fangirls; however, a number of talented writers have done quite well without traditional publishers, and that number is growing every day.

Consider the recent example of Amanda Hocking, who turned to self-publishing her young adult paranormal novels after being turned down by numerous traditional publishers. In March 2010, Amanda started selling digital downloads of her self-published novels on Amazon.com and BN.com at prices ranging from 99 cents to $2.99. Within a few months she was selling hundreds, and then thousands of copies of her books. Just nine months later, Amanda had sold a total of 164,000 books.

But that was just the beginning. In January 2011 — a one-month period of time — she sold 450,000 copies of her nine books, 99 percent of them in the form of e-books. Although we don't have access to Amanda's accounting spreadsheets, we'll take a wild guess based on the typical cut of proceeds that Amazon and Barnes & Noble take from e-book sales through their sites that she has cleared hundreds of thousands of dollars over the past year. And if she hasn't crossed the million-dollar threshold yet, there's no doubt she soon will. This is far more than most authors — even über-bestselling authors of books published by traditional publishers — ever see during the course of their entire writing careers.

All her efforts resulted in enough sales to land her on *USA Today*'s bestsellers list. The publishing house St. Martin's found out about the Trylie Trilogy and re-released the books in traditional print in early 2012. There is a movie option, Amanda has other series in the works as of this printing, and is still selling tons of her 13 books.

So we'll ask the question one more time: Can you really find success through self-publishing? In a word, the answer is "Yes."

Exploring Your Self-Publishing Options

When it comes to self-publishing, you have an almost unlimited number of options for creating your book. A self-published book can be anything from a stapled copy of your manuscript — produced on the printer in your home or at a local copy shop — to an interactive e-book app that can be read on an iPad, Nook, or Kindle, to a top-quality hardcover that is indistinguishable from the best book produced by a traditional publisher or independent press.

Although there are many different self-publishing options, they generally fall into one of two categories: print and digital. Sure, there may be some overlap in the way these two categories of books are created, promoted, and distributed, but ultimately they're completely different animals.

In the sections that follow, we closely examine each of these beasts and provide you with the information you need to make an informed choice as to which route — print, digital, or *both* — is the best for you to pursue.

The print route

Although the world of digital books is expanding rapidly, a lot of people still buy — and prefer to read — good, old-fashioned printed books. These books, sometimes called *p-books* (to differentiate them from those newfangled e-books) are nowhere near extinct, nor are they on anyone's endangered species lists — at least not yet. According to the Association of American Publishers, children's and young adult p-books saw strong double-digit growth in net revenue from January 2011 to January 2012. Specifically, total sales of children's and young adult hardcover books grew to $57.4 million (68.9 percent growth) and paperbacks to $38.0 million (61.9 percent growth). So as you consider self-publishing, don't pass over the print route too quickly — there is still a large (and growing) market for this kind of book.

The following sections consider two of the most common approaches to getting your self-published book into print: working with an offset printer and taking the leap into print-on-demand.

Working with an offset printer — or not

When a traditional publisher actually prints copies of a book, they use a process known as *offset printing*. Offset printing uses indirect image transfer, most often by way of a metal or paper plate that applies ink to a smooth rubber cylinder. The cylinder then transfers the ink to the paper that when assembled becomes your book. Nearly every city — and even many small towns — has one or more printing companies that use the offset printing process to create a wide variety of different products, including flyers, business cards, brochures, restaurant menus, envelopes, sales sheets — and books.

For years, offset printing has been the first choice in self-publishing methods. It is fast and relatively affordable, and the quality of the finished product can be quite good; however, because a printing company is just that, a printing company, you are personally responsible for ensuring that many of the tasks undertaken by a typical traditional publisher are completed. Such tasks include:

- Editing and formatting your manuscript
- Designing a cover (plus or minus an image) and interior page layout
- Proofreading the final copy to make sure there are zero errors of any kind (copyediting as well if your work is nonfiction)
- Deciding on a trim size and binding type
- Choosing paper and other materials

✔ Obtaining an ISBN (the International Standard Book Number, required to sell your book commercially) and a Cataloguing in Publication Number (CIP) from the Library of Congress (LOC)

✔ Warehousing your book if you are handling distribution and sales by yourself or hooking up with a fulfillment and distribution house so they can handle these functions for you

✔ Marketing and promoting your book

Before settling on a particular offset printing company, first do your due diligence. Be sure to get answers to the following questions so you can make an informed decision:

✔ Does the company have experience printing books like yours?

✔ Do samples of their work look well done and professional? Do they guarantee your book will end up the same?

✔ Does the company do its printing in house or is the work outsourced to other companies — or even other countries?

✔ Can the company accommodate your schedule?

✔ Are prices reasonable and payment terms fair?

✔ Can they warehouse and ship out the books per your instructions, if you need them to do so?

Taking the print-on-demand (POD) path

Print-on-demand publishing, or POD for short, can save you time and money when compared to working with an offset printer. The POD process works like this:

1. Send an electronic file of a children's book manuscript (including illustrations, if any) to a print-on-demand publisher.

2. Pay a fee; then the publisher's staff designs and lays out your book and submits it to you for review. (Most bare-bones plans give *you* this responsibility.)

3. After you give the green light, your book is put into production, copies are shipped to distributors, and the book is made available for the world to order through the Internet (including Amazon.com or their own proprietary sites, your own site and Facebook page, to name a few) in any quantity the distributor believes will sell over a reasonable amount of time. Sometimes, POD books are made available one at a time, printed only when a copy has sold; so far, these POD versions don't always look like "real" printed books, but more like copy-shop versions. However, Espresso Book Machines may soon change all that. (See sidebar.)

The primary purpose of a print-on-demand publisher is to sell publishing services to you, the aspiring children's book author. Some services include designing the interior and covers, getting your book listed with the big distributors and online stores, printing on demand as orders come in, and paying royalties on each sale.

Each POD publisher offers a wide variety of publishing packages and services, depending on what you need. In some cases, these packages are clearly set forth on the POD publishers' Web site; in others you need to call or e-mail for a personal consultation. That said, here's what you can expect from most POD publishers:

- ✔ **Basic, bare-bones service:** This level of service puts most of the work in your hands. You can choose from some basic cover and interior templates; you need to edit, format, and proofread your own manuscript; and the finished product is made with the least expensive paper and materials. Your book will be available in a trade paperback edition, though at this price level you probably won't be able to include illustrations. This service costs you around $400 to $500 (although Amazon's CreateSpace will set you up with this basic level of service for free — you pay only for the books you order).

- ✔ **Mid-level service:** You have even more templates to choose from than with basic service, and you get to customize your book's "look" as well as its cover. You can also add illustrations, tables, and an index, and have the option of hardback and trade paperback editions. At this level of service, your manuscript may receive a basic edit, you can expect the paper and materials to be of a higher quality than the basic level of service, and you'll probably receive a nominal number of "free" copies of your book. This level costs you from $750 to $1,250 and up.

- ✔ **Deluxe, top-of-the-line service:** This service offers the highest possible control over your book's design along with the best materials and finishes. Deluxe includes all features of mid-level service as well as a higher level of editing. It allows you to talk to a designer, combining your creative input and their expertise to achieve the personalized page design and cover look, and includes even more "free" copies — which will likely be hardcover. This service costs from about $1,500 on up to many thousands of dollars.

In addition to these upfront fees, you pay every time you order a copy of your book (beyond the author copies included in your plan, if any). Print-on-demand books can be rather expensive — from $15 to $50 or more per copy for a trade paperback.

The print-on-demand scene is in a constant state of flux, and a company that's hot one year may be dead and gone the next. Currently, some of the top print-on-demand companies include CreateSpace (www.createspace.com), which is owned by Amazon.com and therefore plays well with the Amazon Web site; Lulu (www.lulu.com), known for its strong distribution channels; Blurb (www.blurb.com), which is great for books with lots of photographs; and iUniverse (www.iuniverse.com), purchased a few years ago by the parent organization of POD rival AuthorHouse (www.authorhouse.com).

Any of these companies can easily meet your print self-publishing needs — for a price.

Make sure you closely examine *exactly* what you get in return for your hard-earned cash before you commit to any POD publisher.

The digital route

Most of the buzz in publishing today is about the coming of age of the *e-book,* books published in the form of a digital file that can be read on a variety of electronic platforms, including smartphones (think Android and iPhone), tablet computers (iPad and ASUS Transformer, among others), dedicated e-readers (Nook and Kindle), and good old-fashioned laptops and desktops. Five years ago, e-books were just starting to gain a foothold in the world of publishing. Today e-books have arrived in a big way — and are clearly here to stay.

According to the Association of American Publishers, children's and young adult e-book titles surged 475.1 percent from January 2011 to January 2012, to a total of $22.6 million. Long story short, if you've been thinking of self-publishing your own e-book, we would say that you are at the right place at just the right time.

If you've decided to publish your own e-book, you first need to ask yourself these questions — your answers determine the approach you should take to publishing your e-book:

✔ For what platform(s) do I want to publish my e-book?

✔ What do I want to do with my e-book after it's published?

To create a professional looking e-book with all the bells and whistles to offer for sale on Amazon.com or BN.com in significant quantities — while making some money in the process — you need to take your e-book to one of the POD publishers described in the preceding section. Many of these companies also offer e-book publication services that set you up on Amazon.com or other Web sites.

A new twist to POD publishing

When it comes to printed copies, there is one more option: the book machine. Although not yet widely available, the Espresso Book Machine (EBM) allows self-published authors to print as many or as few copies of their book as they like, in person, in real time. For additional information on this alternative to POD publishing, visit the EBM Web site at www.ondemandbooks.com.

If you want to create a professional looking e-book that you can sell on Amazon.com and other Web sites, but you don't want to spend a lot of money — and you're willing to do more of the work yourself — we suggest you consider some of the latest e-book publishing platforms. Each offers pluses and minuses — you need to closely compare the offerings to see which one is best for you:

✔ **Apple iBook Author.** Using this free application, available in the Mac App Store, you can easily create multitouch e-books (currently readable only on iPads and iPhones) that incorporate text, galleries, video, interactive diagrams, 3-D objects, and much more. After you complete your book, you can submit it to the Apple iBookstore for purchase or free download, export it in iBooks format to share on iTunes U, or give to anyone who has an iPad — for free or at whatever price you decide. You can find more info on Apple iBook Author at `www.apple.com/ibooks-author/`.

✔ **Smashwords.** Using its proprietary e-book publishing and distribution platform for e-book authors, publishers, agents, and readers, Smashwords offers multiformat e-books through its Web site, which visitors are able to browse and buy, and then read on any e-reader. Smashwords can also distribute your e-book through the Apple iBookstore, Barnes & Noble, Sony Reader Store, Kobo, and the Diesel eBook Store. Visit Smashwords at `www.smashwords.com`.

✔ **Vook.** Here's what Vook, Inc., says about its product: "Vook is an intuitive and easy-to-use cloud-based e-book publishing platform. Quickly create, edit, style, and publish your e-book — no special software required. When you distribute through Vook, you keep 100 percent of your royalties!" We couldn't have said it better, though we would add that you can also choose to distribute your book through Amazon, Apple iBookstore, and Barnes & Noble — for a fee. Check out complete plans and pricing at `www.vook.com`.

✔ **Kindle Direct Publishing.** If all you want to do is sell your e-book on Amazon.com for the Kindle e-reader, then consider using the Kindle Direct Publishing service. It's free, you'll be able to use your Microsoft Word manuscript files to create your e-book, and your finished product will be available on Amazon.com, which sells far more e-books than any other Web sites. Drop by `kdp.amazon.com` for more information.

If your goal is simply to create a casual e-book to send to friends and relatives and you have no intention of selling the book commercially — at least not now — then you can easily produce it yourself by using standard word processing software (such as Microsoft Word or Apple Pages) and saving your file as a PDF. This approach offers the advantage of using software with which you're probably already familiar — and already own — enabling readers to either print your book or view it on their computers, e-readers, or other digital devices using the commonly available (and free) Adobe Reader software.

Setting a Price for Your Work

Setting a price for a self-published book is the subject of much debate — and sometimes anguish. In our experience, you have three key choices:

- ✓ **Emulate the traditional publishers with your printed book.** You can choose to price your printed book so it is consistent with comparable, traditionally published books. So if your book is a hardcover similar in size and page count to most 32-page hardcover picture books, you can price your book anywhere from $14.99 to $17.99, like a traditional publisher would. If your printed book is a YA novel like Suzanne Collins's *The Hunger Games,* you can try $17.99 like Scholastic Press does.

- ✓ **Charge just a little bit of money.** If it doesn't cost you much to produce your hardcover, paperback, or e-book, you have the flexibility to drop the price far lower than most traditionally published printed books and still make money. A low price of between $.99 and $4.99 can help you generate sales, which can lead to positive word-of-mouth recommendations from readers — and more sales. This was the path taken by successful YA author Amanda Hocking (see the sidebar earlier in this chapter).

- ✓ **Give it away for free.** This is perhaps the most controversial approach to pricing your self-published book, but it can in some cases also be the most rewarding. This strategy is used by many new authors who "sell" their self-published e-books online for free — in some cases generating huge reader interest and buzz in the process. When established and popular, these authors can then charge for future books — or offer a free teaser book and then charge for other books they have written.

Alternatively, you may choose to use a combination of pricing approaches. For instance, when you first launch your e-book, you can give it away for free for a certain period of time — perhaps for a week or even a month — to gain audience traction (while social networking, marketing, and promoting it like mad). Then after you have sold what you determine to be enough at that price, you can up it to 99¢. Then when you really have a solid readership and feel your book can sustain the increased price tag, move on from there. If you write more than one title in a series, perhaps you give away the first title until you publish the second title; at that point your first title goes up to 99¢ or more and the new title sells at $4.99. There are lots of creative pricing structures. You can find out more about promoting and marketing your books in Chapters 19 and 20.

The decision of how to price your self-published book is up to you. Just keep in mind that the more expensive it is, the fewer people are likely to purchase it; and the less expensive it is, the more people are likely to purchase it.

Distributing Your Book

One of your greatest challenges as a self-published author is getting your books into the hands of potential readers. Although traditional publishers have the ability to easily get their books into bookstores, this is not the case for self-published authors. The next sections give you the scoop on getting your self-published book into distribution and out into the world.

Working with distributors

Many bookstores buy their books not directly from publishers, but from a variety of book distributors that work as intermediaries between bookstores and publishers. The good news is that distributors can get your book into most any library or bookstore (both online stores and bricks-and-mortar stores). The bad news is that the large distributors generally don't accept self-published books directly from individual authors — although they may accept self-published books from specific POD publishers. Here are the largest book distributors:

- ✔ **Baker & Taylor.** This Charlotte, North Carolina-based company says that it is "the world's largest distributor of books, digital content, and entertainment products." Although Baker & Taylor primarily serves traditional publishers, the company offers its services to self-published authors via its agreements with companies such as Smashwords (www.smashwords.com) and BookBaby (www.bookbaby.com). Visit Baker & Taylor at www.btol.com.

- ✔ **Ingram Book Company.** The 600-pound gorilla of the book distribution industry, Ingram claims to be "the largest book wholesale distributor in the world, offering immediate access to more than two million titles." Whereas Ingram doesn't work directly with self-published authors (to qualify as a client, publishers have to have at least ten titles in print), the company does handle self-published books by way of its relationships with other organizations, including Publishers Marketing Association (www.pma-online.org), Lightning Source (a POD publisher owned by Ingram — www.lightningsource.com), and others. Stop by Ingram's Web site at www.ingrambook.com.

- ✔ **National Book Network.** This is a smaller distributor that works with about 200 publishers, including a number of children's book publishers. Head to its Web site, www.nbnbooks.com, for more information.

 Many self-published authors skip these distributors altogether and successfully sell their books through their blogs or Web sites, via Amazon.com and BN.com — or by using some of the other approaches we note in the sections that follow.

Getting in the door at traditional bookstores

It's not easy for self-published authors to get their books into traditional bookstores. Why? Because traditional bookstores are used to working directly with large, established traditional publishers, small and independent presses with track records of successful publishing, or with the distribution companies mentioned in the preceding section. These publishers and distributors offer a variety of services (and often promotional cash, known in the book biz as "cooperative advertising funds") designed to make life as easy as they can for bookstores. It's unlikely that you will personally be able to match what the traditional publishers and distributors offer to their bookstore customers.

That isn't to say that self-published authors can't get in the door at traditional bookstores — they can. It helps if you're a local author (many bookstores have shelves devoted to books of local interest) and if you can develop a good working relationship with the bookstore owner or manager. To get your book into a real, live bookstore, make an appointment with the store's manager or book buyer, and bring along the following:

- A sample copy of your book
- A one-page sell sheet that provides
  - Details about your book (author, publisher, ISBNs, cover price, page count, and trim size)
  - A short description of the book and its intended audience
  - A photo of the book cover and author (you!)
  - A brief author (and illustrator, if applicable) bio
  - Information on where the book can be ordered (through a distributor or through you)
- A pitch — the story you're going to tell that will convince the bookstore owner, manager, or book buyer to carry your book. This is the same kind of pitch that is in the query letter described in Chapter 16.

Some new authors think they can get around the seeming taint of self-publishing by making up the name of a publishing house, maybe even creating a corporate identity with a federal tax identification number to legitimize it, putting that self-created publishing house name on the book and/or as the copyright holder, and selling a single title that way. Back in the day, you might have been able to fool some people with this cute trick, but we believe in full disclosure. Imagine what would happen if your self-published book sold enough to get the attention of a traditional publisher who might consider repackaging and selling it, but respectfully stays away because another "publisher" already owns the title?

The first self-published title to hit #1

Some years ago, Richard Paul Evans sent the manuscript of his book *The Christmas Box* to six different publishers, all of which flatly rejected his work. So Evans decided to spend $5,000 of his own money to self-publish 8,000 paperback copies of the book. He distributed these copies to local bookstores, where they were quickly sold at a price of $4.95 each. Flush with his initial success, Evans spent another $13,000 to have 19,000 more copies printed. One thing led to another and within weeks *The Christmas Box* became a bestseller in his state of Utah, selling 240,000 copies nationally by the end of the year and attracting the attention of a novice editor at Simon & Schuster when it became the first self-published book to reach the number-one position on *The New York Times* bestseller list. The editor liked what she saw and signed Evans's book (along with its prequel, *Timepiece*) for $4.25 million.

Persuading online booksellers

Convincing online booksellers — even the big ones like Amazon.com and BN.com — to sell your self-published book isn't all that hard, whether your book is in hardcopy or digital form. We both personally know numerous authors who are selling their self-published books through these sites and others like them. All you need to do is follow the instructions on their Web site in terms of how to format the book for uploading, establish a business relationship, and then supply copies of your book. If you've chosen to print actual copies of your book and sold a certain quantity directly to an online bookseller (yay!), then you'll need to periodically ship more books to them on an as-requested or as-sold basis. If it's an e-Book, you won't have to worry about shipping books at all when you send your online bookseller the e-Book file.

Decide which online booksellers you want to approach, then visit their Web sites and follow their procedures for getting your book into their systems. Here are some of the best:

✔ AbeBooks: www.abebooks.com

✔ Bank Street Bookstore: www.bankstreetbooks.com

✔ Powells: www.powells.com

You can sell your book at as many online bookstores as you like — even creating different versions of your book for each. We believe you'll find that it's easier than you think.

Considering other places to sell your book

Many self-published authors have found success selling their books outside of the traditional bookselling channels. Soon after the first edition of *Writing Children's Books For Dummies* was published, for example, we gave a talk at a local public library on the topic of writing children's books — using *Writing Children's Books For Dummies* as a demonstration and teaching tool throughout the workshop. This three-hour event attracted more than 100 participants, and we signed and sold more than 40 books — brought to the event by a local bookstore that we arranged in advance to help support the talk.

Here are some other places you might consider selling your self-published children's book:

✔ A Facebook fan page or Web site created just for your book

✔ Discount link on Twitter

✔ At school or library readings

✔ Your personal blog

✔ Book fairs

✔ Trade, literary, or publishing magazines

✔ Gas stations, convenience stores, gift shops, car washes, antique dealers — all manner of mom-and-pop venues at which you can speak to an actual owner (just make sure you can tie it into their theme or other merchandise in a logical, sales oriented pitch)

✔ Local crafts fairs or farmer's markets

Chapter 19

Donning Your Publicity Cap

- -

In This Chapter
▶ Recognizing the publisher's role in publicizing your book
▶ Taking charge of your own publicity
▶ Bringing a publicist on board

- -

*G*etting your book onto a bookstore shelf is only one part of the thrill of being a published children's book author. The other part — which is just as important — is getting your book *off* the bookstore shelf and into the hands of a child. And you must play a big part in making that happen.

In this chapter, we present the basics of publicizing and promoting your books. Not only do we address some of the tried-and-true techniques for building a buzz around your books, but we also take a good look the pros and cons of hiring a professional publicist and doing book tours and readings.

Understanding What Your Publisher Will Do to Promote Your Book

Most authors we know expect their publishers to roll out a multimedia marketing blitz that will make their books household names — and *New York Times* bestsellers — overnight. Unless your name is J.K. Rowling or Stephenie Meyer, it's unlikely that you'll get this kind of treatment.

At a minimum, your publisher should engage in the following promotional efforts:

✔ Send out press releases (either hardcopy or online).

✔ Mail copies of your book to key reviewers and review sites.

✔ List your book in its sales catalog and on its Web site.

✔ Create sales copy for Amazon and Barnes & Noble listings.

✔ Support book signings.

This limited amount of publicity is a good start, but much more can be done — by you — to get the word out about your book. This chapter gives you the tools you need to help promote the result of your hard work.

Regardless of what your publisher ultimately agrees to do, make sure you closely coordinate your own publicity efforts with theirs. The last thing you want to do is to duplicate (or leave significant gaps in) your efforts.

Publicizing Your Own Book

The thought of doing your own book publicity can be both exciting and overwhelming thanks to the almost unlimited number of potential tools available, such as Web sites, blogs, videos, radio and television interviews, press releases, podcasts, and social media. Ultimately, though, it's best to take a two-pronged approach to publicity by embracing both the digital and traditional components of publicity campaigns. We outline some of these components in the following sections; for a crash course in using social media to spread awareness of your book, head to Chapter 20.

Focusing on the digital components

When we wrote the first edition of this book, most book publicity efforts were accomplished through good-old-fashioned in-person meetings, phone calls, faxes, and snail-mailed letters and promotional copies. Today most book publicity efforts are accomplished digitally (and inexpensively) by way of e-mail, Web sites, blogs, and social media, which means the digital world is the best place to focus your initial publicity efforts. You can start by creating an online presence for your book and e-mailing your very own press release.

Building an online presence for your book

Nowadays, building an online marketing platform to display, promote, and sell your book is considered an essential element in an effective publicity campaign. Here are the most effective online marketing platforms (for detailed advice on using social media to market your book, see Chapter 20):

✔ **Web site:** You might feature your book on your own existing Web site, or create a new Web site dedicated to your book. You can also try to get other Web site owners to feature your book and link to your site.

✔ **Blog:** You can feature your book on an existing blog or create a new blog dedicated to your book. As with Web sites, you can try to get other bloggers to talk about and link to your book.

✔ **Podcasts:** If you have retained the audio rights to your book (or for use in promotional purposes), you might be able to create a series of podcasts of you, the author, reading chapters of your book aloud.

✔ **YouTube video:** You can create a video based on your book and post it to YouTube. Better yet, you can create a series of videos based on your book and then set up a YouTube channel for potential readers to visit.

✔ **Book trailer:** Used to be only movies got trailers, but now many books do as well. Publishers and authors can go all out with animation or use a simple program such as iMovie to create a catchy trailer to post on YouTube, your Web site, your friends' Web sites — *anywhere.*

✔ **Facebook:** You can create a Facebook page just for your book, make your book a part of your existing Facebook page, or even buy an ad.

✔ **Twitter:** If you have a Twitter account, then you can send out a steady stream of tweets about your book. And if you don't have a Twitter account? Get one.

A well-designed online marketing platform can be a powerful advertisement for your book and — best of all — it's available 24 hours a day, seven days a week, and can be viewed by potential book buyers anywhere in the world.

Sending out press releases

A *press release* (also known as a *media release* or *news release*) is simply a brief, written notice of some newsworthy event — in this case, the publication of your book. Press releases are generally sent out via e-mail or by way of an online press release service.

A press release is most often one — and never more than two — pages in length. Work hard to keep it to only one page. The key parts of a well-written press release are as follows:

✔ **Release date:** Unless you want the end recipient to hold off on using the information for some reason, the release date for your press release should read FOR IMMEDIATE RELEASE (and yes, use all caps).

✔ **Headline:** Write a punchy, one-sentence hook that will make your audience want to read more. Be creative and have fun. Capitalize the first letter of all the words in your headline except articles.

✔ **City, state, date (when you're sending out the release):** Your reader wants to know where you are and how timely the press release is.

✔ **Introductory paragraph:** Write a strong introductory paragraph that includes who, what, when, where, why, and how about your book — as concisely as possible.

✔ **Body:** This is the heart of your press release, and it should be at least two paragraphs long (but remember — keep your press release to no more than a page).

✔ **Biography:** A brief biography of the book's author — you.

✔ **Detailed contact information:** The name, address, phone number, fax number, Web site URL, and e-mail address of the person to contact for more information about the book.

Figure 19-1 shows what a press release using the preceding elements might look like.

Who should you target with your press release? Anyone you think may have an interest in reading it, including newspaper reporters, radio and television talk show hosts and producers, children's book bloggers and Web site operators, magazine editors, bookstore owners, and librarians.

Whenever possible, address your press release to a specific individual in an organization. A press release addressed to a specific person has a much better chance of getting read, which means you have a much better chance of getting the media attention you seek.

In addition to your own list of places to send your press release, you may also consider sending it out using an online press release service, such as

✔ www.businesswire.com

✔ www.prnewswire.com

✔ www.prweb.com

FOR IMMEDIATE RELEASE

New Kid's Book Digs Deep Into the Past

Chicago, IL, January 5, 2020 — Bestselling children's book author Divvy Bobivy digs deep into the Egyptian pyramids in her new book *Who Built the Pyramids*? published by Acme Press in January 2020 and available now for $19.99 at Barnes & Noble, Amazon.com, and other fine book retailers nationwide.

In what promises to be her next blockbuster children's book, Divvy Bobivy blows the lid off centuries of myths and misinformation surrounding the mysterious Egyptian pyramids. An amateur student of archaeology, Bobivy has long wanted to write a book bringing ancient history to life for its young readers, while finding the truth behind these mysterious structures. Says Bobivy, "I've long had a fascination with the pyramids — where they came from, who built them, how they were built. This book brings it all together for me in a fun and fact-filled way."

Author Bobivy has tapped into a huge potential audience with her latest book. A recent study by researchers at Techmasters shows that 79 percent of all readers age 8 to 12 years are interested in learning more about the ancient pyramids. This group of influential potential readers numbers in the millions.

For additional information, contact ChloBo Boochee at 312-555-1212 or chlobo@bestbookpromoters.com.

About Divvy Bobivy: Divvy Bobivy is a bestselling children's book author who has written or co-written more than 25 titles, including the blockbusters *What's That Smell?* and *Baby, You Can Drive My Go-Kart*.

CONTACT INFORMATION:

ChloBo Boochee

Best Book Promoters

312-555-1212 (voice)

312-555-1213 (fax)

chlobo@bestbookpromoters.com

www.bestbookpromoters.com

Figure 19-1:
A sample press release for a children's book.

Touching on the traditional components

Although the Internet and social media are all the rage nowadays, more traditional approaches to getting your book noticed still work. Consider putting together a press kit and arranging promotional radio and television interviews, as described in the following sections.

Put together a press kit

A *press kit* is a collection of press materials that is sent to the media (radio, television, newspapers, magazines, blogs, Web sites) to get them interested in covering your book. The best press kits contain the following:

- A one-page press release that describes your book as breaking news. (We tell you how to craft a press release in the earlier "Sending out press releases" section.)

- A two-paragraph to one-page bio with interesting tidbits describing you and your background. For example, "As a nationally syndicated columnist, Divvy has been interviewed on *Fox & Friends* and CNN. . . ."

- A bulleted fact sheet or essay-style backgrounder about your book. For example, "Two years of research showed that pandas don't actually prefer bamboo leaves. . . ."

- A FAQ (frequently asked questions) of eight to ten suggested questions the reporter could/should ask you during an interview. For example, "How did bells become so important to the story?" or "As a full-time amateur archaeologist, how do you find time to write?"

- Copies of past press clippings (to show that you're newsworthy) and/or a list of past and future signings or events (showing relevance, competence, and experience).

- A sample article (basically, a short version of your press release) that a busy reporter could print verbatim if she desired (make sure you include a copyright release at the bottom of this sheet).

- Photos of the book cover and headshots of the author and/or illustrator.

- A copy of your book (depending on how many free books you negotiated for in your contract, which we explain how to do in Chapter 17).

- Giveaways such as bookmarks, posters, or pencils that your publisher may produce to garner word-of-mouth advertising.

You can drastically reduce the cost of press kits by writing the material yourself, printing it using your own computer and printer, and then making copies at a local copy store. Target your hardcopy recipients carefully, and create a downloadable version of your press kit for your blog, Facebook fan page, or Web site.

Book radio and television spots

In the bang-for-the-buck department, it's hard to beat getting interviewed on a radio or television show. In particular, shows on major radio and television stations reach a very large audience; so do some cable shows. If you get the call for an interview on *Today* or *Good Morning, America,* you'll probably think you've died and gone to heaven.

You simply can't buy this kind of exposure for your book, but you can get your book in front of the producers or hosts — national and local — who are constantly on the lookout for interesting people with fascinating stories.

Here are some tips for getting booked for radio or television interviews:

- ✔ **Understand your market.** Research your local stations, the networks, and the TV shows you're interested in. Get their schedules, check out their Web sites, and tune in. Don't even think about pitching yourself before you've done your research.

- ✔ **Have a hook.** Why should the radio or television producer or radio host book you for this show? If you want to be booked, you need a hook — the aspect of your story that's going to rivet viewers and listeners and keep them from changing the station.

- ✔ **Be selective.** Don't send your press release out to 1,000 random radio and TV stations — instead, pick out the 15 to 25 that might actually be interested in you and your book. Work those prospects thoroughly and then select another batch of stations.

- ✔ **Target a live human.** Target a specific show, get the name and fax number or e-mail address for whoever books guests (usually a producer, program director, or booker — sometimes the host), and send your press release to that person directly.

- ✔ **Be persistent, accessible, and flexible.** You never know when you'll get the call for an interview or appearance. Be persistent — stay in the minds of those doing the booking for your targeted show by sending a press release every once in a while — and be accessible and flexible in the event the show needs someone to fill in unexpectedly.

Promoting Your Work in Person

Sometimes you just need to give your book's publicity a personal touch, and by that we mean getting out in the world and mingling with your readers and the people who are often in charge of your readers' literary choices — namely parents, retailers, and librarians. Whether you want to hit the road for a full-fledged publicity tour or stay closer to home and conduct book signings or readings or targeted workshops, the following sections have you covered.

Interview with Rhonda Sturtz, executive vice president of New York Journal of Books

Rhonda Sturtz is executive vice president of New York Journal of Books (NYJB; www.nyjournalofbooks.com), an influential online book review site. Rhonda worked for many years in advertising sales, including ten years at *TIME* magazine. Rhonda also has eight years of experience in merchandising and retail management, and she has held several positions in the arts. We asked Rhonda to tell us more about the whys and wherefores of book reviews.

WCBFD: Why should children's book authors care about reviews of their books?

RS: One of our esteemed reviewers wrote the following in an essay: "Reviewers interpret, declare, dismiss, and augment — creating the discussion space that books need in order to live. Reviews are the oxygen books breathe." A review guides the potential reader inside the cover, beyond the first impressions, into the guts. A review introduces your book and reveals something about what's inside so the reader can make an informed decision about whether or not to spend the money to buy it or the time reading. A review opens the door, inviting the reader inside.

WCBFD: How should authors attract the attention of reviewers?

RS: With professional reviews like NYJB, typically you must go through administrative channels to get your title assigned to a reviewer. Starting your campaign for a review early is important. The more lead time you provide, the better chance of getting your book on a reviewer's schedule. You can reach out by e-mail. Some authors or publishers mail advance copies, but this is costly and doesn't always work. You can also try to reach out personally by phoning or Skypeing and attempting to set up appointments with publishers of book reviews. Or you can hire a publicist to do this legwork for you. Since they know the points of contact, their ability to cover the industry with notifications is valuable — and they are often the most experienced at getting the good word out when your book has been covered positively. Emphasize a hook, what's important or timely about your book, and how it impacts the cultural or literary dialogue.

WCBFD: Is it true that book reviewers don't pay attention to self-published books? If so, is there something self-published book authors can do to get their books reviewed?

RS: There is a great deal of worthwhile work being self-published today. At NYJB we don't cover self-published titles only because the universe is so large, we would be inundated with requests and do not have the staff to cover that tsunami. There are, however, some review sources today focusing on self-published works.

WCBFD: Some publishers don't do much to get reviews of their authors' books; so what can authors do to facilitate the process?

RS: That is true. Promotion takes time and money. If you feel your publisher doesn't have the resources or is lackluster in their efforts, you can do it yourself. It takes time and effort, but these days you can use social networking Web sites and online press releases to promote your book as well as develop a list of contacts. You can also hire a publicist to do this work for you.

WCBFD: What are some good ways to leverage reviews for publicity?

RS: Network, network — and network some more. Link to them on your Web site, Facebook, and Google+; send out (free) e-press releases with compelling review blurbs; post on Amazon (don't forget to fill in your Amazon author page!); and do e-mail blasts with relevant updates.

WCBFD: What if an author gets a bad review — should he just go in a corner and cry, or is there something he can do about it?

RS: If you're an author, you must have thick skin and understand that not everyone will love your work. I don't like to use the word "bad." I distinguish between favorable and unfavorable reviews. The best you can hope for is a solid review that reflects an understanding of your work. If certain negatives are noted, well, nothing is perfect. A rave review is a gift, but overall you hope that the reviewer will connect with your work and offer constructive commentary. Many authors have contacted NYJB about the reviews of their work, and what they appreciate most is that our reviewers seem to "get it."

One of NYJB's talented reviewers wrote the following in a recent review:

"It is an undisciplined debut novel, but one that showcases great skills and intelligence. To use Mr. Hicks's own phrase, the saving grace of *Boarded Windows* is 'the pleasure of intermittent brilliance.'" This reviewer, while noting that the book has flaws, still lauds the author's potential."

For me as a potential reader, that type of comment actually sparks my interest in that while it does not hesitate to point out glaring weaknesses, it also notes the integrity of the author's talent.

WCBFD: Should authors consider paying for reviews of their books?

RS: We at NYJB feel a paid-for book review is compromised and lacks integrity. How can a reviewer be objective if the opinion they are writing is purchased by the author? At NYJB we feel it is essential to maintain credibility and complete objectivity by keeping an appropriate separation between authors and reviewers. All review requests and scheduling is done through admin. And we do not accept any payment for reviews.

Planning a publicity tour

Many new book authors have the impression that one of the first things their publisher is going to do after a book is published is send the author out on a multi-city publicity tour, complete with media handlers, tour guides, escorts, and travel expenses paid in full. Unless you're a celebrity or an established bestselling book author, it's highly unlikely you'll get this treatment.

You can, however, create your own publicity tour. When you're planning to visit another town or city, line up some publicity while you're there. You can do a little or a lot; it's up to you. Here are some ideas:

- Drop by some bookstores and sign some books.
- Do some readings at local schools and libraries.
- Schedule a radio or television interview or two.
- Make yourself available to local print media.

With a little advance planning, you can accomplish a lot — all on your own schedule.

Joining the signing and reading circuit

One of the key ways that children's book authors get publicity is to do book signings and readings.

- ✔ **Book signings:** Book signings can either be informal, where you drop in unannounced and sign however many books of yours happen to be in stock; or formal, where the bookstore sets up a signing event on a specific date for you to chat with customers and sign books.

  Be sure to bring a couple of fresh, fine-point, permanent markers in whatever color you like — they're great for signing books.

- ✔ **Book readings:** Readings are generally scheduled well in advance so they can be fit into the organizations' routines and announced far enough in advance to generate interest in the event — and attendees.

Whether you decide to pursue a book signing or a reading, simply call the organization you want to work with and ask for the person in charge of arranging author events. You'll soon be on your way to getting the word out about your book.

Hiring a Publicist

Authors love to write books, but many authors aren't similarly inclined to publicize and market them. Selling books may be something you aren't comfortable with or know anything about. For these reasons and more, consider hiring a professional book publicist. A good publicist isn't cheap, but she can make the difference between a book that sells a few copies and a book that sells a few hundred thousand copies. The next sections explain exactly what a good book publicist can do for you, how to find one, and how to get your money's worth.

Discovering what a publicist can do

The most important thing a publicist can do for you is get your foot in the door at a media outlet, generating enough interest to get you scheduled for an interview, profile, or other article. Specifically, a good book publicist can

- ✔ Draft and distribute press releases, press kits, and brochures.
- ✔ Set up interviews with print journalists.

✔ Schedule live and phone-in radio and television interviews.

✔ Build buzz through his network of traditional and social media contacts.

✔ Arrange book signings and readings.

✔ Submit your book to reviewers.

✔ Schedule appearances at conferences and seminars.

✔ Submit your book for consideration for awards and prizes.

When it comes to publicity, a publicist can do just about anything you'd ever need this side of writing your book. What you have your publicist do for you will be limited only by what your publisher plans to do — and the size of your bank account.

Finding the right publicist

Hooking up with the right publicist is a little like dating — you really don't know how things are going to work out until you spend a little time together. If you decide to hire your own publicist, be sure she has the following:

✔ **Significant experience promoting children's books:** Few publicists have specific experience in publicizing books, and even fewer have experience publicizing children's books. Don't fool around; hire publicists who have a solid track record of experience successfully publicizing children's books.

✔ **Established media contacts:** In the publicity business, the Golden Address Book — your extensive network of traditional and social media contacts — is everything. Your ideal publicist has a well-developed list of contacts she can take your book to — contacts who will give it serious consideration.

✔ **Creativity:** The best publicists are always trying out new and creative ways to get the media's attention — and to draw attention to you and your book, while also covering the basics.

✔ **An assertive but pleasant manner:** Assertive is good; aggressive is bad. Someone who is pleasant to work with can get you a lot more interviews than someone your media contacts try to hide from.

✔ **Time for you:** When you're paying someone your hard-earned money, your phone calls should be answered, your e-mail messages should be responded to promptly, and you should always be treated professionally — with dignity and respect.

> ✔ **A personality that meshes with your own:** You not only need to trust this person implicitly, you need to get along with her. Spend some time with your prospective publicist (on the phone or over lunch) before you sign on the dotted line.
>
> ✔ **A knowledge of industry trends:** Books are a business, and the business of books is in constant flux. Your publicist should be up-to-date on the latest trends and constantly adjusting her approach to respond.

To find a publicist, ask other children's book authors for referrals. If you belong to a group like the Society for Children's Book Writers and Illustrators (`www.scbwi.org`), ask around. See whether you can get referrals from your literary agent, your editor, a friend or relative, or someone else you trust who's connected to the business.

Interview with Maryglenn McCombs, publicist

When it comes to publicizing your new labor of love, it's all about making a big splash, and getting noticed in a sea of competing titles. Maryglenn McCombs (`www.maryglenn.com`) is a professional publicist who specializes in creating and executing targeted book publicity campaigns. We asked Maryglenn to give us a professional perspective on publicity.

WCBFD: It's our experience that the publicity provided by publishers is often significantly less than authors expect. What should authors expect from their publishers?

MM: These days, most publishers provide only minimal PR support. Although there are exceptions to the rule, the lion's share of the promotion tends to fall on the author's shoulders. At the very least, most authors should expect, or hope, that their publisher will at least send advance review copies, also known as *galleys,* to the book and library trade media, such as *Publishers Weekly, Kirkus, Booklist, Library Journal,* and/or *School Library Journal,* as well as major media outlets and reviewers who cover books within the genre. Authors should ask the publisher the specifics of promotion strategy and breadth of PR outreach in order to get a sense of what will, and won't, be provided. Authors should be prepared to shoulder at least part of the burden of promotion. One tip I often give to authors is this: Ask not what your publisher can do for you. Ask what you can do for your publisher.

WCBFD: We all know that social media is now an important avenue for publicizing books. Are traditional print and broadcast media dead, or should they still be pursued for publicity?

MM: Both social media and traditional media are vital to successfully promoting a book. I believe the best strategy is a campaign that includes both. From my experience, print media (newspapers, magazines, newspapers, journals), and online media typically generates the most interest in a new book, although there are exceptions with regards to broadcast media. My sense is that book readers typically are people who read papers, magazines, journals, online articles, and reviews. And while readers obviously also watch television and radio, there isn't always the same level of interest among people who prefer watching TV and listening to the radio over reading. Readers read.

WCBFD: What about authors who self-publish their books — how will this affect their ability to get publicity?

MM: If done well, a self-published book should have virtually the same chances of success as a traditionally published title; however, if you are going to self-publish, make sure that you do it the right way. No shortcuts — and no cutting corners! You will need an excellent designer to create a stellar cover for your book and, depending on the book, you may also need a top-notch illustrator. Hire an editor, a proof-reader, and screen printers and e-publishers carefully. Make sure that every single detail of your book is done thoughtfully and professionally, so that your self-published book (and you) will be taken seriously. Cutting corners, producing a less-than-great end product, or trying to promote a book that is poorly designed, poorly edited — or even not edited — and filled with typos is going to result in an end product that will not make a good impression on a consumer, reviewer, or editor.

WCBFD: What is the #1 best thing authors can do themselves to publicize their books?

MM: Write a good book, and make sure it has a top-notch cover design, spectacular interior design, and is appropriately priced for the market. Making sure that your book is a great-looking, well-packaged product is the first step to publicizing your book.

WCBFD: Okay. So what's the #1 publicity mistake authors should avoid at all costs?

MM: The #1 mistake is trying to promote a book that isn't edited, proofread, and is poorly designed. The #2 mistake is trying to get reviews of a book before it is available. Trade review journals — *Publishers Weekly* and others — do provide advance reviews or "forecasts" of upcoming books, but consumer media reviews (all others) shouldn't run before consumers can buy your book. Timing is everything.

WCBFD: Where can authors find a publicist who understands the children's book market?

MM: Ask industry professionals and other authors for recommendations. Your publisher is a great place to start, as most publishers do know publicists they recommend. You can also look online, but there is nothing more valuable that having someone recommend a publicist with whom they've worked. That's why referrals are so important. Ask around! Once you've found a publicist you consider a good fit, have a thorough understanding of what the process is, and understand what services will — and won't — be provided, ask for a written proposal, as well as a list of references. Contact those references, and do not be afraid to ask lots of questions. Make sure you are completely comfortable with your decision before you sign a contract. If you feel uneasy in any way, or don't feel you've gotten answers to the questions you've asked, it might be a good idea to keep looking. After all, you need to trust your publicist with your book, and if you don't feel you can do that, there is no reason to proceed.

Getting the most for your money

You don't want to shell out a ton of money to a publicist without getting results in return. After you've made the decision to engage a publicist, and after you've found a good one, you need to ensure you get your money's worth. Here are a few tips for doing just that:

✔ **Don't wait until the last minute.** Ideally, you should engage a publicist at least three months before your book is published. Six months is better.

✔ **Get a proposal.** Be sure your publicist-to-be gives you a written proposal detailing exactly what services she'll provide and exactly when they'll be delivered.

✔ **Set a fixed price and ceiling.** Publicists usually work in one of two ways: a fixed price for an entire marketing campaign or a fixed hourly rate. If you go with the latter, be sure you set a ceiling price that your publicist may not exceed without first obtaining your written approval.

✔ **Put it in writing.** Get all agreements with your publicist in writing.

✔ **Get reports.** Require your publicist to provide regular (weekly or monthly) reports of what he has done on behalf of your book — phone calls made, press releases sent, producers contacted, and so forth.

✔ **Assess and reengage (or say good-bye).** Take time to periodically take stock of where you're at: Has the publicist done what he promised? What are the results? If you're happy, continue the relationship. If not, don't hesitate to fire your publicist and find a new one.

A good publicist can be your best friend. By taking care of the business side of things up front, your relationship can proceed on a firm foundation of trust. And that's good for you — and for your book.

Chapter 20

Getting Savvy with Social Media

*U*nless you've been living under a rock for the past five years, you've probably noticed that Web sites such as Twitter, Facebook, YouTube, and others like them featuring content created by everyday Joes and Janes — collectively known as *social media* — have taken the world by storm. The result has been a gold rush of people, companies, and other organizations eager to establish social media platforms.

While the jury is still out as to whether having a social media platform is the end-all, be-all for the average children's book author, we personally believe it's a key element in any effective book marketing effort. That's why in this chapter, we look at exactly who to influence, the best places to establish your social media platform, and how to launch a social media campaign.

Influencing the Influencers

The goal of marketing your book via social media is not to do all the talking yourself — it's to get *other* people talking about you. In our experience, it's especially important to get people who can influence others to talk about you.

When the first edition of this book was originally published, Lisa and Peter made a special effort to mail free copies to as many established online children's book bloggers and reviewers as they could find. The hope was that they would talk about this book on their blogs or write book reviews that would appear on influential Web sites. They did. Lisa and Peter's strategy worked, and it helped make this book the #1 book on writing children's books on Amazon.com — where it has remained to this very day.

Little did we know we were practicing a kind of marketing that's relatively new: *social influence marketing.* This new kind of marketing is simply employing social media to gain the attention — and mentions — of *social influencers* (people who have achieved a large social-media presence).

There is no doubt in our minds that social influence marketing should constitute a key part of your book marketing efforts. So where do you start? You start by understanding the basics of influencing others.

The basics of influencing others

Although using social media to influence others is a relatively recent phenomenon, social influence itself is not. People have long sought out the advice of trusted others — friends, relatives, neighbors, colleagues, experts — when they make decisions of all sorts. These decisions can range from something as simple as where to stop for lunch to something much more complex — and potentially risky — as whether or not to buy a house in a particular neighborhood for a particular price using a mortgage with specific terms and conditions.

We influence others every day, just as we ourselves are influenced. We are social creatures, and influencing and being influenced is a perfectly normal and often quite welcome occurrence. We *want* to know if a decision we're about to make is going to be a good one or a bad one — especially if it's a decision with the potential to significantly affect our lives. In the same way, we want to let our friends and significant others (heck, the whole world!) know when a decision we made worked out in our favor — or not, because that information can serve as a cautionary note to others we care about.

When we're thinking about buying something, there are two kinds of products or services that we can buy:

- ✔ **Low-consideration purchases:** These items are generally inexpensive, undifferentiated from one another (one product is pretty much like another), and purchasing them is a low-risk proposition for the buyer. Examples include a pack of chewing gum at a convenience store or a hot dog at a baseball game. These are inexpensive, low-risk purchases. If you don't like the gum or the hot dog, you can toss it out with just a small financial loss. You're probably not going to ask your friends whether you should buy a particular brand of gum, and it's unlikely the opinions of others will influence you much one way or the other.

- ✔ **High-consideration purchases:** These items are usually expensive and highly differentiated. After you buy them, you're pretty much stuck with them. Think about the process you go through when you buy a car. You ask friends and work associates how they like their cars, you read reviews, you comparison shop and take test drives. You know if you make the right decision, you'll be a happy driver for the next five years or more. Make the wrong decision, however, and you could be stuck with a very costly mistake.

Although a children's book is certainly not at the same price level as a new Ferrari, most cost far more than a pack of gum. As such, people often seek out the advice of others when they buy children's books, a behavior that provides children's book authors (like you!) the opportunity to apply the principles of social influence marketing when selling your book.

Understanding the different kinds of online influencers

When it comes to influencing others online, three major kinds of influencers exist — each of whom exerts influence in a particular way:

- ✔ **Positional influencer:** These are influencers who are socially (and often physically) close to you in some way — relatives, spouses or partners, boyfriends, girlfriends, bosses, co-workers. You get the picture. Because these people are closest to the purchasing decision, they have the most influence.

- ✔ **Referent influencer:** These are influencers with whom you hang out (and trust) on social media platforms such as Twitter and Facebook. If someone you follow on Twitter mentions he *loves* his new Brand X mountain bike, then you'll likely take note. And if you're in the market for a mountain bike, then you'll probably automatically include Brand X on your short list.

- ✔ **Expert influencer:** Expert influencers are, well, *experts.* These are the people you consult when you're planning to make a high-consideration purchase and you want to make sure you don't make a costly mistake. It's unlikely you personally know expert influencers (they often have huge followings in social media), but because of their knowledge and expertise, you trust their opinions and give high consideration to their advice.

By understanding how each of these three major kinds of influencers exert their power over others, you can better determine where best to focus your own social influence marketing efforts.

Figuring out where online your influencers live

Deciding *where* to target your social influence marketing efforts is a crucial decision — there are so many blogs, Twitter feeds, message boards, and other social media devoted to children's books that you can't possibly cover them all. You have to be selective when it comes to deciding which influencers to approach and which ones to pass by.

Although a quick Internet search reveals a near-endless list of social media devoted to children's books, not all sites are created equal. Some are probably lucky to attract one or two visitors a month, whereas others attract thousands. Clearly, if you want to influence the influencers it makes more sense to put your focus on the sites that get the greatest number of visitors and attract the most comments and contributions from others.

Knowing Where to Create a Social Media Presence

The world of social media is constantly evolving. The site that's big today may be old news in a matter of months, weeks, or even days. You need to stay aware of what's going on with social media. In particular, keep an eye out for new sites that pop up, particularly ones on which you can establish an influential presence. ***Remember:*** The books you sell may be your own!

The sections that follow clue you in to several currently popular social media tools and offer tips for how to use them to your promotional advantage.

Blogs

Blogs give you the opportunity to write about the process of writing, pass on tips and lessons learned, review the work of other writers and illustrators, and connect with other children's book writers and potential buyers of your books. Many children's book authors make writing a blog an essential part of their social media presence, posting at least a couple times a week — and sometimes much more often than that. Here are some of the very best to consider as models for your own blog:

- Cynsations by Cynthia Leitich Smith, `http://cynthialeitichsmith.blogspot.com`

- Seven Impossible Things Before Breakfast by Julie Danielson, `http://blaine.org/sevenimpossiblethings`

- Jen Robinson's Book Page by Jen Robinson, `http://jkrbooks.typepad.com/blog`

- Read Roger by Roger Sutton, `http://readroger.hbook.com`

- A Fuse #8 Production by Elizabeth Bird, `http://blog.schoollibraryjournal.com/afuse8production`

When creating your own blog, be sure to set up an RSS feed (a Web feed for delivering content). You can then set up your other social media platforms (Facebook, Twitter, and so on) to automatically rebroadcast your blog posts in real time — greatly amplifying the reach of your social media platform.

Facebook

Facebook (`www.facebook.com`) is currently the 600-pound gorilla of social media, and most every children's book author has by now established a presence there. As you consider how exactly you will put Facebook to work promoting you and your books, keep in mind you can create a variety of different kinds of pages on Facebook, each of which has its pluses and minuses.

At minimum, we suggest you create an author page under the "Author, Band, or Public Figure" category of pages. You can then customize this page any way you like, including setting up an RSS feed for your blog posts, excerpts and illustrations from your books, event invitations, your biography and photos, and much more. Visitors can simply "Like" the page to follow you with no further action necessary on your part.

Twitter

Though many people wondered for some time whether there was any real use for a microblogging site that limited posts to no more than 140 characters, Twitter (`www.twitter.com`) looks like it's here to stay — at least for the foreseeable future. That being the case, it has become pretty much essential for children's book authors to create a Twitter feed to keep their followers up to date (by the nanosecond) on their goings on.

We suggest you set up a Twitter account for you as a children's book author, separate from any personal Twitter account you may have already established to keep your friends and family up to date. Use this account to comment on your life as a children's book author, your experiences during the writing or selling process, interesting observations about the publishing industry, and retweets of interesting and informative related posts from others.

YouTube

We're going to bet you've probably spent too much time on the YouTube Web site (www.youtube.com) watching videos of cute cats, funny kids, aspiring singing stars, and who knows what else. As an increasing number of children's book authors get savvy to the power of social media, they are discovering that creating short videos and book trailers based on their books can be very effective selling tools, and that YouTube is a great place to host them.

If you decide to create promotional videos for your children's book, we first suggest you get a hold of a copy of *Video Marketing For Dummies* by Kevin Daum, Bettina Hein, Matt Scott, and Andreas Goeldi (John Wiley & Sons, Inc.), which explains all the ins and outs of creating compelling marketing videos and book trailers, and then hosting them on YouTube. We also suggest you set up your own author channel on YouTube, on which you can host all your videos, making it easy for visitors to find, comment on, and subscribe to your updates.

Pinterest

Pinterest (www.pinterest.com) is one of the newest social media sites to catch the fancy of a large number of users. Essentially, it allows users to bookmark inspirational images they find during their Internet travels. Children's book authors can use it to promote their own personal brands and books. Check out these authors' pins to find inspiration for how you can use Pinterest to promote yourself and your work:

- ✔ Kami Garcia: http://pinterest.com/kamigarcia
- ✔ Mike Mullin: http://pinterest.com/mikemullin
- ✔ Debbie Ohi: http://pinterest.com/inkyelbows

If you have a blog, we recommend including that URL on your Pinterest home page. Simply click the little globe icon and then type in the URL. Oh, and be sure to include a fun description about yourself that makes it clear you're a children's book author worth checking out.

JacketFlap

JacketFlap (www.jacketflap.com) is a meeting place for more than 200,000 authors, illustrators, publishers, and other creators of books for children and young adults. Whether you're a new or established children's book author or illustrator, it's a great place to hang out and meet likeminded people.

Launching a Social Media Campaign

Although a key part of establishing a powerful social media platform is persistently and consistently building your online presence using the various tools at your disposal, you should also plan to make a big social media splash whenever you release a new title. You can make this big splash by launching a social media campaign.

Reviewing the ABCs of a social media campaign

So you've decided to launch a social media campaign — great! Now what? In addition to checking out the nearby "The only book marketing plan you'll ever need" sidebar, we suggest you do the following:

1. Clearly define your goals in advance. You might, for example, want to drive people to your children's book author Twitter feed, increasing your followers from 250 to 1,000 within a two-week period of time. Make sure your goals are SMART, that is: Specific, Measurable, Attainable, Relevant, and Timely.

2. Pick a form of social media you want to target with your social media campaign, for example, "blog," and then do a Google (or use another Internet search engine) search using that form of social media in combination with the search term "children's book." This particular search will generate a (very) long list of children's book blogs.

3. Decide how many social media sites you want to initially target in your campaign, say ten — or ten a day.

4. Visit the sites in rank order of their listing from your Google search. Keep in mind that, in general, the higher the ranking in a Google search, the more visitors the site attracts and the more influence it has on others. Always keep your eye on the prize —you want to leverage your social media efforts to the largest possible audience.

5. Consider each site in turn to determine how you might be able to have an influence on the site's visitors. You might, for example, be able to send a copy of your book to get reviewed on a blog, or you might offer a contest with a signed book as a premium, or you might become an active commenter on that blog — providing valuable insights and influencing other visitors.

6. Create a list of the high-opportunity sites, namely the ones you most want to influence.

7. Execute your social media plan by visiting each of the high-influence sites on your list and accomplishing the actions you have decided will have the greatest impact.

8. Evaluate your results. There's an old saying: Feedback is the breakfast of champions. If your results meet or exceed your goals, then keep doing what you're doing. If not, then adjust your approach and try again. See the section of this chapter titled "Measuring the Effectiveness of Your Campaign" for detailed information on getting feedback and acting on it.

Surveying the unwritten rules of social media marketing

Although there are many different ways to structure your social media campaign, there are four inviolable rules of the road to ensure you get the best possible response — and results.

✔ **What goes around comes around.** Social media depends on the idea of "you scratch my back, and I'll scratch yours." That is, if you're going to ask your prospects to take valuable time out of their day to read your blog, watch your video, or peruse your Facebook page, you have to give them something in return. In some cases, this might just be some great information that they can't get anywhere else. In others, it might be a physical reward, like an autographed book, a free digital copy of another book, or a reading in their child's school.

✔ **Your prospects are all created equal.** When it comes to your social media campaign, you need to treat everyone equally — no one is more special than anyone else. If you decide to reward some sort of premium — say, a free downloadable excerpt from your next book — to people who view your YouTube video on your Facebook author page, then you need to offer the premium to *everyone* who watches your video. In fact, you want to encourage people to pass the link on to their friends, who will in turn pass the link on to *their* friends, and so on. Beware: If you're really good at what you're doing, that premium could number into the thousands, not to mention mailing costs if it is not digitally transmittable.

✔ **Be real.** Be authentic. Be you. Most people will ultimately sniff out a phony.

✔ **If you truly love your campaign, you have to let it go.** The best social media campaigns take on a life of their own, which means you may lose control of them soon after they're released into the wild. This is actually a good thing — you want your campaign to catch fire and take off. Set your goals, design a great campaign, make adjustments if you need to, and then let it go.

The only book marketing plan you'll ever need

Randy Ingermanson (www.advanced fictionwriting.com) knows how to sell books. Known around the world as "The Snowflake Guy" in honor of his Snowflake method for designing and analyzing novels, Randy is the author of six award-winning novels and co-author with Peter of *Writing Fiction For Dummies*. Peter was particularly impressed with the marketing plan Randy rolled out to launch *Writing Fiction For Dummies* to Amazon.com's #1 bestselling book on writing fiction — a position that it has held consistently ever since. Here is Randy's philosophy behind marketing books — and the only book marketing plan you'll ever need.

Sez Randy . . .

When you're marketing your book, you want to excel at two things. You want a great launch and you want your book to continue to sell at a nice steady clip, year after year.

You get the best launch if you have a large e-mail list or a large group of blog subscribers. In my opinion, nothing else is nearly as good as these — not Facebook fans, not Twitter followers.

You can seriously help your steady-state sales if you have a good Web site or blog that attracts people, engages their interest, and convinces them that your book is essential to their life.

Remember that social media are social. It's much better for other people to be talking about you on Facebook and Twitter than for you to be talking about yourself.

Here are the six things I believe give you the most bang for your buck:

✔ Create an engaging author Web site and build an e-mail list of fans who want to be notified when your next book comes out.

✔ Create an engaging blog and build a list of blog subscribers.

✔ Add Facebook and Twitter buttons on every page of your Web site and your blog so people can talk about you.

✔ In each book, put a link to your Web site and blog and tell people why they should visit.

✔ When you launch a new book, create an incentive for your fans to buy it RIGHT NOW and then send an e-mail to your e-mail list of fans. Also blog about it. Make the case that there will never be a better time to buy, and tell them where to get it. Don't be shy, but don't be rude.

✔ Create sales pages for each book on your Web site (or your blog if it isn't part of your Web site) that give people a powerful reason to want to buy your book. Ask for the sale and include links to all the online retailers.

Applying search engine optimization

If you've been tinkering in the social Web for any amount of time, you've probably heard the term *search engine optimization,* which simply means designing your Web site, blog, or other marketing platform in a way that will attract the greatest possible interest of search engines such as Google, YouTube, Bing, Yahoo!, and the like.

How do you do this? Here's a short list of to-do's:

- ✔ Use powerful keywords on your site.
- ✔ Build your Web pages so search engines will love them.
- ✔ Get your pages into the top search engines.
- ✔ Encourage other sites to link to your site.
- ✔ Keep abreast of changes in SEO and adapt your Web presence accordingly.

We could write an entire book on the specifics of how to accomplish this to-do list, but Peter Kent already did: *Search Engine Optimization For Dummies,* 4th Edition (John Wiley & Sons, Inc.). If you're more tech savvy, *The Art of SEO* by Eric Enge (O'Reilly Media) might be worth a look. Check 'em out.

Measuring the Effectiveness of Your Campaign

Is it possible to know how effective your social media campaign was without measuring the results? In a word, no. No matter how many friends complimented you on your new book, how many comments you received on your latest blog post, or how many people pinned a photo of the cover of your book to their boards, you really have no idea how effective your campaign was until you measure the results.

Here are some of the measures you should consider for some of the most common social media platforms:

- ✔ **Blog:** You can measure things such as the number of visitors, the number of comments your visitors make, and the number of times they pass links to your site to other people or other social marketing platforms (by using, for example, the Like button for Facebook, or by retweeting a post of yours on Twitter).
- ✔ **Facebook:** You can measure the number of fans of your author fan page, the average growth in the number of fans, the number of page interactions generated by each post you make, the click-through rate of your stream, and much more.

- ✔ **Twitter:** You can measure the number of mentions of you or whatever it is that you're promoting, the number of retweets of your own tweets, the number of click-throughs, and more.

- ✔ **YouTube:** You can measure the number of views your video generates, the demographics of the viewers (say, 18–24 year olds), and the number of comments and shares your video accumulates during a specific period of time.

Social media measurement tools are constantly being improved. Be sure to keep up with the latest offerings of whatever platforms you decide to target for your social media campaigns.

To properly measure the results of your social media campaign, you have to start with clearly defined SMART goals (goals that are Specific, Measurable, Attainable, Relevant, and Timely).

Interview with Emma Walton Hamilton, author, editor, educator, and arts and literacy advocate

Emma Walton Hamilton (www.emmawalton hamilton.com) is a bestselling children's book author, editor, educator, and arts and literacy advocate. She has co-authored more than 20 children's books with her mother, the actress Julie Andrews, six of which have been on the *New York Times* bestseller list, including The Very Fairy Princess series (#1 *New York Times* Bestsellers), *Julie Andrews' Collection of Poems, Songs and Lullabies* (illustrated by James McMullan); the Dumpy the Dump Truck series; *Simeon's Gift;* and *The Great American Mousical.* Emma is also a freelance children's book editor, host of the Children's Book Hub online, and director of the Children's Literature Workshops for Stony Brook Southampton's MFA in Creative Writing. She has established a particularly strong social media platform and presence, and we asked her to tell us what social media means to her.

WCBFD: Should children's book authors care about social media? Why or why not?

EWH: All authors should care about social media, but especially children's book authors. The role of an author in the marketplace is dramatically different today than it was even ten years ago. The old model where the writer wrote and the publisher promoted is gone. Even in the world of children's books, editors now consider an author's "platform" as much as the quality of the writing when making acquisitions decisions — and they expect authors to play a significant role in the marketing and promotion of their own releases. Those who neglect this part of the job are likely to see lower sales figures and fewer contracts offered — because if a book doesn't sell, publishers are less likely to take a chance on another one by the same author.

The good news is that thanks to social media, it's easier than ever to manage one's own promotional efforts — and for the most part it's free. Children's book authors have an added advantage with respect to their audience demographic in that there is no more powerful way to connect with young people than via the Internet — more specifically, through social media.

(continued)

(continued)

WCBFD: Which social media platforms if any do you consider "must-do's" for children's book authors?

EWH: Facebook and Twitter continue to be essential, with Pinterest coming up quickly as a force to be reckoned with. On Facebook, it's very important to have an author page as well as a profile. This allows your readers to find the information they are looking for without having to wade through personal posts — and it also allows them to follow you without your having to "friend" them.

YouTube is important for book trailers and author videos, and I also like LinkedIn, even though it's more business oriented because of the writers groups one can connect with. JacketFlap.com is a social media site geared solely toward children's authors. And of course one of the best ways to build a following is via an author Web site and a blog.

WCBFD: What is your own approach to social media?

EWH: I maintain several Web sites, and I try to blog once or twice a week (which is widely thought of as the minimum for any effectiveness), though I don't always meet that goal. I have a Facebook profile and an author page, a Twitter feed, a profile on LinkedIn, a Pinterest page, a YouTube channel, and a JacketFlap page.

The key for me lies in linking as much of it together as possible. For instance, when I post something on my blog, it goes out simultaneously to Facebook, Twitter, LinkedIn, and JacketFlap, so I don't have to log on to all four places. Everything I post on Twitter goes to Facebook, and so forth. It's fairly easy to connect everything these days.

I use all these things not just to promote our books, but also to provide information about the Children's Book Hub, the Southampton Children's Literature Conference, and the various courses and editing services I offer. So I strive for a balance between posting news about upcoming releases and events and providing information that is useful to children's book authors and illustrators.

WCBFD: What are the best ways to build a following?

EWH: I think the first question to ask yourself is, "Who is my audience?" Who are you trying to reach? For instance, YA authors are likely to be reaching out directly to their readers, since so many teens use the Internet as their primary source of information. But picture book authors really need to reach out to parents, booksellers, librarians, teachers, and others who put books in the hands of young children. Obviously there's some overlap, but it's important to consider whom you're talking to before you start putting yourself out there.

It's also important to think about what you're going to offer them. The authors who are most successful at using social media provide their readers and followers with added value, something that goes beyond just promoting books and appearances. Perhaps they are encouraging young writers, or expanding upon a specific subject they write about. Maybe they are providing opportunities to further engage with characters beyond the book itself. (I have a good friend who created a Facebook page for one of her animal characters, and she posts on his behalf.) They might offer links to support materials, such as coloring pages or quizzes, or host giveaways or contests. But they are doing more than just self-promotion, which is very attractive.

For those who have a new book coming out, virtual book tours are a great way to build a following. Rather than touring cities, stores, or other real-life venues, authors connect with readers online, via Web sites, blogs, podcasts, vlogs, teleconferences, chats, Web-based articles and reviews, Internet radio and TV, YouTube,

Facebook, and other social networking communities. The key is to ensure that the effort is as structured and coordinated as it would be if you were on a "real" book tour, and that it unfolds over a similar period of days or weeks.

Finally, and perhaps most importantly, the buzzword when it comes to using social media is *reciprocity*. Authors whose posts are purely self-promotional are less likely to develop a following than those who provide the kind of added value mentioned above: who reach out and connect with their followers and industry colleagues. Taking the time to reply to comments, for instance — whether on your blog or your Facebook page — is key, as is posting your own comments on other people's blogs. It's all about building, being part of, and contributing to the online community.

WCBFD: If you could do only one thing in social media to promote your books, what would you do?

EWH: At this point, probably create an author page on Facebook. It's best to have an author Web site as well, but if you're really time- or techno-challenged, a Facebook page can achieve almost as much as a Web site these days. You can create tabs dedicated to individual titles (which become their own sub-pages), and you can post information about and invite followers to events, among many other things.

WCBFD: What fatal errors should authors avoid in social media?

EWH: First of all, if you've been using Facebook or Twitter to tell your friends what you had for breakfast, STOP. Start viewing these sites as the powerful marketing tools that they are. Once you start using them correctly, you won't want your followers looking back at random posts or embarrassing pictures.

Paradoxically, it's really important not to make all your social media efforts about yourself.

Again, aim for community instead of tooting your own horn. Try to provide ongoing value and service to your readers and colleagues, not just information about yourself and your books. In the end, your platform is more than just how many followers you have. It's what you stand on, who you are. It's your value system. That's what your followers are really interested in.

Finally, don't spend so much time on social media that you stop writing! Keep working on your writing first and foremost. Without that, the rest is meaningless.

WCBFD: What do you think the future holds for social media and children's books?

EWH: I think we will see the KidLit Blogosphere — already a formidable force in today's children's book industry — becoming an even greater influence. Mostly composed of librarians, educators, booksellers, and authors, these bloggers have become so powerful that many publishers today believe a good review from one of them is as important as one from the *New York Times*. I expect this trend will continue to grow.

I also think that we will see more traditional publishers offering "boutique" services for self-publishers, which will dramatically change the publishing landscape and which will make promotional efforts even more important for authors. And I suspect that as we read more on electronic devices, we will start sharing our reading choices in the same way we do our music ones.

Some people worry that as we engage more in social media, we will read less and books will eventually become obsolete. I'm more optimistic. I think that our society has always been, and always will be deeply invested in storytelling . . . it's just that the mediums are diversifying. With so many ways to create, communicate, and connect, it's truly an exciting time to be a writer!

Part VI
The Part of Tens

The 5th Wave   By Rich Tennant

"Is this where the breakout session for children's book authors meets?"

In this part . . .

Here are a couple of quick reference chapters to help you negotiate not only writing a children's book but also getting it the recognition it deserves. These short and sweet chapters are great for generating ideas or solving problems (and they're also pretty fun to read, if we do say so ourselves). Prepare to be inspired with a ton of story-line sources and a rundown of some of the most important and well-known children's book awards you can aim to win one day.

Chapter 21

More Than Ten Great Sources for Storylines

In This Chapter

▶ Using folk tales, mythology, and more

▶ Looking at kids' brand-new experiences and everyday concerns

▶ Sifting through contemporary history and science

Certain premises for story lines can be employed time and again. Whether your take on an existing story sounds derivative is up to you and your writing skill. But ever since we writers started scratching our stories on the walls of caves or sitting around a fire listening to a tale told with a good cup of tea, we've been sharing our experiences and imaginings with others. And some of these experiences and imaginings are more universal than others. They may have happened to us, or to a friend, or perhaps we heard them told as children and the tales still captivate us. Some are just great stories with action and adventure, good and evil, magic and exploration. And some are pure urban (or rural) myth.

To find out whether anyone owns a story — and whether you can retell it in your words without getting in trouble — use this fairly reliable test: If you can find three different sources of adaptations or retellings in the public domain, then you can fairly assume the story is up for grabs. (A story falls into *public domain* if it's a creative work no longer protected by copyright and can be used by anyone.) Just make sure to get your hands on the three physical books the story comes from because online sources can't always be relied upon to correctly credit material. Check the copyright and permissions pages and ascertain that the publisher or author hasn't obtained permission from someone else to use the story. If they did, they would have to credit it, and if the credit is in the book, they may have had to pay for the privilege of using it or adapting it — something you may not want to do.

In this chapter, we list some fabulous resources for story lines that you're welcome to pilfer and tinker with to your heart's content because no one — and everyone — owns them.

Tales of Yore

Fairy tales, folk tales, and fables are all fictional stories told generation after generation (some hundreds of generations). They're usually short (the length of short stories as opposed to novels) and often devoid of description or con-text-setting narrative, focusing only on character and action. They vaguely capture a bygone period of time or history — when read in the original. And they often embody a lesson or moral — or can be deconstructed to reveal one.

Although it can be difficult to discern one from the other, and subjects in one mirror subjects in another, each of these three categories can be distinguished by a few salient differences.

Fairy tales

Fairy tales are, of course, fanciful and imaginary stories about people, animals, things, or magical beings who have magical powers. They are always made up and are intended to amuse and entertain. They have satisfying themes, such as good triumphing over evil. Fairy tales follow certain conventions: There is no question who the good guys are, magic often abounds, and the bad guys usu-ally get their due. Although these and other conventions can make fairy tales somewhat predictable, that predictability and familiarity provide the perfect setup for deviations. For example, what if you were to take the well-known tale of Goldilocks and set it in the present day with a young bear who breaks into a house of humans? Or how about a tale about a young male Sleeping Beauty instead of a female one?

Fairy tales don't have to be relegated to picture books only. Middle grade novels and young adult novels often take a premise or a character from a fairy tale and then tweak and update it to create stories relevant to today's audiences. Consider Robin McKinley's *Spindle's End* (Ace Trade), a contemporary take on *Sleeping Beauty);* or *Ella Enchanted* by Gail Carson Levine (HarperTeen), a Cinderella story; or even books that take more than one fairy tale and weave them together such as Emma Donoghue's *Kissing the Witch: Old Tales in New Skins* (HarperTeen); or Francesca Lia Block's *The Rose and the Beast: Fairy Tales Retold* (HarperTeen), a collection of stories with both traditional and contemporary fairy tale retellings.

If you choose to adapt fairy tales, go back to the originals and not to the Disney adaptations, because certain additions to the Disney tales aren't public domain.

Fables

Fables are stories that have a point, a lesson, that's supposed to help the reader live better, understand something about a specific culture, or comprehend the natural world. Fables are heavy-handed morality tales in which animals and humans are taught obvious little lessons. Although we don't advise preaching to children in your haste to teach them everything you know or believe (a very common mistake made by first-time writers), we do think fables provide interesting moral dilemmas and lessons that can be disguised by good writing.

We don't suggest that you submit an adapted fable to a publisher using the word *ass* in the title or the text. Why? Because although children of a certain age will find it hilarious, the gatekeepers (publishers who acquire the manuscripts in the first place, booksellers who stock the books, librarians who shelve them, and then parents who buy the finished product — more about them in Chapter 3) may not share your delightfully childlike sense of humor. On the other hand, books such as *Walter the Farting Dog* and *Everybody Poops* are bestselling titles that have become *evergreens* (backlist titles that sell consistently year after year).

Fables provide life lessons in proper behavior and human nature. They also open the door to story lines based on teaching lessons in the most obvious of ways, for how much more obvious can you get than a stated moral at the end of a story? Unless you're writing a traditional fable in the traditional format, which includes a fablelike title and an obviously spelled out moral at the end, avoid preaching to children. They don't like lectures any more than you do. If you must have a moral to your story, it's better to be subtle about it, elegantly writing it into your plot and character development and letting the reader discern its validity on her own.

Folk tales

Folk tales involve the traditional beliefs, practices, lessons, legends, and tales of a culture or a people passed down orally through stories. Folk tales have ways of explaining basic natural truths for each culture, such as where the world came from, why humans have power over animals, why animals act the way they do, why the seasons change, and so on. They tend mostly to be based in the natural world, but, like fables, they can also focus on human behavior; however, they rarely have that preachy, moralistic tone of fables. Often, folk tales require the characters to use their wits to solve a problem.

Folk tales are generally written by people from certain regions and reflect those cultures in some way. For instance, trickster tales have their origins in cultures as diverse as West African and Native American Indian. Anansi tales, a specific form of trickster tale involving Anansi, a spider, has its roots in the Caribbean. Br'er Rabbit is also a trickster figure, originating from folklore of the peoples of south and central Africa; Br'er Rabbit made his way to the American South via the North American slave trade. In other words, folk tales come in many shapes and forms — many of which are similar in nature to each other — regardless of origin or adaptation.

Mythology and Mythological Heroes

The Greeks and Romans (and every other ancient culture) developed heroes and antiheroes that populated exciting stories of adventure, magic, and power — covering every imaginable activity, behavior, hope, and emotion that humans or immortals could conceive. These mythologies, regardless of origin, have been adopted into nearly every culture and religion in the world in some way or another, representing universal experiences.

Nursery Rhymes

Nursery rhymes — those little ditties from your childhood — are great sources for characters and story lines. Imagine Mary, Mary Quite Contrary as the star of her own hip-hop troupe. Or what if Little Miss Muffet wasn't arachnophobic and instead befriended the spider? How would Jack and Jill have approached the hill if one of them were physically challenged? Nursery rhymes are also perfect for getting you in that kid-space, rhyming, upbeat, fun-time, story line–writing mood.

Bible Stories

The Bible, both the Five Books of Moses and the New Testament, is full of exciting stories. Miracles were born in the Bible and provide great launch pads for children's stories. And if you want to be really controversial, how about tackling evolution versus creationism?

Sibling Issues

Certain experiences in a child's life are definitive. Those involving siblings can even be life altering. What better story line for a sibling in need than one that revolves around issues facing siblings, such as when a new baby comes home, or when one sibling is favored over another, or when a sibling becomes seriously ill?

Family Changes

Most children must face changes that alter the delicate balances of the family unit in subtle and not-so-subtle ways. Because children seem to thrive with structure (which ultimately allows them to fly free and experiment in the world in healthful, appropriate, and constructive ways), and because family is the most basic and important structure in their lives, any issue facing a family affects them. Some issues to write about include separation or divorce, remarriage, adoption, nontraditional families, moving to a new neighborhood, abusive situations, and more.

Situations such as going through a divorce, moving to a new neighborhood, or dealing with the abuse of a parent or sibling could be the basis for a story line appealing to children and their parents. Think of situations that your family faced as you were growing up or situations that made you feel unsure or uncomfortable. Chances are, you could write a book to help some other child who feels the same way you did.

First Experiences

Few things are more touching than thinking about a child facing an experience for the first time. For some reason, we sentimentalize (as in "How cute!") these situations, when in actuality such experiences are more often exhilarating or frightening (or something in between) to a child. In other words, anything but *cute!*

Many books out there are about the first day at school, but you may be able to write a better one. Or you can write about other firsts, such as first haircuts, first crushes, first bicycle rides, first sleepovers, first times in the principal's office, or first trips to the dentist.

The list of firsts is endless — and continues way past babyhood. Scour your memories for some memorable firsts in your own life or in the lives of your family members for some potent story line material.

Common Childhood Fantasies

Who hasn't longed to live in different circumstances or wished to be a different person altogether? Children move in and out of their fantasy worlds many times during a given day. More importantly, fantasies are great starting points for interesting story lines. Consider fantasies built around astronauts, fairies, princesses, mad scientists, pirates, monsters, secret agents, wishes, and so forth.

Friendship and Social Issues

From the first time they attend a "Parent and Me" class to their first sleepover, children are thrust into social situations that become more and more integral to their well-being as they get older. Soon friends supplant parents as favorite people to spend time with. If you can come up with a ton of issues facing families, imagine a child trying to figure out all the ins and outs of being a friend or navigating middle school or dealing with mean kids. Just take yourself back to elementary school, junior high school, or high school days, and it should all come rushing back to you. Some classics include peer pressure, cheating, smoking, drugs, religious or racial differences, bullying, and more.

Growing Pains (Emotional and Behavioral)

Children, even the tiniest ones, experience new and powerful emotions all the time and don't know how to handle them. Some children seem to just barely survive, whereas others make these experiences seem easy. But wouldn't it be great if there were wonderful stories starring a relatable someone who has to deal with these same issues in their own lives? Then children could explore their options without leaving the comfort of their favorite secret fort. Some of our favorites include feeling shy, being left out, losing a friend to a different clique, having a disability, experiencing fears, and dealing with mean kids.

Bodies: Their Functions and Changes

Children of all sizes and ages have to learn to deal with bodily functions and changes. In the last decade, quite a few books about bodily functions that were considered taboo in polite society have become raging bestsellers. Consider content, fictional or nonfiction, about body types and differences, disease and sickness, the uses of your five senses, or potty training.

History Makers and History in the Making

Sure, some history teachers could bore the prickles off a porcupine, but history is filled with great stories about heroes and heroines, villains and do-gooders, and just plain-old folks like you and us. Have you ever felt captivated by a time in history or wondered what it felt like to be in the shoes of an especially fascinating contemporary or historical figure of note? There is lots of material for children on the usual suspects (think presidents, pilgrims, and scientists of yore), but what about today's makers of history? What about the visionaries of the recent past, such as entrepreneurs and modern-day game changers? Consider inventors of newer medical devices, people and cultures in developing countries, talented singers and dancers, contemporary writers and poets, and more.

And don't forget that you can find a rich vein to mine in history in the making. Current events can be plucked from daily news sources; they present a wealth of new and interesting topics to write about.

Your audience is not just preschoolers and elementary school-age children; tweens and teens need good, timely books, too!

Nature, Science, Technology

Stories with natural, scientific, or technological content are highly coveted by publishers. If they're well-written, cover a contemporary topic, and adopt a unique approach, you have a better-than-average chance of getting published. Teachers, librarians, and parents are always looking for new and exciting material to supplement what's taught in school — as in material that doesn't reek of lessons to be learned or homework to be done. If you can couch learning about photosynthesis in a story about a young boy's adventures in the Amazon or craft a biography of Steve Jobs for the picture book audience, then you might be onto something good. Think about story lines or content revolving around fossils and dinosaurs, insects, trees and plants, earthquakes and hurricanes, evolution versus creationism, and more.

Check out the latest national school curricula requirements, compare them to supplemental literature already out there, and fill in the gaps. Librarians, teachers, parents, and students will hail your efforts if they're done well and approach timely topics such as the future of technology or new advances in stem cell research and its possibilities or consequences (what a great new take on *Frankenstein* the latter might provide!).

Chapter 22

Ten Recognitions Children's Authors Dream of Receiving

*B*ook prizes and awards look good on your living room wall *and* help you sell your book. This chapter fills you in on some of them, plus a couple key lists.

Newbery Medal

Sponsored by the Association for Library Service to Children, a division of the American Library Association, the Newbery Medal is awarded each year to the author of the most distinguished contribution to American literature for children.

Caldecott Medal

The Caldecott Medal is awarded each year by the Library Service to Children to the illustrator of the most distinguished American picture book for children.

Coretta Scott King Book Award

The Coretta Scott King Award is presented each year to honor the authors and illustrators of outstanding books about the African-American experience written for children.

Printz Award

The Michael L. Printz Award for Excellence in Young Adult Literature is given each year to the best book written for teenage readers.

Belpré Medal

The Belpré Medal is awarded each year to the Latino or Latina author and illustrator whose work of children's literature "best portrays, affirms, and celebrates the Latino cultural experience."

Geisel Award

The Theodor Seuss Geisel Award is awarded each year by the Association for Library Service to Children to the author(s) and illustrator(s) of "the most distinguished American book for beginning readers published in English in the United States during the preceding year."

Stonewall Book Award

The Stonewall Book Award-Mike Morgan & Larry Romans Children's & Young Adult Literature Award is awarded by the Gay, Lesbian, Bisexual, and Transgender (GLBT) Round Table of the American Library Association. This award is presented each year to the author(s) of a book of "exceptional merit relating to the gay/lesbian/bisexual/transgender experience."

Sibert Medal

Each year, the Robert F. Sibert Informational Book Medal is given to the author(s) and illustrator(s) of "the most distinguished informational book published in the United States in English during the preceding year."

ALA Quick Pick

The purpose of this honor is to highlight fiction and nonfiction books "aimed at encouraging reading among teens who dislike to read for whatever reason."

Texas Bluebonnet Award

Being nominated for a state book award — especially the Texas Bluebonnet Award — can help an author sell tens of thousands of books. And you don't even have to win; you just have to get on the master list.

Index

• *N* •

• *O* •